Windows 95 Power Tools

Martin S. Matthews

RANDOM HOUSE
ELECTRONIC PUBLISHING

Windows 95 Power Tools

Cover art by Henk Dawson

Interior design by Emil Ihrig, VersaTech Associates
Book composed and produced by Sybil Ihrig, VersaTech Associates

Windows 95 is a trademark of Microsoft, Inc.

Published in the United States by Random House, Inc., New York, and simultaneously in Canada by Random House of Canada, Limited.

Manufactured in the United States of America

Third Edition

0 9 8 7 6 5 4 3 2 1

ISBN 0-679-75587-X

Trademarks

New York   Toronto   London   Sydney   Auckland

To William A. Dunn, Bill,
always my Leader and mentor,
for all the great lessons
and the great times learning them!

Contents

Part V: Windows 95 Advanced Topics

407

Part VI: Windows 95 Power Tools Companion CD

471

Acknowledgments

This book, like most others, has had a number of people involved in it who have materially added to the book and the quality of its production. The author could not do the book without them, and for their efforts he is exceptionally grateful.

Brent Ethington, Microsoft Product Manager on the Windows 95 team, always tried to get answers to even the dumbest questions.

Emil Ihrig of VersaTech Associates in Prescott, Arizona, created the excellent design used here, while Sybil Ihrig of the same firm produced the book with much expertise and a lot of patience for the author's foibles and schedule changes.

Harriet O'Neal had the painstaking task of copy editing and not only did it with great skill but in great humor, always trying to make up for the author's slipped schedules.

John Cronan, author and technical writer, expertly wrote Chapters 7 and 8, as well as technically reviewed the entire book twice.

Patricia Shepard, author and neighbor, took on the daunting task of pulling together the many pieces of shareware and their documentation.

Susan Lawson, the Random House Editor, never lost faith even when it might have been prudent.

Carole Boggs Matthews, an author in her own right, the author's partner and mother of his son, once again bailed him out by jumping in and writing Chapter 11.

To these and the many others behind the scenes, the author gives his heartfelt thanks.

Martin S. Matthews
June, 1995

Introduction

ndependent of all the hype, the advent of Windows 95 is a major milestone in personal computing. It represents the end of the PC- and MS-DOS foundation layer in IBM-compatible personal computers. It is the transition between 16-bit and 32-bit personal computing. It is the culmination of over three years work, the largest software testing program in history, and a major investment on the part of Microsoft. More than all that, Windows 95 brings significant new capability and usability to the end user. Among the many new features and capabilities in Windows 95, the following are the most important to the typical end user:

- Full compatibility with the vast majority of existing Windows and DOS software, as well as hardware based on the Intel 386 and above

- A simpler, more intuitive user interface that makes using a personal computer faster, easier, and more fun

- Improved speed and efficiency in many areas including running multiple programs, file handling, and printing

- A much easier means of adding and configuring new hardware using Plug and Play technology

- The addition of a universal electronic mail handler for receiving, creating, and sending messages over local area networks, the Internet, and various information services, as well as sending and receiving faxes

- The addition of many less prominent, but no less valuable, features including long filenames, built-in networking, direct Internet connectability, support for mobile computing, improved multimedia, and many more

The purpose of *Windows 95 Power Tools* is to give you the means to quickly and fully utilize all of Windows 95's new features and capabilities.

Its objective is to go beyond just showing you how to use Windows 95 and to give you the added tools to become a true power user of the product. The book does this with

- In-depth explorations of all the important topics in Windows 95 including the new user interface, file management, printing, customization, networking, communication, e-mail, the Internet, The Microsoft Network, multimedia, managing, optimizing, using DOS, and the command language

- Detailed steps to perform hundreds of different functions

- Tips, notes, or cautions on hundreds of different items

- Many extensive tables explaining the options or alternatives in a given area

- Lavish use of screen, window, and icon illustrations

- A bundled CD-ROM with many programs and utilities to extend what you can do with Windows 95

How This Book Is Organized

Windows 95 Power Tools is divided into six parts that build upon one another while covering all aspects of Windows 95. The six parts, along with a description of their contents, are as follows:

- **Part I, Windows 95 Introduction**, introduces you to Windows 95 and provides an overview of what is changed or new and how best to use the changes and new features. This part is the foundation for the rest of the book and covers the Windows 95 environment and new user interface, file management, setting up and customizing, and printing.

- **Part II, Windows 95 Networking**, describes networking and how to install and fine-tune a Windows 95 network, as well as how to make the best use of it. Part II also looks at remote access to a network and the networking accessories available in Windows 95.

- **Part III, Windows 95 Messaging and Communications**, describes communications and how to set up and use your modem and the Windows 95 HyperTerminal program. Part III also looks at how to use Microsoft Exchange for e-mail and faxing, as well as how to use The Microsoft Network, CompuServe, and the Internet.

- **Part IV, Windows 95 Multimedia and Accessories**, examines both the software and hardware aspects of multimedia, as well as all of the Windows 95 accessories not discussed elsewhere in this book.

- **Part V, Windows 95 Advanced Topics**, addresses the areas of system management, optimization, using DOS, and the Windows 95 command language.

- **Part VI, Windows 95 Power Tools Companion CD**, describes and provides documentation for the programs on the CD.

What is on the CD

The compact disk that is enclosed with this book contains a number of powerful and useful programs and utilities. Among these are a complete Windows batch programming language and interpreter (WinBatch), along with an editor (WinEdit), to create batch scripts for automating anything that you can do in Windows 95 (a big void in Windows 95 itself). There are also two screen-capture programs (Grabit Pro and Professional Capture Systems), a paint program (Paint Shop Pro), three Internet-related programs (MKS Enhanced Mosaic Web Browser, Pping, and WFTP32), a Windows activity monitor (Win, What, Where), a very powerful application and information toolbar (RipBAR) and disk-space analyzer (RipSpace), and a Windows compressed file manager (Zip Manager). In addition there are nine utilities (File View for Windows, IconCalc, INIedit, Mem, Print Switch, RegFind, WinClock, WinImage, and WinPrint), a set of fonts (RRKeyFonts/PC), and a game (Hop). All of these programs and utilities are power tools for a wide variety of needs.

In the very back pages of this book, there are several promotional offerings related to the shareware on the CD.

Conventions Used in This Book

To make this book easier to use, these conventions were followed:

- Words or characters in **boldface** are either part of a heading or are to be typed on your keyboard.

- Words or characters in *italics* need special emphasis, are being defined, or are words or characters used as themselves.

- Individual keys on the keyboard are shown as keycaps, like this: ⎣←Enter⎦ or ⎣Shift⎦. If two keys are to be pressed together, they have a line joining them. For example, ⎣Ctrl⎦-⎣S⎦ or ⎣Shift⎦-⎣F2⎦.

- Messages and other direct quotes from the screen are in a display font, like this:

  `Press any key when ready.`

PART I

Windows 95 Introduction

When you first start Windows 95, *a small message appears that says* Starting Windows 95 . . . *In previous versions of Windows this same message read* Starting MS-DOS . . . *This simple change is indicative of the very profound change that is Windows 95—a totally new and complete operating system.*

Prior to Windows 95, you needed a combination of DOS as your operating system and Windows as your user interface. DOS, which directly controlled your hardware, provided the foundation layer of software. Windows provided the graphical user interface that determined what you saw and how you entered commands.

Windows 95 combines both the operating system and the graphical user interface into one package. Windows 95 also provides many improvements to both functions and adds new features and accessories.

Part I of this book introduces you to Windows 95 and provides an overview of what is changed or new and how best to use them. This part is the foundation for the rest of the book.

The Windows 95 Environment

The Windows 95 screen that appears after loading has completed is extremely simple, as you can see in Figure 1–1. In this simplicity, though, there is the power to do virtually anything you want. That is its beauty. It is also very different from Windows 3.1, its most recent predecessor. The Windows 3.1 shell, the Program Manager, is nowhere to be seen, but it is available if you really must use it (see Chapter 3).

The Windows 95 Screen

The Windows 95 screen has only two primary components: the desktop, which covers the screen, and the Taskbar, which is by default at the bottom of the screen.

The Desktop

The *desktop* is an area on which you can place items you are working on or items that are awaiting your attention. Normally these items are contained in windows, such as programs that you are using or files that you are looking at. The desktop, though, can also contain icons, dialog boxes, and the mouse pointer.

Figure 1–1

*Initial
Windows 95 screen*

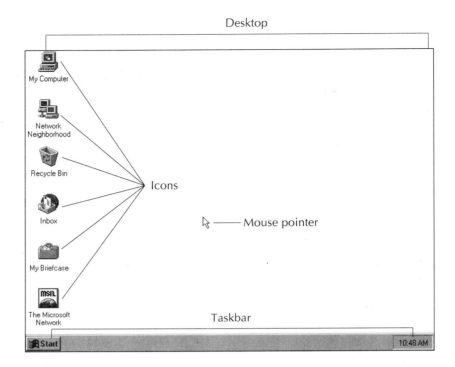

- **Windows** are variable areas of the screen with a border around them that contain the programs or files that you are currently using.
- **Icons**, such as those on the left of Figure 1–1, are small graphic objects that represent items waiting to be used.
- **Dialog boxes** are fixed areas of the screen with a border that contain messages to you or that ask you to supply some information that is needed.
- **Mouse pointer** shows where the mouse is currently pointing.

Objects on the desktop can be moved around, opened up, put away, or deleted. Further discussion of the objects on the desktop and how they are handled is provided later in this chapter and in Chapters 2 and 3.

The Taskbar

The Taskbar at the bottom of the screen is the primary device for controlling Windows 95. With it you can start a program, switch among programs already running, open the Control Panel (where you can set options for many different functions), find a file, get help, shut down Windows, run DOS commands, add or remove printers, and tell time. In addition to the Start button on the left and the clock on the right, the Taskbar has the bar itself in which active tasks—programs that are currently loaded or open file folders—are displayed. Also, the area containing the clock can expand to include a notification area that will tell you there is information waiting to be printed, newly received electronic mail, or that an accessibility feature is turned on. It also provides a good volume control for a sound board. A more fully utilized Taskbar is shown here:

The tasks on the Taskbar will expand or contract to fill the space, depending on how many tasks there are. If the tasks become too small, the Taskbar can be expanded to make them readable. Also, if you move the mouse pointer to a task, the full task name is displayed. As you'll see in this chapter, the Taskbar is quite flexible. You can move it to any of the four sides of the screen, you can hide it, or you can allow it to be covered by a window.

THE START BUTTON

The Start button opens the Start menu, which provides much of the functionality of the Taskbar. The Start menu has seven *options* or choices from which you can select. These options and their purpose are as follows:

- **Programs** allows you to choose a program to start.
- **Documents** allows you to choose a document to load and, in so doing, start its associated program.

- **Settings** allows you to open the Control Panel and other objects where you can change the settings on many Windows features.

- **Find** allows you to search for a file or folder on your computer or a computer on your network.

- **Help** opens the Windows Help facility, where you can review topics from a table of contents, search for a word in the index, or search for words or phrases used in help topics.

- **Run** allows you to type in the path and filename of a program, file, or folder to open, or of a DOS command to run.

- **Shut Down** prepares your computer to be turned off.

 **Do not turn off your computer without first selecting Shut Down from the Start menu and waiting until Windows tells you it is OK. If you do not shut down in this way, it is possible that information will not be saved on your disk and therefore will be lost.**

The first four menu options have an arrowhead on the right. This means that if one of those options is selected, a second menu (a submenu) will open. In the Programs option you can do this several times, as shown in Figure 1–2. The last two options have an ellipsis, or three

Figure 1–2

The Programs option with several submenus

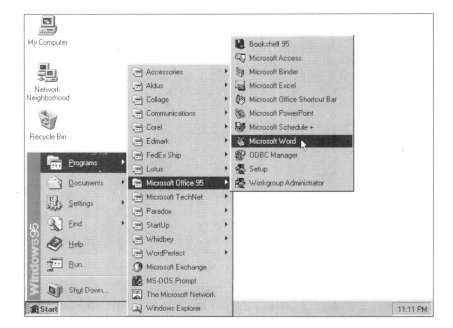

dots, after them. This means that a dialog box will open if you select one of those options. For example, if you select Run, a dialog box, like this one, opens asking you to enter the command you want to run.

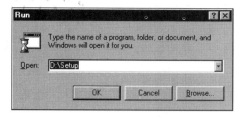

Windows and Dialog Boxes

Other than icons and the mouse pointer, everything else that appears on the desktop appears in a window or a dialog box. They are the containers for all that is done within Windows. Dialog boxes and windows are the same in that they both define an area of the screen with a border around it, and they both present information with which you can do something. Their dissimilarities, though, are significant. Dialog boxes are a fixed size, do not have a menu, and are used for displaying messages or getting information from you. Windows, on the other hand, can change their size, generally have a menu, and are used to contain a program, a data file, or a folder with other folders and/or files in it.

Parts of a Window

Most windows have a common set of features and controls similar to those shown in Figure 1–3. This window contains an open folder showing the files and other folders within it. As you might expect, this window is called a *folder window*. This window, with all its components, is also used to display objects that are not obviously folders. The term *folder window* is therefore used to refer to all of these types of windows independent of whether they display folders or not. The parts of the folder window and their purposes are as follows:

- **Title bar** contains the name of the program or the path and name of the folder in the window and is also used to move the window.

Figure 1–3

Folder window

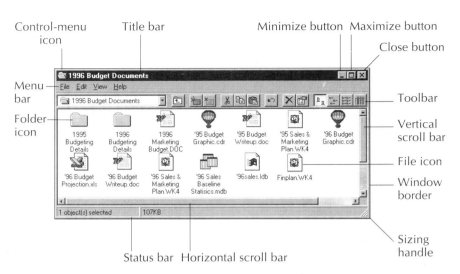

- **Control-menu icon** opens the control menu from which you can move, size, and close the window.
- **Menu bar** contains the menus that are available in the window.
- **Toolbar** contains tools related to the contents of the window.
- **Folder icon** represents a folder which can contain other folders or files.
- **File icon** represents a program or data file.
- **Horizontal scroll bar** allows moving the contents of the window horizontally.
- **Status bar** provides messages and information about what is displayed or selected in the window.
- **Sizing handle** allows sizing of the window in two dimensions.
- **Vertical scroll bar** allows moving the contents of the window vertically.
- **Window border** separates the window from the desktop and is used to size the window.
- **Close button** closes the window.
- **Maximize button** increases the size of the window to fill the desktop.
- **Minimize button** decreases the size of the window so you only see the task on the Taskbar.

Figure 1–4

Folder Options dialog box

Title bar
Tabs
Option buttons
List box
Check boxes

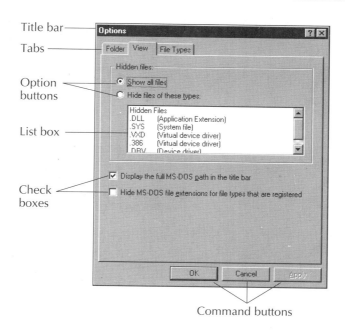

Command buttons

Not all windows have all of these features and some of them are optional. For example, in the folder window shown in Figure 1–3, the toolbar and status bar can be turned on or off.

Parts of a Dialog Box

Dialog boxes are not as standard as are windows. There are almost as many different dialog boxes as there are reasons to have them. All dialog boxes, though, use a common set of controls, which are shown in Figures 1–4, 1–5, and 1–6. These controls and their purposes are as follows:

- **Title bar** contains the name of the dialog box and is also used to move it.

- **Tabs** allow you to select among several pages in a dialog box.

- **Option buttons**, also called *radio buttons*, allow you to select one among mutually exclusive options.

- **List box** allows you to choose one or more items from a list, which may have a scroll bar to move the list.

- **Check boxes** allow you to turn features on or off.

Figure 1–5

*Properties for
Display dialog box*

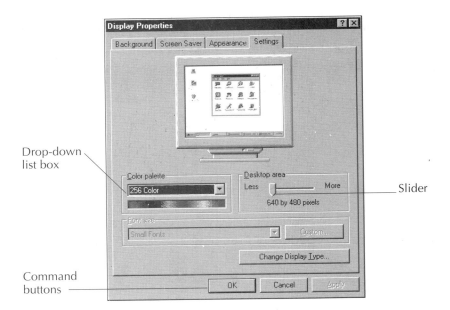

■ **Command buttons** perform immediate functions such as
closing the dialog box and accepting the changes made in it
(the OK button) or closing the dialog box and ignoring any
changes (the Cancel button).

■ **Drop-down list box** opens a list of items from which you can
choose one that is shown when the list is closed.

■ **Slider** allows you to select from among several continuous
values.

■ **Spinner** allows you to continuously vary a number up or
down.

■ **Text box** allows you to enter and edit text.

Figure 1–6

*Find All Files
dialog box*

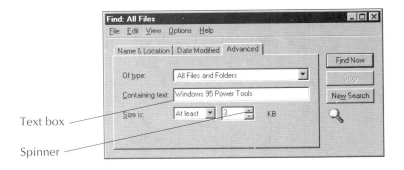

The Mouse and the Keyboard

The parts of Windows 95 described so far represent how Windows presents information to you—how it communicates from the computer to the user. The mouse and the keyboard provide the other half of the equation—how you communicate back to the computer. The mouse and the keyboard allow you to enter data as well as control what the computer is to do. Much of what you see on the screen, especially the controls in windows and dialog boxes, were created with the mouse in mind, but almost all of them can also be used with the keyboard.

Using the Mouse

The *mouse* is used to move the mouse pointer on the screen and to indicate a choice by pressing a button. There are a number of alternative pointing devices including trackballs, pointing sticks, and graphic tablets with one, two, three, or more buttons. The most common, though, is a two-button mouse similar to the Microsoft Mouse, and that is what is assumed in this book. As you'll see, Windows 95 requires at least two buttons to make the best use of all of its features.

The mouse may be used by either the left or right hand and the meaning of the left and right buttons may be switched to facilitate this. (Switching the meaning of the buttons is done in the Mouse Control Panel, which you reach by choosing Settings and Control Panel from the Start menu—see Chapter 3.) In normal usage, the right hand controls the mouse and the left mouse button is the primary one. The left mouse button is therefore called "the mouse button." The right button is always called the "right mouse button." If you switch the meaning of the buttons, you will have to mentally change how you interpret these phrases.

There is also standard terminology for using the mouse. These terms and how they are used in this book and in most other sources are as follows:

- **Point on** means to move the mouse until the tip of the pointer is on top of the object you want to select.
- **Click on** means to point on an object you want to select and quickly press and release the left mouse button.
- **Right-click on** means to point on an object you want to select and quickly press and release the right mouse button.

- **Double-click on** means to point on an object you want to select and quickly press and release the left mouse button twice in rapid succession.

- **Drag** means to point on an object you want to move and press and hold the left mouse button while moving the mouse and dragging the object with you. When you get the object where you want it, release the mouse button.

In most instances, you select an object on the screen by clicking on it. When you do that, the object becomes *highlighted* to indicate its selection, as the My Computer icon is highlighted below, whereas the Network Neighborhood is not.

You also open the Start menu by clicking on it or select a task in the Taskbar by clicking on it. You operate most of the controls in a window or a dialog box by simply clicking on them. For example, tabs, option buttons, check boxes, list boxes, drop-down list boxes, sliders, spinners, scroll bars, command buttons, and the close, maximize, and minimize buttons are all operated by clicking on them. To activate a text box, click on it and then type the desired text. You drag the scroll box in the middle of the scroll bar and you drag sliders. Finally, you open some of the icons in the notification area of the Taskbar (next to the clock) by clicking on them.

Like the Start menu, all menus are opened by clicking on them, and once open, you select an option by clicking on it. Also, while a menu is open, you can open another menu by simply moving the mouse pointer to it; you don't have to click until the option you want is highlighted. To open a submenu, you only need to move the mouse pointer for it to open. Here are other tasks that you can perform with the mouse:

- **Start a program** by double-clicking on its icon.

- **Load a document** and start its associated program by double-clicking on its icon.

- **Open a folder** by double-clicking on its icon.
- **Select text** by dragging across it.
- **Move a window** by dragging its title bar.
- **Size a window** by dragging one of its sides or corners.
- **Select multiple items** on the desktop or in a list by dragging a rectangle or *selection box* around them.
- **Select multiple items** in a list by holding down Ctrl while clicking—called Ctrl-*click*.
- **Select multiple contiguous items** in a list by holding down Shift while clicking—called Shift-*click*.

USING THE RIGHT MOUSE BUTTON

Prior to Windows 95, the right mouse button had very little use. Now, however, the right mouse button will open an object specific (context sensitive) *popup* menu for the object you right-click on. For example, right-clicking on the Taskbar opens the Taskbar popup menu shown here:

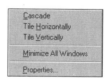

Almost every object on the desktop has its own popup menu, including the desktop itself. (The popup menus for the desktop and for a folder are shown next.) Notice that every popup menu has a Properties option. This opens a properties dialog box that allows you to set options for the object on which you right-clicked. Figure 1–5 showed the properties dialog box for the desktop.

You can also drag an object with the right mouse button and, when you do, you will get a popup menu that asks you how to interpret the drag. For example, if you drag a file from one place to another with the right mouse button, you get the following popup menu that asks what you want to do (this operation is further discussed in Chapter 2):

Using the Keyboard

As much as Windows 95 is designed to be used with a mouse, you can do almost everything with the keyboard. While a lot of keyboard operations are not as efficient as using the mouse, there are a number of keyboard shortcuts that are faster than using the mouse. The shortcut keys that are available in Windows 95 itself are shown in Table 1–1. Many of the Windows 95 accessories and most programs have their own set of shortcut keys, and most of them share the Cut, Copy, and Paste keystrokes. Of the keystrokes shown here, three are of particular importance: Alt-Esc, which allows you to switch among the programs and folders that are shown on the Taskbar; Alt-Tab, which also allows you to switch among folders and programs on the Taskbar, but does so through a dialog box and restores the folder's or program's window if it is minimized; and Ctrl-Esc, which opens the Start menu.

If two or more tasks (loaded programs or open folders) are active when you press Alt-Tab, the Task Switcher dialog box opens, as

Table 1–1.

Shortcut keys available in Windows 95

Keystroke	Purpose
Alt-←Enter	Switches the active DOS program between full screen and operating in a window
Alt-Esc	Switches among the folders and the programs on the Taskbar
Alt-F4	Closes the active window
Alt-Prt Sc	Captures the image of the active window and places it on the Clipboard
Alt-Spacebar	Opens the Control menu for the active window or selected Taskbar object; same as clicking on the far left of the active window's title bar or right-clicking on a Taskbar program or folder
Alt-Tab	Switches among programs and folders on the Taskbar using the Task Switcher dialog box
↑ ↓ ← →	Moves the selection in the direction of the arrow
←Backspace	Activates the parent folder of the active window
Ctrl-A	Selects all the objects in a window
Ctrl-C	Copies selected objects to the Clipboard
Ctrl-V	Pastes the contents of the Clipboard at the current insertion point
Ctrl-X	Cuts (removes) the selected objects and place them on the Clipboard
Ctrl-Z	Undoes the last copy, move, delete, paste, or rename operation you performed
Ctrl-Esc	Opens the Start menu
Delete	Places the selected object in the Recycle Bin
←Enter	Activates the selected object or menu option in the way that clicking or double-clicking would; also closes the active dialog box implementing any changes that were made
End	Moves the selection to the last object
Esc	Closes the active menu or the active dialog box without making a selection
F1	Opens the Windows Help facility
F2	Edits the name of the selected folder or file
F4	Opens the drop-down list in the toolbar of a folder window

Table 1–1. (continued)

Shortcut keys available in Windows 95

Keystroke	Purpose
F5	Refreshes the active window with the most recent information
F6 or Tab	Moves the selection among major areas within a window, a dialog box, or on the desktop
F10 or Alt	Activates the menu bar on the active window
Home	Moves the selection to the first object
Letter keys	Moves the selection to the object beginning with that letter
Prt Sc	Captures the current image on the screen and places it on the Clipboard
Shift-Delete	Deletes the selected object; it cannot be undone
Shift-F10	Opens the context sensitive popup menu for the selected object; same as right-clicking on the object

shown next, and you can switch to another task by holding down Alt while continuing to press Tab. If only one task is active and it is currently open, then nothing happens when you press Alt-Tab. If you are currently looking at the desktop and have only one active task, then Alt-Tab will take you to that task.

Neither Alt-Esc nor Alt-Tab will take you to the desktop. With several active tasks, you must minimize them to work on the desktop. You can use Minimize All Windows in the Taskbar popup to get to the desktop and then Undo Minimize All to return to open windows you had.

Not all of these keys are active under all circumstances. F2, for example, only works when you have a file or folder selected that you have created (the names of the system folders My Computer, Network Neighborhood, and Recycle Bin cannot be changed). Also, if the toolbar is turned off in a folder window, Tab does not do anything. With the toolbar turned on, Tab switches you between the selected object in the window and the drop-down list box in the toolbar.

The very best way to become familiar with the keyboard is to try out the effect of various keystrokes for yourself.

Using Windows 95

When you first start Windows 95, the Welcome message in the center of the screen tells you to click on the Start button to begin. That is all you need to know to begin to use Windows 95. The Start button will open the Start menu from which you can start any program that has been installed in Windows 95, change the settings or defaults on most features in Windows 95, find a file or a computer on your network, get help, or shut down Windows. That is a lot to be so readily available. There are, of course, many other facets of Windows 95. The next few paragraphs will introduce you to some of the other things that you can do.

Accessing Information

The icons that initially appear on your desktop—My Computer, Network Neighborhood, Microsoft Exchange Inbox, and Recycle Bin—provide access to the information that is stored on your computer or on other computers in your network. If you are not connected to a network, you will not have Network Neighborhood, and if you have neither a modem nor a network, you will not have an Exchange Inbox. (You may also have icons for My Briefcase and The Microsoft Network. These are not pertinent to the current discussion and will be discussed in Chapters 2 and 9 respectively.)

MY COMPUTER

My Computer

My Computer provides access to the disk drives that have been installed or defined on your computer, as shown in Figure 1–7. This includes floppy disk drives, hard disk drives, and CD-ROM drives that are physically on your computer (drives A, B, C, and D in Figure 1–7). It also includes drives or folders on other computers in your network that have been *mapped* to drive letters on your computer. These are shown with a cable beneath them and are drives E, F, G, and H in Figure 1–7 (these are physical drives on other computers). Additionally, the My Computer window contains folders for Control Panel, Printers, and Dial-Up Networking. Control Panel and Printers

Figure 1–7

Disk drives available in My Computer

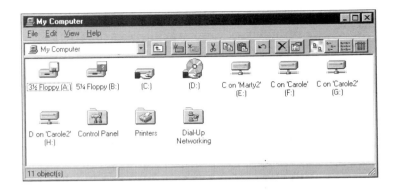

are the same as the options with the same name in the Start menu Settings option. Chapter 3 will discuss the Control Panel and Chapter 4 will cover the Printers folder. Dial-Up Networking is discussed in Chapter 6.

When you double-click on a disk drive in the My Computer window, a new window opens and displays the files and folders that are on that disk drive. You can then double-click on a folder to open it and keep doing that until the final folder contains only files, as shown in Figure 1–8. (If

Figure 1–8

Opening a series of folders to find a file

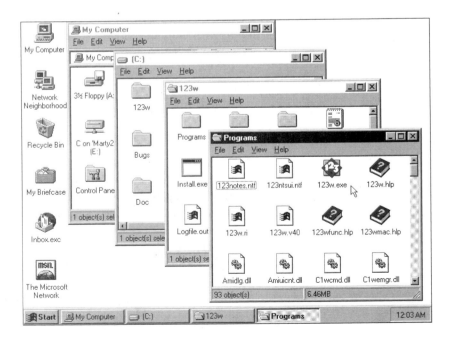

you do not see separate windows but rather a single window with the contents changing, you can change it as you will learn later in the chapter.) *Folders*, then, are the Windows 95 replacements for directories in previous versions of DOS and Windows. Folders can contain other folders and files as well as electronic mail (e-mail) and other objects. Folders are the primary container in Windows 95.

NETWORK NEIGHBORHOOD

Network
Neighborhood

The Network Neighborhood provides access to information located on computers to which you are connected. This includes computers in your immediate workgroup, which are shown as computer icons in the Network Neighborhood window (see Figure 1–9); computers in other workgroups connected to your network, which are reached through the Entire Network icon; and computers to which you can gain remote access through telephone lines and a modem.

When you double-click on one of the computers in your workgroup, you see the disk drives (represented by folders), folders, and printers that are on that computer and being shared with you. Each person on the network as well as the network administrator can determine what you see in the Network Neighborhood. Opening one of the disk drives begins a process exactly like opening a disk drive in My Computer, as you can see in Figure 1–10. Part II of this book contains an in-depth look at networking Windows 95.

MICROSOFT EXCHANGE

Inbox

The Microsoft Exchange (or just Exchange) provides access to all the messaging sources to which you are or can be connected. For example, if you are on a network with an e-mail system, the Exchange will allow you to send, receive, store, and retrieve your e-mail; if you have a modem and a CompuServe and/or Internet account, the Exchange

Figure 1–9

*Network
Neighborhood
window*

Figure 1-10

*Network
Neighborhood
provides access to
disk drives on
other computers.*

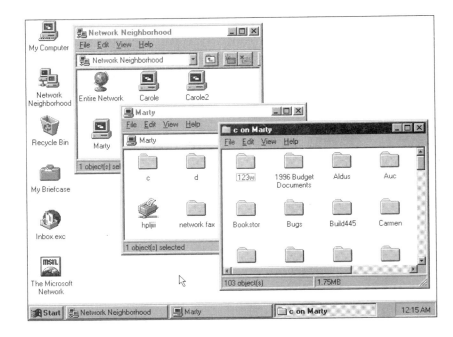

will allow you to send, receive, store, and retrieve CompuServe and/or
Internet messages; and if you have a fax/modem you can send, receive,
store, and retrieve faxes. All e-mail, information service messages, and
faxes are stored together in a common set of folders in the Exchange, as
shown in Figure 1–11. Opening one of the folders shows the messages
from various sources like those in Figure 1–12. Double-clicking on a
message allows you to read it, send a reply, forward it to another person,
or move, copy, or delete it. This allows you to take a fax that you have
received and send it out as e-mail, or to fax a CompuServe message.

The Exchange provides a miniature word processor to create e-mail,
as shown in Figure 1–13. Also, an integrated address book is available

Figure 1-11

*Common set of
folders in
the Exchange*

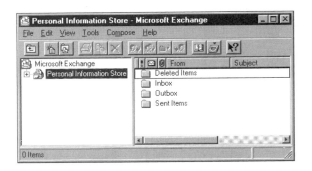

Figure 1–12

Exchange messages from several sources

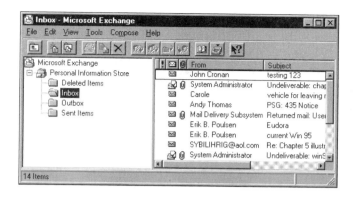

that can be used across all forms of communications. Part III of this book provides in-depth coverage of communicating with Windows 95.

RECYCLE BIN

Recycle Bin

The Recycle Bin provides a safety net that protects you from inadvertently deleting something you want to keep. All files and folders that you delete go into the Recycle Bin. Under the default settings, the items stay in the Recycle Bin until you "empty" it or restore the items to another folder. You can tell something is in the Recycle Bin because you can see paper sticking out the top, like this:

Recycle Bin

You can empty the Recycle Bin by either right-clicking on it and selecting Empty Recycle Bin from the popup menu or by opening the

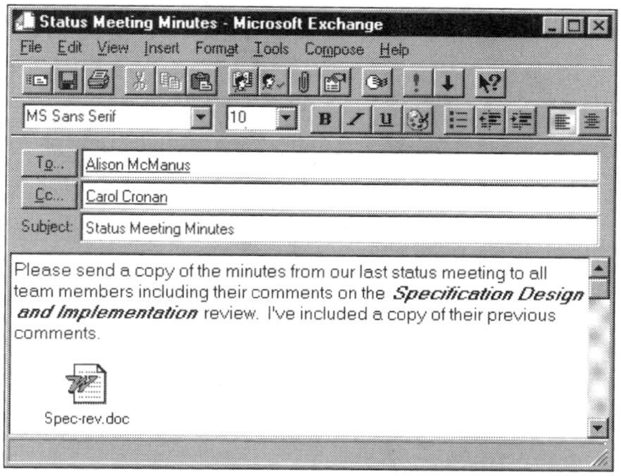

Figure 1–13

Creating e-mail

Recycle Bin window and choosing Empty Recycle Bin from the File menu. Although opening the Recycle Bin window to empty it takes a couple of extra steps, it allows you to confirm visually what it is you are permanently deleting, as you can see here:

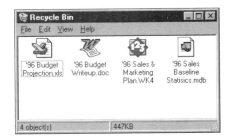

To undelete one or more objects still in the Recycle Bin, you need to select the objects in the window and then choose Restore from the File menu. You can also undo the last object you deleted, renamed, copied, or moved by choosing Undo from the Edit menu of any folder, or the Explorer window, or by pressing Ctrl-Z.

You do not have to use the Recycle Bin if you are comfortable working without the safety net it provides. To immediately delete an object when you press Del or choose Delete or Clear from a menu, right-click on the Recycle Bin, choose Properties, and then in the dialog box click on Do not move files to the Recycle Bin. In this same dialog box, shown next, you can select the maximum amount of disk space that you want to allocate to the Recycle Bin. It is a good idea to keep this fairly small so your Recycle Bin does not end up taking over your disk.

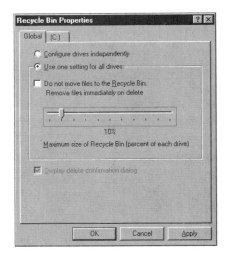

 **Caution**

When the contents of the Recycle Bin approaches the disk space allocated for it, anything else you delete that causes the Recycle Bin to exceed its allocated disk space will immediately and literally delete (you cannot undo it) enough current contents of the Recycle Bin to make room for the new deletion. You will *not* be given a warning.

Using Windows and Dialog Boxes

When you open My Computer, Network Neighborhood, or any of their folders, you get the folder window with the same menus and the same controls as the ones you can see in Figure 1–14. Other than the programs that you run, it is the most common window in Windows 95.

FOLDER WINDOW MENUS

The four folder menu menus, File, Edit, View, and Help remain constant, but the contents of the File menu change depending on what is selected. If nothing is selected in the window, the File menu is the leftmost menu in Figure 1–15. If a folder is selected, the File menu looks like the middle one, and if a file is selected, the File menu is similar to the one on the right in Figure 1–15.

The purpose of each of the File menu options is described in Table 1–2. In the table you will see the term *shortcut*. A shortcut is a link or pointer to a folder or file that allows you to open the folder or file remotely. For example, if you create a shortcut to the Microsoft Access program file MSACCESS.EXE, you can start Access by double-clicking on the shortcut, which can be placed on the desktop or in another folder. If you create a shortcut for a folder, you can open the

Figure 1–14

The folder window

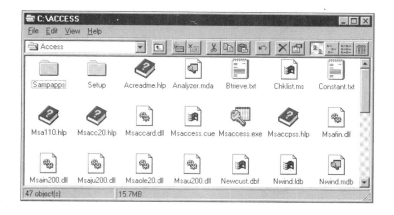

Figure 1–15

Three forms of the folder window File menu

Nothing selected   Folder selected   File selected

Table 1–2.

Folder window File menu options

Option	Purpose
New	Creates a new folder, shortcut, or file of various types
Open	Opens and/or starts the selected objects depending on whether it is a file, folder, or program
Explore	Opens the Explorer window for the selected folder (see Chapter 2 for a discussion of the Explorer window)
Find	Opens the same Find All Files dialog box available from the Start menu (see Chapter 2)
Sharing	Allows you to specify whether you want to share a folder
Send To	Copies the selected folder or file to a floppy disk drive or a fax recipient
Print	Prints the selected file
Quick View	Displays the selected file on the screen, often without starting the program that created it
Create Shortcut	Creates a new shortcut for the selected object in the same folder with the original object
Delete	Deletes the selected object
Rename	Allows you to rename the selected object
Properties	Opens the property dialog box for the selected object
Close	Closes the active window

Figure 1–16

*Folder Window
Edit, View, and
Help menus*

Edit menu

View menu

Help menu

folder by double-clicking on the shortcut. All of the entries that create the list of programs in the Start menu Program options are shortcuts. Both Chapters 2 and 3 will discuss shortcuts further.

The Edit, View, and Help menus are shown in Figure 1–16 and the purpose of each of the options is described in Table 1–3.

The Options dialog box that is opened by choosing Options in the View menu has three tabs. The first, Folder, shown in Figure 1–17, lets you determine if you want a new window created each time you open a new folder. The top option opens a new window; the bottom option replaces the contents of the first window each time you open a new folder. The second tab, View, allows you to determine the type of files you want displayed and to set several options for the folder window, as you can see in Figure 1–18. The third tab, File Types, shows

Figure 1–17

*Options dialog
box, Folder tab*

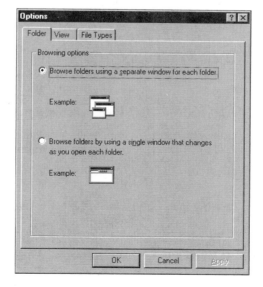

Table 1–3.

Folder Window Edit, View, and Help menu options

Option	Purpose
Undo	Reverses the last copy, move, delete, or rename you performed
Cut	Removes the selected object(s) from the window and places it on the Clipboard so it can be pasted elsewhere
Copy	Copies the selected object(s) to the Clipboard so it can be pasted elsewhere
Paste	Places a copy of the Clipboard contents into the active window; may be done multiple times into different windows
Paste Shortcut	Places a shortcut to the file or folder that has been copied to the clipboard.
Select All	Selects all of the objects (files and folders) in the window
Invert Selection	Selects all of the objects in the window not currently selected
Toolbar	Turns the toolbar on or off beneath the menu bar in the active window
Status Bar	Turns the status bar on or off at the bottom of the active window
Large Icons	Displays the windows contents as large icons, as shown in Figure 1–14
Small Icons	Displays the windows contents as small icons, as shown in Figure 1–20
List	Displays the windows contents as a brief list, as shown in Figure 1–21
Details	Displays the windows contents as a detailed list, as shown in Figure 1–22
Arrange Icons	Sorts the icons in the window by name, type of file, size, or date and allows you to toggle the automatic arrangement feature
Line up Icons	Aligns all objects in the window to an invisible grid
Refresh	Revises the contents of the window with the latest information from the disk
Options	Opens the Options dialog box shown in Figures 1–17 through 1–19
Help Topics	Opens the Help Topics dialog box, discussed later in this chapter
About Windows 95	Opens a message window that, among other things, tells you the physical memory and system resources that are left

Figure 1–18

Options dialog box, View tab

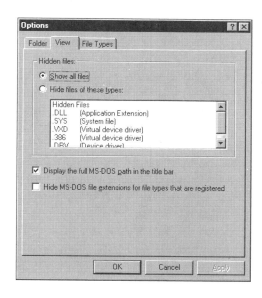

you the registered file types, the program with which they are opened, and allows you to add or remove types, as shown in Figure 1–19.

If you want to select all but a few objects in a folder window, select the objects you *do not want* to select and choose Invert Selection from the Edit menu.

Figure 1–19

Options dialog box, File Types tab

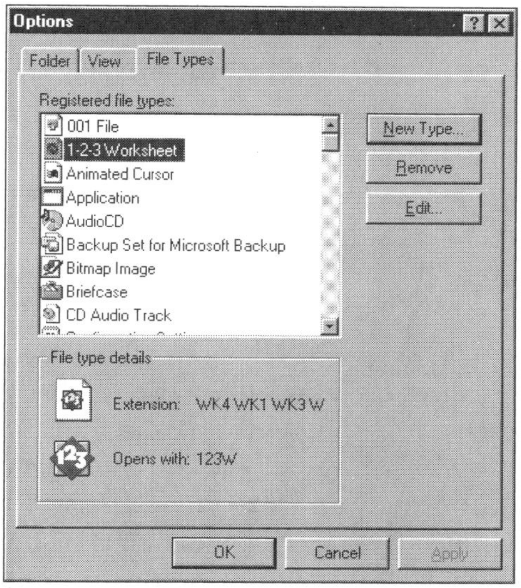

The difference between small icon view (Figure 1–20) and list view (Figure 1–21) is the difference between a vertical and a horizontal orientation. The icons and the information shown are the same, but small icon view is scrolled vertically and list view is scrolled horizontally. In the Details view (Figure 1–22), you can sort the objects by clicking on the button at the top of the list for the field by which you want to sort. For example, if you want to sort by size, from smallest to largest, click on the Size button; if you want to sort from largest to smallest, click on the Size button a second time. In other words, you get an ascending sort the first time you click on a button and a descending sort the second time. Also in the Details view, if you want to change the width of a column, you can drag the vertical line between the buttons at the top of the list. When the mouse pointer is on a vertical line between buttons and ready to change a column width, the mouse pointer becomes a vertical line with a horizontal double-headed arrow running through it like this:

Name	Size	Type
Chklist.ms	1KB	MS File
Constant.txt	4KB	Text Document
Msa110.hlp	129KB	Help File

In Details view of a folder window, click once on the button at the top of a column for an ascending (A–Z, 1–9) sort of the column, or click twice for a descending sort.

FOLDER WINDOW TOOLBAR AND CONTROLS

If you select Toolbar in the View menu of a folder window, a toolbar will appear below the menu bar at the top of the window. The folder window toolbar has seven groups of controls. On the left is a drop-down list box that lets you quickly get to any drive or drive-level folder on your computer. To the right of the drop-down list box are six sets of buttons that are described in Table 1–4.

The drop-down list box, shown next, is the most versatile and therefore most valuable of the toolbar elements. It will always show the chain of folders from your selected folder to the selected drive, as well as all the drives and folders that you have available. This places information even on a large network only a few clicks away. The default high-level folders are Control Panel, Printers, and Dial-Up Networking, but as you will see in Chapter 3, you can place other

Figure 1–20

*Folder window in
small icon view*

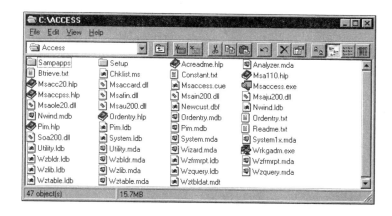

Figure 1–21

*Folder window in
list view*

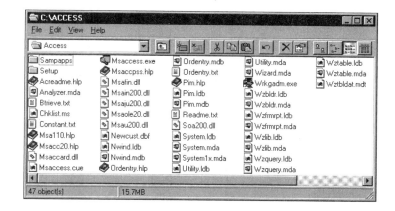

Figure 1–22

*Folder window in
detail view*

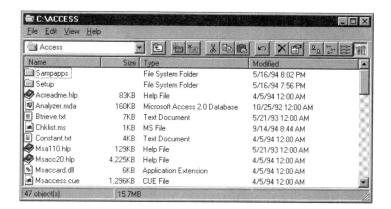

Table 1–4.

Buttons in the folder window toolbar

Button	Name	Description
	Up One Level	Takes you up to the next-higher-level folder or disk drive
	Map Network Drive	Gives a drive on another computer a letter on your computer
	Disconnect Net Drive	Removes the drive letter on your computer and breaks the network connection
	Cut	Removes the selected object(s) from the window and places it on the Clipboard so it can be pasted elsewhere
	Copy	Copies the selected object(s) to the Clipboard so it can be pasted elsewhere
	Paste	Places a copy of the Clipboard contents into the active window; may be done multiple times into different windows
	Undo	Reverses the last copy, move, delete, or rename operation you performed
	Delete	Removes the selected object(s) from the window and places it in the Recycle Bin, if activated; otherwise permanently deletes it
	Properties	Opens the Properties dialog box for the selected object
	Large Icons	Causes the window to display files and folders as large icons
	Small Icons	Causes the window to display files and folders as small icons
	List	Causes the window to display files and folders in a short list
	Details	Causes the window to display files and folders in a detail list

folders at either the My Computer or Desktop levels.

Using Help

Windows 95 includes an extensive Help facility that is also very easy to use. You can open this facility from a number of different places, but most simply by clicking on Help in the Start menu or by pressing F1 . Also, the Help Topics option in the Help menu of all folder windows opens the same general Help Topics dialog box, shown in Figure 1–23. This dialog box provides three ways of getting help on a particular problem.

Figure 1–23

*Help Topics
dialog box*

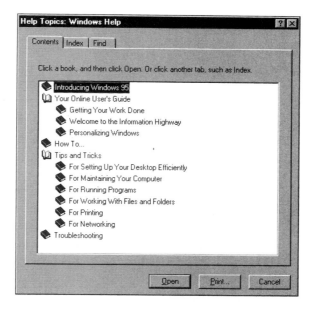

Figure 1–24

*Detail topics with
"how-to" steps*

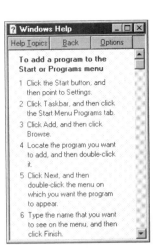

- You can look through a hierarchical table of contents for articles that pertain to the subject on which you want help.

- You can look up a word or phrase in an index to find either a series of steps that tell you how to do something, or an article on that subject.

- You can search for specific words or phrases in help topics.

HELP CONTENTS TAB

In the Contents tab shown in Figure 1–23, you double-click on a topic to see related subtopics and articles. This may provide another list of topics, each of which opens a small explanation window. Sometimes these smaller windows have a series of steps that tell you how to perform some function, as you can see in Figure 1–24.

The Options menu of a how-to window allows you to copy the topic to the Clipboard, print the topic, keep the how-to window on top of other windows, and change the font and color used by the window. Most importantly, you can add your own annotation to a help topic using the Annotate option in the menu. An annotation is your own notes on the subject, so if by trial and error you discover how to do something better, you can add the explanation of your findings to the topic. When you choose Annotate from the menu, a small dialog box opens in which you can enter the text you want to use to annotate the help topic. When you save the annotation, a small paper clip icon appears in the how-to window, and when you click on the paper clip, the annotation appears as shown next.

 **Adding annotations allows you to customize Windows Help.**

HELP INDEX TAB

If you select the Index tab, you can type one or more characters to find a particular index entry, as shown in Figure 1–25. You can also use the scroll bar. When you find the entry you want, you can double-click on it or select it and click on Display. If there are several topics related to an entry, you will be asked to choose one and then you will be shown a small how-to window. Often the how-to window will have a button to access related topics. In all cases, the how-to window lets you return to the initial Help dialog box by clicking on Contents, or to the previous topic you looked at by clicking on Back.

Figure 1–25

Searching for an index entry

Figure 1–26

Finding a word or phrase in Help

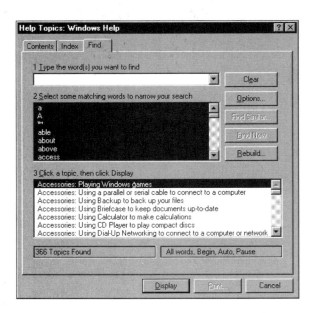

HELP FIND TAB

The first time you select the Find tab, the Help facility builds an index of all the words and phrases used in Help topics. You are then shown the window in Figure 1–26, which allows you to either enter or select the words and/or phrases that you want to find. When you do that, a detail Windows Help window will open with information related to your search, as shown in Figure 1–27. This includes steps to reach an objective, tips, warnings, and one or more Related Topics buttons, which open similar windows with a related topic described.

Figure 1–27

The result of using Help Find

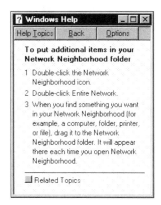

What Is in Windows 95?

Windows 95 comes with a large number of smaller programs, or *applets*, which are discussed in depth in other chapters of this book. The following paragraphs and tables, though, will give you an overview of what is in Windows 95. Most of these applets are started from the Programs Accessories option of the Start menu, but to give this list some organization, the applets are divided into file management, printing, networking, communicating, multimedia, productivity, system, games, and other. Each of the applet entries will give a brief description of the applet, show its icon, tell where it is started and in which chapter of this book it is discussed more fully.

File Management Programs

Icon	Name	Description
	Windows Explorer	Provides access to all folders and files; Started from Start menu Programs; Discussed in Chapter 2
	Backup	Backs up folders and files to floppies and tape; Started from Start menu Programs Accessories System Tools; Discussed in Chapter 2
	Briefcase	Synchronizes the same file on two different computers; Started from the desktop; Discussed in Chapter 2
	File Manager	Provides Windows 3.1-like access to folders and files; Started with WINFILE.EXE in Windows folder; Discussed in Chapter 2
	Disk Defragmenter	Optimizes the storing of files on hard disks; Started from Start menu Programs Accessories System Tools; Discussed in Chapter 2
	DriveSpace	Compresses files stored on disks and manages that compressed drive; Started from Start menu Programs Accessories System Tools; Discussed in Chapter 2

| | ScanDisk | Checks for and repairs disk errors;
Started from Start menu Programs Accessories
System Tools;
Discussed in Chapter 2 |

Printing Programs

Icon	Name	Description
	Printers	Allows adding and deleting printers and managing print queues; Started from Start menu Settings; Discussed in Chapter 4
	Fonts	Allows adding and deleting fonts; Started from the Control Panel; Discussed in Chapter 4

Networking Programs

Icon	Name	Description
	Direct Cable Connection	Allows transferring files and folders over a serial or parallel cable; Started from Start menu Programs Accessories; Discussed in Chapter 11
	Dial-Up Networking	Allows access to a computer and a network from a remote computer over phone lines; Started from Start menu Programs Accessories; Discussed in Chapter 6
	Chat	Allows a two-way conversation over a network link; Started from the Other folder on CD; Discussed in Chapter 6
	ClipBook Viewer	Allows sharing multiple Clipboard objects over a network; Started from the Other folder on CD Discussed in Chapter 6
	NetWatcher	Provides a view and control of who is connected to your computer and the folders and files that are being shared; Started from Start menu Programs Accessories System Tools; Discussed in Chapter 6

Communicating Programs

Icon	Name	Description
	HyperTerminal	Provides transfer of files and messages with a modem; Started from Start menu Programs Accessories; Discussed in Chapter 7
	Phone Dialer	Allows the computer to dial a phone number for you; Started from Start menu Programs Accessories; Discussed in Chapter 7
	Fax Cover Page Editor	Allows you to create a fax cover page; Started from Start menu Programs Accessories; Discussed in Chapter 8
	Fax Viewer	Allows you to look at and print faxes that have been received; Started from Start menu Programs Accessories; Discussed in Chapter 8

Multimedia Programs

Icon	Name	Description
	CD Player	Allows you to play audio CDs; Started from Start menu Programs Accessories Multimedia; Discussed in Chapter 10
	Media Player	Provides control for playing digital audio and video clips; Started from Start menu Programs Accessories Multimedia; Discussed in Chapter 10
	Sound Recorder	Allows you to digitally record sound; Started from Start menu Programs Accessories Multimedia; Discussed in Chapter 10
	Volume Control	Provides control of sound volume; Started from Start menu Programs Accessories Multimedia; Discussed in Chapter 10

Productivity Programs

Icon	Name	Description
	WordPad	Provides a reasonably featured word processor; Started from Start menu Programs Accessories; Discussed in Chapter 11
	NotePad	Provides a text editor for unformatted files; Started from Start menu Programs Accessories; Discussed in Chapter 11
	Paint	Provides a bitmap drawing program; Started from Start menu Programs Accessories; Discussed in Chapter 11

System Programs

Icon	Name	Description
	Regedit	Allows you to view and edit the Registry; Started with REGEDIT.EXE in the Windows folder; Discussed in Chapter 12
	Sysedit	Allows you to view and edit AUTOEXEC.BAT, CONFIG.SYS, WIN.INI, SYSTEM.INI, and other files; Started with SYSEDIT.EXE in the Windows/System folder; Discussed in Chapter 12
	System Monitor	Allows you to monitor system resource usage; Started from Start menu Programs Accessories System Tools; Discussed in Chapter 12

Game Programs

Icon	Name	Description
	FreeCell	A solitaire card game of logic and skill; Started from Start menu Programs Accessories Games; Discussed in Chapter 11
	Hearts	A card game for play over a network; Started from Start menu Programs Accessories Games; Discussed in Chapter 6

| | Minesweeper | A game of figuring out where the mines are; Started from Start menu Programs Accessories Games; Discussed in Chapter 11 |
| | Rumor | A game where a rumor can be passed around a network; Started from Start menu Programs Accessories Games; Discussed in Chapter 11 |

Other Programs

Icon	Name	Description
	Calculator	Provides the functions of either a simple or scientific desktop calculator; Started from Start menu Programs Accessories; Discussed in Chapter 11
	Character Map	Provides access to all of the special characters in all of the fonts on your computer; Started from Start menu Programs Accessories; Discussed in Chapter 11
	Clipboard Viewer	Allows you to view and save the contents of the Clipboard; Started from Start menu Programs Accessories; Discussed in Chapter 11
	Object Packager	Allows you to package an object that was created by an OLE-ignorant program so the object can be used as if it were OLE compliant; Started from Start menu Programs Accessories; Discussed in Chapter 11

Windows 95 File and Disk Management

indows 95 has divided the files and folders you can access into three groupings:

- Those files that are accessible from your computer and are found in **My Computer**
- Those files that are stored on other computers on the network to which you are connected and are found in **Network Neighborhood**
- Those files that are messages you send and receive over a network or a modem and are stored in special folders kept in the **Exchange**

Networking and the Network Neighborhood is the subject of Part II of this book, beginning with Chapter 5. Messaging and the Exchange is the subject of Part III, beginning with Chapter 8. This chapter, then, will deal with file management as it relates to files and folders that you can access through My Computer. While, as you learned in Chapter 1, this does include network drives that have been mapped to your computer, these will not be emphasized in this chapter. The purposes of this chapter are to explore how to locate and handle files and folders and how to work with your disks.

Locating Files and Folders

In Chapter 1 you saw how you can open My Computer, select a drive, select one or more folders, and finally find the file or files you want. Each time you select a new object (drive, folder, or file), a new window opens or the contents of the current window are replaced. This is a very simple and intuitive approach, but it does not give as broad a view of your file system as you might want, and file handling is not as efficient as it might be. For this reason, Windows 95 has provided another view of your files and folders that not only is broader, but also provides some efficiencies in file handling. This other view is called the Explorer.

Explorer

The Explorer takes the familiar folder window that you saw in Chapter 1 and splits it vertically, as you can see in Figure 2–1. In the left pane there is a hierarchical structure of computers, drives, and folders, and in the right pane there are the drives, folders, and files contained in the object selected on the left. This is similar to the File Manager in Windows 3.1 with the major difference being that the left pane of the Explorer contains all of the objects on your desktop, not just the currently selected drive, which was shown in the left pane of the File Manager. This means that the Explorer exposes the full continuum of everything you can

Figure 2–1

Explorer window

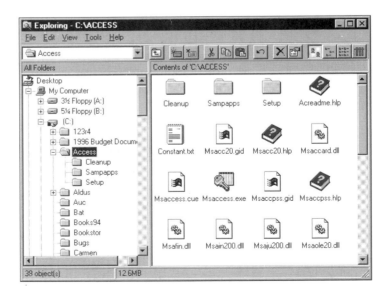

Figure 2–2

*The left pane of
the Explorer
showing all the
objects on
the desktop*

access on your computer, including all of your Network Neighborhood, as shown in Figure 2–2. Within the Explorer you can drag a file from any object to any other object you can access—a very efficient way of moving files around—as you will see later in this chapter.

The toolbar and status bar are exactly the same in the Explorer as in the folder window, and the menu bar is the same except for the Tools menu that is shown next.

The Tools menu provides four options, two of which are similar to options on the Start menu: Find and Go to. Find allows you to locate a file, a folder, or a computer as described later in this chapter. The Go to option, which is similar to Run on the Start menu, allows you to open a folder by typing the path and the name of the folder in the Go To Folder dialog box, as shown here:

The Map Network Drive and Disconnect Network Drive options allow you to attach or remove a drive letter on your computer to a drive on another computer on the network to which you are connected. It is not necessary to map a network drive in order to use information on a remote computer, but mapping allows you to treat the remote drive like any drive on your computer. This is especially helpful within a program like a word processor. Chapter 6 will explain mapping further.

LOCATING FILES WITH EXPLORER

The Explorer's primary function is to locate files and folders when you don't know their exact path and filename or to simply explore the files and folders that are available to you. You do this by selecting the computer, disk drive, and folders that you want to open in the left pane. If a folder has a plus sign to the left of it, you can click on the plus sign and subordinate folders will appear. The plus sign will then change to a minus sign. You can do this for as many levels as necessary, like this:

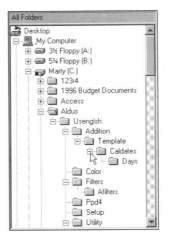

Once you are in the correct folder, you can then use the scroll bars in the right pane to find the file you want, and, finally, double-click on it to open or start it. If you then want to go to another folder that is not immediately visible in the left pane, you can use the scroll bars in that pane to find it, or, more quickly, you can use the drop-down list box in the toolbar to locate another drive, as shown next:

As you saw in the folder window in Chapter 1, the right pane can be in any one of four formats: large icons, small icons, list, and details. You can change the format with either the rightmost four buttons in the toolbar or with the View menu.

Find

Besides My Computer and Explorer, there is a third way of locating files and folders that provides more than just the location of the objects. This is the Find option in the Start menu or in the Tools menu of the Explorer window. When you select Find, a second set of menu options appears that lets you choose to find files, folders, or computers on the network, as you see next. Additionally, you can search for items located in The Microsoft Network, which is covered in Chapter 9.

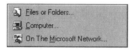

The most common task is to find a file. Selecting that option opens the dialog box shown next. This allows you to search for a file based on its name and where it is located; based on the date it was created or modified; or based on its file type, the text it contains, or its size.

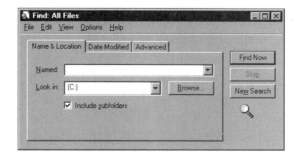

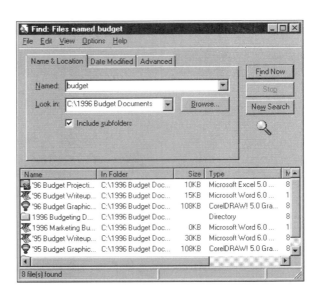

If I were to look for all the files and folders accessible from My
Computer with the word *budget* in the filename, the results on my
system would look like Figure 2–3.

In the name field you can enter a fragment of a name, like *bud*, and
get all the files whose name contain that fragment, like *Budget*, *bud96*,
and *Salesbud*. In this case the fragment can be anywhere in the name.
You can also use the wild card character *, which stands for any number of characters, to select only matches where the name fragment is
at the beginning or at the end of a name. For example, *bud** will
return *Budget* and *bud96*, but not *Salesbud*, whereas **bud* will return
1996bud and *Salesbud*, but not *Budget*.

The Options menu allows you to make the search case sensitive and to
save the results. A default search is not case sensitive, meaning that if
you search for files named *bud**, you still get both *Budget* and *bud96*. On
the other hand, if you turn on Case Sensitive, you would only get
bud96. Saving the results places an icon on the desktop that you can
drag to a folder. When you open this icon, you will have the Find window with the results of the find in it. From the results of a find you can
do most file handling functions, as you will see later in this chapter.

USING FIND

The Windows 95 Find option is very adaptable, allowing you to find a wide variety of files and then to manipulate what you found. The following sections provide several examples of this capability.

Group similarly named files If you have several files in different folders all associated with a project and each of the files have some common name fragment, for example *proj* (for *project*), you can gather all of the files into one folder using the following steps:

1. From either My computer or Explorer, select New Folder from the File menu, then type a folder name that contains the name fragment you are searching for, and press ⏎Enter. This creates the folder that will hold the files. You can rename the folder after the search if you wish.

2. From the Start menu open Find (if Find is already open and displays the results of a search, click on New Search and answer OK to clear the current search).

3. In the Named drop-down list box, type the name fragment being sought.

4. Open the Look in drop-down list and make sure that the appropriate drive or computer is selected. (If you select a computer, all the drives accessible to that computer will be searched.)

5. Click on Find Now.

6. When the list of found files has been returned, select the ones you want to be in the new folder (press and hold Ctrl while clicking on them), and then drag them to the folder, which should also have been found.

Finding by type and date Say you created a Microsoft Word 6.0 document in the last month, but you forgot the name. To find it you would follow these steps:

1. Open Find or select New Search and choose the Date Modified tab.

2. Click on Find all files created or modified, click again on During the previous month, and make sure that 1 is in the numeric entry box.

3. Click on the Advanced tab, open the Of type drop-down list, and select Microsoft Word 6.0 Document.

4. Click on Find Now.

The Find Files dialog box will display a list of Word 6 files you created in the last month.

Finding by content and size If you want to delete several early drafts of files that contain a phrase and you know these files are less than 64 KB in size, whereas the final files you want to keep are larger, you can use the following instructions to delete these drafts:

1. Open Find or select New Search and click on the Advanced tab.

2. In the Containing text box, type the text you want to search for without quotation marks unless they are to be included in the search.

3. Open the Size is drop-down list box and select At least if you know the lower size limit, or At most if you know the upper size limit.

4. Press Tab to move to the size itself, and type the size you want to be the limit (for example, if you want to search only files over 64 KB, type 64 after selecting At least in the drop-down list).

5. Click on Find Now.

6. When the search is complete, select the files you want to delete and either drag them to the Recycle Bin or press [Del].

The Computer option of Find will be discussed in the Networking chapter in this book (Chapter 6).

File Manager

As useful as Windows 95 and the Explorer are, you may find yourself wishing for the old File Manager that you had in Windows 3.1. The File Manager did have several features that you may long for, such as File Move and Copy, and the drive icons in the toolbar across the top. If so, you can still use the old File Manager in Windows 95. Hidden in your Windows folder is a file named Winfile.exe. If you find this folder and file using the Explorer and then double-click on it, the File Manager will open, as shown in Figure 2–4.

Figure 2–4

The File Manager in Windows 95

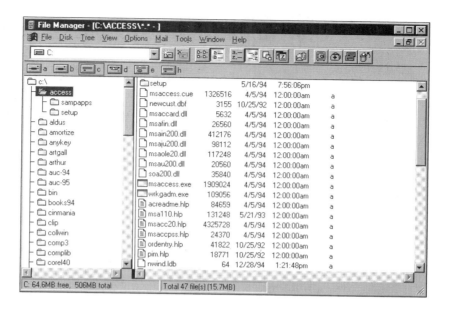

 The File Manager will not display long filenames. All you'll see is the 8.3 names created by Windows.

The menus and tools in the Windows 95 File Manager are the same as the Windows 3.1 versions except that you cannot share and unshare files in the Windows 95 File Manager. Also, you will have the Microsoft Tools (Backup, Antivirus, DriveSpace, and Undelete) only if you installed Windows 95 on top of Windows 3.1.

 If you delete a file in the File Manager, the deleted files do NOT go into the Recycle Bin and cannot be undeleted.

Handling Files and Folders

There are many tasks that you perform on files while using your computer. This includes copying, moving, naming, renaming, deleting, retrieving, and backing up files and folders. How easy and efficient these tasks are go a long way in determining how satisfied you are with your computer system. Windows 95 has many improvements in this area and a few that still need some work.

The following paragraphs will explore all of the major file handling tasks and describe how they are performed in Windows 95.

Copying and Moving Files and Folders

There are three primary ways to copy or move files in Windows 95 and two more if you include the File Manager and DOS. These are, in order of their ease of use, dragging within the Explorer, using cut or copy and paste, dragging between folder windows or the desktop, File Manager File Move or Copy, and DOS commands.

DRAGGING WITHIN THE EXPLORER

By all means the easiest way to copy or move a file or folder from one folder to another is to drag it from a folder that is open in the right pane of the Explorer to another folder or disk in the left pane. The trick is to display both the source folder in the right pane and the destination in the left. One of the great beauties of the Explorer is that every disk and folder that you can access from your computer can be displayed in the left pane of the explorer. Therefore, any file or folder that you can display in the right pane can be dragged and thereby copied or moved to any disk or folder you can access.

Simply dragging a file or folder from one folder to another *in the same disk drive*, as you see in Figure 2–5, will *move* that file or folder and not leave a copy in the original folder. If you press and hold Ctrl while dragging, you will copy the file or folder leaving the original where it was. (A copy action displays a small plus sign in a box next to

Figure 2–5

Moving a file to a different folder by dragging it

the dragged item.) If you drag a file or folder from one disk drive to another, you will always make a copy of the object you drag.

 If you use the right mouse button to drag a file or folder from one folder to another, you will be asked if you want to copy or move it.

 When dragging a file or folder in the Explorer, you can automatically scroll the left pane by dragging the object to just inside the top of the pane to scroll up, or to just inside the bottom of the pane to scroll down. The alternative, which is often more straightforward, is to manually scroll the left pane before beginning to drag.

USING THE EDIT MENU

You can use the Edit menu options to copy and move files both in the Explorer and in normal folder windows. This is done by first selecting the file or folder to be moved or copied. Then, from the Edit menu, choose Cut if the file is to be moved (no copy left behind) or Copy if the file is to be copied. Then select the destination folder or disk and choose Paste from the Edit menu. This technique works well when you cannot see or do not immediately know what the destination of the copy or move will be.

 Independent of how you copy or move a file, you can undo the last ten copies or moves using the Undo option in the Edit menu, as shown next, or by pressing (Ctrl)-(Z).

OTHER FORMS OF COPYING AND MOVING

Copying and moving files and folders between folder windows means simply that you open the receiving folder window, open the sending folder window, and then drag the file or folder from one to the other. If having two windows open at a time is a problem, you can open the sending folder, drag the file or folder to the desktop, close the sending folder, open the receiving folder, and drag the object to it.

Within the File Manager you can drag a file or folder from the right pane to the left one, but unlike the Explorer, the left pane only contains the folders on the selected drive. The real benefit in the File Manager is the Copy and Move options in the File menu that allow you to enter the source and destination and change the name in the process. This is very useful and is a major omission in Windows 95. DOS, of course, allows you also to enter a Copy or Move command where you can specify the source and destination.

Naming and Renaming Files and Folders

One of the most desired features since the earliest days of the IBM PC has been to have filenames longer than the eight-character filename and three-character extension (this is abbreviated as the 8.3 format) that began its life before the PC. Windows 95 finally provides for long filenames and does so in a manner that allows for backward compatibility with older systems. It gives every file two names: a long filename and an 8.3 alias.

USING LONG FILENAMES

The long filename can be up to 255 characters long and can include any combination of the following:

- Numbers 0–9
- Upper- and lowercase letters *A–Z* with case differentiation
- Blank (Spacebar, character 32)
- The special characters allowed in the 8.3 format:
  ! # $ % & ' ( ) - @ ^ _ ` { } ~
- The additional special characters, valid in a long filename but not in an 8.3 alias:
  + . = [ ] , ;
- All of the characters above character 127
- But the following characters may *NOT* be included:
  " * / : < > ? \ |

When you name a file, Windows 95 looks at the name. If your name fits the 8.3 format *and is all uppercase*, then both the filename and the alias are the same. Otherwise, Windows 95 generates an 8.3 format alias out of the long filename. This is not something you can control and the resulting alias depends on many things. Blanks are removed, lowercase is converted to uppercase, characters not allowed in the 8.3 format are removed, and the long name is truncated at eight characters. If this causes a duplicate filename, then a number is added to the end of the name. For example, if you have two Word for Windows files named 1996 Marketing budget.doc and 1996 Marketing plan.doc, the first will have an alias of 1996MARK.DOC and the second an alias of 1996MA~1.DOC.

A long filename can have multiple periods within it. When an alias is generated from a long filename with several periods, all but the last period will be removed and an extension will be created using the first three characters after the rightmost period.

Both My Computer and the Explorer display only the long filename. But, there are two ways you can see both the alias that Windows 95 has assigned a file and the long filename. First, right-click on the file and choose Properties. The Properties dialog box will open and you can see the long name at the top next to the icon and the short name opposite MS-DOS Name, as shown in Figure 2–6.

The second way of seeing both the filename and the alias is from the DOS prompt from *within Windows 95* (open the Start menu, select

Figure 2–6

File Properties dialog box showing both the filename and the alias

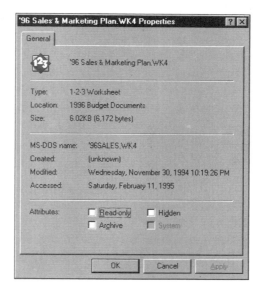

Figure 2–7

A DIR at a DOS prompt from within Windows will show both an alias and the long filename

```
C:\1996 Budget Documents>dir

Volume in drive C is MARTY
Volume Serial Number is 1CC5-8A01
Directory of C:\1996 Budget Documents

.              <DIR>         08-14-95   1:32p  .
..             <DIR>         08-14-95   1:32p  ..
96SALES  MDB      425,984    08-14-95   1:29p  '96 Sales Baseline Statisics.mdb
96BUDGE  XLS       10,240    08-14-95   1:22p  '96 Budget Projection.xls
96BUDGE  DOC       30,720    08-14-95   1:25p  '96 Budget Writeup.doc
96SALES  WK4        6,244    08-14-95   1:26p  '96 Sales & Marketing Plan.WK4
96BUDGE  CDR      110,450    08-14-95   1:19p  '96 Budget Graphic.cdr
1996BUDG <DIR>                08-14-95   1:34p  1996 Budgeting Details
1996MARK DOC            0    11-07-95  10:48p  1996 Marketing Budget.DOC
1996MA~1 DOC            0    11-07-95  10:49p  1996 Marketing Plan.DOC
95BUDGE  DOC       30,720    08-14-95   1:25p  '95 Budget Writeup.doc
95SALES  WK4        6,244    08-14-95   1:26p  '95 Sales & Marketing Plan.WK4
95BUDGE  CDR      110,450    08-14-95   1:19p  '95 Budget Graphic.cdr
1995BUDG <DIR>                10-10-95   3:48p  1995 Budgeting Details
        10 file(s)         731,052 bytes
         4 dir(s)       67,502,080 bytes free

C:\1996 Budget Documents>
```

Programs and then MS-DOS Prompt). If you then type DIR in a folder that has long filenames, you will see the short aliases on the left in the normal position of the DOS filename, and the long filename on the right, as you can see in Figure 2–7. Files that do not have a long filename, have the same name on both the left and the right.

When you use long filenames there are several considerations to keep in mind. Most importantly, you should not use older Windows or DOS utilities to copy, move, backup, rename, or sort files or folders with long filenames. They will strip off the long filename. This problem will *not* occur with older file editors, such as word processors that run under Windows 95, because of a feature called *tunneling*. With tunneling, programs that normally open a file, save temporary files during their process, and end up renaming a temporary file for the permanent save file will operate on the alias, and Windows 95 will preserve the long filename in the background. However, if you do this editing outside of Windows 95 (for example, on another computer or in DOS), you will lose the long filename.

Using an older file-management utility to back up, copy, move, rename, or sort files with long filenames will strip off the long filename.

Another potential problem when using long filenames is that a file manipulation can change the alias. For example, if you copy a file from a folder with potential duplicate aliases to a folder without potential duplicates, the copy will have a different alias. This situation also can occur when you edit a file and save it to a different folder or when you restore a backup file to a different folder.

A search of filenames may produce results that are not expected. This is because, in some instances, both filenames and aliases are searched but only the filenames are shown. Take, for example, the following aliases and filenames:

MANUFACT.DOC	Manufacturing plan.doc
MANUFA~1.DOC	Manufacturing budget.doc
ENGINEER.DOC	Engineering plan.doc
ENGINE~1.DOC	Engineering budget.doc
PLANNING.DOC	Planning summary.doc
PLAN-1.DOC	Plan-1.doc

If you did a DIR *1 at the DOS prompt, you would get this:

MANUFA~1.DOC

ENGINE~1.DOC

PLAN-1.DOC

This appears reasonable, but if you do a similar search and only get back the long filename, it does not appear so obvious, like this:

Manufacturing budget.doc

Engineering budget.doc

Plan-1.doc

 **The Find option on the Start menu searches only the long filename and in the above example would return only Plan-1.doc.**

Prior to Windows 95, only one date/time was maintained for a file. This was initially the date/time created and then, as the file was changed, the last date/time modified. Windows 95 now maintains three figures: the date/time that a file was created, the date/time that a file was last modified, and the date the file was last opened. All of these are displayed in the Properties dialog box for the files, as you can see in Figure 2–8, and are available to be used in new utilities such as backup utilities.

Figure 2–8

File Properties dialog box showing the three dates associated with a file.

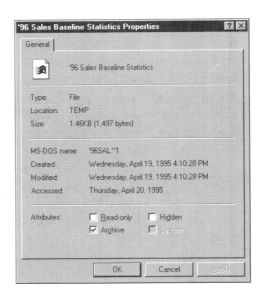

CHANGING FILE AND FOLDER NAMES

Changing file and folder names could not be easier. Simply select the file or folder, click on the filename, and type the new name or edit the existing name. This can be done in the Explorer, in My Computer, on the desktop, or any place you see a file or folder name, like the results window of the Find option.

If you initially select the file by clicking on it, you must wait for a brief moment and then click again to change the name. You do not want to double-click or you will open the file instead of being able to edit. You need to pause between clicking for selection and clicking to change the name.

If a file is selected, you can press F2 to begin editing the name.

When a name is available for editing, a vertical line, called the *insertion point*, appears in it. This tells you where the next character you type will be placed. If any characters in the name are selected (highlighted), they will be replaced by whatever you type.

Once you have the name available for editing, you can drag across the characters you want to change and either press Del to remove the characters or type the replacement characters. You can also use the keystrokes in Table 2–1 to edit a folder- or filename.

Table 2–1.	Keystroke	Function Performed
Editing keys	↑ ↓ ← →	Moves the insertion point in the direction of the key pressed
	Home / End	Moves the insertion point to the left (Home) or right (End) end of the name
	←Backspace	Deletes the character to the left of the insertion point
	Del / Delete	Deletes the character to the right of the insertion point
	←Enter	Completes editing, accepting any changes made
	Esc	Completes editing, ignoring any changes made

Creating and Using Shortcuts

Windows 95 has added a feature, not available in earlier versions of Windows, that allows you to open a folder or start an application without finding and double-clicking on the actual folder or on the actual program file (a file with the extension .EXE, .COM, or .BAT). This new feature is called a *shortcut*. Shortcuts allow you to leave all the files related to a given program in a folder for that program and yet start the program or open the folder from a variety of locations. All you need in each location is a small (under 1 KB) shortcut file.

A shortcut is a link or a pointer to the original program file or to the original folder. When you double-click on a shortcut, Windows 95 opens the original folder or starts the original program to which the shortcut points. The Programs option of the Start menu is composed of folders containing shortcuts, as you can see in Figure 2–9. Shortcuts can be anywhere. You can place them on the desktop, in a folder that you create just to hold program shortcuts, and/or in the Start menu. Chapter 3 will show you several examples of how you might set up your computer using shortcuts so that you can easily get at your programs, files, and folders.

You can create shortcuts in several ways. The easiest is to drag a program file or a folder to the Start menu. This creates a shortcut in the \Windows\Start Menu folder and places the program name on the top of the Start menu. The result is that you can start a program or open a folder by opening the Start menu and clicking on the program or folder name without using the Programs option.

Figure 2-9

Shortcuts and folders that make up the Programs option of the Start menu

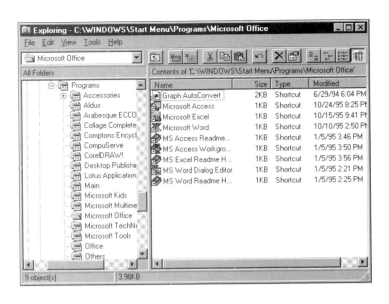

Two other ways to create shortcuts you can use anywhere are to right-click on a program file or a folder to open the popup menu, or select a file or folder and open the File menu. Then, in either case, choose Create Shortcut as shown here:

A new file is then created with the words *Shortcut to* in front of the name of the file or folder you clicked on. The new file is in the folder that contained the original file or folder, but you can drag it anywhere.

If you right-click on this new file and select Properties, the Properties dialog box will open. The General tab, for most files, shows the normal name, size, and dates that are part of the properties of all files. The Shortcut Tab (or Program Tab for shortcuts to DOS programs), though, is unique and shows the original file to which the shortcut is pointing, the starting folder, and any hot key that has been assigned to the shortcut, as shown in Figure 2–10. This tab also allows you to find the original file or folder (display the file or folder in its containing folder) by clicking on the Find Target button and to change the icon that is used with the shortcut.

To quickly start an application or open a folder, press a key you want to use as a hot key while the Hot Key text box is selected in the Properties for Shortcut dialog box.

A shortcut for a DOS program is the Windows 95 replacement for a PIF file. (A PIF is a program information file that is used to facilitate running DOS programs under Windows.) A DOS shortcut's properties dialog box has a number of additional tabs that allow you to determine the screen font, memory handling, screen characteristics, and other facets of how Windows interacts with the program. If a Windows 3.1 PIF file exists for the DOS program, look at that file to get the settings for a shortcut to that program (you'll not be allowed to create a shortcut to a PIF file because that is like having a PIF for a PIF). If no PIF exists, try running the program without any changes in the shortcut; it is highly likely that none are needed. If all fails, you will have to ask the publisher of the DOS program what the settings should be.

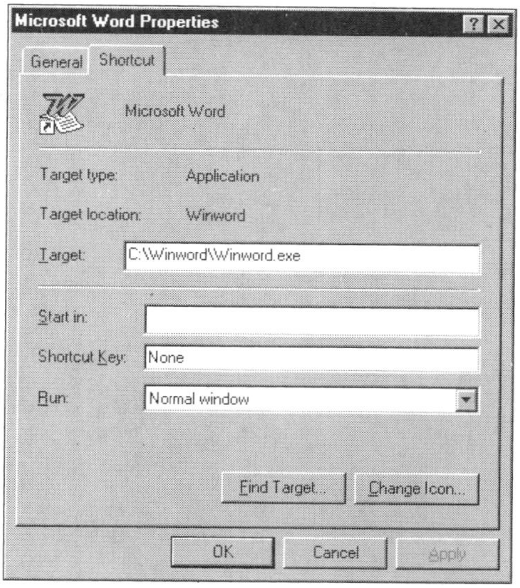

Figure 2–10

*Shortcut
Properties
dialog box*

Microsoft Word Properties	? ✕

General | Shortcut

Microsoft Word

Target type: Application

Target location: Winword

Target: C:\Winword\Winword.exe

Start in:

Shortcut Key: None

Run: Normal window

Find Target...   Change Icon...

OK   Cancel   Apply

If you create a shortcut for a DOS program or a nonprogram file, you can get additional icon choices from \Windows\System\Iconlib.dll, \Windows\System\Pifmgr.dll, \Windows\System\Shell32.dll, and \Windows\Moricons.dll.

Associating Files

Associating, or registering, files is the process of identifying the program that is used to create and edit a type of file, so that if you activate (double-click on) that type of file, the program will start and load the file. For example, Word for Windows is used to create and edit most files with the .DOC extension. DOC files are therefore associated with Word for Windows, and if you double-click on one of them, Word for Windows will start and load the file so it is ready for you to edit.

Most associating is done automatically when a program is installed. You can see which file types are associated with what programs in the File Types tab of the Explorer Options dialog box, shown in Figure 2–11. You can open this dialog box from either the Explorer or My Computer View menu.

If you want to associate a file type that is not automatically registered when a program is installed, use the following steps:

Figure 2–11

File associations are registered in the File Types tab of the Options dialog box.

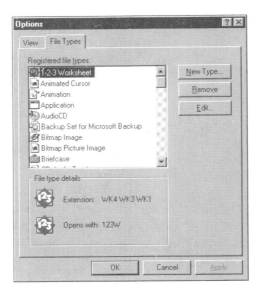

1. Select a file of the type you want to register, and open the Options menu from either My Computer or the Explorer.

2. Click on the File Types tab and then on New Type. The Add New File Type dialog box opens, as shown in Figure 2–12.

    For example, say you wanted to create a file type for "zipped" files that have been compressed with PKZip, and that whenever you double-clicked on that file type, you wanted PKUnzip to decompress them.

3. Type **Zipped file** and **zip** for the description and the extension. The description will appear in the Type column in the Explorer detail view and in the Properties dialog box for the files. The extension should be the extension used by all files in the file type.

4. Click on New, type **Open** in the Action text box, use Browse to locate PKUnzip on your computer, double-click on the filename, and finally click on OK.

5. Back in the Add New File Type dialog box, click on Change Icon, choose the file cabinet icon from the Moricons.dll file (see most recent tip above) to select the icon to be used with the file type, and then click on OK twice to complete the process.

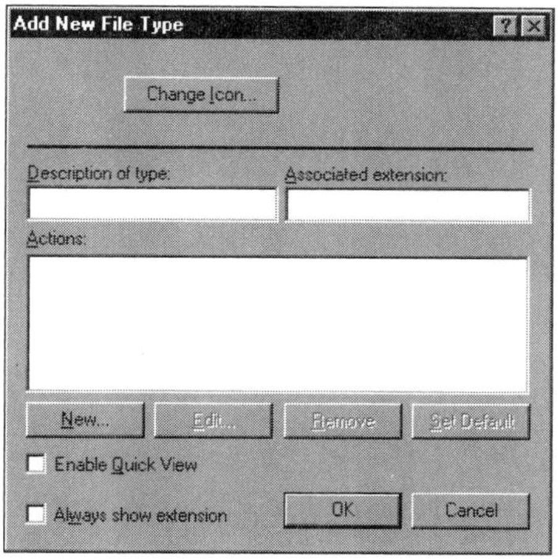

Figure 2–12

Dialog box to associate a new file type

Deleting Files and Folders

Deleting a file or a folder is as simple as selecting it and pressing `Del` or choosing Delete from the File menu, right-clicking on it and choosing Delete, or dragging the object to the Recycle Bin—or is it? In Windows 95, everything you delete goes into the Recycle Bin independent of how you deleted it. This is a safety feature that allows you to undelete whatever you deleted until you empty the Recycle Bin. But it also means that you must take the extra step of emptying the Recycle Bin.

USING THE RECYCLE BIN

By adding the Recycle Bin to Windows 95, Microsoft has taken Windows a step closer to the Apple Macintosh, where the broadly appreciated feature, called the Trash Can, has been a permanent fixture since the first Mac. The Windows 95 Recycle Bin is like a special purpose shortcut to the Recycled folder in your primary hard disk. All files and folders that you delete by one of the above methods are automatically placed in this folder unless you take an action to prevent it (you will see how to do that in a moment). The Recycled folder can be viewed like any other folder, as you can see in Figure 2–13. This is the same view you get if you double-click on the Recycle Bin to open it.

Figure 2–13

The Recycled folder in the Explorer

As in virtually all Windows 95 objects, you control the Recycle Bin by right-clicking on it and opening its Properties dialog box, as shown here:

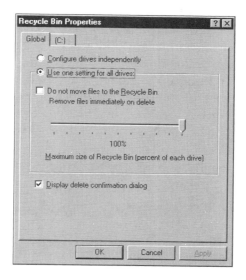

You can set the Recycle Bin properties either globally, for all drives on your computer, or for each drive independently (of course, if you have only one hard drive, that is the same thing). In either case, you can purge the files immediately upon deleting them and thus inactivate the Recycle Bin, and you can determine the amount of your disk space you want to allocate to the Recycled folder. If you purge files immediately upon deletion, you will get a warning message, shown next, every time you delete a file or a folder using any of the techniques. The same is *NOT* true if you set your disk allocation too small and then delete more files than can fit. You get no message and the earliest-deleted files simply disappear. The default Recycle Bin is 10 percent of your hard disk space, which, in most circumstances, should be adequate.

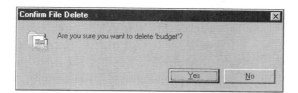

 If you delete more files than can be held in the disk space allocated for the Recycle Bin, your earliest-deleted file(s) will disappear without warning.

Synchronizing Files with My Briefcase

My Briefcase provides a means to synchronize files between two computers. It is a special folder that keeps track of the change status of the files it contains. This allows you to work on the same file on two computers, and have Windows remember which is the latest file, and then update the older one so the two are the same. For example, if you use My Briefcase to take files from a computer at work and work on them on a computer at home, when you return the briefcase to the computer at work, the original files can be updated for the changes you made at home, as shown next. The steps to do this are as follows:

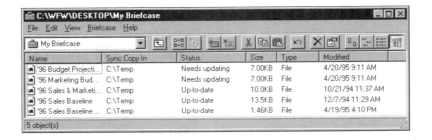

   If you do not have a Briefcase on your screen, you may have elected not to install it when you installed Windows 95. You can add it by using Add/Remove Programs in the Control Panel.

1. Drag or copy the files you want to keep synchronized to My Briefcase.

2. Drag or copy My Briefcase to a floppy disk and carry it to a second computer, or drag My Briefcase to another computer on your network.

3. Open My Briefcase on the second computer and edit the files while they remain in the briefcase. Alternately or in addition, you can edit the original files on the first computer.

4. Open My Briefcase back on the original computer, either while it is still on the floppy or by dragging it to the original computer's hard disk, and choose Update All or Update Selection from the Briefcase menu. The Update My Briefcase dialog box will open, as shown in Figure 2–14.

    The Update My Briefcase dialog box shows you what Windows believes to be the direction of the updating you want done. If

Figure 2–14

*Notification of
updating to be
done from
My Briefcase*

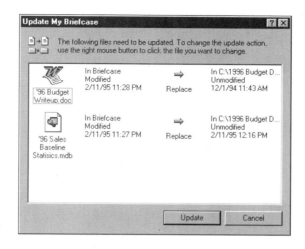

Figure 2–14

*Notification of
updating to be
done from
My Briefcase*

you want to change the file that is updated, right-click on the entry you want to change, and then, in the popup menu that opens, either select the opposite direction or Skip to not update either file.

5.   After assuring yourself that the updating that Windows is proposing is correct, or after changing it, click on Update to synchronize the files between My Briefcase and the original files.

If both files have changed, Windows will suggest that you skip updating either file. You can change this and update either one you want. Also, it is planned that some programs will allow you to look at two files and identify the differences.

Handling Disks

Disk drives provide for storing your folders and files and for transporting these objects on and off your computer. Most computers have at least one floppy-disk drive, one hard-disk drive, and possibly a CD-ROM drive. The CD-ROM drive will be discussed in depth in Part IV on Multimedia, but some of what will be said here about floppy and hard drives also applies to CD-ROMs.

Floppy- and hard-disk drives can be thought of as just large folders, and some of the discussion earlier in this chapter that related to folders also pertains to disks. Most importantly, you can drag and copy files and folders to disks just as you can to other folders. But there are also many unique features about disks. They can be formatted, copied, scanned for errors, defragmented, compressed, and backed up. Those are the subjects of this section.

Formatting and Labeling Disks

Formatting prepares a new disk so that it can be used or erases a used disk so it can be reused. In Windows 95 you can format a disk by right-clicking on it in either My Computer or the Explorer and choosing Format from the popup menu. The Format dialog box appears, as shown in Figure 2–15. In it you can select the capacity of the disk you are formatting and the type of formatting you want to do. The options for format type and their purposes are as follows:

- **Quick** format does not check the disk for bad sectors (similar to ScanDisk discussed in a moment). It only erases the existing information and prepares the disk for use.

- **Full** format completely scans the disk for errors and, if it doesn't find any, erases the old information on the disk and prepares it to be used.

Make sure the disk you are trying to format isn't currently opened in the Explorer. You cannot format the disk while its contents are displayed.

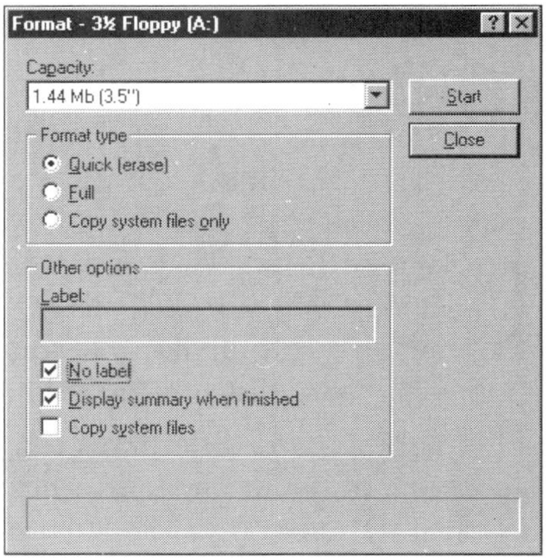

Figure 2–15

Format dialog box

- **Make Bootable Only** does not format the disk but only writes the four system files (Command.com, Drvspace.bin, Io.sys, and Msdos.sys) on the disk that make it able to start your computer. These files take 325 KB of disk space.

 Use Quick format only if you are very sure you have a disk with no bad sectors. The extra time it takes to scan and let you know about bad sectors could save you problems later.

If you choose Quick or Full for the Format Type, you can optionally add a label to the disk of up to 11 characters and get information about the formatted disk telling you how much space is available and how much is used by system files and bad sectors. Also, you can add the system files in addition to formatting. The formatting information looks like this:

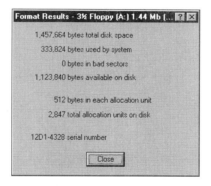

If you add a label to a disk in formatting, you can see the label in the Properties dialog box for that disk (where you can also change the label or add one if it was not done in formatting). If a used disk has a label and you want to remove it during formatting and have no label, click on No label.

Analyzing and Repairing Disks with ScanDisk

As disk size increases, the chance of something happening to the information you have written on the disk increases proportionally. To ease this problem with today's larger disk sizes, Windows 95 has included a general disk-diagnostic-and-repair program called

ScanDisk. ScanDisk will work on hard disks, floppy disks, and RAM drives, but not CD-ROM disks, and it will detect and fix problems in the following areas:

- Directory tree structure
- DriveSpace or DoubleSpace compression structure, volume header, volume file structure, and volume signatures
- File allocation table, or FAT
- File structure (cross-linked files and lost clusters)
- Long files names
- Physical drive surface (bad sectors)

To load ScanDisk, open the Start menu and choose Programs, Accessories, System Tools, and ScanDisk. You can also right-click on a drive in either the Explorer or My Computer, select Properties, and click on Check Now in the Tools tab. Once started, the ScanDisk dialog box opens, as shown in Figure 2–16. This allows you to select the drive to scan and to choose between the Standard scan, which checks for file and folder problems but not for physical damage to the disk, and Thorough scan, which adds the physical disk analysis. The scan for physical damage takes considerably longer than the Standard scan (depending on the size of your drive and what is found, this can be

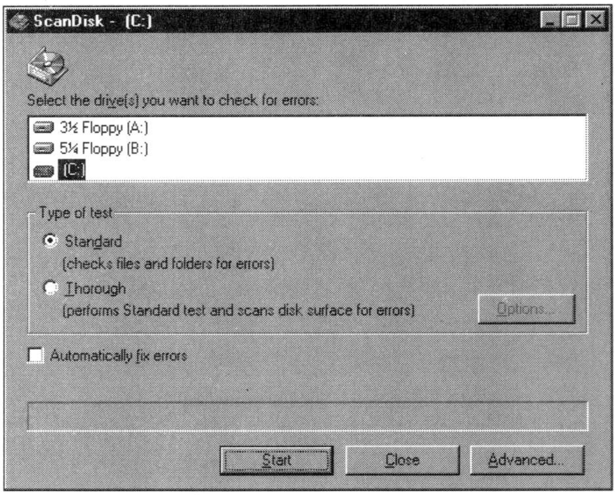

Figure 2–16

ScanDisk dialog box

the difference between less than a minute or more than 20 minutes), so normally you may want to do a Standard scan.

You can see how long it has been since you last ran ScanDisk on a drive by right-clicking on the drive in the Explorer or in My Computer, choosing Properties, and opening the Tools tab.

If you encounter an error while running ScanDisk, under default settings you will be notified of the error and asked what you want to do, as shown here:

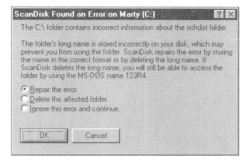

Depending on what the error is, you will be given a choice of fixing the error, deleting the offending file or folder, or doing nothing. In most instances the dialog box will tell you what can be done with the error (repairing it is the most common), and what is recommended here. Repairing works most of the time and should be tried before the other alternatives. If you wish, you can have ScanDisk automatically fix most errors without asking you by clicking on the Automatically fix errors check box in the ScanDisk dialog box. Unless there is a lot of repetition in the repairing process, it is a good idea to look at the error messages to see what is happening on your disk. A rash of problems could indicate it's time to get a new hard disk.

You can control some aspects of what ScanDisk does through the Advanced button in the ScanDisk dialog box. Clicking on this button opens the ScanDisk Advanced Options dialog box, shown next. The first option, Display summary, determines when the ScanDisk Results (shown after the ScanDisk Advanced Options dialog box) are displayed. This summary provides feedback on how your disk is doing.

The second option in the ScanDisk Advanced Options dialog box determines what to do with lost file fragments. Files are stored in multiple pieces, or *fragments*, and sometimes a fragment becomes detached from the rest of the file. In most instances where the rest of the file exists, ScanDisk can reattach the fragment and all is well. But, if the rest of the file has been deleted or if for some reason ScanDisk can't reattach it, the fragment is considered lost. There is very little chance that if the fragment can be converted to a file (very difficult in and of itself), you can determine what it is and use it. In most cases, the fragments result from deleted files and are of no value. It is therefore recommended that lost file fragments be deleted and their space converted to free space. As a result, the Free option is the default for handling lost file fragments.

Cross-linked files occur when two files share the same fragment, although the fragment is probably only correct for one file. In most instances this corrupts both files and they need to be deleted. The other option is to make a copy of the fragment and attach one to each file. This allows you at least to try to read both files and decide which file, if either, is worth keeping. The final possibility is to ignore cross-linked files. This is not a good idea because it can cause an application to crash, potentially bringing down the entire system and losing more files.

The fourth option in the Advanced Options dialog box asks you if you want to check for invalid filenames and invalid dates and times on files. Invalid filenames, such as might occur on files you brought over from a Unix or Macintosh computer, might not be readable by your applications and therefore need to be fixed. Invalid dates and times can cause files to be sorted incorrectly or cause backup and setup programs to make incorrect assumptions.

The final option asks you if you want to check your host drive, which is your uncompressed drive if you are using DriveSpace or DoubleSpace disk compression. If this box is not checked, the host drive is ignored. If you are using disk compression, you should check your host drive before checking the compressed drive. Therefore, the box should be checked. Disk compression is discussed further later in this chapter.

PHYSICAL SURFACE SCAN

If you choose a Thorough disk scan, ScanDisk will analyze the disk for physical defects. The Options button next to the Thorough option opens the Surface Scan Options dialog box. This allows you to determine what area of the disk you want to scan: the system area, the data area, or both. When ScanDisk finds a physical error on the disk, it flags that sector as a bad one so nothing will be written there in the future and writes any information found in the original sector, in another. This works well in the large data area, but the system area is very small, so there is often not room to move a file. Also, some older programs look for their information in a specific location in the system area, and if it is moved, the program will not work. Often if errors occur in the system area, you will need to replace the disk. The Surface Scan Options dialog box is shown in the illustration at the top of the next page.

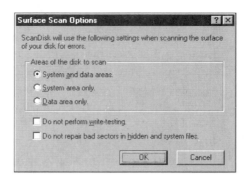

The Surface Scan Options dialog box has two check boxes that allow you to disable write testing and to not repair bad sectors that contain hidden or system files. When ScanDisk does a surface scan, it reads a sector, then writes back the information that was in the sector and compares the two. This fully tests the ability of the disk to be read from and written on. There is a chance that this process can corrupt data, and therefore the reason for the check box is to turn off write testing. The problem is that you will not know if you have a bad sector that should have been corrected. In most cases the data is read correctly, and then if a write error is detected, the sector is flagged, and the data is correctly rewritten in a new location.

The reason you may not want to repair bad sectors containing hidden or system files has already been discussed—because of the limited size of the system area and because some older programs expect the files in a specific location. The alternative, though, is to buy a new disk, so it is recommended that you try the repair process and see whether or not you have a serious problem.

While it is possible to run other programs while running either ScanDisk or Disk Defragmenter, each time you write to the disk the utilities will restart, causing the process to go very slowly. This is also true with the Screen Saver. You should therefore turn off the Screen Saver and not run other programs while running either of these utilities.

Optimizing or Defragmenting Disks

Files are stored on a disk in pieces, or fragments, the size of which depends on the size of your drive; the larger the drive, the larger the fragments. If there is enough room in one location on your disk to store an entire file, then the entire file is stored in one contiguous location. If there is not enough room in one spot, then the file is broken up and stored in fragments throughout the disk. In this latter case, reading the file can take much longer and fragments can become lost, as you just read about under ScanDisk. If you add and delete a lot of files, fragmentation of your files can become a serious problem and significantly slow down your disk access. To fix this problem, Windows 95 has included Disk Defragmenter. This program goes through your disk rearranging files so that all of their fragments are contiguous, thereby, speeding up disk access.

Start Disk Defragmenter by opening the Start menu and choosing Programs, Accessories, System Tools, and Disk Defragmenter. You can also right-click on a drive in the Explorer or My Computer, choose Properties and Tools, and then click on Defragment Now. If you enter through the Start menu, you will be asked to specify a drive you want to defragment, and then, in either case, the Defragmentation dialog box will open as shown here:

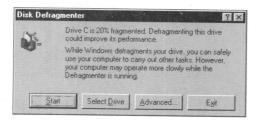

You can control some of what Disk Defragmenter does by clicking on Advanced to open the Advanced Options dialog box shown next. In this dialog box (Figure 2–17) you can choose to defragment only files, only free space, or both. Also, you can choose to have this decision for one time only, or to be a default that is used every time you defragment a drive.

If your drive is approximately ten percent or less fragmented, you will get a message telling you it's unnecessary to defragment your drive. You can still defragment it by clicking on Start.

Click on Start to begin the process. When you do, the Defragmenting Drive dialog box opens, as shown in Figure 2–17. This allows you stop or pause the process and to show the details of the defragmentation. While it is fun to see the enlarged detail display, it significantly slows

Figure 2–17

*Advanced Options
dialog box*

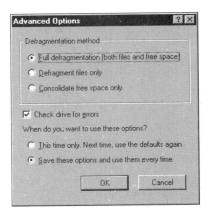

the task down. To get the fastest performance from Disk Defragmenter, it is best to minimize the dialog box so that you only see it in the task bar (it still tells you the percentage complete).

Disk Defragmentor will work with DriveSpace and DoubleSpace compressed drives (the host drive should be defragmented first), but it will not work with other compression utilities such as Stacker or SuperStor.

Compressing Disks

Compressing a disk squeezes the contents down so they fit in roughly one-half the space they took before being compressed. Thus the storage space on the disk is roughly doubled. Disk compression is accomplished by a complex algorithm that eliminates unused space and repeated characters or patterns of characters. When a disk is compressed, it behaves and looks to you, the user, and to programs using it like any other disk; it just contains approximately twice as much data. In reality, the compressed disk is a newly created virtual drive that is given the name of the original uncompressed drive. In addition, a new uncompressed drive, often called drive H or the *host* drive, is created that contains at least one file, the entire contents of the compressed drive. If for some reason you need other uncompressed files, they also can be placed on the host drive.

Do not in any way change the compressed file on the host drive (called Drvspace.000 or Dblspace.000), or you will risk losing all of your files on the compressed drive.

You can compress a hard drive or a floppy drive or change the compression on an existing DriveSpace or DoubleSpace drive by opening the Start menu and choosing Programs, Accessories, System Tools, and DriveSpace. You then choose what disk you want to compress in this dialog box:

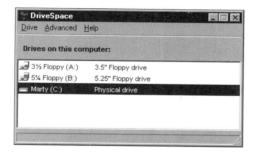

DoubleSpace is the original Microsoft disk compression routine that was first available with MS-DOS 6.0. For legal reasons, it was replaced by DriveSpace in MS-DOS 6.22. Windows 95 contains DriveSpace, but it can fully utilize disks that were compressed with DoubleSpace.

Double-clicking on a drive in the DriveSpace dialog box opens the Compression Properties dialog box, shown in Figure 2–18. This tells you if the drive is compressed, the amount of used and free space, the compression ratios, and the parent drive if the drive is compressed. The Compression Properties dialog box is just an information box similar to the drive Properties dialog box, and the only option you have is to hide the host drive. (Only under rare circumstances, where a new user might get into trouble, should you hide a host drive. Otherwise, hiding a drive only leads to confusion.) To do anything else with a drive, you must return to the DriveSpace dialog box. There, after selecting a drive, you can compress, uncompress, or adjust the amount of free space with the Drive menu. The Advanced menu allows you to mount (open) or unmount (close) a compressed drive on removable

Figure 2–18

Compression information for a compressed drive

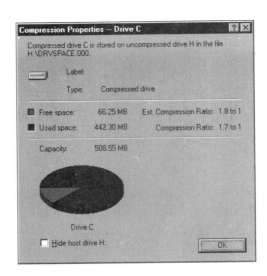

media like floppies, create a new (empty) compressed drive using the free space on an existing drive (which may or may not be compressed), delete an existing compressed drive, and change the compression ratio assumption used to figure free space on a compressed drive.

If you start with an uncompressed drive, you can either compress all of the data and free space on the drive and end up with a single compressed drive plus a host drive, or you can create a new, empty compressed drive from the free space and end up with an uncompressed drive, a compressed drive, and a host drive. For example, if you have a 160-MB hard disk with 100 MB of files and 60 MB of free space and you compress the entire drive, you would then have a 320-MB compressed drive with 100 MB of files (see note below) and 220 MB of free space plus a 160-MB host drive with little or no free space. (These are approximate numbers—in actual fact you seldom get the full 2:1 compression ratio, and you will use one or two megabytes of the host drive for system files.) On the other hand, if you create an empty compressed drive using the free space, you will have a 100-MB uncompressed drive with no free space, a 120-MB empty compressed drive, and a full host drive. It is obvious that you can get more free space by compressing the entire drive. It also takes considerably longer because all of the existing files must be compressed.

The file sizes that you see reported in My Computer or the Explorer, after you have compressed a drive, are the uncompressed size of the files—the size the files would be if you copied them to an uncompressed drive.

Figure 2–19

*Compress a Drive
dialog box*

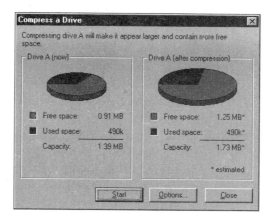

When you choose to compress a drive, the dialog box shown in Figure 2–19 opens showing you the current space on the drive and the space after compression, as well as the space on the host drive to be created. Clicking on the Options button, you can change the drive letter of the host drive, but you cannot change the allocation of space until the compression process is complete. You can also hide or expose the host drive in the Options dialog box. If the host drive has less than 20 MB of free space, DriveSpace will hide the host drive by default. You can change that.

Compressed drives are limited to 512 MB. If you compress a drive with more than 256 MB, you will not get the 2:1 compression ratio that you get with smaller drives, as shown in Figure 2–18. A larger host drive will make up for this somewhat.

As DriveSpace begins the process of compressing a drive, it first scans the disk for errors, both with the files and with the surface; it then defragments the files and finally compresses the drive. Depending on the size of the drive and the speed of your processor, this can take up to several hours. It is very safe, though, and can even recover from a power outage in the middle of the process. You should close all open files and applications, or you will be reminded to do so once DriveSpace starts. If you are compressing the drive that contains Windows 95, DriveSpace will restart your computer with a limited version of Windows 95 to complete the compression. Upon completion you are told how much free space was created on the disk. Then after completion, your computer will be restarted again with the full version of Windows 95.

Always back up all data files before compressing a drive that contains them.

Compressing and using compressed floppy drives works the same as with hard drives. Under the default settings, if you insert a compressed floppy in the drive, Windows 95 will automatically see it is compressed and allow you to work with the files as if they were not compressed. This is called *automounting*. You can control whether compressed floppies are automatically mounted (opened) or not by opening the DriveSpace Advanced menu, choosing Settings, and checking Automatically mount new compressed devices in the Disk Compression Settings dialog box, as shown next. If automounting is turned off, you can manually mount the drive again through the DriveSpace Advanced menu.

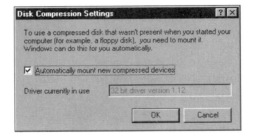

If you infrequently use compressed floppy disks, turn off automounting and save about 4 KB of memory.

You can adjust the amount of free space on the host drive and on the compressed drive by opening DriveSpace's Drive menu and choosing Adjust Free Space. This opens the dialog box you see in Figure 2–20. By dragging the slider to the left, you will increase the amount of free space on the compressed drive and decrease the amount on the host drive. Dragging the slider to the right has the opposite effect. As you drag the slider, one drive will go up as the other goes down using the compression ratio (2:1 by default) between the two. Instead of the slider, you also may type a number in one of the Free Space number boxes.

You should leave at least 2 MB on the host drive for your hard disk. Some DriveSpace operations require at least 1.5 MB on the host drive.

One other DriveSpace adjustment that you can make is to change the compression ratio for a compressed drive. This is done through the

Figure 2–20

Adjust Free Space dialog box

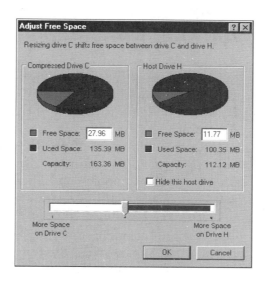

Advanced menu and the Compression Ratio dialog box, shown next. By dragging the slider you can change the ratio used in estimating the amount of free space. Since there is no way to know the types of files you will be storing in the free space, and different files compress to different degrees, you must use a rule of thumb to estimate the amount of free space on a compressed drive. By default, this ratio is 2:1. Your experience may be different. Look at the actual compression ratio, and decide how representative it is of what you might place in the free space. Also, consider the types of files you may place there. Program and word processing files do not compress very much, while drawing and bitmapped files compress a lot. Then, set the compression ratio to fit your beliefs. Only the estimated amount of free space will be changed.

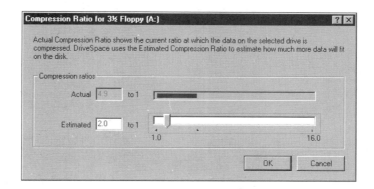

Backing Up Files and Folders

Backing up a hard drive or even floppies is something we are all told to do numerous times but don't do until we lose a valuable file. *Backing up* is simply copying a disk or disks to other disks or to tape. Backing up a hard drive used to require the flipping of a lot of floppies. Today, a 250-MB tape drive costs less than $200 and greatly reduces the amount of effort. Even better, Windows 95 includes a backup program that automatically recognizes these inexpensive tape drives, as well as floppies, and provides a high degree of compression and file management in backing up your files. You can keep track of the files you backed up and retrieve a single file, if you wish.

You start the backup process by opening the Start menu and choosing Programs, Accessories, System Tools, and Backup. After the Welcome to Microsoft Backup message, the Microsoft Backup dialog box will open, as shown in Figure 2–21. For a backup, the first step is to select the files to be copied. You do this either by selecting entire folders on the left (by clicking in their check boxes), or by opening a folder (by clicking on it) and then selecting files on the right (by clicking on their check boxes). At the bottom of the Backup dialog box you can see the total number of files selected and the total size of those files. Once you have completed selecting the folders and files

Figure 2–21

*Microsoft Backup
dialog box*

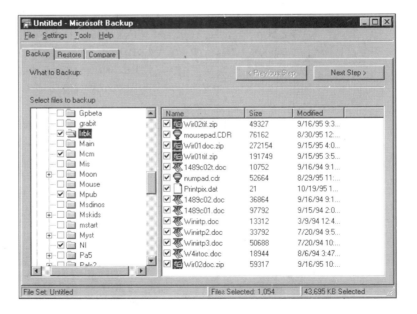

you want to back up, click on the Next Step button in the upper right of the dialog box.

 **You will speed up the backup process and reduce the size of the back-up files by not backing up program files which you already should have on disk anyway.**

The second step is to select where you want to place the backup, on a floppy disk drive or, if available, a tape. To do this, simply click on the drive you want to use and click on Start Backup. You are next asked to enter a name for the backup set and then click on OK. As the backup is in progress, you are given a continuous status report of the number of files and bytes backed up, as well as the elapsed time, as shown here:

 **Most tapes drives cannot be used to back up files from floppy disks because both the tape drive and the floppy use the same controller.**

Once you have backed up a set of files and folders, you can restore them either to their original location or to a new location. Also, you can compare the backup files to the original files to see if there is any difference. The restore process is particularly useful because you can restore individual files as well as the entire set. To start the restore process, click on the Restore tab, choose the device from which you want to restore, and then select the fileset to use, as you can see in Figure 2–22. After clicking on Next Step, you can then select the folders and files as you did in the backup process. When you are done, click on Start Restore. The compare operation works in the same manner.

After selecting all the files you want to back up and the destination of the backup, you may want to save that set of specifications so that you do not have to specify it again. Do this by selecting Save As from the

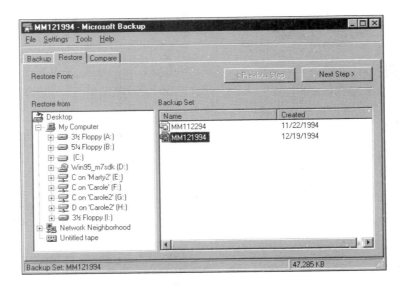

Figure 2–22

Selecting a fileset to restore

Microsoft Backup File menu and entering the name. You can also print the list of files being backed up by selecting Print from the File menu. Be warned, though, it is a single-column list, and if you have many files, it could be a number of pages long because it gives you only 59 files per page.

The Settings menu allows you to select the type of files and folders that you want to consider for backup and then a number of options for backup, restore, and compare. Of importance, the Backup tab allows you to select between a full backup and a backup of only those files that have changed since the last full backup. (Doing full backups less frequently and incremental backups more frequently is an excellent way to do backups.) Also of importance, both the Restore and Compare tabs allow you to choose a location for restoring and comparing, other than the original location. There are a number of other options for all of the processes, but they are self-explanatory, and the defaults are what you usually will want.

Copying Disks

Copy Disk allows you to copy data from one floppy disk to another of the *same* type. For example, you can copy data from a 3.5-inch disk to another 3.5-inch disk, but you cannot copy from a 3.5-inch disk to a 5.25-inch disk. If you have two floppy drives of the same type, you can copy files directly between them. Otherwise, you will be prompted to remove the *source* disk and insert the *destination* disk in the same drive. Disk copying is activated by right-clicking on any of your floppy disk drives in the Explorer or My Computer and choosing Copy Disk, or in My Computer, selecting the drive and choosing Copy Disk from the File menu. Using either method, the Copy Disk dialog box opens, as shown next.

 **Any data on your destination disk will be deleted, regardless of the size of the file(s) being copied.**

Select the source drive in the Copy From list box and the destination drive in the Copy To list box. Click on Start to begin the process, and when prompted, remove the source disk and insert the destination disk. When complete, you can repeat the process for other disks you have to copy by clicking on the Start button.

Setting up and Customizing Windows 95

indows 95 is designed to operate the way you operate. To accomplish this, a great deal of flexibility has been built into Windows 95. This allows you to custom-tailor it to behave the way you want it to. Of course you must take the time to learn how to do that and then carry it out. The purpose of this chapter is to identify the areas that can be customized, to describe what the options are, and to show you how customizing can be accomplished.

Setting up Windows 95

You can tailor Windows 95 in two very broad ways: by setting up or organizing your screen, disk, folders, and files the way you want them; and by customizing the many settings that are available in the Control Panel. In this section you'll look at setting up and organizing your Windows 95 system, and in the next major section you'll look at customizing it using the Control Panel.

Figure 3–1

Opening screen with the Welcome window

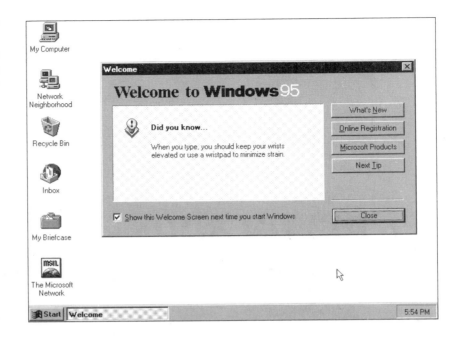

Arranging Your Screen

The obvious place to start tailoring your system is with the Windows 95 screen. When you first start Windows 95, your screen looks approximately like that shown in Figure 3–1 (yours may have fewer icons on the left depending on what Windows' options you have installed, and you may or may not still see the Welcome message). There are many things you can do to this screen and its components to make them fit what you want.

Your first decision is whether you want to see the Welcome message each time you start Windows. The tips it provides are worthwhile and so you may want to keep Welcome appearing until you have run through all the tips several times.

If you have already turned off the Welcome message, you can restart it by double-clicking on Welcome.exe in the Windows folder.

WORKING WITH DESKTOP ICONS

The second change you can make to the desktop is to rearrange the icons, possibly remove some, or add to them. If you want to change their placement on the screen, you must first open the desktop popup menu (by right-clicking on the desktop) and turn off Auto Arrange, as shown next. (Auto Arrange forces the icons into one or more columns on the left.)

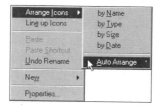

With Auto Arrange off, you can drag the icons anywhere on the desktop and they will remain there, as shown in Figure 3–2. This is particularly valuable with a large screen (19 to 21 inch) operating at higher resolutions (1024 × 768 and above) where you have lots of real estate for various windows. Remember, though, that icons on the desktop can be covered over by windows and, in that case, the only way to get to the icon is to minimize or close the window. For this reason, placing all the icons in the default position on the left side and leaving the remainder of the screen for windows has substantial merit. Of course, even on the left side, you still can drag the icons into any order you choose.

Figure 3–2

Desktop icons can be dragged anywhere on the screen.

Among the initial six desktop icons the ability to delete or move them to another folder is not consistent. My Computer, Network Neighborhood, and Recycle Bin cannot be deleted or moved to another folder. You can create shortcuts for any of the desktop icons and place the shortcuts in any folder or disk drive you want to use. You can delete My Briefcase, Microsoft Exchange (Inbox), and Microsoft Network and you can move them to other folders. Also, if you delete Microsoft Exchange or Microsoft Network, you can add them back by selecting them in the Add/Remove Programs Properties dialog box reached from the Control Panel (opened from the Start menu Settings option). My Briefcase, however, can only be reinstalled from the Windows 95 Setup program.

You can add as many icons to the desktop as you want or as can fit. Again, you must consider that desktop icons get covered over by windows and can be accessed only by minimizing the windows. Two icons you might want to add are Explorer and a printer. Explorer is so heavily used that it is a natural, and having a printer on the desktop allows you drag a document to it in order to print the document. To add the Explorer to the desktop, right-drag the Explorer.exe file from the Windows folder in the Explorer or My Computer window, and select Create Shortcut(s) Here from the popup menu that appears. To add a printer, open the Printers folder in My Computer, drag the printer you want to the desktop, and click on OK to create a shortcut.

CUSTOMIZING THE TASKBAR

The Taskbar can be tailored to fit your wishes. You can expand and contract it, move it to any of the four sides, have it always visible or only visible when you want it. See this for yourself with the following steps:

1. Open the Start menu, and from the Programs option select eight or more programs to start. Notice that the tasks on the Taskbar get smaller as you add more of them, until the tasks are so small that you cannot read much of the label, like this:

2. Move the mouse pointer to the top edge of the Taskbar so the mouse pointer becomes a two-headed arrow, and then drag the top edge up about a quarter of an inch. The Taskbar will

double in size vertically making the labels easier to read, as you can see here:

3. By pointing on a blank area of the Taskbar, drag the Taskbar to each of the four sides of the screen. The Taskbar will jump to each side. When the Taskbar is on the right side, the screen looks like Figure 3–3. When you are done, return the Taskbar to the bottom of your screen.

4. Right-click on a blank area of the Taskbar and click on Properties. The Taskbar Properties dialog box will open wih the Taskbar Options tab displayed, as shown in Figure 3–4.

The purpose and use of each Taskbar option are as follows:

■ **Always on top** keeps the Taskbar visible no matter how many windows you have open or the placement of those windows. If Always on top is not checked, the Taskbar will be

Figure 3–3

Taskbar moved to the right side

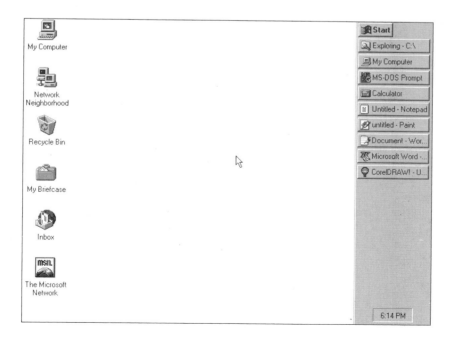

Figure 3–4

Taskbar options

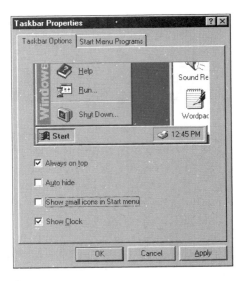

covered over by a maximized window and the only way to get to the Taskbar will be by closing or minimizing the window.

■ **Auto hide** hides the Taskbar unless the mouse pointer is moved to the edge of the screen containing the Taskbar, in which case the Taskbar pops up. If Always on top is not also checked, and if you have a maximized window on your screen, you will not be able to see the Taskbar when you move the mouse to the edge because the Taskbar will be created beneath the maximized window.

 **Both Always on top and Auto hide must be checked for Auto hide to work properly.**

■ **Show small icons in Start menu** makes the icons in the Start menu small so more options can fit in a smaller area.

■ **Show Clock** allows you to control the display of the clock.

5. Click on Auto hide and make sure Always on top is also checked. Then click on OK to close the dialog box. If your mouse is not in the Taskbar area and some other object, for example, a window, is active, the Taskbar will disappear.

6. Move your mouse pointer to the bottom edge of the screen and your Taskbar will reappear. You now can use the Taskbar as you could before you turned on Auto hide. If you move

your mouse pointer above the Taskbar without clicking on it, the Taskbar will disappear. If you click on the Taskbar, it becomes the active object on the screen, and when you move the mouse pointer away, the Taskbar remains on the screen until you click on some other object (window or icon).

7. Right-click on a blank spot on the Taskbar and open the Properties dialog box. Click on Always on top to turn it off and then close the dialog box. Now if you load and maximize a program, you can no longer get the Taskbar to appear by moving the mouse pointer to the bottom edge of the screen. If you make the program window a size where you can see the bottom part of the desktop, the Taskbar will appear if you move the mouse pointer to the bottom edge.

8. Again open the Taskbar Properties dialog box, turn off Auto hide, and close the dialog box. Now the Taskbar is permanently on the desktop; however, if you maximize a window, the Taskbar will be covered over, and the only way to get to it is to reduce the size or close the program window.

9. Open the Taskbar Properties dialog box for a final time, and set the options in the manner that best suits you. The default is that only Always on top is on.

Starting Programs

Windows 95 has so many ways of starting programs that, as you are setting up Windows 95, you need to take several minutes to consider which of the starting methods you want to use with what program. The various methods consist of selecting a program from one of the following sources:

- The Programs option in the Start menu
- The Start menu itself
- The desktop
- A special folder
- The Program Manager
- The Explorer or My Computer

The last option, using the Explorer or My Computer, is the most cumbersome and therefore should be used only as fallback for programs that you very seldom use. Look at each of the other methods and consider how they should be used.

THE PROGRAMS SUBMENU

If you installed Windows 95 on top of a previous version of Windows, your Programs option of the Start menu was automatically loaded with all of the programs you could start from the Program Manager. Also, if you install a new or updated program in Windows 95, that program is added automatically to the Programs option. The Start menu Programs option, then, is the default or most common way that Windows 95 expects you to start your programs. Look at the steps involved in this method:

1.   Click on the Start menu.
2.   Move the mouse pointer to the Programs option.
3.   Move the mouse pointer to the folder that contains the program.
4.   Click on the program.

There are four steps, although Steps 2 and 3 are admittedly very simple. (If you want to use an accessory, it goes to five steps.) The Programs option provides reasonable access to a large number of files and, except for the programs that you use most often, it represents a good choice for the bulk of your programs.

While most programs are automatically placed in the Programs option, you can add programs on your own, and you can remove or change what is automatically placed there. If you look in the Windows folder, you will find a folder labeled Start Menu, and within it the Programs folder, as you can see in Figure 3–5. The Programs folder is the same as the Programs option in the Start menu. Any folders or files that you place in the Programs folder will appear on the Programs submenu. If the files are shortcuts, then you can activate the shortcut by clicking on it in the Programs option of the Start menu. To add a program to the Programs option, simply add its shortcut (see Chapter 2 for creating shortcuts) to the Programs folder, either directly or to a new or existing folder in the Programs folder. Similarly you can delete shortcuts and folders to remove them from the Programs option. Notice the similarity between the Programs option submenus in Figure 3–6 and the folder layout in Figure 3–5.

Figure 3–5

The source of the Start menu Programs option

Figure 3–6

The resulting Programs submenus

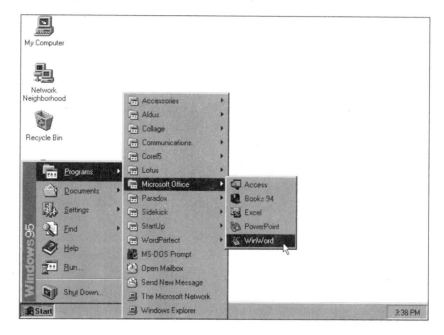

THE START MENU

In addition to the Programs option, you can place folders and short-cuts directly on the Start menu itself so that when it opens you can immediately see them, as shown in Figure 3–7. The steps to start a program whose shortcut is directly on the Start menu are as follows:

Figure 3–7

Figure 3–7

*Shortcuts and
folders directly on
the Start menu*

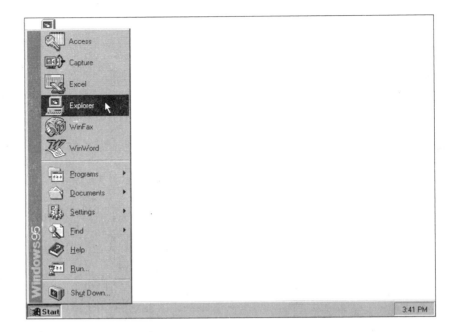

1. Click on the Start menu.
2. Click on the program.

There are two steps, half as many as it takes to start a program in the Programs option of the Start menu. Of course, if you put a folder directly on the Start menu, you add an extra step to open the folder. The downside to the Start menu is that you have very limited space, especially if you use large icons on the Start menu (the Taskbar Properties dialog box allows you to select small icons). Because of this limitation, the Start menu should only be used for your most frequently used programs.

If you place more items on the Start menu than there is room to hold them, the topmost items disappear off the top of the screen.

You can add programs to the Start menu in several ways. The easiest is to drag a program file itself (a .EXE file) from the Explorer or My Computer window to the Start menu button on the Taskbar. Windows will automatically create a shortcut and place it in the Start menu, and the original file will remain in its original folder. Staying within the Explorer, you can create a shortcut and drag it to the Start Menu folder

Figure 3–8

*Start Menu
Programs tab*

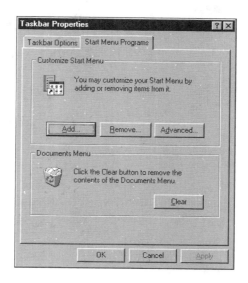

in the Windows folder. Finally, you can open the Start Menu Programs tab of the Taskbar Properties dialog box from the Start menu's Settings Taskbar option, as shown in Figure 3–8.

If you click on Add in the Start Menu Programs tab, the Create Shortcut dialog box will open. This allows you to type in the path and filename of the program you want on the Start menu. The real benefit of this method of adding to the Start menu comes from the Browse button, which allows you to search for and select a path and filename. Then, by clicking on Next, you can create or select a folder, either on the desktop or within the Start menu, in which you want to place the shortcut. Clicking on Next again allows you to enter or edit the name of the shortcut. In this way, the Start Menu Programs tab leads you through each of the steps used to create a shortcut and to place it on the Start menu from within the Explorer. As a matter of fact, the Advanced button of the Start Menu Programs tab opens the Explorer with the Start menu displayed. This allows you to directly change the Start menu as you would had you started out in the Explorer.

The Remove button in the Start Menu Programs tab displays the detail entries of the Start menu, as shown in Figure 3–9. By clicking on the plus sign next to each folder, you can see the shortcuts that are within the folder. By selecting a folder or a shortcut and clicking on Remove, you can remove an entry from the Start menu. You can, of course, do this directly from the Explorer or My Computer.

Figure 3–9

*Removing
shortcuts and
folders from the
Start menu*

THE DESKTOP

If a program has a shortcut on the desktop, as shown in Figure 3–10, you can start it with a single step:

1. Double-click on the icon.

This is obviously the easiest way to start a program *unless* there are windows covering the icon. In this case you must first move, close, or minimize the window to get to the icon, and the steps become the following:

1. Minimize the covering window
2. Double-click on the desktop icon

While this is only two steps, minimizing a window is comparatively slow, and if you have restore it again, it will add an even slower third step. All of a sudden the advantage is at best negated and is potentially a liability. If you have many windows open, you can right-click on the Taskbar, choose Minimize All Windows to get to the desktop, and then use Undo Minimize All to restore the windows, but that is still three steps. Except for programs that you normally start before other programs are started, using the desktop to start programs does not make a lot of sense. Other methods are more efficient.

You can place shortcuts on the desktop by dragging them either from the Explorer or My Computer to the desktop or, within the Explorer, by dragging them from any other folder to the Desktop icon. If you just drag a program file (ones with a .EXE, .COM, or .BAT extension)

Figure 3–10

*Placing program
shortcut icons on
the desktop*

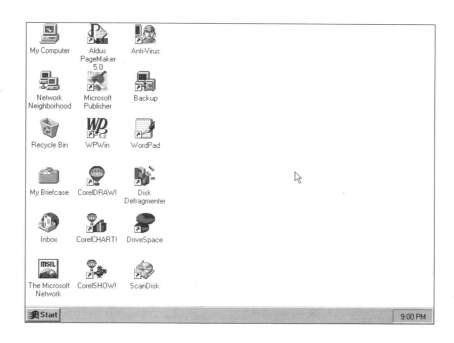

to the desktop, you will automatically create a shortcut without any
further steps. If you right-drag any file, you will be asked, among several other options, if you want to create a shortcut. Also, of course, you
can create a shortcut within the Explorer or My Computer and drag it
to the desktop.

**Quickly create shortcuts by normal dragging of a program file (one with
a .EXE, .COM, or .BAT extension) to the desktop or the Desktop icon.**

A SPECIAL FOLDER

Another way to set up your system for easy access to your programs is
to create a special folder in which you place the shortcuts for those
programs and then leave that folder open on the desktop. Such a
folder is shown in Figure 3–11. The major advantage this folder has
over the desktop itself is that you can quickly get to it by either clicking on the folder's task on the Taskbar (most direct way if the Taskbar
is visible) or by pressing [Alt]-[Tab] and going through the task switcher. The steps to start a program with a special folder are as follows:

1.   Click on the special folder's task on the Taskbar.

2.   Double-click on the program you want to start.

Figure 3-11

*A special folder
containing the
shortcuts for the
programs you use*

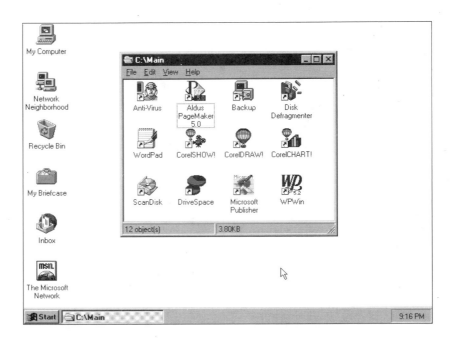

These two steps are faster than the two that include closing or minimizing a window to get to the desktop, and about the same as the two
that include opening the Start menu. The special folder steps assume
that the special folder is open on the desktop. If you leave the folder
open when you shut down Windows, it will be open when you start it
back up. Also, as long as you don't put an icon on the desktop under
the special folder, there should not be any reason why you would ever
want to close it.

 There are several ways to create a new folder on the desktop. You can
right-click on the desktop and then choose New and then Folder from
the popup menu that appears. Alternatively, you can click on Desktop
on the left side of the Explorer and then choose New Folder from the
File menu. You can name the new folder anything you like as long as
there is not another folder on the desktop by the same name.
Examples of names you can use are Programs, Main, and Desktop.

To load the special folder with program shortcuts, you simply need to
drag the program files from either My Computer or Explorer to the
folder, and the shortcuts will automatically be created. If you want a
shortcut to a folder to be in the special folder, you will have to first
create the shortcut and then drag it to the special folder. Remember

that placing a folder in the special folder adds another step to get to the program you want to start.

THE PROGRAM MANAGER

If you are really captivated by the Windows 3.*x* Program Manager's approach to getting at the programs you want to start, you can use the Program Manager in Windows 95, as shown in Figure 3–12. To start the Program Manager, open the Windows folder in either My Computer or Explorer and double-click on Progman.exe. You can place a shortcut to the Program Manager on either the desktop or the Start menu to quickly get to it in the future. If you want the Program Manager to be automatically started every time you start Windows 95, you can drag a shortcut to the Windows\Start Menu\Programs\Startup folder.

Other than your personal tastes, there is no compelling reason to use the Program Manager. It is at best equivalent to a special folder, and unlike a folder, you cannot just leave it on the desktop and have it automatically opened the next time you start Windows 95. All of the tools, such as Copy, Move, and Rename, that are in the Program Manager are 16 bit rather than 32 bit in Windows 95, and Rename only works on the short filename. The Program Manager was a good approach in Windows 3.*x*, but it has been superseded by better approaches in Windows 95.

In day-to-day usage, programs directly on the Start menu turn out to be the easiest to get to. This is definitely where you should place the programs you use every day. Since the Start menu is limited, you are

Figure 3–12

Windows 3.x Program Manager in Windows 95

going to have to use one or more of the other methods. All things considered, the special folder is the next easiest to use, followed by the desktop and finally the Programs option of the Start menu. Since the Programs option is automatically built for you, you need only to build and maintain a special folder.

 **You can have several shortcuts for the same program in different places. Shortcuts take less than 1 KB of disk space.**

Document-Centricity

The last section described how to start programs. The historical approach to computing has been to start a program and then load a document. Windows 95 accelerates a trend begun in Windows 3.*x* to allow you to select a document to work on and have its program automatically started and the document loaded. This is called *document-centricity*. Its purpose is to allow you to concentrate on the documents you are creating and not worry about the programs you are using. Many documents now are created by several programs, and as this trend progresses, it will not be easy to determine, from looking at the screen, what program you are using.

Document-centricity results from associating a document file with a program, as you read about in Chapter 2. When you do that, you can simply double-click on a document, and its associated program is started and the document loaded. As a result, most of the things that you can do to quickly start programs, you also can do with documents. You can drag a document or its shortcut to the desktop (a shortcut is not automatically created for you); you can drag a document to the Start menu where a shortcut is automatically created; and you can create a special folder to hold documents or use the same special folder you created for programs. Finally, Windows 95 provides an option on the Start menu to allow you to select one of the last 15 documents that you started by double-clicking on the document, as shown in Figure 3–13. (Figure 3–13 also shows a document directly on the Start menu.)

Directly starting a document saves you the steps it takes to load a document once a program is loaded, which may or may not be significant to you. If it is, then you should look at the previous section again and consider how you want to set up your documents to easily load the ones you use most often.

Figure 3–13

The Start menu Documents option shows the last 15 documents you directly started.

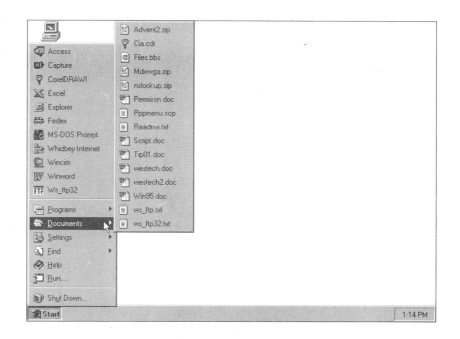

Customizing with the Control Panel

The Control Panel is the primary place in Windows 95 where you set the defaults and parameters that determine how the many functions will operate. It is your primary tool for customization. In the Control Panel shown in Figure 3–14, there are 20 functions with settings that you can tailor to your needs. (The number of functions in the Control Panel depends what you have installed on your computer. Yours may be more or less.) Of these 20 functions, ten pertain to functions that are discussed in other chapters. These ten are: Fonts, Joystick, Mail and Fax, Microsoft Mail Postoffice, Modems, Multimedia, Network, Printers, Sounds, and System. The remaining ten will be discussed in the remaining sections of this chapter.

You can open the Control panel in several ways. The most common method is to open the Start menu, move your mouse pointer to Settings, and then click again on Control Panel. A simpler method (although slower because of the time to open My Computer) is to open My Computer and double-click on the Control Panel icon. You can also open the Explorer, click on My Computer in the left column, and then double-click on the Control Panel in the right column.

Figure 3–14

The
Control Panel

Figure 3–15

The Explorer
showing the
description of the
functions in the
Control Panel

Once the Control Panel is open, you can open any of the functions by double-clicking on it.

If you click on the Control Panel in the left side of the Explorer, you will get a description of each of the icons in the Control Panel, as shown in Figure 3–15.

Accessibility Options

Accessibility
Options

The Accessibility Options allow you to set up the keyboard, mouse, screen, and sound to compensate for various physical challenges you may have. When you open the Accessibility Options control panel, the Accessibilities Properties dialog box appears, as shown in Figure 3–16. This dialog box has five tabs, one for each of the four areas addressed, plus a General tab for settings that relate to all areas. Each of these tabs are discussed in the following sections.

KEYBOARD

The Keyboard tab allows you to turn on or off three functions that can make the keyboard easier to use: StickyKeys, FilterKeys, and ToggleKeys. In addition, by clicking on the check box at the bottom, you can have Windows tell the programs you use to display additional help topics relating to the keyboard.

Shortcut:
Press either Shift key five times in succession.

StickyKeys StickyKeys allows you to press Shift, Ctrl, or Alt plus another key, one at a time, so you do not have to press two keys together. When StickyKeys is turned on and you press Shift, Ctrl, or Alt, the computer thinks the key is held down even though you have physically removed your finger from the key. You can turn on StickyKeys by either clicking on the Use StickyKeys check box in the

Figure 3–16

Accessibilities Properties dialog box

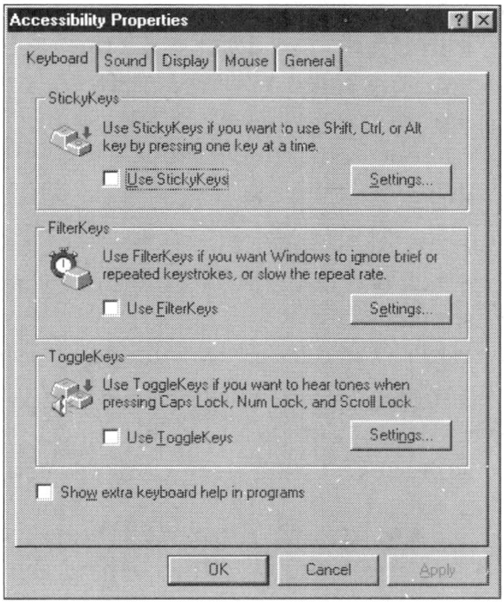

Figure 3–17

*Settings for
StickyKeys
dialog box*

Figure 3–17

*Settings for
StickyKeys
dialog box*

Accessibilities Properties dialog box or by pressing the shortcut keys. If you click on Settings under StickyKeys, the Settings for StickyKeys dialog box will open, as shown in Figure 3–17.

The Settings for StickyKeys dialog box allows you to turn on or off the shortcut keys and to enable several options and notification schemes. The StickyKeys status on the screen is the StickyKeys icon displayed in the notification area next to the clock, as shown on the left.

Shortcut:
Hold down
Right [Shift] for
eight seconds.

FilterKeys FilterKeys allows you to reduce double keystrokes, slow down key repetition, and reduce accidentally hit keys. The purpose of FilterKeys is to desensitize the keyboard so that it is less likely to give you unwanted keystrokes. It does this by ignoring repeated or short duration keystrokes, or by slowing the rate at which a keystroke can be repeated. FilterKeys is valuable for people with tremors or a tendency to "bounce" keys.

You can turn on FilterKeys by either clicking on the Use FilterKeys check box in the Accessibilities Properties dialog box or by pressing the shortcut key. If you click on Settings under FilterKeys, the Settings for FilterKeys dialog box will open, as shown in Figure 3–18.

The Settings for FilterKeys dialog box allows you to turn on or off the shortcut keys and to enable several options and notification schemes. The Filter options provide the following alternatives:

- **Ignore Repeated Keystrokes** allows you to lengthen the amount of time before the start of automatic key repetition

Figure 3–18

*Settings for
FilterKeys
dialog box*

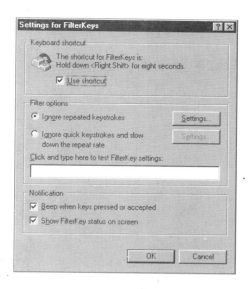

that occurs when you hold down a key. Click on Settings to set
the Ignore keystrokes repeated faster than option to determine
the amount of time you must hold down a key before repeated
keystrokes begin. Drag the slider to a time from 0.5 to 2 seconds. You can test the time setting from the same dialog box.

- **Ignore Quick Keystrokes and slow down the repeat rate**
  reduces the possibility of double keystrokes. It determines the
  minimum amount of time that must exist between two keystrokes (from releasing one key to pressing another) before they
  are considered two actual keystrokes. Another keystroke within
  the minimum time is ignored. Click on Settings to open the
  Advance Settings for FilterKeys dialog box, shown in Figure
  3–19, and determine the specific characteristics of the Ignore
  quick keystrokes and Slow down keyboard repeat rate option:

  - No keyboard repeat eliminates repeated keystrokes occur-
    ring when you hold a key down.

  - Slow down keyboard repeat rates specifies both a Repeat
    delay between keystrokes and a Repeat rate. These set-
    tings reduce the possibility that a key which is accidentally
    hit will be considered a valid keystroke. This is done by
    adjusting the amount of time between pressing a key and
    accepting a valid keystroke. The slider beneath the options

Figure 3–19

*Advanced Settings
for FilterKeys
dialog box*

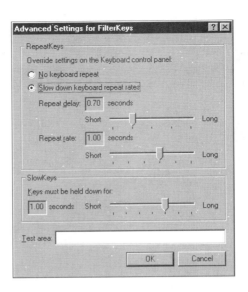

allow times between 0.3 and 2 seconds for both Repeat delay and for Repeat rate.

- SlowKeys sets the length of time which keys must be held down to be recognized. The slider establishes a time from 0.0 to 2 seconds. Keystrokes which are not held down for the specified time are not recognized.

The FilterKeys status on the screen is the FilterKeys icon displayed in the notification area next to the clock, as shown on the left.

Shortcut:
Hold down
Num Lock for
five seconds.

ToggleKeys ToggleKeys allows you to hear a sound when you press Caps Lock, Num Lock, or Scroll Lock to turn them on or off. When ToggleKeys is turned on and you press Caps Lock, Num Lock, or Scroll Lock, you will hear a sound to let you know you have turned on or off one of these keys. You can turn on ToggleKeys by either clicking on the Use ToggleKeys check box in the Accessibilities Properties dialog box or by pressing the shortcut key. If you click on Settings under ToggleKeys, the Settings for ToggleKeys dialog box will open and allow you to turn on or off the shortcut key. ToggleKeys does not display an icon in the notification area when it is turned on.

SOUND

The Sound tab of the Accessibilities Properties dialog box, shown in Figure 3–20, allows you to enable or disable two features that help compensate for hearing impairment. These are SoundSentry, which

Figure 3–20

Accessibilities Sound tab

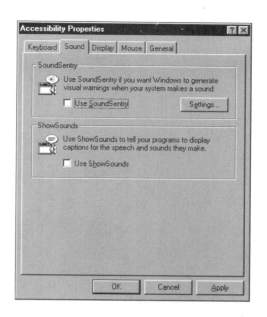

flashes a part of the screen when making a sound, and ShowSounds, which tells applications to display sounds on the screen. You can turn either of these features on or off by clicking in their check box. The SoundSentry Settings button allows you to determine the part of the screen you want to flash.

DISPLAY

Shortcut:
Press Left Alt, Left Shift, and Prt Sc all together.

The Display tab of the Accessibilities Properties dialog box allows you to change into High Contrast mode, where the colors and fonts used on the screen make it easier to read for those who are visually impaired. You can turn on High Contrast mode either by pressing the shortcut keys or clicking on the check box. By clicking on the Settings button, the Settings for High Contrast dialog box opens, as shown in Figure 3–21. This allows you to enable the shortcut keys and to select a high contrast color scheme.

MOUSE

Shortcut:
Press Left Alt, Left Shift, and Num Lock all together.

The Mouse tab of the Accessibilities Properties dialog box allows you to turn on or off MouseKeys. This enables the numeric keypad on the right of most keyboards to perform all of the functions that can be performed with a mouse. MouseKeys, which can be used at the same time you are using a mouse, is not only useful for those that

Figure 3–21

Settings for High Contrast dialog box

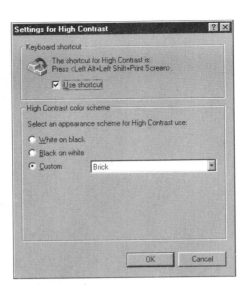

have problems using the mouse, but it is also valuable when you are trying to position the mouse very precisely. MouseKeys redefines the numeric keypad, as shown in Figure 3–22. The specific key assignments are as follows:

- **The** ⑤ **key** is the same as clicking the left mouse button once, unless either the ✱ key or the − key was pressed first.
- **The other number keys** move the mouse pointer in the direction indicated.
- **The** ＋ **key** is the same as double-clicking the left mouse button, unless either the ✱ key or the − key was pressed first.
- **The** Ins **key** locks down the left mouse button for dragging.
- **The** Del **key** releases the left mouse button after dragging.
- When ／, ✱, or − is pressed, it causes the ⑤ and ＋ keys to function as though the left, right, or both of the mouse buttons are being used.
- Ctrl **and a number key** except 5 jumps the mouse pointer in large increments. This can be turned off in the Settings for MouseKeys dialog box.
- Shift **and a number key** except 5 moves the mouse pointer one pixel at a time. This can be turned off in the Settings for MouseKeys dialog box.

Figure 3–22

Numeric keypad with MouseKeys

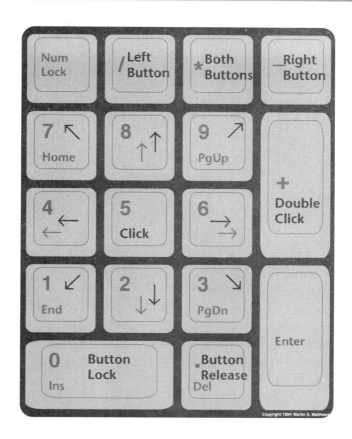

- Num Lock switches between MouseKeys and a normal numeric keypad in whatever state (numeric entry or cursor movement) that is chosen in the Settings for MouseKeys dialog box.

The Settings button opens the Settings for MouseKeys dialog box, which you see in Figure 3–23. This enables or disables the use of the shortcut key, turns on or off Ctrl and Shift as described above, and allows you to choose how Num Lock will work and whether the MouseKeys icon, shown on the left, will appear in the notification area when MouseKeys is turned on. Additionally, the Settings for MouseKeys dialog box has two sliders that let you determine how fast the mouse pointer will move in response to your pressing the keys. Top Speed is the maximum speed that the mouse pointer will travel across the screen. Acceleration is the time delay before achieving maximum speed.

Figure 3–23

*Settings for
MouseKeys
dialog box*

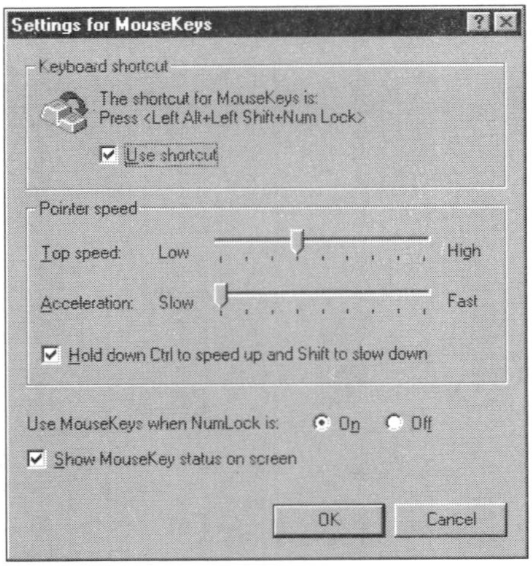

Figure 3–24

*General Tab of
the Accessibilities
Properties
dialog box*

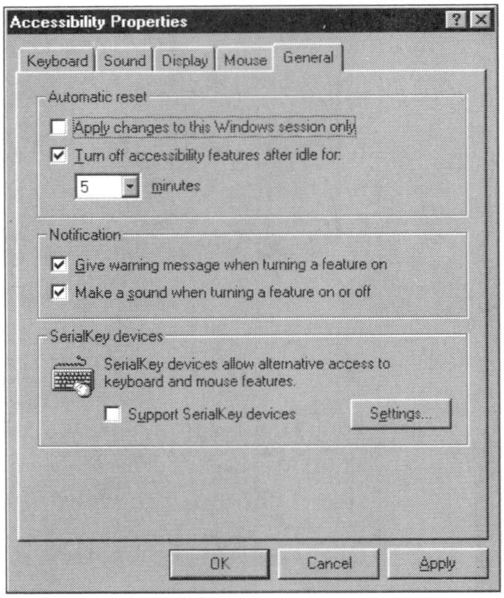

GENERAL

The General tab of the Accessibilities Properties dialog box allows you
to set several options that apply to all accessibility features, as shown in
Figure 3–24. It also enables or disables SerialKey devices, which allows
connection of an alternative input device in place of a keyboard.

Within the General tab, you can determine if the accessibility features you have turned on apply only to the current Windows session (they are turned off when you next use Shutdown in the Start menu) or if they should remain enabled until you turn them off. Alternatively, you can choose to have the enabled accessibilities features turn off after your computer is idle for a period of time. Both of these options allow two people with different access needs to use the same computer. The General tab also allows you to determine the kind of visual or audio notification you want when you turn a feature on or off.

SerialKey devices allows you to connect an alternative input device using a serial port in your computer. That device can send to the computer information which is treated as keystrokes and mouse events. The SerialKey Settings button is used to select the serial port (COM1 through COM4) and baud rates that you want to use (300 to 19,200).

Add New Hardware

Add New
Hardware

The Add New Hardware control panel starts the Hardware Installation Wizard, which walks you through the steps of configuring Windows 95 for a new piece of hardware. It is best to physically install the new hardware in your computer and then run the Add New Hardware Wizard. The first window welcomes you and tells you to press Next. The second window asks you if you want Windows to try and detect the new hardware. If you have not already installed the item, choose No and click on Next to select the type of hardware, as shown in Figure 3–25. If the hardware is installed, you can still choose No and save time by selecting the type of hardware from the list. Letting

Figure 3–25

Selecting the type of new hardware being installed

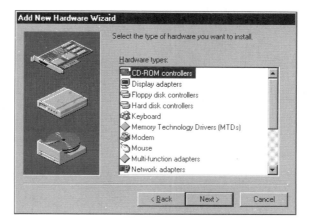

Windows detect it, though, will help answer questions that you will be asked about the item.

You should not be running any other programs while you are trying to install new hardware, especially if you let Windows try and detect it. Your computer may have to be restarted, and you could lose anything you are in the middle of in another program.

If you let Windows detect the new hardware and click on Next, you will be warned that it may take a while and you may have problems. You must click on Next again to actually start the detection process. You will see a status indicator telling you how the detection is progressing. If the status indicator stops for several minutes (say more than three), you may have a problem and you will need to restart (reboot) your computer. When the detection process is complete, you will be told what Windows has found and asked if you want to install that hardware. If you do, click on Finish, otherwise click on Cancel.

If you select a specific piece of hardware and click on Next, Windows will either try to detect that specific piece of hardware or present a list of manufacturers and models from which to select your hardware. Most of the hardware lists are very extensive and you should find your device. If not, the list will have a Generic entry under Manufacturers with several models that represent various varieties of this item. Select the one that's closest to yours. If Windows tries to detect the hardware, it may ask you several questions concerning the device; then it will tell you what it thinks the new piece of hardware is, and you can accept it or go back and try again.

If Windows detects a conflict between a new piece of hardware and hardware you already have installed, it will tell you about it and offer to start the Conflict Troubleshooter, shown next. The Conflict Troubleshooter will lead you through the process of resolving the conflict.

Add/Remove Programs

Add/Remove
Programs

The Add/Remove Programs control panel allows you to add programs for which you have floppy disks or CD-ROMs, to remove programs that you have installed from Windows 95, to add or remove components of Windows 95, and to create a Windows 95 Startup floppy disk. When you click on the Add/Remove Programs control panel, the Add/Remove Programs Properties dialog box will open, as shown in Figure 3–26.

INSTALL/UNINSTALL TAB

To install a new program from the Install/Uninstall tab, insert a floppy or CD-ROM in the appropriate drive, click on Install and then on Next. Windows will search your drives for an install or setup program and tell you what it has found. If it has found the correct program, click on Finish. If not, click on Back and then on Next to have Windows search again. When you click on Finish, Windows will start the setup or install program that was identified, and you can carry on with that program. This saves you from having to search out the name of the install program and type it in the Run dialog box.

To uninstall a program, it must be installed through Windows 95 and, as a result, be on the list at the bottom of the Install/Uninstall

Figure 3–26

*Add/Remove
Programs
Properties
dialog box*

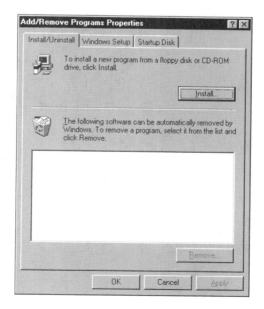

tab. If a program is there, click on it to select it, and then click on Remove to begin the process.

WINDOWS SETUP TAB

The Windows Setup tab, shown in Figure 3–27, allows you to add or remove the Windows 95 components that are displayed in the list box. Beside each component there is a check box that, if it has a check mark, says the component is currently installed. If it isn't installed and you want it to be, click in the check box to add the check mark. If it is and you don't want it to be, also click in the check box to remove the check mark. After you have made all of the changes you want, there should be check marks in the check boxes for the programs that are either currently installed and you want to leave them there, or are not installed and you want to add them. When you are satisfied with the list, make sure the Windows 95 CD-ROM or first floppy disk is in the correct drive, and then click on OK. The Windows 95 Setup program will start and carry out your changes.

STARTUP DISK TAB

If something happens to your hard disk, you will not be able to start your computer and possibly fix the problem because the files needed to get started are on your hard disk. Therefore it is very important that

Figure 3–27

Add/Remove Programs Windows Setup tab

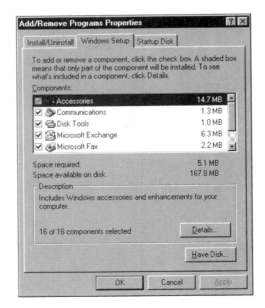

you have an emergency floppy disk with the files needed to start. When you installed Windows 95, you were asked if you wanted a startup disk. If you did not create one then, or something happened to that disk, you can create a new one using the Startup Disk tab in the Add/Remove Programs Properties dialog box. Click on Create Disk. You will see a progress bar appear in the dialog box. Then, when you are asked, insert a disk that can be written over into drive A. When the progress bar reaches the right side and disappears, the Startup disk has been created. Remove the disk and label it "Windows 95 Startup Disk."

Date/Time

Date/Time

As you might expect, the Date/Time control panel allows you to set the date and time. It also allows you to select your time zone. You can open the Date/Time Properties dialog box, which you see in Figure 3–28, either by double-clicking on the Date/Time control panel icon or by double-clicking on the time in the lower right of the Taskbar. To change the time, you need to click on the hour, minute, second, or AM/PM segment that needs adjustment and then use the spinner (up and down arrows). To change the date, you need to select the correct month and year and then click on the correct day.

The Time Zone tab, shown in Figure 3–29, besides being a neat "gizmo," gives Windows 95 the ability to work in a worldwide communications environment. Saying it's 10 AM anywhere in the world can be related to where you are. To set your time zone, you can click

Figure 3–28

Date/Time Properties dialog box

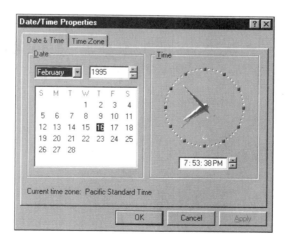

Figure 3–29

Time Zone tab

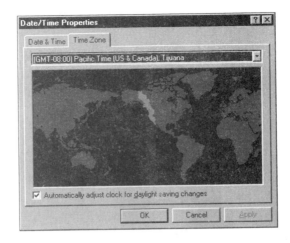

Figure 3–30

Display Properties dialog box

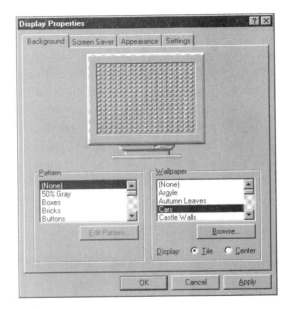

on the map in your time zone or select your time zone from the drop-down list box.

Display

Display

The Display Properties dialog box, which you see in Figure 3–30, can be opened by either double-clicking on the Control Panel icon or by right-clicking on the desktop and selecting Properties. Display

Properties has four tabs. They allow you to set the default patterns and wallpaper used on the desktop; select a screen saver; choose the colors used for various parts of a window; and select a screen resolution, number of colors, and font size.

BACKGROUND TAB

The Background tab lets you determine how the desktop will look. You can choose from a large selection of either patterns or wallpaper that comes with Windows 95, edit one of the standard patterns to create a new one, or browse through your disk looking for wallpaper that has been included in other programs. While you can have both a pattern and a wallpaper, if the wallpaper fills the screen (the Tile option), the wallpaper will cover the pattern. (Patterns are geometric shapes, while wallpaper is pictures.)

SCREEN SAVER TAB

A screen saver places a moving pattern on your screen that replaces the normal screen contents if your computer is left idle for a set amount of time. The Screen Saver tab, shown in Figure 3–31, allows you to choose the screen saver you want to use, see how it looks, make changes to its settings (speed, pattern, and so forth), set the time your computer must be idle before the screen saver comes on,

Figure 3–31

Screen Saver Tab

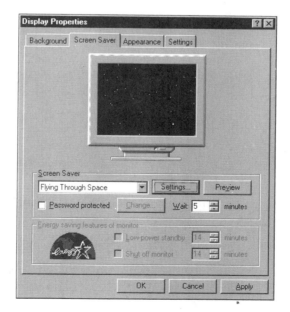

Figure 3–32

Appearance Tab

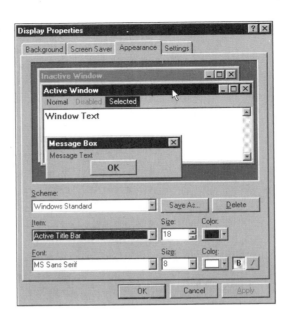

and potentially set a password that must be entered before the screen saver is turned off. Also, if you have an Energy-Star-compliant monitor, the Screen Saver tab allows you to enable the energy-saving features of your monitor.

APPEARANCE TAB

The Appearance tab, which you can see in Figure 3–32, allows you to set the color and shading as well as the font size and style used in various parts of the screen. You can choose one of many existing schemes that come with Windows 95, or you can build one yourself by clicking on the area of the screen you want to change, or by selecting it from the Item drop-down list box and then choosing size, color, and font characteristics. After you have selected your scheme, you can save it with the Save As button.

SETTINGS TAB

The Settings tab, which is shown in Figure 3–33, is very dependent on the display adapter and monitor that you have. If your equipment has the capability, you can change the color palette from 16 colors to 256 colors, to even larger numbers of colors; change the screen resolution (pixel area) from 640 by 480 pixels to 800 by 600 pixels as well as to 1024 by 768 pixels, or a higher resolution; and change the font

Figure 3–33
Settings Tab

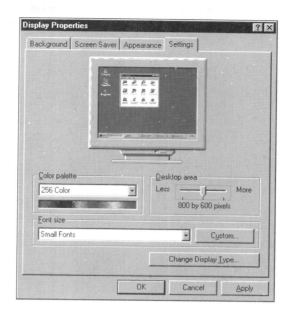

size. If you change your display adapter or have more than one driver available for it, you can change the driver through the Change Display Type button. (A better way to change your display driver is to use the Add New Hardware control panel. The wizard will, under most circumstances, automatically detect the type of adapter you have and will install the correct driver for it.)

Keyboard

Keyboard

The Keyboard Properties dialog box, shown in Figure 3–34, is opened by double-clicking on the Keyboard icon in the Control Panel. This dialog box allows you to change the speed at which repeated keys appear, the language your keyboard is built for, and the type of keyboard you have. The character repeat speed is set in two ways: the Repeat delay, which determines how long the computer waits before beginning the repetition; and the Repeat rate, which is how fast the letters appear once they have started repeating. If you frequently get repeated characters when you don't want them, then you want to lengthen (drag to the left) the Repeat delay. If you get more characters than you want when you repeat characters, then you want to slow down (drag to the left) the Repeat rate.

Figure 3–34

Keyboard Properties dialog box

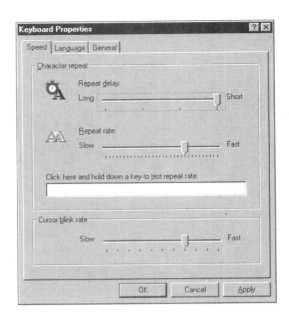

The best speed for cursor blinking is determined by what is most pleasing, or least displeasing, to your eye. Look at several settings to see the difference. When you set up Windows 95, the normal language and type of keyboard you use were determined. In the Language tab you can add and remove additional languages, set the shortcut keys used to switch language, and determine if you want to see the keyboard layout on the screen and be notified of the language you are using in the notification area of the Taskbar. In the General tab you can select a different keyboard type from a list of choices if you happen to install a different keyboard.

The accessibilities features, described earlier in the chapter, override the keyboard speed settings if the accessibilities features are enabled.

Mouse

Mouse

The Mouse Properties dialog box, which you see in Figure 3–35, lets you determine how your mouse will behave. In the Buttons tab you can switch the left and right mouse buttons so you can use the mouse with your left hand and change the double-click rate to one that is more comfortable for you. When you exchange the left and right mouse button, like all dialog box changes, it doesn't take effect until

Figure 3–35

*Mouse Properties
dialog box*

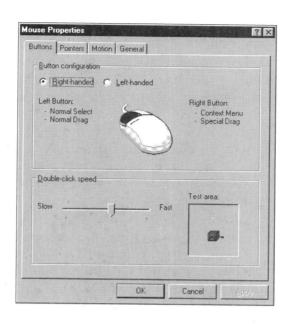

you click on Apply or close the dialog box. The Double-click speed is how quickly you must press the mouse button a second time to have it considered a double-click. You can test your double-click speed by clicking on the jack-in-the-box and seeing if it opens or closes. If not, you'll need to change the speed.

The Pointers tab lets you choose the pointer scheme you want from seven alternatives that come with Windows 95. You may find that one of these is easier for you to see. The Motion tab allows you to set how fast the pointer image moves on the screen, to turn on or off the showing of the trail of the mouse pointer's path, and to set the length of that trail. If you set the pointer speed too fast, you may find that the pointer will overshoot where you are aiming, and if it is too slow, you may get impatient. The purpose of pointer trails and their length is to make it easier to see where the mouse is moving. The General tab allows you to select the type or brand of mouse or other pointing device (trackball or writing tablet) that you have and set any specific option that may be available.

If you are using a laptop or notebook computer, you may want to turn on the pointer trail to make the mouse pointer easier to see on an LCD display.

Passwords

Passwords

The Password Properties dialog box, shown in Figure 3–36, allows you to set and change the passwords that allow you to log on to Windows as well as other passwords to, for example, log on to a network and/or an e-mail system. To change a password, click on the button for Windows or Other, enter the existing password (this is a null, or the absence of any password, when you first install Windows), and then enter and confirm the new password. Logging on to Windows occurs when you initially start (boot) Windows or when you shut down to log on as a different user.

Also, from the Passwords Properties dialog box, you can enable the remote administration of your computer and set it up so multiple users can have their own settings based on their logon password. Remote Administration allows you to use a notebook computer that you have taken home to log on and fully control your computer at work, using modems and phone lines or satellite communications. If you choose to have multiple-user settings in the User Profiles tab, you can then choose two additional items, desktop icons and Start menu components, that can optionally be included in each user's settings. Remote access service (RAS) is discussed in Chapter 6.

Figure 3–36

Password Properties dialog box

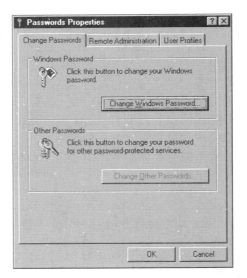

Regional Settings

Regional
Settings

The Regional Settings Properties dialog box, which is shown in
Figure 3–37, allows you to make choices that can be passed along to
application programs so they use the correct formats for numbers,
currency, time, and dates. You can start this by clicking on the part of
the world in which you live (or in which you want the computer set
up). Based on this choice, the remaining tabs in the Regional Settings
Properties dialog box are automatically set for that part of the world.
You can, if you wish, go into each of Number, Currency, Time, and
Date tabs and further customize such things as decimal and thousands
separator, currency symbol, and date format. But to use all of
the standards for a given part of the world, you only need to click on
that part of the map in the Regional Settings tab.

Figure 3–37

*Regional Settings
Properties
dialog box.*

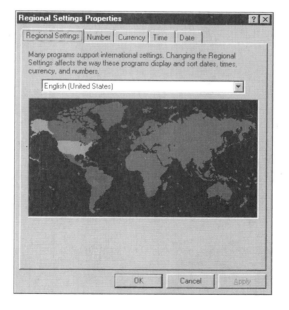

Windows 95 Printing

Printers

Printing, like many other functions, has gone through a major metamorphosis in Windows 95. Gone are the Print Manager and Print Control Panel from Windows 3.*x* along with the confusion about which to use for a particular printing function. All Windows 95 printing functions are consolidated in the Printers folder shown on the left.

Behind this simple Printers folder there is great depth in the Windows 95 printer functions. Central to this is a new 32-bit print engine that provides the following:

- Smooth background printing, which feeds the printer only what it requests

- Improved printing performance, which returns to the application sooner

- Support for over 800 printer models (versus 300 in Windows 3.*x*) including PostScript Level II printers

- Spooling for MS-DOS applications as well as for Windows applications

- Support for image color matching between your screen and your printer

- Deferred printing that allows you to spool your printing while you are on the road and automatically print when you are connected to a printer

- Simplified printer installation and configuration through a single-user interface and full Plug and Play support

In summary, Windows 95 provides faster printing that is easier to use and truly operates in the background, allowing you to do meaningful work while your computer is printing. In this chapter, you'll learn about installing and configuring printers with Windows 95, as well as printing and managing your print queue. Additionally, you'll see how to add and delete fonts, how to use them, and how to manage the fonts you have on line.

What Is a Printer?

Asking "what is a printer?" may sound like a dumb question. On the surface a printer is any device that converts digital information into a form that you can carry away with you and read. There are many forms of these electro-mechanical devices including laser, ink-jet, and dot-matrix printers. To Windows 95, though, these devices are merely part of what it considers to be printers. A network address may be considered a printer, and usually there is a physical printer on the other end. But, if you can "print" to a disk file, then that is considered a "printer," and if you can "print" to a fax modem, then that also is considered a "printer." A physical printer, a network printer, a disk file, and a fax modem have three things in common: a name, a port address, and a driver program. A port address may be a hardware port address like COM2 or LPT1, but it may also be a network path, or a software port address like FILE or FAX. A driver program is a piece of software that can take digital information and convert it in such a way that a device or another program can use it. This then makes for a very broad definition of a printer. It also gives Windows 95 great flexibility in dealing with new devices and computing capabilities.

 **A printer is anything that has a name, has been assigned a port address, and has a driver program that can feed it information.**

Installing Printers

All printer functions, including installing a new printer, begin by opening the Printers folder. You can do that in one of several ways. The easiest is to open the Start menu and select Settings and then

Figure 4–1

Printers folder

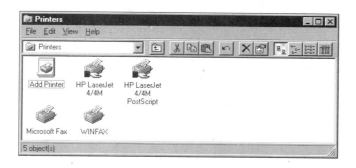

Figure 4–2

*Add Printer
Wizard
initial message*

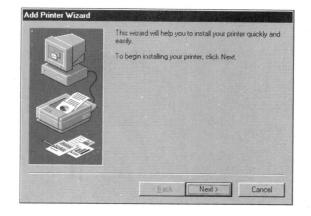

Printers. The other ways are to open My Computer, the Explorer, or the Control Panel and double-click on the Printers folder. In any case, the Printers folder will open and display the printers you have available as well as an icon for adding printers, as shown in Figure 4–1.

By double-clicking on the Add Printer icon, you start the Add Printer Wizard, which you see in Figure 4–2. This leads you through the process of installing the printer driver that is correct for your printer. Click on Next to begin.

Your first decision is to determine how the printer you want to use is connected to your computer. As you can see in Figure 4–3, you have two choices: Local printer and Network printer. A local printer has a cable that is directly connected to your computer. A network printer is connected to another computer or to just the network through its own adapter card and you use it over the network. Determine which you want, click on it, and click on Next.

Figure 4–3

*Local versus
network
printer decision*

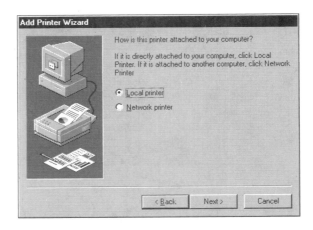

Figure 4–4

*Choosing the
printer
manufacturer
and model*

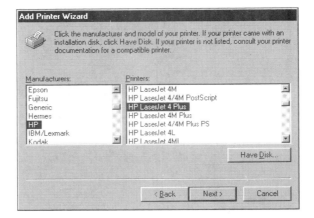

Local Printer Installation

If you are installing a local printer, you must next choose the manufacturer and model of your printer, as shown in Figure 4–4. First
choose the manufacturer in the left column and then the model in the
right column. If you have a recent driver disk from the manufacturer,
you can use that by clicking on Have Disk. After clicking on Next,
you are asked to identify the port you want to use with your printer,
as you can see in Figure 4–5. LPT1, which is the standard parallel
printer port, is the default selection.

If you choose a serial port (COM1 through COM4), you will want to
configure the port by clicking on the button of that name. A COM*x*
Properties dialog box will open, similar to that shown in Figure 4–6.

Figure 4–5

Choosing the printer port

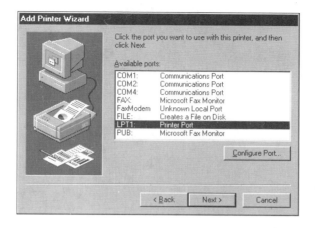

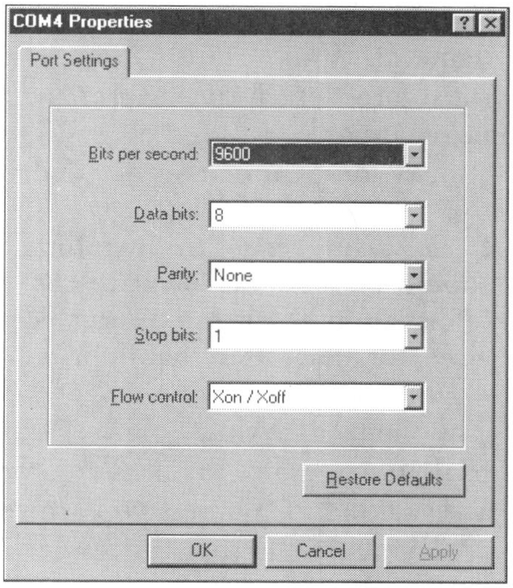

Figure 4–6

Configuring a serial port

You may need to consult your printer manual to make the correct settings. If they are incorrect, your printer probably will not work correctly. If you are using a parallel port (LPT1 or LPT2), your only configuration option is whether to spool your DOS print jobs. The other available ports do not have configurable settings. When you have chosen the port you want to use and made any necessary configuration settings, click on Next.

The Add Printer Wizard window then asks what name you would like to give this printer and if you would like to make it your default printer, as shown in Figure 4–7. The purpose of this is for you to give

Figure 4–7

*Naming
the printer*

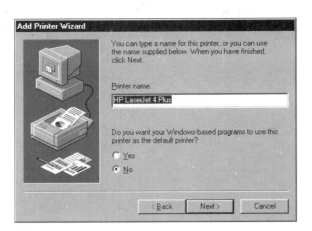

the printer a name that is meaningful to you. For example, you could name a printer "Third Floor LaserJet" or "Marketing's Printer" if those are descriptive names for you. If this printer is the primary printer that you use, then it should be your default. When you have named the printer and decided if it is your default, click on Next.

If the printer you are installing is Plug and Play compliant (there should be a sticker on it to that effect), then you will not be asked information about the printer port—Windows will have automatically gone out and gotten that information for itself.

The final Add Printer Wizard window asks if you want to print a test page to make sure the printer is working the way you set it up. This is a very good idea unless you are very sure of the printer setup. There are many things that can go wrong in connecting and setting up a printer. If you do try it and it doesn't work, see "Trouble Shooting Printers" later in this chapter. After deciding on whether to test the printer, click on Finish. You will see a message box appear that tells you the progress of installing the necessary printer drivers. If you don't see any messages to the contrary, when the Add Printers Wizard closes, the printer has been successfully installed.

Network Printer Installation

If you choose Network printer in the second Add Printer Wizard window, then your third window will look like that shown in Figure 4–8. Here you are asked to enter the network path to the printer you

Figure 4–8

*Establishing the
path to a
network printer*

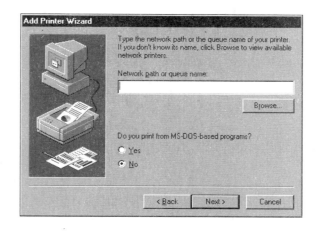

Figure 4–9

*Shared printers
on your network*

want to use. If you know the path you can type it in, but in most circumstances it is easier to click on Browse. You'll be shown the computers in your workgroup. If you click on the plus sign beside a computer, you'll see the shared printers on that computer, as you can see in Figure 4–9. Click on the printer you want to use and then click on OK. When you return to the Add Printer Wizard, the path will be filled in for you. Decide if you want to print from DOS programs on that printer and then click on Next.

As you saw with a local printer, you are next asked to enter a name for the printer and if you want to use it as your default. After doing that, click on Next. Finally you are asked if you want to test the printer. When you click on Finish, the appropriate printer driver files will be copied to your computer, and the printer will become available for you to print on, just as if it were attached directly to your computer.

Configuring Printers

Once a printer is installed, you can change its configuration through the printer's Properties dialog box, a sample of which is shown in Figure 4–10. You can open your printer's Properties dialog box by right-clicking on the printer in the Printers folder and choosing Properties. The Properties dialog box that opens for your printer may be different than the one shown in Figure 4–10, although many of the elements will be the same. In the next several sections, the HP LaserJet 4 Plus Properties dialog box will be described. This should be instructive in making the settings for your printer. If your printer is Plug and Play compliant, much of the printer configuration will be done automatically for you.

General Tab

The General tab of the printer Properties dialog box shows you the printer's name at the top and allows you to enter a comment about the printer, identify a page to print between each print job, and print a test page. The printer's name is the one you gave it when you installed the printer. You can change this name in the Printers folder

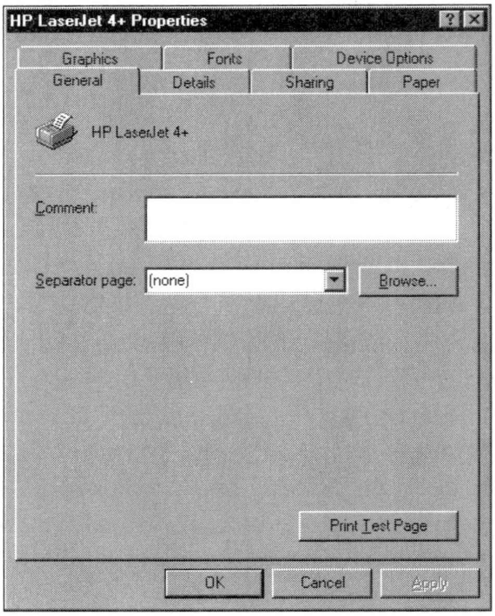

Figure 4–10

Printer Properties dialog box

by editing the name as you would a file or folder name, or you can use the Rename command in the popup menu opened by right-clicking on the printer.

The Comment field is used to pass on any necessary information about the printer; for example, where the printer is physically located, what kind of paper or forms it has loaded, what the printer is to be used for, and the hours it will be turned on. The Comment field is transferred to all the users that install your printer on the network, although if you change the comments, they will not see the change unless they reinstall the printer.

Changes to a printer's Comment field are not seen by other users who have already installed the printer.

If you have multiple people using your printer or if you are printing multiple documents at the same time, then inserting a separator page between each document may help you separate the various users and documents. You have two built-in choices for a separator page in the drop-down list box: Full and Simple. The Simple option is just text that tells you the document name, the computer that printed it, and the date and time it was printed. The Full option adds the Windows 95 graphic at the top of the page and therefore takes longer to print. You can create your own separator page by using a draw program such as CorelDRAW! to create and then export a Windows metafile image (with the extension of .WMF). Then use the Browse button to locate this file and identify it as the separator page you want to use. Only the computer that is directly connected to a printer may set up a separator page.

Details Tab

The Details tab, shown in Figure 4–11, allows you to select the printer port and driver to use with a printer as well as define the ports and drivers that are available. The Details tab also allows you to set various port, spooling, and timing characteristics. The options available in this dialog box will be grouped into printer ports, printer drivers, print spooling, and timeout settings.

PRINTER PORTS

A printer port in Windows 95 can be a hardware port on your computer, either serial (COM1 through COM4) or parallel (LPT1 or

Figure 4–11

*Printer Properties
Details tab*

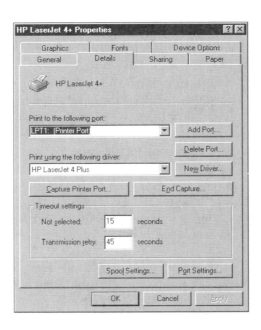

LPT2); it can be a network path leading to a printer on another computer; or it can be a software port, like FAX for a fax modem or FILE for a disk file, which is not a printer at all. If you open the Print to the following port drop-down list box, you will see a list similar to this:

You can assign a printer to any one of these ports. If you don't find the port you want, you can add a port by clicking on the Add Port button. The Add Port dialog box opens, as shown in Figure 4–12. Here you can enter a network address, or, as you saw in "Network Printer Installation," you can use the Browse button to locate it. Alternately, you can define a new local port such as FILE or FAX. If you want to remove a port, you may do so by clicking on Delete Port in the Details tab and selecting the port to remove.

Besides entering the path to a network printer, you may define a local port address that you are not using, for example LPT3, to be a network

Figure 4–12

*Add Port
dialog box*

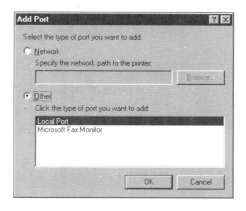

printer address. This is similar to mapping a network disk drive to a
drive letter on your local machine. For printers, though, it is called *capturing a printer port*, and the Capture Printer Port button in the Details
tab opens the dialog box of the same name. Here you can choose a port
from LPT1 through LPT9 and identify the network path to associate
with that port, as you can see next. If you want to continue to use this
port address the next time you start Windows, then click on Reconnect
at logon. If you want to disconnect the network path from the port
address, click on the Release Printer Port button in the Details tab and
select the port to be released.

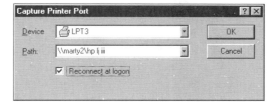

The Port Settings button in the Details tab (see Figure 4–11) opens
the port configuration dialog box that you saw above in "Local
Printer Installation." For a serial port there are several significant settings, like baud rate and bit pattern. For a parallel port, you can
determine if you want to spool DOS printing. For other types of
ports it is not used.

PRINTER DRIVERS

Printer drivers are the programs that put the data in your computer
in a form that can be printed and then control the printer while it is

Figure 4–13

Dialog box for selecting a printer driver

printing. Generally there is a printer driver for each type of printer. If you open the Print using the following driver drop-down list box, you'll see a driver for each type of printer you have installed. If you select New Driver, you'll see the pair of list boxes for manufacturers and models that you saw in "Local Printer Installation" and that is shown in Figure 4–13. It is very important that you use the correct driver for your printer.

PRINT SPOOLING

Theoretically, print spooling quickly writes your printed output on disk and then allows you to go back to work while the actual printing takes place in the background. In early versions of Windows this was a joke. Writing the output to disk took as long as printing, and you couldn't get anything done while the "background" printing took place. All you accomplished was to double your print time. In Windows 3.*x*, and especially Windows for Workgroups 3.11, print spooling became a real benefit. Windows 95 carries that several steps further. For non-PostScript printers, Windows 95 quickly writes the printer output on disk as *enhanced metafiles* (EMF). This is faster than the raw printer data written by Windows 3.*x* and allows a quicker return to your application. The background printing makes full use of the 32-bit multithreaded architecture of Windows 95 to provide smooth printing while you are working in the foreground. The net result is that, if you haven't used print spooling before, you'll want to do so in Windows 95.

Print spooling is controlled in the Spool Settings dialog box, shown in Figure 4–14 and opened with the button of that name in the Details

Figure 4–14

Spool Settings dialog box

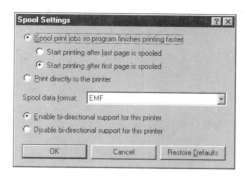

tab. Your first choice in this dialog box is whether to spool print jobs or print directly. If you spool printing, you can choose to start printing after the first or after the last page has been spooled to disk. If you start after the last page, you will get back to your application quicker, but the overall printing will take longer. Another option in this dialog box is whether to use the EMF format for spooling or to spool raw printer data. The EMF format is faster, but if you are having trouble printing, try switching to raw printer data. Finally, with newer printers and computers, you can enable or disable a bidirectional printer port that allows your computer to interrogate your printer and have your printer respond with information needed by the computer.

TIMEOUT SETTINGS

The Timeout settings in the lower half of the Details tab determine how long the computer should wait before reporting that a printer is not ready. The first of these, Not selected, is the number of seconds to wait for a printer to be online. The second, Transmission retry, is the number of seconds to wait for a printer to be ready. Normally whether a printer is online is up to you: have you plugged it in, turned it on, and placed it online? You therefore want the timeout on this to be short, so the computer will tell you sooner that you need to go turn on the printer. On Transmission retry, you are waiting for the printer to digest the last data you sent it. You therefore want Transmission retry to be longer. If you are having problems with big print jobs being cut-off, you need to make this time even longer (say 60 to 100 seconds).

Sharing Tab

The Sharing tab of the printer Properties dialog box, which is shown in Figure 4–15, allows you to determine if you want to share your

Figure 4–15

Printer Properties
dialog box
Sharing tab

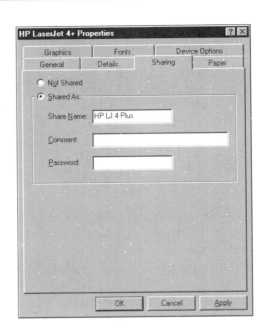

printer with others on your network. If you do, you can enter a name, a comment, and a password for the shared printer. Only if you share your printer can others use it, and the name you give it will be the name they see. You cannot share a printer without giving it a name. The comment is displayed in the list of printers seen by all on the network. You might enter the physical location of the printer in the Comment field. The password starts out to be null, the absence of any password, so if you do not enter one, a password will not be used for that printer.

Paper Tab

The Paper tab, which you see in Figure 4–16, allows you to set several printer defaults that can be overridden by settings the end user may make. This is particularly important if a printer is dedicated to a certain form, for example, envelopes. Otherwise you probably will want to leave this set to the printer's defaults, and let the end user set these items. You can restore the defaults by clicking on that button at the bottom of the tab.

The Paper Size list box shows the sizes your printer can handle. If your printer supports a custom size, you'll have a Custom icon you can select along with a Custom button where you can specify the size.

Figure 4–16

*Printer Properties
dialog box
Paper tab*

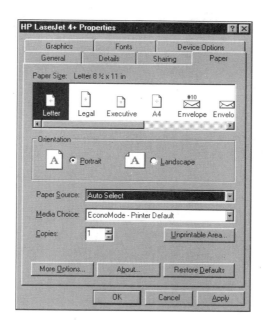

If you select a particular form, especially envelopes, you can see the size at the top of the list box.

The Orientation, Paper Source, and Media Choice are those available for your printer. If you have a media choice of Transparency, only select it when printing transparencies or you may cause smearing and waste ink.

Most laser printers cannot print to the very edge of the largest paper size they can handle. If you have a laser printer, you'll see an Unprintable Area button, which opens a dialog box that allows you to set the margins that cannot be printed upon. It is unusual to change the defaults for this, which are set by the manufacturer.

Some printers will have a More Options button, which provides additional printer specific settings you can change.

Device Options Tab

The Device Options tab allows you to make several settings that are directly related to your particular printer. The settings for an HP LaserJet 4 Plus are shown in Figure 4–17. If you have a Plug and Play compliant printer and a bidirectional port, settings like Printer Memory will be set for you. If you have an older printer without Plug

Figure 4–17

*Printer Properties
dialog box Device
Options tab*

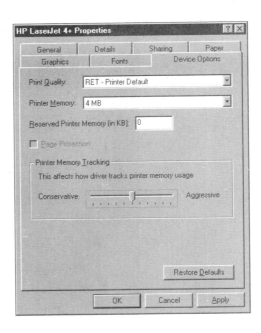

and Play, you should check such settings as Printer Memory, otherwise you may not utilize the full capability of your printer.

Fonts Tab

The Fonts tab, shown in Figure 4–18, allows you to identify the hardware-related font characteristics. These include identifying any font cartridges you have installed and how you want to download TrueType fonts. Simply click on the cartridges you have. If your printer can handle two cartridges, you will be allowed to select two. For TrueType fonts, if your printer can handle outlines, you'll want to download outline fonts; you'll find it faster. Bitmaps are next fastest and graphics least fast.

Graphics Tab

The Graphics tab, which you see in Figure 4–19, allows you to determine how graphics are sent to your printer. Unless speed is more important than quality, you normally will want to print at the highest resolution you can, although this affects only graphics.

Figure 4–18

*Printer Properties
dialog box
Fonts tab*

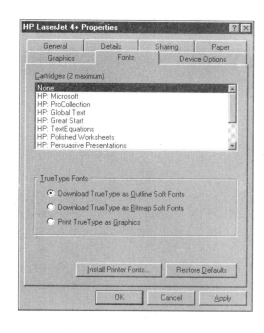

Figure 4–19

*Printer Properties
dialog box
Graphics tab*

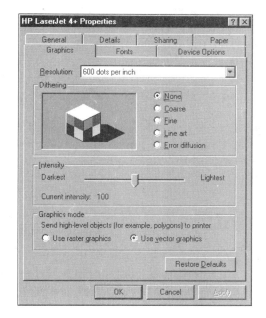

Text is always printed at the printer's highest resolution.

Dithering is a way to give the appearance of more colors or more shades of gray than you can otherwise produce. Use the following settings under the conditions given:

- **None** if you are satisfied with your existing colors or gray scale
- **Coarse** if you are printing at a resolution of 300 dots per inch (dpi) or higher
- **Fine** if you are printing at a resolution of less than 300 dpi
- **Line Art** if you are printing drawings with well-defined borders between black and white
- **Error Diffusion** if you are printing pictures that don't have sharp, well-defined edges

Do not base your Dithering setting on the example in the dialog box. Your printed result should look much different.

The Intensity setting is simply how dark or light you wish to print graphics. Graphics Mode, on the other hand, determines how your printer creates a graphic. Vector graphics describe an image in terms of the position, length, width, and direction of the lines that make up the image. Raster graphics describe an image in terms of the position, size, and pattern of dots that make up the image. Vector graphics are faster and, for certain images like line art, can produce a more pleasing result. Raster graphics are simpler for the printer to produce and, for photographic-like images, can be more pleasing.

If your image is not being printed correctly (for example, two objects are printed on top of one another when they are not supposed to be), switch to raster graphics.

Using Printers

One normally thinks of using printers from within a program—loading or creating a document and then selecting the print command. For example, in WordPerfect, with a document open, you click on the

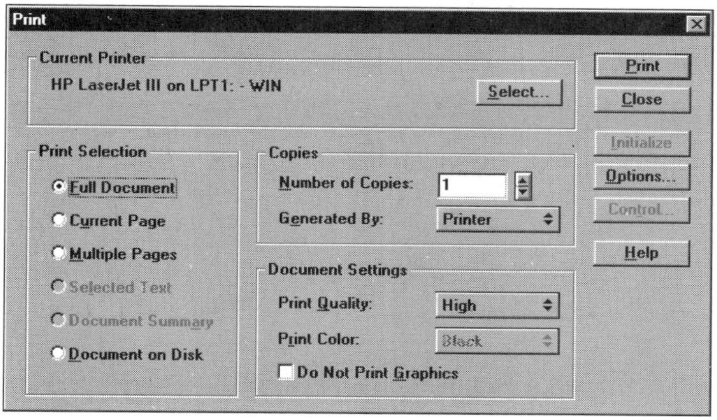

Figure 4–20

*WordPerfect's
Print dialog box*

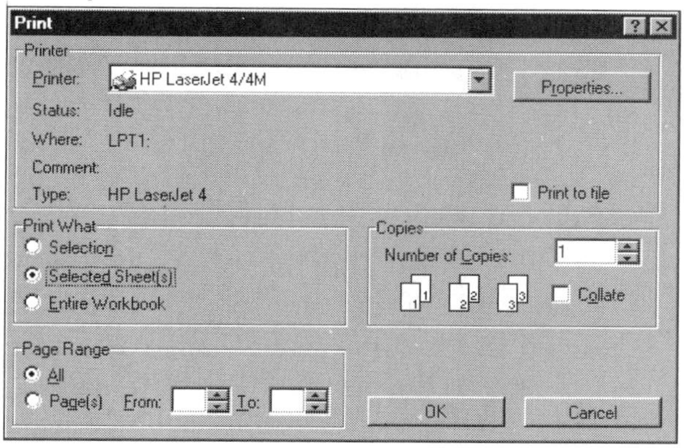

Figure 4–21

*Excel's Print
dialog box*

printer icon in the toolbar and the Print dialog box opens, as shown in Figure 4–20. Here you can select what within the current document to print, the number of copies, and so forth. Most Windows programs that produce a document have a similar function and dialog box. Excel's is shown in Figure 4–21. The settings in these dialog boxes will override the settings in the printer's Properties dialog box.

Drag-and-Drop Printing

Windows 95 provides another, simpler way to print. You can drag a document file to a printer icon, and the document will be printed. In some cases the document will print directly. In other cases the program that is associated with the document (and probably created it) will be loaded, the document printed, and then the program closed. In the process you may or may not see a Print dialog box (a WordPerfect document pauses and lets you make changes to its Print dialog box; Word and 1-2-3 do not). As you saw in Chapter 3, you can drag a printer shortcut to the desktop and leave it there. Then from either My Computer or the Explorer, you can drag a document to the printer's shortcut icon and have the document printed. Of course, the document must be associated with a program, normally the one that created it, that is registered with Windows 95 to provide drag-and-drop printing. Many Windows programs are registered that way.

Managing Print Spooling

As you read above, if you accept the default, Windows 95 spools your printing onto your disk and then feeds it to your printer in the background while you are doing other things. If you or others on your network are sending enough work to your printer, you will build up a print queue of jobs waiting to be printed. Windows 95 has provided a way for you to manage the print queue with the print spooler window, similar to that shown in Figure 4–22. You open this window by double-clicking on the printer icon, which can be a shortcut.

The body of the print spooler window lists the print jobs in the queue with the document name, status, the name of the computer that sent the job to the printer, the job size, and the time it arrived in the queue. You can rearrange the order in which the jobs are printed by dragging the jobs up or down in the print queue. The print spooler window also gives you the ability to pause and restart either the printer or just one job, and to cancel a job or purge all jobs from the printer. Here's how:

- **Pause a job** by selecting the job and choosing Pause Printing in the Document menu.
- **Pause a printer** by choosing Pause Printing in the Printer menu.

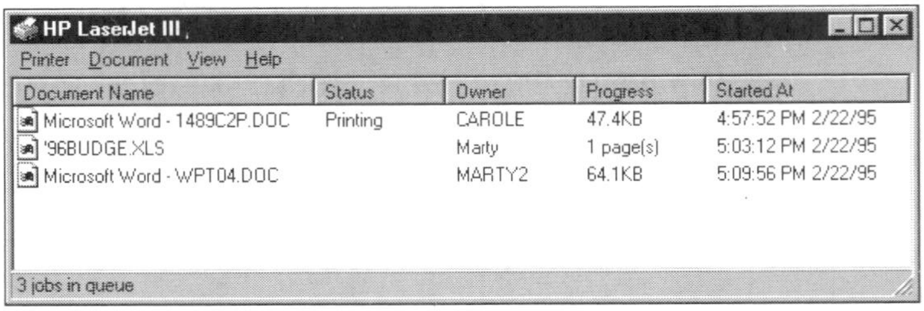

Figure 4–22

Print spooler window

Document Name	Status	Owner	Progress	Started At
Microsoft Word - 1489C2P.DOC	Printing	CAROLE	47.4KB	4:57:52 PM 2/22/95
'96BUDGE.XLS		Marty	1 page(s)	5:03:12 PM 2/22/95
Microsoft Word - WPT04.DOC		MARTY2	64.1KB	5:09:56 PM 2/22/95

3 jobs in queue

- **Cancel a job** by selecting the job and pressing $\boxed{\text{Del}}$ or by choosing Cancel Printing from the Document menu.
- **Purge all jobs** in the queue by choosing Purge Print Jobs from the Printer menu.

 **Drag a job in the print queue to rearrange the order in which it will be printed.**

The Printer menu also allows you to open the printer Properties dialog box, to set the printer as the default, and to close the window. If the printer is a network printer, you will also have the option to work offline. This way, if you are not currently connected to the network (for example, if you are out of the office), you can store your printing on disk and defer it until you are next connected to the network. Most of the options on the Printers menu can also be found on the popup menu that opens when you right-click in the print spooler window, as you can see here:

 **If you are using a laptop or notebook computer away from the office, you can still print by setting the printer to Work Offline. This way the printing is spooled to disk and deferred until you are next connected to a printer.**

Printer Popup Menu

The popup menu that opens when you right-click on a printer has many of the same options as the Printer menu in the print spooler window, as shown next. In addition, you can open the print spooler window, display the Sharing tab of the Properties dialog box, create a shortcut for the printer, and delete or rename the printer.

Trouble Shooting Printers

If your printer is not printing or not printing correctly when you send it information to be printed, you have three broad steps you can take to solve the problem: look at the physical attributes of the printer; look at the online messages you are getting; and look at the Printer Troubleshooter in Windows 95 Help.

Physical Attributes

The physical attributes to consider are those obvious things that are often assumed to be OK but sometimes are not. Here is a check list for you to use:

- Is your printer plugged into a working electrical outlet?
- Is your printer connected to your computer? Is there a cable securely fastened both to your printer and to your computer?
- Is your printer turned on? Is the power light lit or is there some other indication of power being on?
- Is your printer online? Does the online switch show that it is enabled?
- Is your printer properly supplied with paper and ink or toner or a ribbon?

There is one other physical attribute that is very important but not always easy to check: the port on your computer to which your printer is connected. First determine if the printer is connected to a parallel or serial port and then which one. A parallel port will have a 25-pin female connector on the computer. A serial port will have either a 9-pin male connector or a 25-pin male connector on the computer. Most printers use a parallel port and most computers only have one parallel port: LPT1. If you think your printer is using a serial port, determine what else is using a serial port. Two good candidates are your mouse and a modem. If you have a serial mouse, it is often using the 9-pin connector and is COM1. If your printer is then using the 25-pin male connector, it is probably COM2. Your mouse could be a bus mouse and not use a serial port, and therefore your printer would be using COM1.

If you have a modem, it could be connected to any port. If it is working, it is easiest to open the Control Panel, double-click on the Modems icon, select your modem, and click on Properties. The General tab should show you the port to which the modem is connected. Unfortunately there is not such a handy place to find the port to which your mouse is connected.

Once you have a pretty good idea of the port your printer is using, then review the port assignment you made during installation, as described above under "Local Printer Installation."

Online Messages

One obvious way to find a problem is to look at the messages that you get when you try to print. Some messages are more helpful than others. Four of several possible messages you can get are shown next. The first two are not very specific and could almost be caused by the same thing. In fact, the first message was caused by the printer being not physically connected to the computer, while the second message was caused by the printer being turned off (being turned on but offline caused the same message). Since the second message mentions checking the printer cable, you might think the first two messages are reversed. The third message is very specific about being out of paper, and that is in fact what caused the message. The fourth message was caused by a network setup problem, as it implies.

1   

2   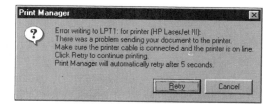

3

4

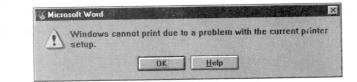

Messages give you surface facts that start you looking for the problem, and they may or may not be very helpful about where specifically to look. Sometimes all you need to know is that there is a problem. For example, the first message above resulted because I had my printer connected to another computer, and when I saw the message I instantly knew that I had forgotten to switch the cable. The message didn't need to specifically tell me what the problem was.

With the newer printers and bidirectional printer ports, much more information is passed to the computer and therefore displayed in messages.

Print Troubleshooter

Windows 95 has an excellent Print Troubleshooter in its Help system. To use it, click on Help in either the Start menu or in any Windows menu bar and choose Help Topics. When the Help Topics window opens, select the Contents tab and double-click on both Troubleshooting and If you have trouble printing, as shown in Figure 4–23. The Print Troubleshooter will open, as shown in Figure 4–24.

By following the instructions and answering the questions in the Print Troubleshooter, you will be able to learn a lot about what is causing your printing problem and how to fix it. There is, of course, no guarantee that you will be able to solve all possible printing problems. With the combination of looking at the physical attributes, considering the online messages, and studying the Print Troubleshooter, you have a number of tools to solve your problems.

Figure 4–23

Opening the Print Troubleshooter

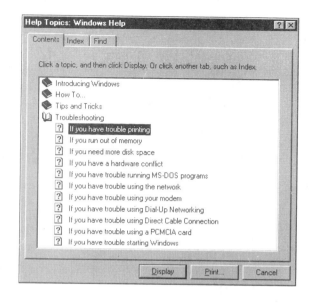

Figure 4–24

Print Troubleshooter

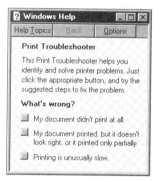

Printer Fonts

The majority of text printing utilizes type fonts that are separately downloaded from your computer to your printer when you print text. As you create the text, you specify the fonts to use, their size, and their style (normal, bold, italic, or bold italic). Then when you print the text, the fonts you have chosen are downloaded. The fonts you have available depends on what fonts you have added to your computer. Windows 95 comes with nine typefaces: Arial, Courier, Courier New, MS Sans Serif, MS Serif, Small Fonts, Symbol, Times New Roman, and WingDings. Four of these typefaces are primarily for the screen: Courier, MS Sans

Serif, MS Serif, and Small Fonts. Of the remaining five typefaces, three come in four styles: normal, bold, italic, and bold italic. Since a *font* is a combination of a typeface and a style, you have a total of 18 fonts in Windows 95. Many other packages come with additional fonts, and you can buy inexpensive fonts from many sources. The problem becomes how to add the new fonts you get and how to manage fonts on your disk.

Adding and Managing Fonts

Windows 95 has consolidated the installation and management of fonts into a single Fonts folder. You can open this folder by opening the Control Panel (Start menu, Settings, Control Panel) and clicking on the Fonts folder icon, shown on the left. The folder window shown in Figure 4–25 appears.

ADDING FONTS

Occasionally, additional fonts are automatically added to your system when you install programs, whether you want the additional fonts or not. WordPerfect is particularly notorious for this. Normally the fonts are just made available to you, and you must determine which you want to install and then do the installation yourself. CorelDRAW!, for example, comes with several hundred fonts on a CD-ROM and a book that shows you what each font looks like. You can go through the book and decide which you like and then copy them to the Fonts folder on your hard disk. A problem, though, becomes obvious when

Figure 4–25

Fonts folder window

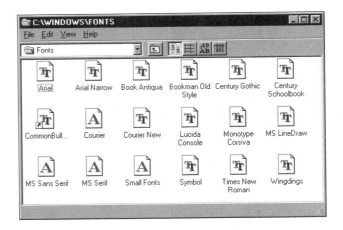

Figure 4-26

CorelDRAW!
font filenames

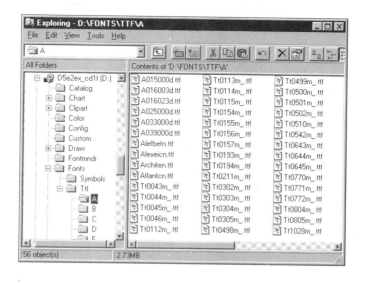

Figure 4-27

Add Fonts
dialog box

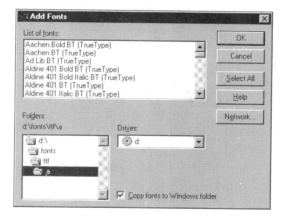

you look at the CorelDRAW! CD-ROM—the filenames of the font files do not tell you a thing, as you can see in Figure 4–26. Windows 95 has the solution for this in a font installation program that shows you the name of the font.

You start the font installer by opening the File menu in the Fonts window and choosing Install New Font. The Add Fonts dialog box opens. When you select the correct drive and folder, a list of fonts appears—this time in human readable form, as shown in Figure 4–27. You then can select the fonts you want and click on OK to copy them to the Fonts folder on your hard disk (the dialog box says "Copy fonts to Windows folder" but this means they're copied to the Fonts folder). If you want several noncontiguous fonts, hold down Ctrl while selecting them. If you want several fonts in succession, click on the first font, press and hold Shift, and click on the last font. When you have selected all the fonts you want, click on OK. The fonts will be copied to your Fonts folder.

The font names do not immediately appear. Instead a message appears that says Retrieving font names: *xx%*. **When it reaches 100%, the names will appear.**

Font files can be fairly large, over 100 KB. If you select very many of them, you can easily take up a lot of space on your hard disk.

MANAGING FONTS

Fonts are files, and anything you can do with a file you can do with a font. You can drag a font to another folder or to the Recycle Bin. You can select a font and press Del. You can copy a font onto a floppy disk. For all these tasks, the Fonts folder provides a source that shows you the full font name so you can know what you are doing.

If you drag (move) a font to another folder, it will no longer be available to be used in applications. Fonts must be in the Fonts folder to appear in the list of fonts displayed by applications.

The Fonts windows has several other features that help you manage your fonts. Best of these is that by double-clicking on a font you open up a dialog box that displays the font, as shown in Figure 4–28. This way you can see what the font looks like. You can open this same dialog box by right-clicking on the font to open the popup context menu and then choosing Open.

Double-click on a font to see what it looks like.

From the View menu of the Fonts window, you can select List Fonts By Similarity and see other fonts that look similar to a given font. For example, Figure 4–29 shows fonts that are similar to Times New Roman. Also, from the View menu, you can select Hide Variations and list only the typeface names and not all their styles (bold, italic, and bold italic). This can make it easier to see the typefaces you have, as you can see by comparing Figure 4–30, which shows only the typefaces, and Figure 4–31, which shows all of the fonts.

Figure 4–28

*Font display
dialog box.*

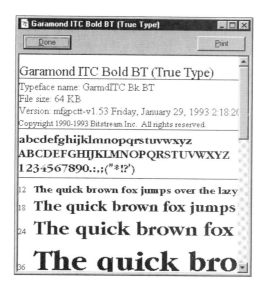

Figure 4–29

*Fonts similar
to Times
New Roman*

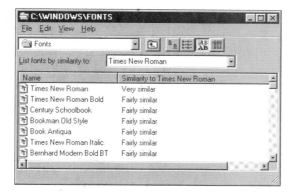

Figure 4–30

*Only the typefaces
are displayed, not
the styles*

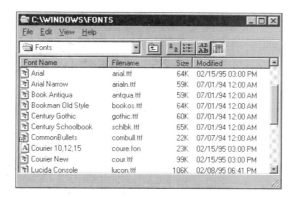

Figure 4–31

*All of the fonts
are displayed*

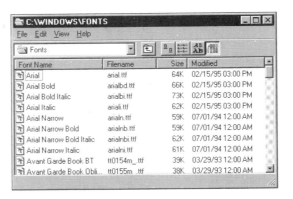

TrueType and Type 1 Fonts

The printer fonts that come with Windows 95 are scalable TrueType fonts. By being *scalable*, only one size font is sent to the printer, and it is then scaled in the printer to make the other sizes necessary for a particular document that is being printed. *TrueType* is the font rendering technology that is built into Windows 95. This technology takes the font outlines (really mathematical descriptions) that are on your disk and uses them both to display the font on the screen and to provide the font to the printer. This technology works with any TrueType font independent of its source. There is a competing *scalable* font technology called Adobe Type 1 from Adobe Systems Inc. To use it you must have the Adobe Type Manager (ATM) software to do the rendering for both the screen and the printer. ATM is frequently given away with Type 1 fonts, and so long as you are using the latest version (Version 3.0 as of this writing), the Adobe technology is very comparable to TrueType. If you really want to split hairs, Type 1 may have a slight edge on the quality of type it produces, and TrueType may have a slight edge on the speed at which the fonts are produced. The only negative is that Type 1 requires ATM, another piece of software to maintain.

PART II

Windows 95 Networking

If the 1980s were the era of the PC, then the 1990s are the era of networking PCs. The isolated, stand-alone PC is increasingly becoming a connected part of a larger system. This connectedness gives each user access to data, programs, hardware, and communications not readily available to the stand-alone PC. With this sharing and communications come improved efficiency, lowering of costs, and faster responsiveness. The cost is additional hardware, additional software, and greater complexity.

Windows 95 addresses these issues by not only providing networking, but by improving the benefits from it while reducing the cost. All the software you need for networking is a standard part of Windows 95, making it very inexpensive. Windows 95 also greatly eases the setup burden while providing all the necessary features.

Part II describes networking and how to install and fine-tune a network, as well as how to make the best use of it. Part II also looks at remote access to a network and the networking accessories available in Windows 95.

Networking
and Its Installation

With all the growth in networking, its installation and management has remained the province of networking professionals. Windows 95 provides an alternative for smaller firms by offering full-featured networking that is relatively easy to install and maintain. Windows 95 can be all the networking software you need, or it can be a well-integrated client in a larger network using other software from Microsoft or other manufacturers. Some of the important networking improvements in Windows 95 are as follows:

- Full 32-bit networking with 32-bit software, 32-bit file and printer sharing, and 32-bit network card drivers

- Full built-in support for Novell NetWare networking, including a Microsoft 32-bit NetWare client for connecting to either NetWare 3.*x* or 4.*x* servers

- Support for an environment with multiple networks, including simultaneously using multiple network card device drivers

- Full capability for remotely connecting to and using, or even managing, a network including accessing NetWare and Unixservers

- Support for many industry standard networking protocols, including TCP/IP and IPX, as well as client support for a

157

number of other networking systems, including Artisoft Lantastic, Banyan Vines, DEC PathWorks, and Sun NFS

The key advantage of Windows 95 networking is that you can take it to any depth that you want. At one extreme, Windows 95 can provide the means for the simple sharing of files or a printer among a couple of computers. At the other extreme, Windows 95 can easily be integrated with several other networking schemes in a large networking complex. In between are the sharing of other devices including CD-ROMs, tape drives, and modems; the implementing of various security and control schemes; and the using of Windows 95 as a Windows NT or NetWare client. Windows 95 has the capability; your needs are the determinant of what you do with it.

This chapter will introduce you to networking in general and Windows 95 networking in particular. The chapter will then lead you through the installation and setup of a network using Windows 95, including some of the hardware alternatives and the possible software options.

Networking

Computer networking (or just *networking*) is the connecting of computers in order to share resources, exchange data, and communicate among the users. Resources that can be shared include printers, disk and tape drives, programs, and databases. Exchanging data is the sending of information files from one computer to another, and communicating is the transferring of messages among the computers on the network. The primary reasons for networking are

- Sharing and/or controlling hardware and software
- Working on common data
- Improving communication among users

These can lead to reduced costs and improved efficiency. The sharing of hardware allows the purchase of better, more expensive devices than if each person on the network had one of the devices. The sharing of software facilitates its control, so for example, it performs in a consistent way for all users; and sharing software may be what allows multiple users to work on common data. Working on common data allows the maintenance of a large body of information, like a database or an accounting system, by several people.

Improved communications with electronic mail, or *e-mail*, facilitates the coordinating of schedules and, often, the more efficient sharing of information.

Types of Networks

Computers in a network can be connected in several different ways including using modems and phone lines. Except for the discussion of remote, or dial-up, networking in Chapter 6, networking in this book refers to a group of computers that each have a network adapter card and dedicated cabling (or wireless channel) connecting them and that run Windows 95 or other networking software. Within this framework there are two classes of networks: wide area networks and local area networks.

Wide area networks (*WANs*) generally connect other networks or larger computers at some distance from one another using dedicated telephone lines, satellite links, or microwave links. WANs can connect *nodes*, or end points, across the street or around the world from one another. WANs are professionally managed, highly complex networks and are not within the scope of this book.

Local area networks (*LANs*) generally connect computers or smaller LANs within a single office or building with dedicated cabling or wireless channels. LANs are more common and come in two types that differ in the way they distribute networking tasks. These are peer-to-peer LANs and client-server LANs.

PEER-TO-PEER LANS

In a peer-to-peer LAN all computers (nodes) equally share networking tasks, with equal ability to provide resources and use resources on other nodes. Any of the computers may store programs and data used by others, and any of the computers may have a printer or other resource shared by all. For example, the peer-to-peer LAN in Figure 5–1 has a shared printer on one computer and a shared tape drive on another.

Peer-to-peer LANs tend to be smaller and more localized to a single *workgroup* (people working together) than client-server LANs although this is not a requirement. When a workgroup first decides to utilize a network, it often is a peer-to-peer LAN, because it causes the least disruption and is the least expensive. Everyone can continue to do what

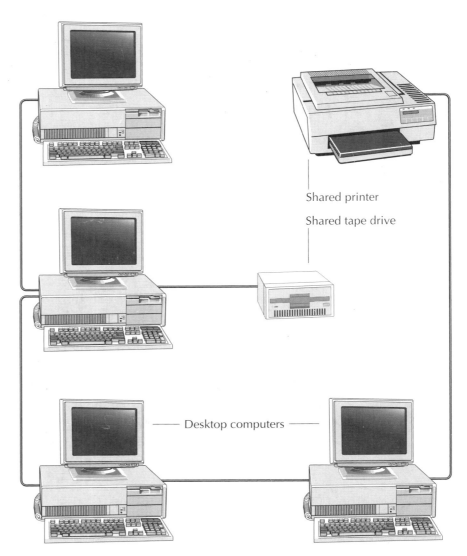

Figure 5–1

A peer-to-peer LAN with a bus topology

Shared printer

Shared tape drive

Desktop computers

they previously did on their same computers, and in addition, they can share resources, exchange data, and communicate.

A peer-to-peer LAN requires only network adapter cards for each computer, cabling to link the computers, and Windows 95. Of course each computer must be able to run Windows 95, so it must have at least a 386 processor, 4 MB of memory, and about 40 MB of free disk space.

CLIENT-SERVER LANS

In client-server LANs there are two types of computers: *clients*, or *workstations* for the individual users on the network, and *servers* that provide the central facility for managing the network, storing programs and data, and providing common resources. The network management done by the server includes managing network files, network communications, and network resources such as printers, tape drives, and CD-ROMs. A server is usually dedicated to its task and cannot be used for normal end-user tasks such as word processing. Nevertheless, the server normally is more powerful than the average desktop computer, with more memory, a faster processor, and a lot more disk space. Client workstations, on the other hand, can be less powerful and even may not have a disk, although that is unusual. Workstations usually are normal desktop computers on which normal computing tasks can be run, and they may even have their own peripherals such as a printer (referred to as a *local printer* to distinguish it from a network printer), as shown in Figure 5–2.

Peer-to-peer LANs generally are less expensive than client-server LANs in terms of both hardware and software. Although the workstations may be cheaper in a client-server LAN, a peer-to-peer LAN does not require a dedicated server. Also, the server requires special software and more technical expertise on the part of the people running it. Common server software includes Novell NetWare and Microsoft Windows NT Server. Windows 95, though, works excellently as the client with either server software.

The decision of whether to use a peer-to-peer LAN or a client-server LAN is not black and white. Larger LANs (more than ten nodes) generally tend to be client-server LANs, because at that point the economies of scale allow for the purchase of a reasonable server by having only slightly less capability in each workstation. There is nothing that prevents larger peer-to-peer LANs, but at about a dozen users, a peer-to-peer LAN is usually too slow in most situations. If you are running a centralized application, like an accounting system, where several people are working on it at one time, a client-server LAN makes a lot of sense. While you can run such a system on a peer-to-peer LAN, one node will be dedicated mostly to the central disk activities, so you might as well make it a server.

Figure 5–2

*Client-server
LAN with
a star topology*

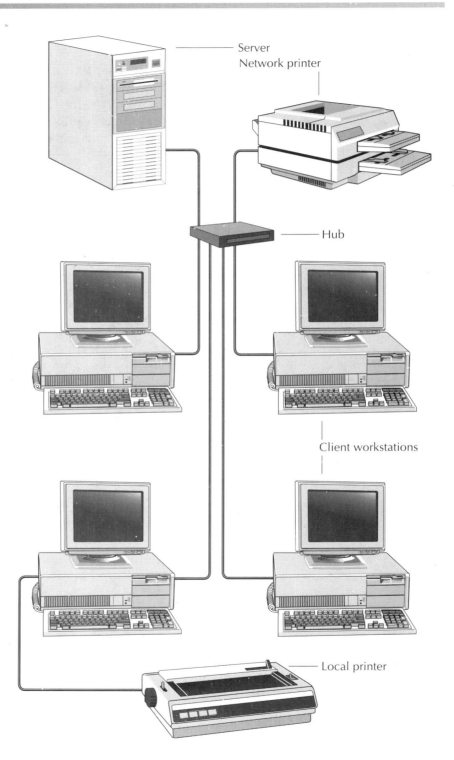

Server
Network printer

Hub

Client workstations

Local printer

Network Hardware

Independent of the type of network, each node in the network must include a computer (or an intelligent peripheral such as some printers) with a network adapter card and the necessary cabling to connect them.

NETWORK COMPUTERS

The size and configuration of network computers, over and above the minimum necessary to run Windows 95, depend almost exclusively on what you are going to do with the computers. Look at each workstation or computer in a peer-to-peer LAN, and decide what tasks it will be performing and the hardware required for those tasks. Other than the network adapter card, there is no special hardware required for networking.

The server, if one is desired, must also be sized to fit its tasks. The processor does not have to be the absolutely fastest available. A 66-MHz 486 or a 60-MHz Pentium are good choices. The server's memory must be adequate for the software you are running (a minimum of 8 MB for NetWare and 12 MB for Windows NT, although most servers have at least 16 MB), and the disk space must satisfy the storage needs of the applications you are running. In addition you might want to provide tape backup in the server and an uninterruptable power supply (UPS), so that the server and its files are protected. The only absolute requirement for networking in the server, like in a workstation, is a network adapter card.

NETWORK ADAPTER CARDS

A *network adapter card* (also called a network card, network board, LAN adapter, or network interface card) is the electronic interface between your computer and the cabling that joins the network. The network adapter cards manage the traffic on the network to make sure that information gets to its destination. The network adapter card is plugged into one of the expansion slots on the *motherboard* (main circuit, or system, board) in your computer and the network cabling plugs into the card.

The network adapter card takes information that is to be sent over the network and packages it in *packets*, or *frames*, with an address of where it is going, much like an envelope with an address on the front. The packets are then sent out over the cables and intercepted by the node to which they are addressed. The receiving node then extracts the information and gives it to its computer.

There are a number of variations in network adapter cards. This results from different types of cards, different card slots on the motherboard into which the network adapter card connects, and different types of cabling.

Types of Network Adapter Cards   Three common types of network adapter cards are used in LANs: Ethernet, Token Ring, and ARCnet. ARCnet is typically used in smaller peer-to-peer networks and is being challenged even in that market by Ethernet. Ethernet is common in small to reasonably large networks of both peer-to-peer and client-server LANs. Ethernet is no longer significantly more expensive than ARCnet, and in most situations, it is at least twice as fast. Although ARCnet is slow, it is very reliable. Token Ring is used in larger, more mission-critical client-server networks. Token Ring adapters cost three to four times what an Ethernet adapter costs and are more than 1.5 times faster. The other benefits of Token Ring are that it is more reliable than Ethernet and can provide built in diagnostic and network management capabilities that are valuable in managing larger networks. The decision on the type of network card probably points to Ethernet, unless you have a mission-critical situation that makes it worthwhile to pay the price for Token Ring.

All network adapter cards in your network must be the same type with the same type of cabling.

Types of Motherboard Card Slots   The slots on the motherboard are determined by the bus architecture used. Four bus architectures are in common use today: ISA, EISA, VESA, and PCI. ISA is the oldest bus architecture and can be either 8 or 16 bits (the data path is either 8 or 16 bits wide). ISA network adapter cards can also be 8 or 16 bits, with 16-bit cards being twice as fast for a small additional cost. ISA cards can be used in both EISA and VESA slots but without the added benefits of those architectures. EISA, VESA, and PCI are different implementations of a 32-bit bus. EISA is the oldest and the most expensive. VESA is the cheapest and the least sophisticated. PCI is the newest and probably the wave of the future for high performance network adapter cards. For most networking needs, a 16-bit ISA is probably adequate. In heavily used servers, you might go to a 32-bit PCI bus card.

Windows 95 can fully drive a 32-bit network adapter card, should you have the need.

NETWORK CABLING

Two types of cable are used in Ethernet networks: coaxial and twisted pair. Coaxial cable is similar to (but not the same as!) television cable. Twisted-pair cabling is similar to four-wire telephone cabling and *might* be the same—you need to check the specifications of the wire that you have (or that is already installed in your building) against those recommended for your network adapter cards. Token Ring networks commonly use one of two types of twisted-pair cabling: Type 1, which is shielded and runs at 16 megabits per second (Mbps), and Type 3, which is unshielded and runs at 4 Mbps. Additionally, both Ethernet and Token Ring can use fiber optic cable with special adapters or converters for particularly long distances—1.2 miles for Ethernet and 2.5 miles for Token Ring. ARCnet uses either twisted-pair or coaxial cable.

Do not use existing telephone twisted-pair cabling without checking its specifications against those recommended for your network adapter cards.

Coaxial Cable   Coaxial cable, or *coax*, has wire braid surrounding a central wire with plastic insulation in between and a plastic jacket on the outside. Ethernet coaxial cable can be thin (about 0.2 inch in diameter), called *10Base2* or *ThinNet*, or thick (about 0.4 inch in diameter), called *10Base5* or *Standard* Ethernet. Thick coax, which was the original Ethernet cabling, can connect workstations up to 1640 feet apart versus up to 600 feet for thin coax. Thick coax is several times more expensive than thin, is harder to find, and harder to handle. For these reasons thick coax is primarily used to connect other networks or over longer distances. Thin coax is generally easy to find and inexpensive. ARCnet cards use a slightly different thin coaxial cable, and you can tell the difference by the number stamped on it. Ethernet thin coax is RG-58A/U; ARCnet is RG-62A/U.

Ethernet thin coax uses a BNC twist-to-lock connector. You can buy the cables with the connectors on them, or you can add the connectors as you install the cable if you have or want to buy the necessary tools. Depending on the network topology (see "Network Topology" later in this chapter) you are using, the cable

Figure 5–3

*Ethernet thin
coax cabling
components with a
bus topology*

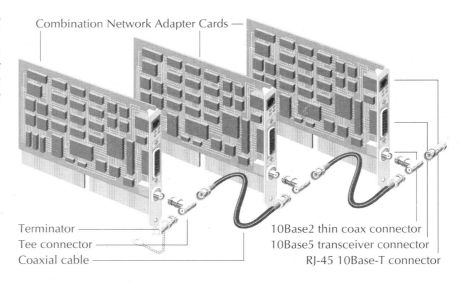

Combination Network Adapter Cards —

Terminator ———
Tee connector ———
Coaxial cable ———

10Base2 thin coax connector
10Base5 transceiver connector
RJ-45 10Base-T connector

either connects directly to the network adapter card (star topology), or more commonly, uses a tee connector (bus topology), as shown in Figure 5–3. When you are using a bus topology, the computers in the middle have a cable connected to each end of the tee connector, while the computers on the ends have only one cable and require a 50-ohm terminator on the unused half of the tee connector.

Twisted-Pair Cable   Ethernet twisted-pair cabling (called 10Base-T or UTP for unshielded twisted pair) has four individual wires (two pairs—one for transmitting and one for receiving data). Each wire is insulated and twisted with its mate in a pair, and then the two twisted pairs are covered by a plastic outer cover. The twisting of the pairs provides some amount of shielding against electrical and radio interference. If this is not sufficient to keep noise off the network, you can get shielded twisted-pair cable that has a braided jacket enclosing the two pairs of wires. Twisted-pair cable uses a modular connector, known as an RJ-45 plug, similar to a modular phone plug except that it has eight pins, or conductors, instead of four as in a standard (RJ-11) phone plug.

For twisted-pair cabling to work, the transmitting pair of wires on one end of the cable must become the receiving pair on the other end. This *crossover* function is handled normally in the hub (see "Network Topology" later in this chapter) in a star topology, which is

Figure 5–4

*Ethernet twisted-
pair cabling
components with a
star topology*

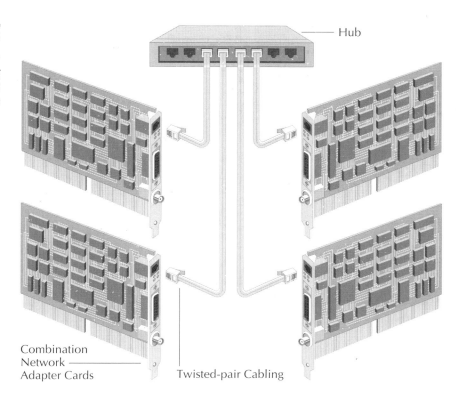

Hub

Combination
Network
Adapter Cards

Twisted-pair Cabling

commonly used with twisted-pair cabling, as shown in Figure 5–4. If
you want to network only two computers with 10Base-T, you may do
so without a hub by using a special crossover cable, which provides
the crossover function.

Unshielded twisted-pair cabling is cheaper and is easier to install than
coaxial cable, but it is more susceptible to electrical and radio interference. Twisted-pair cable can be shielded, but it substantially
increases the cost and reduces the availability and ease of installation.
Often when you are installing twisted-pair cabling, you can simply be
careful about *not* running the cable along side any motorized equipment (fans, water coolers, machine tools) or fluorescent light fixtures
and solve most of the problems.

Cabling Summary   Table 5–1 provides a summary of network
cabling specifications. It is useful information, but it is to some
degree like trying to describe apples and oranges with the same
terms. An Ethernet twisted-pair *segment* is the distance between two
nodes, and only two nodes can be on it. An Ethernet coaxial *segment*

Table 5–1.

Summary of network cabling specifications

Type of Cabling	Maximum Segment Length	Maximum Network Length	Minimum Cable Length	Maximum Speed	Maximum Network Nodes	Maximum Nodes/ Segment
Ethernet:						
Twisted Pair (10Base-T)	328 ft	NA		10 Mbps	1024	2
Thin Coax (10Base2)	600 ft	3000 ft	2 ft	10 Mbps	90	30
Thick Coax (10Base5)	1640 ft	8200 ft	8.5 ft	10 Mbps	300	100
Fiber Optic (10Base-F)	1.2 mi			10 Mbps		
Token Ring						
Type 1 - Shielded	328 ft	NA		16 Mbps	NA	260
Type 3 - Unshielded	148 ft	NA		4 Mbps	NA	72
Fiber Optic	2.5 mi			16 Mbps		
ARCnet						
Twisted Pair	400 ft	4 mi	6 ft	2.5 Mbps	255	10
Thin Coax	1000 ft	4 mi		2.5 Mbps	255	8

is the maximum length of a single run of coaxial cable and can have up to 30 or 100 nodes depending on the type of coax. A Token Ring *segment* is the length of one ring and can have up to 72 or 260 nodes on it. There is a limit of five Ethernet coaxial segments, and only three of them can have nodes. Therefore, the maximum network length for Ethernet coax is five times the segment length, and the maximum network nodes is only three times the number of segment nodes. Both Token Ring and Ethernet twisted pair can be expanded virtually forever. Therefore there is no maximum network length, and for Token Ring, there is no maximum number of nodes. The Ethernet specification itself limits the total number of nodes in the network to 1024, although you can join multiple networks to increase that number. While there is no specified minimum cable length for Ethernet twisted pair, Token Ring, or ARCnet coax, as a practical matter, you should not cut a cable shorter than two feet.

There are many ways to implement a large network and many ways around the limits shown in Table 5–1. These involve various types of hubs, repeaters, and bridges, all electronic devices that allow you to expand your network. For more information see the book *LAN Times Encyclopedia of Networking* by Tom Sheldon, published in 1994 by Osborne/McGraw-Hill, (800) 822-8158, or the *Black Box Catalog* from Black Box Corporation, P.O. Box 12800, Pittsburgh, PA 15241, (412) 746-5500.

NETWORK TOPOLOGY

Network topology describes how the nodes or devices on a network are connected. For Ethernet, there are two topologies: bus and star.

Bus Topology   In a *bus topology*, which is used with coaxial cable, each of the devices are connected in a line on a single run of cable. This is a daisy-chain arrangement where the cable goes from device (computer, workstation, or server) to device. With thin coax cable, the tee connector provides the joining of the two cables at each device except on the ends, where a 50-ohm terminator is used on one side of the tee connector, as you can see in Figure 5–5. With thick coax, a clamp-on connector goes over a continuous run of cable and provides the signal to a transceiver, which sends the signal through a separate multiconductor cable to the network adapter card, as shown in Figure 5–6. Again, on either end of the thick coax cable there is a 50-ohm terminator. (This complex, costly configuration, needed with thick coax, is part of the reason that it is not widely used any more.)

Star Topology   A *star topology*, which is used by both Ethernet 10Base-T twisted-pair cabling and Token Ring cabling, uses a *hub* to fan out the network from one incoming signal to two, four, eight, or more outgoing signals. You can have a server feeding several hubs that each feed several hubs that each feed a number of workstations, allowing you to get very quickly to a large number of nodes, as shown in Figure 5–7. The benefits of a star topology are as follows:

Figure 5–5

Bus topology with 10Base2 thin coaxial cable

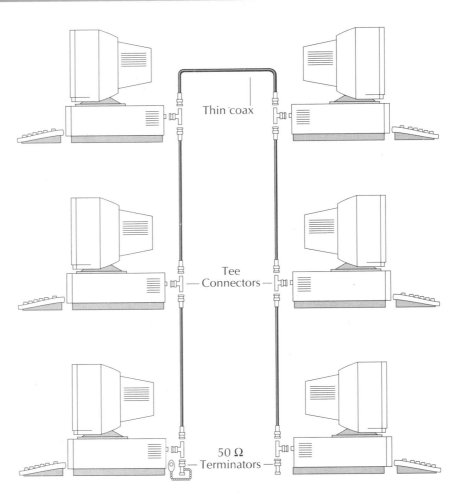

- The loss of one segment generally does not bring down the entire network.
- Network traffic seldom hits a bottleneck since each node has its own cable.
- Network design is very flexible and is easily expanded.
- Cable problems are easy to find by observing what is working and what isn't.

In a star topology, you can daisy chain from one star to another and another, creating four or more layers. You will find you improve your reliability if you fan out from one hub to many hubs and have only two, or at the very most three, layers.

Figure 5–6

Bus topology with 10Base5 thick coaxial cable

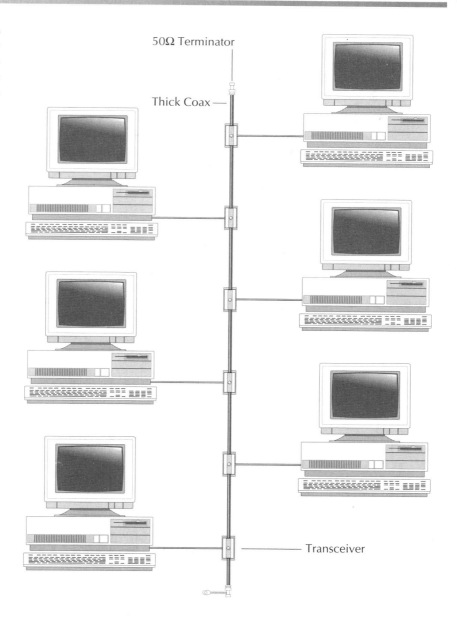

50Ω Terminator

Thick Coax —

Transceiver

On the negative side, hubs are expensive, and if one fails, the entire network will go down. Also, there is a lot of cable in a star topology, and while it is cheaper per foot than coaxial cable, the quantity of it may more than make up for the lower cost per foot.

In summary, Ethernet twisted-pair (10Base-T) in a star topology is the predominate networking scheme in use today. This means that

Figure 5–7

Star topology with 10Base-T twisted-pair cable

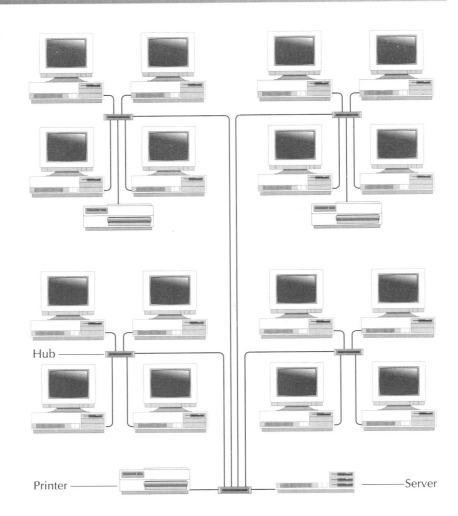

you will find a large number of competitively priced components on the market and a lot of knowledge on their use.

In all but the simplest network installations, usually a combination of topologies are used. Within a given workgroup the typical network uses a 10Base-T star topology and then uses a 10Base2 or 10Base5 bus topology to run between workgroups or floors in a building.

Setting Up Network Adapter Cards

For your network adapter card to work with your computer, the card must have two or three settings correctly made on it. These settings, which include the interrupt request line, the I/O port address, and possibly the upper memory address, determine how the card communicates with the computer. To make the settings, you will need to know the settings of these items for other devices in your computer. To find that out, given that you are already running Windows 95, follow these instructions:

1. Open the Start menu, choose Settings, and then click on Control Panel.

2. Double-click on the System icon and then on the Device Manager tab.

3. Click on Print in the lower right, and then when the dialog box opens, make sure that System summary is selected, and then click on OK.

You will get a list of what device is using which interrupt request line, port address, and upper memory address. With this information, you can see what is available for the network adapter card.

 **Before handling a network adapter card or any electronic circuit card, be sure to ground yourself by touching some grounded object to make sure that static electricity does not damage some component on the circuit card. An even better idea is to get, connect, and wear a grounding wrist strap while working with the circuit card.**

Different cards use different methods of changing the settings. Some have a small set of pins sticking up, called a *DIP header*, with little plastic or metal blocks, called *jumpers*, connecting some of the pins. Others have tiny banks of numbered switches, called *DIP switches*. Still others (the newest and the best) use software to configure themselves. This last kind are called *jumperless* or *switchless*, and while they cost as much as fifty percent more, they make setup very easy. When you run the software, it does the same thing as the Windows 95 Device Manager in that you get a list of what device is using which setting. The software then recommends the setting you should use for the network adapter card. You can change or accept this and click on OK—the card will then be set up for you.

If you need to set up a card with either jumpers or switches, you'll need to study the manual that came with the card to determine the purpose of each jumper or switch. Then with your list of what other devices are using, read the following sections to determine how to set up your card.

INTERRUPT REQUEST LINE

The *interrupt request line* (*IRQ*) determines which interrupt line on your computer the network adapter card uses to request service. On all the computers on which Windows 95 will run, there are 16 interrupt request lines numbered 0 through 15. Table 5–2 shows some default and possible uses of these lines. Some possible choices for the network adapter card are IRQ 7, 10, and 11. Look at what your other devices are using, and then decide what you want to use for this card. Next, look at your card's manual, and decide how your choice translates into pins or switches on your card.

With a DIP header, you need to lift off the jumpers (you may need to use a small screwdriver to pry it up or needle-nose pliers to grasp it) and then place the jumper back on the correct pins. With a DIP switch, note which side is *ON*, and then press down or slide across (depending on the type) the correct switches so they are on.

	IRQ	Standard or Typical Use
Table 5–2.	**0**	System timer
Interrupt request lines and their normal use	**1**	Keyboard
	2	Programmable interrupt controller (implements IRQ 9–15)
	3	Serial ports COM2 and COM4
	4	Serial ports COM1 and COM3
	5	Possibly a bus mouse or a sound card
	6	Floppy-disk controller
	7	May be available
	8	System CMOS and real-time clock
	9	May be available
	10	May be available
	11	May be available
	12	Possibly a SCSI hard-disk or device controller
	13	Math coprocessor
	14	IDE or ESDI hard-disk controller
	15	May be available

I/O PORT ADDRESS

The *I/O port address* is the address through which the computer, the card, and the driver software for the card all communicate. It is actually a range of numbers that are expressed in hexadecimal notation (base 16), so you often see them with a small *h* after the number. Table 5–3 shows some default and possible uses of these addresses. Some possible choices for the network adapter card are 300h–31Fh, 320h–33Fh, and 340h–35Fh. Look at what your other devices are using, and then decide what you want to use for this card. Next look at your card's manual, and decide how your choice translates to pins or switches on your card.

 Hexadecimal (hex) numbers go from 0 to 15 instead of 0 to 9 for decimal numbers. Alphabetical letters A–F are used to represent the hexadecimal numbers beyond 9. The range of hexadecimal numbers then is 0, 1, 2, 3, 4, 5, 6, 7, 8, 9, A, B, C, D, E, and F. The I/O port address range 300h–31Fh represents 32 decimal (20 hex) addresses: 300–309 is 10, 30A–30F is 6, 310–31F is 16 (310 follows 30F).

 Most network adapter cards and their manuals identify only the base I/O port address. This is the left-hand number in the address range shown in Table 5–3. For example, for the range 300h–31Fh, 300h is the base I/O port address.

 A network adapter card takes 32 (20 hex) address positions, for example, 300h–31Fh. Therefore, if you have a SCSI controller at 340h, you cannot put the network adapter card at 330h because it will take up 330h–34Fh, overlapping the SCSI controller and causing serious problems.

UPPER MEMORY ADDRESS

The *upper memory address* is an area of upper memory (between 640 KB and 1 MB) that some network adapter cards use. Ethernet cards only use this if you have a diskless workstation and boot the computer from a *boot PROM* in the network adapter card. (The boot PROM is a chip that allows you to boot off of files in the server.) ARCnet cards use upper memory as buffer memory as well as for a boot PROM. The address, which is a range, is expressed in hexadecimal like the I/O port address. Table 5–4 shows some default and possible uses of these addresses. Two possible choices for the network adapter card are CC000h–DBFFFh and E0000h–EFFFFh. Look at what your

Table 5–3.

I/O port addresses and their normal use

Port Address	Standard or Typical Use
000h–0DFh	System components like system timer, keyboard, speaker
0F0h–0FFh	Numeric coprocessor
1F0h–1F7h	IDE/ESDI hard-disk controller
200h–20Fh	Gameport—Joystick
220h–22Fh	Sound card
230h–23Fh	Bus mouse or Sony CD-ROM
278h–27Fh	LPT2 printer port (LPT3 if present)
2E8h–2EFh	COM4 serial port
2F8h–2FFh	COM2 serial port
300h–31Fh	May be available, may be used by a sound card
320h–33Fh	May be available, may be used by a SCSI controller
340h–35Fh	May be available, may be used by a SCSI controller
378h–37Fh	LPT1 printer port (LPT2 if LPT3 present)
388h–38Fh	May be used by sound card
3B0h–3BBh	Display adapter (Monochrome area)
3BCh–3BFh	(LPT1 printer port if LPT3 present)
3C0h–3DFh	Display adapter (Color area)
3E8h–3EF	COM3 printer port
3F2h–3F5h	Floppy-disk controller
3F6h–3F6h	IDE/ESDI hard-disk controller
3F8h–3FFh	COM1 serial port

other devices are using, and then decide what you want to use for this card. Next look at your card's manual, and decide how your choice translates to pins or switches on your card.

NODE ADDRESS

Each network adapter card in a network must have a unique node address. Ethernet cards have this address built into the card, and it

Table 5–4.	Upper Memory Address	Standard or Typical Use
Upper memory addresses and their normal use	A0000h–AFFFFh	VGA and EGA display adapters
	B0000h–B7FFFh	MDA and Hercules display adapters
	B8000h–BFFFFh	CGA and Hercules display adapters
	C0000h–C7FFFh	VGA, EGA, and 8514/A display adapters
	C8000h–CBFFFh	8514/A display adapters
	CC000h–DBFFFh	Normally available (was used by exPanded memory pages)
	DC000h–DFFFFh	May be available if not used by SCSI disk controller
	E0000h–EFFFFh	Normally available except in PS/2 computers
	F0000h–FFFFFh	System ROM BIOS

cannot be changed. ARCnet cards have a DIP switch that allows you to enter the address for each card. When you do this, be sure to keep a log, so you can see that no two computers have the same address.

Setting Up Windows 95 Networking

Under many circumstances, when you set up Windows 95 on a computer properly connected to a network, Setup will detect the network and the network adapter card you are using and correctly configure Windows to use the network. You have to do nothing but use the network. Part of the reason that so much of this chapter is devoted to hardware is that 70 to 80 percent of all networking problems are with the hardware. This is especially true with Windows 95. If your network has either a NetWare or Windows NT server, Setup will automatically provide the correct client software to run in your computer. If you are running Windows for Workgroups in a peer-to-peer network, or if you are setting up a Windows 95 peer-to-peer network, Setup will normally do all the work for you.

Add New Hardware

If you add a network adapter card and a network connection after setting up Windows 95, use the Add New Hardware control panel, shown on the left, (open the Start menu, choose Settings Control Panel, and double-click on Add New Hardware) to start the Add New Hardware

Figure 5–8

*Add New
Hardware Wizard*

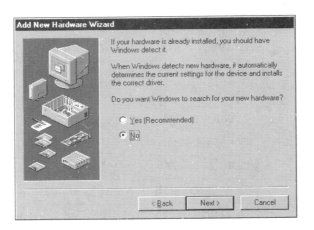

Wizard. This will lead you through the process of identifying and configuring your card and the networking software you are using, as shown in Figure 5–8. Again, in most instances your task is no greater than clicking on Next. Setup should find the card and its resource usage (IRQ and I/O port address) and install the necessary driver software.

If your Windows 95 networking setup did not go perfectly, or if for some reason you want to make a change to your network, then the Network control panel provides all of the settings to configure your networking software. This same set of dialog boxes is used by Setup to enter network settings, so any setup questions you have can be answered by the next series of sections on the Network control panel.

Network Control Panel

Network

The Network control panel is reached by opening the Control Panel and then double-clicking on the Network icon, shown on the left. This opens the Network dialog box, which you can see in Figure 5–9.

The primary work in the Network dialog box is done in the Configuration tab. Here you can add, remove, and configure components. The components are shown in the list box at the top of the dialog box. By selecting a component, you can remove it (click on Remove) or change its properties (click on Properties). You can also add components by clicking on Add. When you do that, a list of the four components is displayed, as shown next. Each of these components is discussed next.

Figure 5–9

*Network
dialog box*

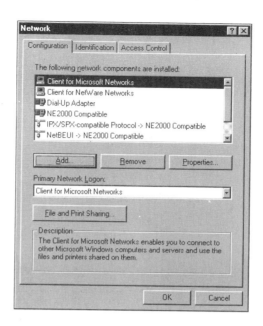

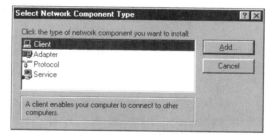

 You can also open the Network dialog box by right-clicking on the Network Neighborhood and then choosing Properties in the popup menu that appears.

NETWORK CLIENTS

A network client is the primary software component necessary for your computer to operate on a network. It provides the ability within Windows 95 to access files and print to printers located on other computers. Windows 95 comes with a number of network clients that allow you to connect to and utilize many different networks. If you are physically connected to a network when you run Setup, it is

Figure 5–10

Select Network Client dialog box

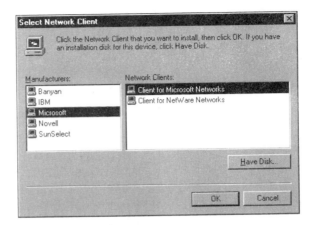

likely that Setup will detect the network and install the appropriate client. If, for whatever reason, Setup cannot determine what client to install, or if you want to install a client, you do so through the Select Network Client dialog box, which is shown in Figure 5–10. You open the Select Network Client dialog box by choosing Client and clicking on Add in the Select Network Component Type dialog box discussed above.

Selecting a Network Client   If you want to create a Windows 95 peer-to-peer network, connect to or replace a Window for Workgroups network, or if you want to be a client on a Windows NT or LAN Manager network, you need to use the Client for Microsoft Networks. If you want to be a client on a Novell NetWare network, you can use either the Microsoft Client for NetWare Networks or one of the Novell clients. If you are on another manufacturer's network, then you need to select the manufacturer and appropriate client for your network.

 **Both Novell and Microsoft have NetWare clients, and you should probably try both to see which works best for you.**

The Select Network Client dialog box lists the manufacturers that have contributed clients to operate within Windows 95, as well as the clients Microsoft has written for Windows 95. If you want to use other client software that you got separately from Windows 95, you may do so by clicking on Have Disk. Otherwise, select the manufacturer and client software you want to use, and then click on OK.

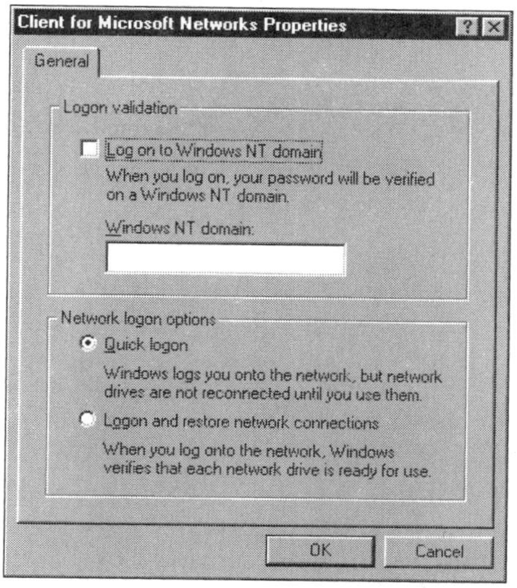

Figure 5–11

*Client for
Microsoft
Networks
Properties*

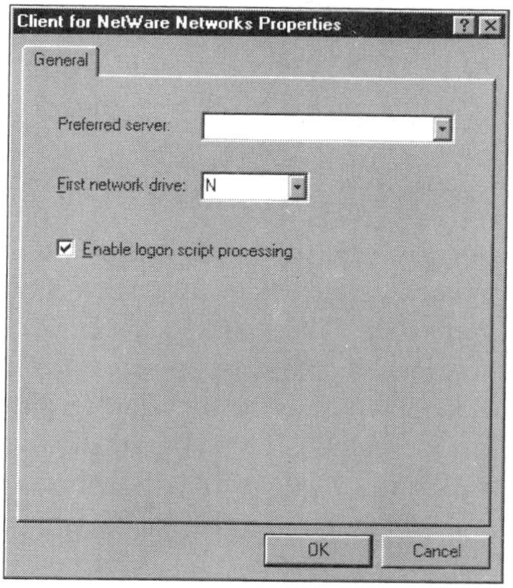

Figure 5–12

*Client for
NetWare
Networks
Properties*

Setting Client Properties Once you have installed a client, you can set its properties by double-clicking on it in the Network dialog box or selecting it and clicking on Properties. Each type of client has its own set of properties, as shown in Figures 5–11 and 5–12.

The client for Microsoft Networks Properties allows you to log on to an identified Windows NT domain and to determine how much checking you want to do of available network drives at logon. If

Figure 5–13

Auto detection of a new network adapter card

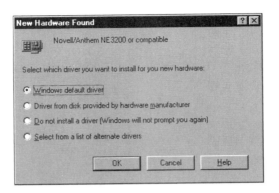

your network drives (those that you have mapped to your computer) are mandatory for your work, then you probably want to do the more time-consuming Logon and restore network connections. If you have several network drives that are often not up when you start up, then you will want to use the Quick logon. If you don't use Quick logon in the latter case, you will be asked about each network drive that is not available. After you have done that several times, you'll want to switch to Quick logon.

NETWORK ADAPTERS

As you saw in the first part of this chapter, a network adapter is a piece of hardware that allows you to connect your computer to a network. This can be a network adapter card that connects to a dedicated cable or wireless link using Ethernet, Token Ring, or ARCnet, or it can be a modem that allows you to connect to a telephone line. When you run through Setup or Add New Hardware, the system will try to determine what type of adapter card you have and its settings (IRQ, I/O port address, and so on). Also, if after setting up Windows 95 you install a network adapter card, Windows may detect the new card on startup, as shown in Figure 5–13. In any case (Setup, Add New Hardware, or startup), if the card adheres to the Plug and Play standard, Windows 95 will be able to identify it and its settings; otherwise, you will have to manually do the identification. From within Setup or the Add Hardware Wizard, you'll be shown the Select Network adapters dialog box, which you see in Figure 5–14. You can open the same dialog box by selecting Add from the Network dialog box, choosing Adapter, and clicking on Add.

Figure 5–14

*Select Network
adapters
dialog box*

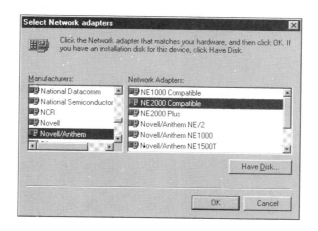

Selecting a Network Adapter   The Select Network Adapters dialog box lists many of the manufacturers of network adapter cards as well as their various models. If you are using a generic network adapter card that is NE1000 (8 bit), NE2000 (16 bit) or NE3200 (32 bit) compatible, you can find these adapters under Novell/Anthem, as shown in Figure 5–14. If you want to use a network adapter card not on the list and for which you have a floppy disk or a CD, you may do so by clicking on Have Disk. Otherwise, select the manufacturer and network adapter you want to use, and then click on OK.

Setting Network Adapter Properties   While running Setup or Add New Hardware, after selecting a network adapter card, you will be shown a Properties dialog box, similar to the one you see in Figure 5–15 but for your adapter card. The settings in the dialog box will vary for each type of card, but the NE2000 settings are representative. There are two to four tabs, with all cards having Driver Type and Bindings tabs, with some cards having Resources and/or Advanced tabs. The Driver Type tab allows you to select between enhanced-mode and real-mode drivers. Enhanced-mode drivers are by far the best choice. Bindings allows you to attach ("bind") one or more protocols to a particular adapter. See the discussion later in this chapter about protocols. Resources is where you tell Windows the IRQ and I/O port address to use for this card. With some Plug and Play compliant cards, resource information is automatically provided to Windows, so a Resource tab is not necessary. The Advanced tab allows you to set values for specific properties, which vary among adapter cards.

Figure 5–15

A network adapter card properties dialog box

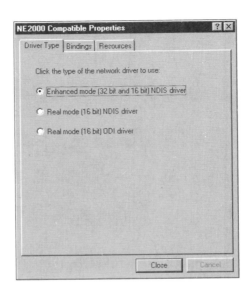

NETWORK PROTOCOLS

A network protocol is the method of communication used on the network. For the network to function, all computers on the network must employ the same protocol. A protocol is like a human language—to communicate, people must speak the same language. When you choose a client and an adapter, or they are selected for you by Setup, one or more protocols are installed and attached, or "bound," to the adapter. You can add a protocol by clicking on Add in the Network control panel, selecting Protocol, and clicking on Add again. The Select Network Protocol dialog box opens, as shown in Figure 5–16.

Selecting a Network Protocol   Many protocols were developed for specific types of networks, such as IPX/SPX for Novell NetWare. Over time these protocols have evolved and are now being used on several types of networks. With Windows 95, you can simultaneously use several protocols, but each takes loading time and computer resources. Windows 95 includes five 32-bit protected mode (able to address large memory space with multitasking) Microsoft implemented protocols as follows:

- **IPX/SPX** Internetwork packet exchange/Sequenced packet exchange, developed by Novell for NetWare

- **Microsoft DLC** Data Link Control protocol, used primarily to connect to IBM mainframe computers

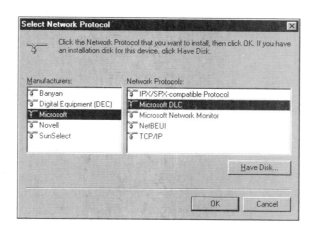

Figure 5–16

*Select Network
Protocol dialog box*

- **Microsoft Network Monitor** Microsoft Systems Management Server component, used to detect and troubleshoot LAN problems
- **NetBEUI** Network basic input/output system (NetBIOS) extended user interface, developed by IBM and Microsoft
- **TCP/IP** Transmission control protocol/Internet protocol, developed for UNIX and Internet

Additionally, Windows 95 includes two Microsoft 16-bit real-mode versions of NetBEUI and IPX/SPX as well as several protocols contributed by other vendors such as Banyan, DEC, and Novell. The question becomes which protocol is best under different circumstances. For the five Microsoft 32-bit protocols, their primary use and considerations are as follows:

- **IPX/SPX** Use with Novell NetWare and combined NetWare, Windows NT networks; slower, with more overhead than NetBEUI on smaller LANs
- **Microsoft DLC** Use with IBM mainframe computers to connect to computers running Windows 95; use also to provide connectivity to printers connected directly to the network
- **Microsoft Network Monitor** Use to direct Remote Access Service (RAS) problems on networks (first you need to install Microsoft Network Monitor Agent, described later in this chapter)

- **NetBEUI** Use with smaller (100 or less nodes) IBM and Microsoft networks; fast, small memory usage, and good error protection; poor performance over WANs

- **TCP/IP** Use with Internet, UNIX, and with multiple hardware/operating system platforms; most widely accepted protocol; slower than NetBEUI on smaller LANs, but good for larger LANs and WANs

The Select Network Protocol dialog box lists some of the manufacturers of network protocols as well as the protocols they provide. If you want to use a network protocol not on the list and for which you have a floppy disk or a CD, you may do so by clicking on Have Disk. Otherwise, select the manufacturer and protocol you want to use, and then click on OK.

Setting Network Protocol Properties   Each of the protocols has a unique set of properties and a unique Properties dialog box, as you can see in Figures 5–17 and 5–18. All of the dialog boxes have at least two tabs: Bindings, where you identify where the protocol will be used, and Advanced, where you make detail settings. Other tabs are unique to specific protocols. The default settings work under most circumstances.

If you are using TCP/IP, be sure to check the IP Address in the TCP/IP Properties dialog box, and if you are not connected to a DHCP server, be sure to specify an IP address. If you don't, you'll find that the system will pause periodically for a couple of seconds while it tries to get an IP address off a nonexistent DHCP server.

Figure 5–17

NetBEUI Properties dialog box

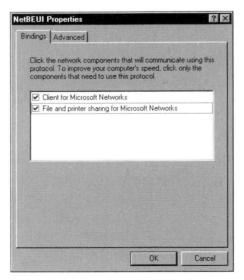

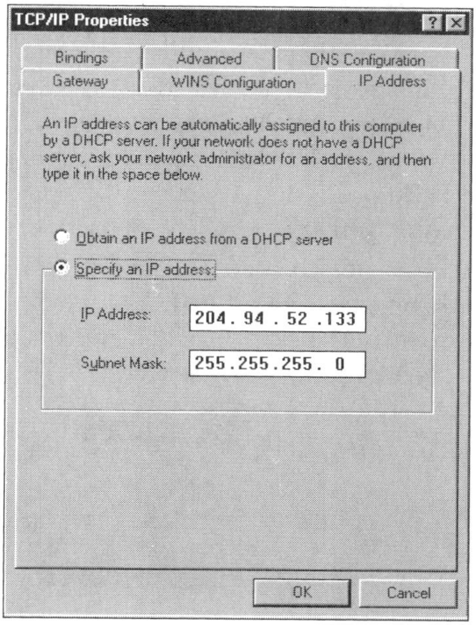

Figure 5–18

*TCP/IP
Properties
dialog box*

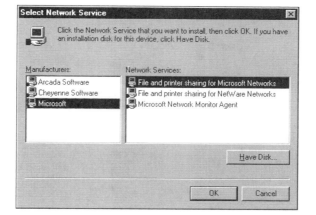

Figure 5–19

*Select Network
Service dialog box*

NETWORK SERVICES

Network services provide the means for you to share the disks, files, folders, and printers on your computer with others on the network (to perform the server function in a peer-to-peer network). Also, network services can set up your computer to allow for automatic system backup or for maintaining a remote registry for your computer. From the Select Network Component Type dialog box, you can select Service and Add to open the Select Network Service dialog box, shown in Figure 5–19.

Microsoft provides file and printer sharing for both Microsoft and NetWare networks, although you can install only one at a time, and the Microsoft Network Monitor Agent, a component of the Network Monitor that screens data flow in and out of the computer using Windows 95. Other manufacturers provide other services such as system backup. If you have a network service on a disk or CD, click on Have Disk. Otherwise, select the service you want to use, and click on OK.

Each of the services have a unique set of properties and a unique Properties dialog box, as you can see in Figures 5–20 and 5–21. As with network protocols, the property defaults are a good place to start with network services.

Figure 5–20

File and printer sharing for Microsoft

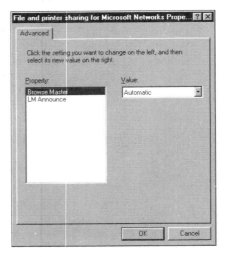

Figure 5–21

Backup Exec Agent Properties dialog box

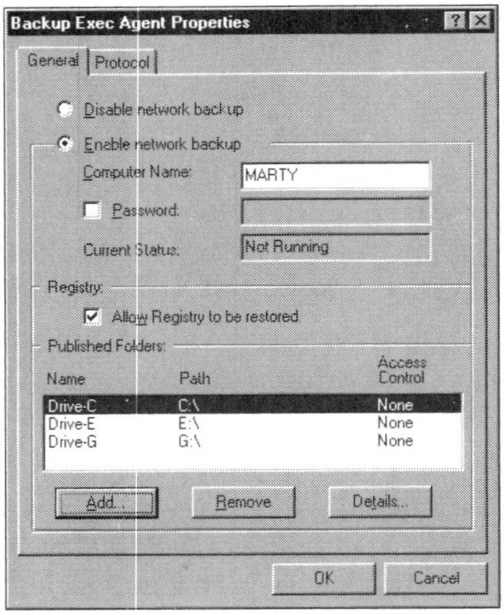

Using a Windows 95 Network

There are many ways to use a network. You can share the resources (data, folders, disks, CD-ROMs, and printers) on or connected to your computer with others in your workgroup; you can utilize the resources on other computers in your workgroup or on servers to which you have access; and you can transfer files and send messages to anyone to whom you are connected. You can also share some software on a network and use *groupware*, which is software that is meant to be worked on by several people in a workgroup. Examples of groupware are Lotus Notes, which defined this type of software, and Microsoft Schedule+.

In this chapter you will see how to share your resources and how to control that sharing. You will also see how to find and utilize resources elsewhere on the network to which you are connected, including the transferring of files. Sending messages over networks as well as all other aspects of electronic mail (e-mail) are the primary subjects of Chapter 8, so they are not covered here. This chapter does cover dial-up, or remote, networking and the several networking accessories that are part of Windows 95.

Sharing Your Resources

You can share most of the hardware, software (programs), and data that are on your computer. For your protection and the protection of your programs and data, you have a reasonable degree of control over how these resources are shared and by whom. There are two levels of sharing control available in Windows 95: a summary level where you can turn sharing on or off for your entire computer and all of its resources, and a detail level where you can turn sharing on or off individually for each specific disk, folder, or printer.

Turning Resource Sharing On or Off

Network

In order to share any of the resources on your computer, you must turn on sharing at a summary level. Windows 95 allows you to turn on or off the sharing of files and, separately, the sharing of printers. The *sharing of files* means that others on your network can read and potentially modify the files in the disks and folders that you have identified as being shared. The *sharing of printers* means that others on your network can print their documents on the printer(s) that you have identified as being shared. The summary level enabling of file and printer sharing is done through the Network control panel with the following steps:

1. Open the Start menu, choose Settings Control Panel, and after the Control Panel opens, double-click on the Network control panel icon. The Network dialog box will open, as you can see in Figure 6–1.

2. Click on the File and Print Sharing button just below the middle of the Network dialog box. The File and Print Sharing dialog box will open, as shown here:

3. To share your resources, select either or both of the check boxes. Select the top box to share disks, folders, and files;

Figure 6–1

*Network
dialog box*

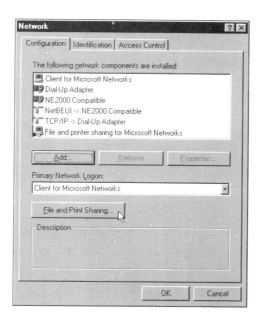

select the bottom box to share the printers connected to or on your computer (such as a fax).

If the check boxes are selected (check marks in them) and you don't want to share either or both types of resources, click in the boxes to turn off sharing.

4. Click on OK after you have set the summary level sharing status the way you want it.

Sharing Individual Resources

Although you may have turned on file and/or printer sharing on your computer at a summary level, nothing is shared until you specifically enable sharing for a particular resource. You must do this on a resource-by-resource basis except that if you share a disk, all folders and files on that disk are automatically shared.

If you do not want to share all the files on a disk, do not share the disk drive. You must specifically share the individual folders to which you want to provide access.

SHARING DISKS AND FOLDERS

Disks and folders are shared through either My Computer or the Explorer using these steps:

1. Open either My Computer or the Explorer and right-click on the disk or folder you want to share. The popup menu for that object will open, as you can see in Figure 6–2.

2. Select Sharing from the popup menu. The object's Properties dialog box will open with the Sharing tab selected, as shown in Figure 6–3.

Figure 6–2

Selecting Sharing from a drive's popup menu

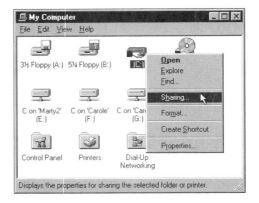

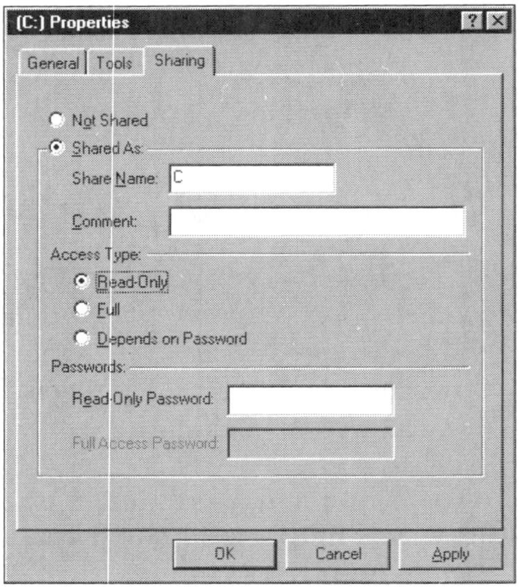

Figure 6–3

Sharing tab in a disk's or folder's Properties dialog box

3. Select Shared As to share a disk or folder, and either accept the default name or enter a new name that will be what the object is called on other computers. You can also enter a comment that will help identify your computer. The comment can be seen in the Details view of the Explorer's view of the Network Neighborhood.

4. Select the type of access you want to provide from among the following choices:

    ▪ **Read-Only** access allows people to read and copy files but not to modify or delete them.

    ▪ **Full** access allows people to modify and delete files as well as add and read them.

    ▪ **Depends on Password** access allows you to give different individuals different passwords, some of which allow full access and some read-only access.

5. Enter the passwords you want to use for the type of access you have chosen, and click on OK.

SHARING PRINTERS

Printers

Sharing a printer is very similar to sharing a disk or a folder except that it begins in the Printers folder. Use the following steps:

1. Open the Start menu and choose Settings, Printers. The Printers dialog box will open.

2. Right-click on the printer you want to share, and in the popup menu that opens click on Sharing. The Sharing tab of the printer's Properties dialog box will open, as shown in Figure 6–4.

3. Select Shared As and either accept the Share Name or enter a new one. Enter a comment if you want to provide one and a password if you want password protection on the use of the printer.

4. When you are satisfied that the dialog box is the way you want it, click on OK.

Using Resources on Other Computers

A major benefit of networking to you personally is that you now have access to all of the resources that have been shared on your network.

Figure 6–4

*Sharing tab of a
printer's
Properties
dialog box*

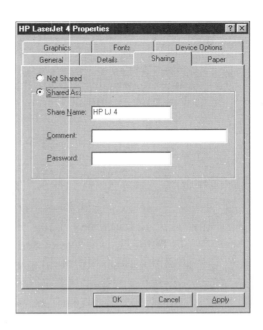

To realize this benefit, you must locate the resources and utilize
them. You can do that through the Network Neighborhood or by
mapping the resources to your computer.

Accessing Resources through the Network Neighborhood

The Network Neighborhood is the primary path to network resources.
It performs the same functions for your network resources as My
Computer does for the resources on your computer. When you open
the Network Neighborhood, you see the computers in your immediate
workgroup as well as an icon representing the rest of your network, as
you can see in Figure 6–5. If you open the Entire Network, you'll see
the other workgroups and servers that you can access. If you open these
workgroups, you'll see the individual computers that are available within them.

If you click on a computer, either directly in the Network
Neighborhood or within a workgroup under the Entire Network, you
will see the resources that have been shared on that computer, as
shown in Figure 6–6. By double-clicking on one of the disk resources
you can open it and see the folders and files that are available within it,

Figure 6–5

Network Neighborhood

Figure 6–6

Resources shared on a particular computer

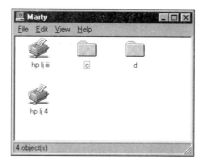

just as you could by double-clicking on a disk in My Computer. Depending on how the disks and folders are shared, you will be able to read and copy files and possibly modify and delete them. If you want to copy a file onto your own computer, you need only drag it from its original folder to one on a disk in your computer. Use the following steps for that purpose:

Dragging a file between disks copies it, unlike dragging a file between folders on the same disk, which moves the file.

1. Open the Network Neighborhood from the desktop, and select the network computer from which you want to copy the file.

2. Open the network computer, and select the disk and folder containing the file. You should be able to see the file. If not, use the scroll bar until you see the file.

3. Open My Computer, and select first the disk and then the folder that are to receive the file. You should now be able to see both the receiving folder and the file. If not, drag and size the windows until you can see both, as shown in Figure 6–7.

Figure 6–7

Windows set up for copying between a network computer and yours

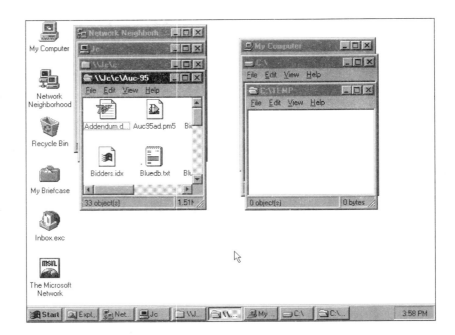

Figure 6–8

Network Neighborhood within the Explorer

4. Drag the file from the network computer's folder to your computer's folder. A copy of the file will be on your computer for you to use as you wish.

USING EXPLORER WITH NETWORK NEIGHBORHOOD

The Explorer provides full access to the computers, disks, folders, and files within the Network Neighborhood, as you can see in Figure 6–8. This makes searching for and copying files easier, because you

Figure 6–9

Explorer set up for copying between a network computer and yours

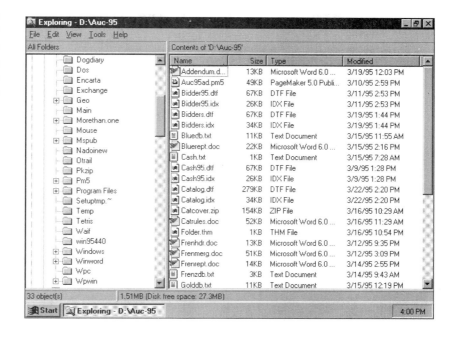

can get at and align the sending and receiving folder more simply. Compare the following steps with those immediately above:

1. Open the Network Neighborhood in the left pane of the Explorer and select the computer, drive, and folder from which you want to copy the file.

2. Adjust the right pane so you can see the file you want to copy.

3. Adjust the left pane so you can see the folder to which you are going to copy the file, opening the necessary parent disks and folders. The Explorer window shown in Figure 6–9 is set up for the same source and destination as the windows in Figure 6–7.

4. Drag the file in the right pane to the correct folder in the left pane.

While the number of steps for the Explorer approach and the Network Neighborhood/My Computer windows approach are the same, the Explorer one is significantly easier to carry out and is more intuitive.

PRINTING THROUGH THE NETWORK NEIGHBORHOOD

In a manner similar to the copying of a file by dragging it between the Network Neighborhood and My Computer windows, you can

Figure 6–10

Dragging a file to print it on a network printer

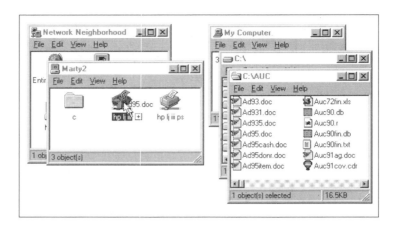

print by dragging a printable document file to a network printer. Use the following steps to do that:

1.   Open the Network Neighborhood, and select the computer with the printer you want to use.

2.   Open My Computer, and select the disk and folder containing the file you want to print.

3.   Adjust the windows so you can see both the file and the printer.

4.   Drag the file to the printer, as shown in Figure 6–10. The file will be printed on the printer you chose.

For *drag-and-drop printing* to work, the file to be printed must be associated with a program that is registered in Windows with a print action. See "Associating Files" in Chapter 2.

USING FIND OVER A NETWORK

Finding a file over a simple network, such as those shown in the figures here, is fairly simple, but in a large network you may have a difficult time finding the correct computer, let alone the correct file. You can use the Find command in the Start menu to locate computers and find folders and files on a network. The Computer option, which you can select immediately after choosing Find from the Start menu, allows you to enter a computer name and, optionally, a disk or folder. Windows then will tell you the workgroup the computer is in and any comments associated with that computer, as you can see in Figure

Figure 6–11

Finding a network computer gives you the workgroup it is in.

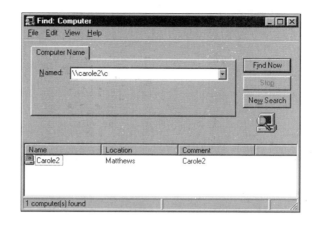

6–11. You can enter either the full network path name (see tip below) if you want to specify a disk or folder, or just a computer name without any backslashes. If you search for a computer by itself within your workgroup, you will get Network Neighborhood as the Location.

 **A network path name that includes the computer name has the following format: \\\computer name\drive letter\folder name\filename.**

To search for a file or a folder on a network computer, you must know the computer it is on, or the network drive must be mapped to your computer (see the next section). With a known computer, you can use the Network Neighborhood from within Find to locate the computer and then search for the file on that computer. The steps to do that are as follows:

1. Open the Start menu and choose Find Files or Folders. The Find: All Files dialog box will open.

2. Click on Browse, scroll the list until you see Network Neighborhood, and then open the Network Neighborhood and, if necessary, the Entire Network.

3. Select the workgroup and the computer, as you see in Figure 6–12, and then click on OK.

4. Enter the file or folder name to search for and click on Find Now. The results will be displayed as in any other Find, like those shown in Figure 6–13.

Figure 6–12

*Selecting a
network computer
to search*

Figure 6–13

*Results of a
network search*

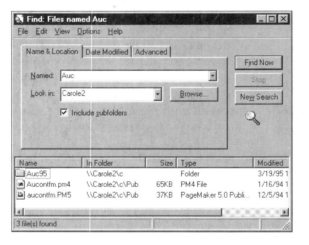

Mapping Network Resources to Your Computer

If you use the same network resources very often, you will find that the above procedures become cumbersome, and you will long for a more direct approach. Mapping network resources to your computer, which you first read about in Chapter 1, is such an approach. Mapping creates a pseudoresource on your computer that you can treat just as if it were physically there. You can do this for both disks and printers.

Windows 95 has menu options for mapping network disk drives, but a similar procedure for printers is called *capturing a printer port.*

MAPPING A NETWORK DRIVE

One of the major benefits of mapping a network drive is that you can directly address the drive from within an application, just as if it were a drive on your computer. To map a network drive to your computer, use the following instructions:

1. From My Computer, Network Neighborhood, or the Explorer, click on the Map Network Drive button shown on the left. Alternately, from the Explorer you can open the Tools menu and choose Map Network Drive. The Map Network Drive dialog box will open as you see here:

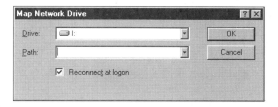

2. Select the drive letter to which you want the network drive mapped on your computer. This can be any unused drive letter.

3. Type the full network path to the drive you want mapped (see the tip on network paths earlier in this chapter). Here's an example: **\\Planning\c** where *Planning* is a computer in your workgroup and *c* is the drive on that computer that you want mapped.

    If you have recently mapped the drive, it will be on the list that is displayed when you click on the down arrow at the right of the Path text box, like this:

4. When the drive letter and the path are the way you want them, click on OK. The new drive letter will be available on your computer and it will refer to the network drive.

Figure 6–14

*Capture Printer
Port while adding
a new printer*

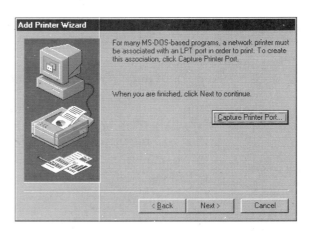

A slightly easier approach to mapping a network drive is to display the
drive in the Network Neighborhood and right-click on it. In the
popup menu choose Map Network Drive. The Map Network Drive
dialog box will appear with the Path filled in.

MAPPING A NETWORK PRINTER

In Chapter 4 you saw how to add a network printer to your computer, allowing you to print directly to it. This provides a printer path
such as *\\Sales3\HpLJ4* where *Sales3* is the computer name and
HpLJ4 is the printer name. There are certain situations and applications, especially DOS applications, where you cannot use a printer
path like this and instead you need to specify a port address, such as
LPT2. Windows 95 allows you to map network printers to an unused
port address. As noted above, this is called *capturing a printer port*. You
can do this in two different ways. The first is at the end of adding a
new printer (started from the Printers folder) where the Add Printer
Wizard displays a Capture Printer Port button, as shown in Figure
6–14. The second way is in the printer's Properties dialog box where
the Details tab also has a similar button. In both cases, the Capture
Printer Port dialog box will open, as shown next. The Add Printer
Wizard has the added benefit of having the Path already filled in.

In the Capture Printer Port dialog box, open the Device drop-down list box, and choose the port address you want to use. If you have a local printer attached to your computer, it probably will be using LPT1, although this dialog box will not alert you to that. In this instance, you would not want to use LPT1 for a network printer. If you have already mapped other network printers, they will be displayed like this:

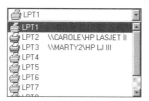

If you entered the Capture Printer Port through the Properties dialog box, you will need to enter a printer path. See the discussion at the start of this section on printer paths. When the port and path are the way you want them, click on OK to complete the network printer mapping. You can then refer to the port address to use the network printer.

Dial-Up Networking

Dial-up networking, or *remote access* (*RAS*—pronounced "razz"), allows you to remotely access a network via a modem and phone lines or other communications links. With RAS you can be on the road with your laptop, dial into your office computer, and not only access that computer but the entire network to which it is connected, just as if you were using your office computer. As long as your laptop and office computers are running Windows 95 and are both configured for dial-up networking, you can access any network (peer-to-peer, client-server, NetWare, or Windows NT) to which your office computer is connected. You can get and send mail; you can access shared data; you can remotely print; and you can transfer shared files. RAS also allows you to connect to public networks, such as the Internet, that are not running Windows 95. With the explosion of mobile computing, dial-up networking becomes a significant part of Windows 95.

To use dial-up networking, you need to set up your mobile or remote computer (the *remote client*) with a dial-up connection to your office or connecting computer (the *dial-up server*), and you need to set up your office or connecting computer to be a server so it will receive incoming calls and serve as a gateway to the network to which it is connected.

Setting Up a Remote Client

Dial-Up
Networking

You set up dial-up networking through the Dial-Up Networking folder in My Computer or the Explorer. To create on your computer a remote client that can call in and connect to another computer, use these instructions:

1. Open My Computer and then open the Dial-Up Networking folder. Your folder should look like this:

2. Double-click on the Make New Connection icon. The Make New Connection dialog box opens, as shown in Figure 6–15.

3. Type in a name of the computer you are calling; make it a name that is meaningful to you.

Figure 6–15

*Make New
Connection
dialog box*

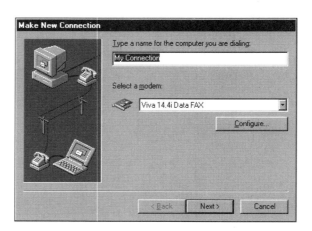

Figure 6–16

Dial-Up Networking folder with connection icons

 The name you give the computer you are dialing appears as an icon label in the Dial-Up Networking folder.

4.   If your modem is not displayed in the Select a modem drop-down list, then you need to install your modem in Windows 95. See Chapter 7 on how to do this. The Configure button allows you to make settings pertaining to your modem. These are also described in Chapter 7.

5.   Click on Next, and enter the area code and telephone number of the computer you want to call.

6.   Click on Next again. You'll be told that you have successfully created a new connection. Click on Finish to complete the process. The Dial-Up Networking folder will reappear with an icon for your new connection, as you can see in Figure 6–16.

Setting Up a Dial-Up Server

Any computer with a modem running Windows 95 can be set up to act as a dial-up server. It can receive one call at a time and provide access to both its own resources as well as those on the network to which it is attached. Use the following instructions to set up a dial-up server:

1.   From the Dial-Up Networking folder, open the Connections menu and choose Dial-Up Server, as you see on the left. The Dial-Up Server dialog box will open, as you see in Figure 6–17.

2.   Click on Allow caller access to enable that function.

3.   If you want to define a password for remote access, click on Change Password, enter the old and new passwords, and click on OK. The default password is a null, the absence of any password.

Figure 6–17

Dial-Up Server dialog box

4. If you want a comment displayed when someone connects to the server, enter that in the Comment text box.

5. Click on Server Type for access to several advanced settings, which you can see next. Under most circumstances, you should keep the default settings shown here. Click on Cancel to return to the Dial-Up Server dialog box.

6. Click on Apply to turn on the Dial-Up Server. You will see the Status change from Idle to Monitoring, as you see in Figure 6–18. Click on OK to close the dialog box.

Using Dial-Up Networking

Once you have the client and server set up, using dial-up networking is as easy as double-clicking on a connection icon. When you do that, the Connect To dialog box opens, as shown in Figure 6–19. This should reflect the entries that you made when you set up the connection. One important new aspect of this dialog box is that it lets you establish and

Figure 6–18

Dial-Up Server waiting for an incoming call

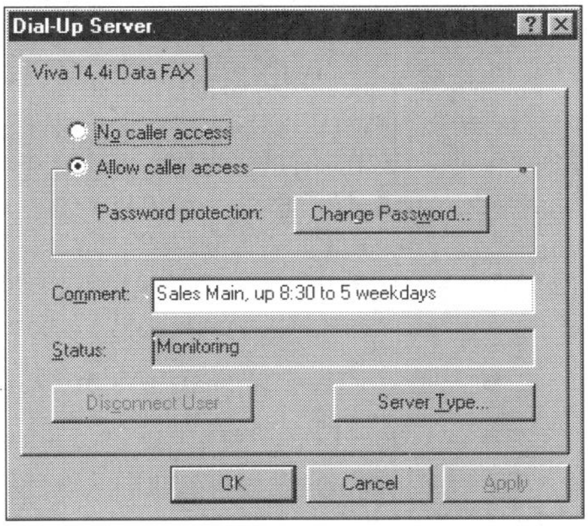

Figure 6–19

Connect To dialog box

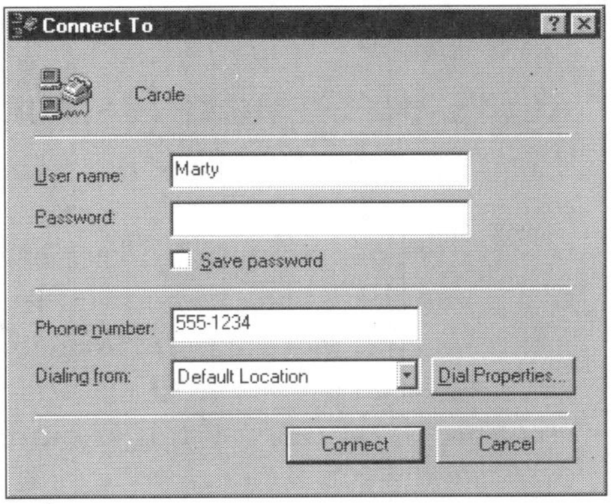

utilize various locations from which you can call. This way you can have places from which you frequently call already established, with their peculiar settings such as area code and digits to get an outside line. You can establish new locations and their characteristics through the Dial Properties button as described in Chapter 7.

When the Connect To dialog box is the way you want it, click on Connect. You will hear your modem dialing, and a dialog box will appear indicating your progress. When a connection is made, the Connecting to dialog box changes to Connected to and shows the speed and duration of connection like this:

In addition to explicitly using a dial-up connection by double-clicking on it, you can implicitly do it by trying to use a remote resource that requires a dial-up connection, for example, a mapped disk drive or a network printer. In any case, once you have connected to a dial-up server, you have the following three functions you can perform:

- Access information on the disk drives attached to either the server or its network
- Print on the printers attached to either the server or its network
- Use the Exchange to send and receive mail via the dial-up network connection

Using the Exchange, including its remote access, is the principal focus of Chapter 8, so that topic is left for the later chapter.

ACCESSING REMOTE DISK DRIVES

To access individual disk drives on either the computer to which you are connected or its network, you must map those drives to drive letters on your computer as described earlier in this chapter. The difficult part is knowing the correct network path of the drive you want to use. The path has the same format as described earlier, namely *computer name**drive name*. Once you have mapped the drive(s) to your computer, you can use the Explorer or My Computer to access files over the dial-up connection, just as if you were directly using the server computer, with the only penalty being the slowness of the modem.

PRINTING ON REMOTE PRINTERS

To use a printer over a dial-up connection, simply establish the connection, and then use Add Printer in the Printers folder to create a new network printer using that connection. You can then print to that printer as you would to any network printer. If you are not physically connected when you print, the output will be spooled to your disk until you are next connected, at which time it will print. As with remote drives, the difficult part is knowing the correct network path for the printer. The format is *computer name**printer name*.

CONTROLLING A DIAL-UP SERVER

Anytime you leave an enabled modem on a computer that is receptive to calls, as is the case with a dial-up server, you need to be concerned

Figure 6–20

*Dial-Up Server
dialog box
showing someone
connected to
your computer*

with security. The first step is to turn off caller access in the Dial-Up Server dialog box whenever you do not need it. The second step is to use password protection. You can do this at both the dial-up server level as well as at the drive- and folder-sharing levels giving you a double protection. As with any passwords, keep them secure and change them often. The final and not always possible step is to watch who is using the server. You can do this through the Dial-Up Server dialog box, as you can see in Figure 6–20, as well as in the Net Watcher, which is described at the end of this chapter.

 **Be sensitive to the security needs of a dial-up server.**

PROTOCOLS TO USE WITH DIAL-UP NETWORKING

Depending on the network behind the dial-up server to which you want to connect, and what you want to do on that network, you will need to have different protocols bound to the dial-up adapters in *both* the server and the remote client. Chapter 5, under "Network Protocols," discusses this topic and how to install, or bind, protocols to an adapter. For dial-up networking, use the guidelines in Table 6–1 for selecting the protocols that are correct for your situation. Other than when you want to use the Internet or a NetWare network, NetBEUI is the best choice. Also, you can have multiple protocols bound to the dial-up adapter, but it will slow down the loading time.

Table 6–1.	Protocol	Circumstances
Protocols to use in dial-up networking	Any	Accessing only the resources in the dial-up server
	TCP/IP	Accessing the Internet
	IPX/SPX	Accessing a NetWare network
	NetBEUI	Accessing a Windows NT, Windows 95, or other Microsoft or IBM network

Networking Accessories

Windows 95 includes five networking accessories; however, the media that your copy of Windows 95 came on will dictate whether you have access to three of these. The first three accessories discussed in the following sections—Chat, ClipBook Viewer, and Hearts—are available only if your version of Windows 95 came on a CD-ROM disk.

- **Chat** allows two or more people on the network to directly communicate by typing messages to each other.

- **ClipBook Viewer** allows you to store and transfer over the network multiple pages of clipboard contents.

- **Hearts** is a card game that can be played by as many as four people on the network.

- **Net Watcher** allows you to see who on the network is accessing your resources and what they are accessing.

- **WinPopup** allows you to send a quick message to someone on the network and have it pop up on their computer.

As of the date this book was written, files for Chat, ClipBook, and Hearts were on the CD-ROM version of Windows 95 in a folder called Other. If you cannot locate the files on your hard disk after you install Windows 95, open the Other folder on your Windows 95 CD-ROM, and copy the files to the Windows folder on your hard disk. Then create shortcuts in the Accessories submenu for those programs that you use often.

Using Chat

Chat is started by running the Winchat.exe file located in either your Windows folder or in the Other folder on your Windows 95 CD-ROM disk. Open the Start menu and choose Run. In the Run dialog box, use Browse to search for Winchat.exe, and click on Open when you find it. Then click on OK in the Run dialog box. This opens the Chat window, shown in Figure 6–21.

  You can initiate a conversation by clicking on the Dial button in the toolbar or choosing Dial from the Conversation menu. This brings up a dialog box in which you can enter the name of the computer you wish to call. If the person you are calling has their Chat set to automatically answer incoming calls (done in Preferences under the Options menu), then that person's Chat window will open, and you will be able to type messages between the two computers. If you want to add another person to the conversation, click on Dial, and enter the name of the additional computer. On your screen the Chat window will split into the same number of panes as there are people in the conversation, and you can see what each party is typing. You can quickly clear the screen of all contents by clicking on the Delete button or choosing Clear All from the Edit menu. The Edit menu also offers the standard Cut, Copy, and Paste options.

  You can answer an incoming call by clicking on the Answer button or selecting Answer from the Conversation menu. Similarly, you can end a conversation by clicking on the Hang-up button or selecting Hang up from the Conversation menu.

Figure 6–21

Chat conversation between two computers

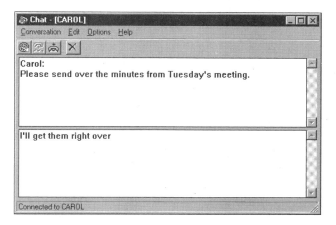

Using the ClipBook Viewer

The ClipBook Viewer is started by running the file Clipbrd.exe (see the comments and note in the previous section, "Using Chat," to locate and execute the file). This opens the ClipBook Viewer window, shown in Figure 6–22.

Both the Clipboard viewer and the ClipBook viewer have the same file-name: Clipbrd.exe. Neither are installed by default. The Clipboard viewer is available through the Add/Remove Programs control panel and the ClipBook viewer is available only by copying it from the \Other\ClipBook folder on the Windows 95 CD. The ClipBook viewer is a networking tool and allows you to temporarily or permanently store several items and to access them across the network. The Clipboard viewer only allows you to look at and save one item at a time.

The ClipBook Viewer performs three primary functions:

- Allows you to view the contents of your Clipboard (where objects from cut and copy operations are temporarily stored).
- Allows Windows to hold and store multiple objects from cut and copy operations on multiple pages of the ClipBook
- Allows you to share objects in the ClipBook with other users on the network

When you first open the ClipBook Viewer, you see the Clipboard view, as shown in Figure 6–22. The results of your most recent cut or copy are displayed. You create ClipBook pages by pasting the Clipboard contents to a page in the ClipBook that you name. Each

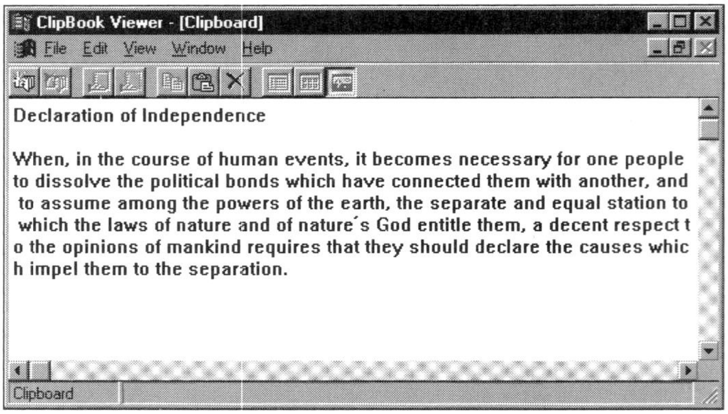

Figure 6–22

ClipBook Viewer Window

> **ClipBook Viewer - [Clipboard]**
>
> File Edit View Window Help
>
> **Declaration of Independence**
>
> When, in the course of human events, it becomes necessary for one people to dissolve the political bonds which have connected them with another, and to assume among the powers of the earth, the separate and equal station to which the laws of nature and of nature's God entitle them, a decent respect t o the opinions of mankind requires that they should declare the causes whic h impel them to the separation.
>
> Clipboard

page of the ClipBook can be shared or not. First, select the Edit menu Paste option, provide a name for the ClipBook page that the current Clipboard contents will appear in, and then choose whether to share this page with other networked computers, as shown next. After clicking on OK, the Share ClipBook Page dialog box opens and provides sharing options much like sharing a drive, folder, or file. Select whether to open the program that created the shared object when you connect to another ClipBook, the level of security you want, and click on OK.

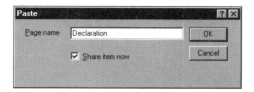

You can view your ClipBook pages by choosing Local ClipBook from the Window menu, as shown in Figure 6–23. From the View menu you can change how you view the pages: thumbnails (reduced images), a page listing by choosing Table of Contents, the contents of a selected page by choosing Full Page. The toolbar provides quick access to these three representations as well as other commonly used menu options that allow you to open and close ClipBooks on other computers; to share or unshare selected pages; and to copy, paste, and delete pages. You can view the shared ClipBook pages of other computers on your network in the same manner and then copy their contents into your own files.

Figure 6–23

ClipBook pages shown as thumbnails

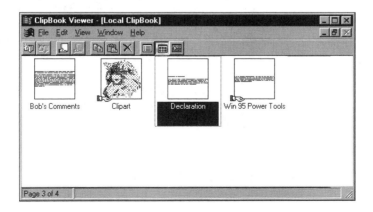

Using Hearts

Hearts is started by opening the Start menu and choosing Programs, Accessories, Games, Hearts. This opens the Hearts Network window and a dialog box that asks your name and whether you want to join another game or start your own and be the dealer. If you elect to join another game, you will be asked for the dealer's computer name. If you elect to be the dealer, Hearts will then wait for others to join the game. When you are ready to start, press F2 or choose New Game from the Game menu. You may have from zero to three other players. The computer will play the hands not taken by live participants. When the game begins, the Hearts window looks like that shown in Figure 6–24.

The objective of the game is to have the lowest score by *not* taking tricks with hearts or the queen of spades in them *unless* you can take all such tricks. You take a trick by playing the highest card in the suit led for that trick. You begin the game by passing three cards from your hand to one of the other players. Every fourth hand no cards are passed. Normally you want to pass your highest hearts or any spade queen or above (select a card to play by clicking on it). Then the person with the two of clubs leads with that card. You must follow suit if you can. If you can't follow suit, you may throw away your high hearts or spades or any other card you wish. Whoever takes a trick plays the first card for the next trick.

Figure 6–24

Hearts window

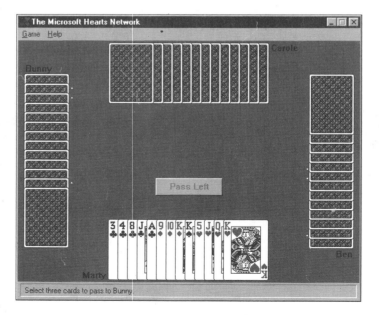

Play continues until all cards have been played. At the end of a game, one point is assessed for each heart in the tricks you took plus 13 for the queen of spades. If you get all of the hearts plus the queen of spades, you get zero points, and all other players get 26 points.

Using the Net Watcher

The Net Watcher is started by opening the Start menu and choosing Programs, Accessories, System Tools, Net Watcher. This opens the Net Watcher window, shown in Figure 6–25. This initial window shows users currently connected to your computer and the folders and files they have open. There are two other views available in Net Watcher: one showing shared resources, as you see in Figure 6–26, and the other showing files opened by network users, as shown in Figure 6–27. The Net Watcher, through the toolbar buttons or the Administer menu, allows you to perform the following tasks:

Change the computer ("server") that you are looking at (you must have administrative authority over a computer to view it)

Disconnect a user who is currently logged on to your computer

Close files that are opened by a network user

Share or stop sharing a resource

Displays view shown in Figure 6–25

Displays view shown in Figure 6–26

Displays view shown in Figure 6–27

Figure 6–25

Net Watcher showing the activity of users on your computer

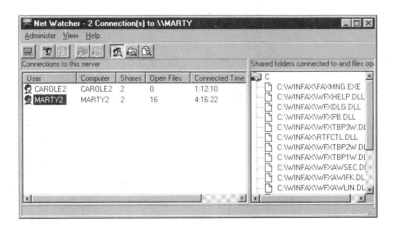

Figure 6–26

Net Watcher showing shared resources on your computer

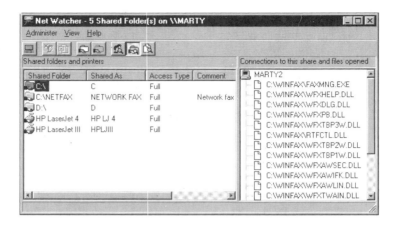

Figure 6–27

Net Watcher showing files opened by others on the network

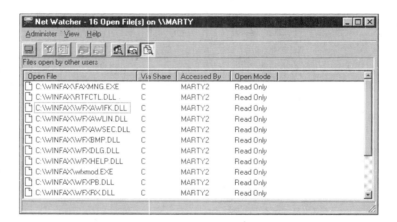

Using WinPopup

WinPopup is started by running the Winpopup.exe file, located in your Windows folder. By clicking on the Send icon or choosing Send from the Messages menu, the Send Message window opens, as shown in Figure 6–28. Here you can send a message to one person (computer) or to everyone in your workgroup. If you are sending it to just one person, you must type in the computer name; to send it to your workgroup, click on Workgroup, and then, in either case, type the message and click on OK. The person(s) receiving the message must have WinPopup running in order to receive the message. If WinPopup is loaded but minimized when a message is received, the window will open ("popup") with the message, as shown in Figure 6–29.

Figure 6–28

WinPopup message creation dialog box

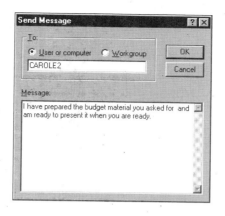

Figure 6–29

WinPopup window with a message that has been received

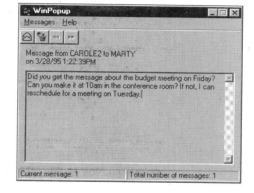

You can automatically start WinPopup every time you start Windows 95 by putting a shortcut to WinPopup in your \Windows\Start Menu\Programs\StartUp folder. The Program file for WinPopup should be in your \Windows folder.

PART III

Windows 95 Messaging and Communications

While Windows 95 networking allows you to connect with other computers immediately around you, *Windows 95 communications allows you to connect with other computers anywhere in the world. The connection you make can be with an information service, like CompuServe or the Microsoft Network; another PC; a mainframe computer; or the Internet, which provides a connection to literally thousands of computers of all types.*

With either Windows 95 networking or communications, Windows 95 messaging allows you to create and manage electronic mail (e-mail) and faxes using the Microsoft Exchange. This single program is a messaging hub for handling normal network e-mail, as well as mail using Microsoft Network, CompuServe, and the Internet.

Part III describes communications and how to set up and use your modem, as well as how to make best use of HyperTerminal, a Windows 95 communications program. Part III also looks at how to use Microsoft Exchange for messaging and faxing, as well as how to use Microsoft Network, CompuServe, and the Internet.

Modem Communications and Hyperterminal

indows 95 offers substantial opportunities for its users to expand the capabilities of their PC from the desktop to literally the world. Complementing the various networking schemes that were mentioned in previous chapters, Windows 95 incorporates the ability to communicate with anyone that has a communications link (phone line or microwave or satellite link) attached to a modem installed in or attached to their computer. While this capability has been available for some time, it has not been widely used. A growing number of people subscribe to an online service such as CompuServe or the Internet, but very few people use the more basic level of direct PC-to-PC communication. The reason is simple—the same thing that keeps people away from computers in general: unreasonable complexity coupled with more than occasional frustration.

Windows 95 offers three significant telecommunication capabilities that reduce the complexity, shield you from many areas of frustration, and help you tap the full potential of your computer:

- Single-point modem installation (previous versions of Windows required each telecommunication program to configure the modem separately)

221

- HyperTerminal, a basic but capable and easy-to-use telecommunication program
- Phone Dialer, a handy tool that transforms your modem and basic telephone into a full-featured system with speed dialing, calling-card capabilities and other telephoning conveniences.

Setting Up a Modem

Windows 95 includes a Modem Wizard that assists you in setting up your modem. The Modem Wizard uses Plug and Play technology to make setting up a modem as easy as possible. If your modem is Plug and Play compliant, it will respond to queries during its set up and relay information that you would otherwise have to enter. Even if you don't own a Plug and Play device, Windows 95 can determine much about your modem and how it is connected to your computer.

There are several different ways to initiate the setup of a modem. All routes, though, lead to the same destination, the starting of the Modem Wizard.

Modems

- If you have a modem installed prior to setting up Windows 95, you will be prompted during setup to configure your modem using the Modem Wizard.
- If you add a modem after installing Windows 95, you can open the Modem Wizard by clicking on either the Modems control panel or the Add New Hardware control panel.
- If you try to run a communications program such as Hyper-Terminal or Phone Dialer without first configuring your modem, the Modem Wizard will open.

Whichever path you take displays the Install New Modem dialog box, shown in Figure 7–1.

Modem Wizard

The Install New Modem dialog box gives you the option of having Windows 95 try to detect your modem, or letting you pick your model from an extensive list. Your best bet is to allow Windows 95 to begin the configuration process on its own. If it doesn't detect

Figure 7–1

*Install New
Modem dialog box*

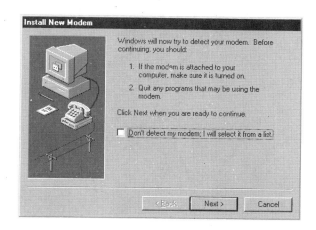

your model you can always search the list and select the closest match to your modem. The documentation that came with your modem might offer some alternate choices if your particular model is not detected or listed. Selecting a modem from the list is described in more detail after Step 1.

If you have an external modem, make sure it is turned on before you try to set it up.

To install and configure a modem using the Modem Wizard, follow these steps:

1.   Click on the Next button.

Windows 95 begins by checking your communication ports to locate a modem. If you have an internal modem, you set (or might now need to set) the communication port (COM1, COM2, COM3, or COM4) that you want the modem to use. This is normally accomplished by setting a jumpered or DIP switch on the modem circuit card. An external modem is connected by cable to a serial port that is already designated as COM1, COM2, COM3, or COM4.

COM1 and COM3 share the same interrupt request line (IRQ4) and COM2 and COM4 share IRQ3. If two devices are concurrently trying to use the same interrupt, you will experience significant problems. The most common conflict occurs when a serial mouse and modem share an interrupt.

Figure 7–2

Verify Modem
dialog box

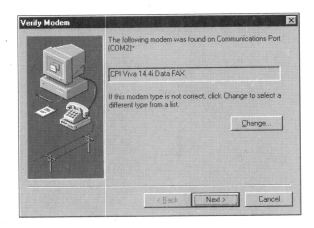

Figure 7–3

List of modems
by manufacturer
and model

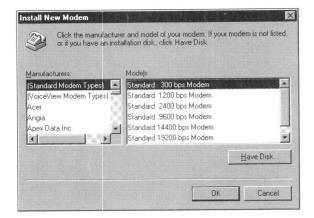

After a short time the Modem Wizard will recognize the presence of your modem and ask you to verify the model, as you see in Figure 7–2, or fail to recognize your modem and ask you to choose a model from its list of manufactures and models, which is shown in Figure 7–3.

2.   If the Modem Wizard recognized your modem correctly, click on Next to finish the configuration process. If you need to select a modem or change the Modem Wizard's selection, click on Change, select the modem manufacturer and model that you want to use, and then click on OK or Next depending on how you got to the selection dialog box. If that brings you back to the Verify Modem dialog box, click on Next again to go on to the final Modem Wizard dialog box.

Tip If you cannot find a manufacturer and model that match your modem, try using the most generic driver by selecting the first manufacturer listed (Standard Modem Types) and the speed of your modem in the Models list box.

3. The next Modem Wizard dialog box informs you of a successful installation. Click on Finish or Next to complete this stage.

If you have set up a modem previously, you have already defined a dialing location. You are then finished with the Modem Wizard, have used Finish in Step 3, and the Modem Properties dialog box is displayed, so you can change current settings or add new modems and dialing locations. Skip ahead to the next section, "Dialing Properties."

If this is your first modem installation, you used Next in Step 3 and need to continue with the next few steps to set up your dialing location.

1. The Location Information dialog box opens and asks you questions that pertain to your dialing location. Select or type in the information that pertains to your most common dialing location. You can set up multiple locations in the Modems Properties dialog box, which is discussed shortly.

2. Click on Next. The Dialing Properties dialog box opens as shown in Figure 7–4.

Figure 7–4

The Dialog Properties dialog box

Dialing Properties	? X

My Locations

Where I am:

I am dialing from: Default Location   New...   Remove

The area code is: 360

I am in: United States of America (1)

How I dial from this location:

To access an outside line, first dial: for local,   for long distance.

☐ Dial using Calling Card: Change...

☐ This location has call waiting. To disable it, dial:

The phone system at this location uses: ● Tone dialing ○ Pulse dialing

OK   Cancel

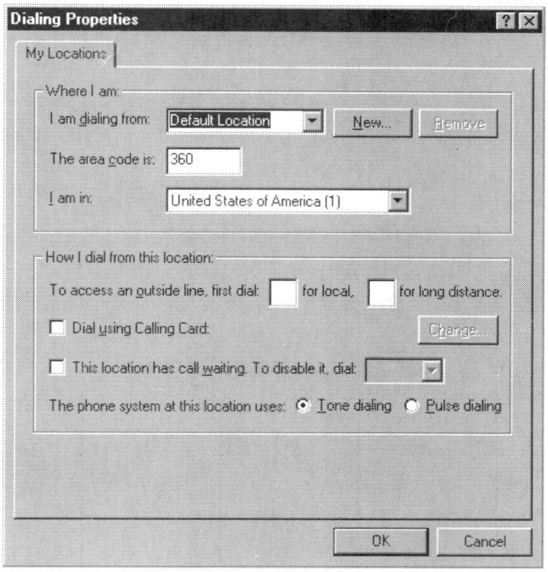

Dialing Properties

The Dialing Properties dialog box, which you can also open by clicking on Dialing Properties in the Modems control panel, is a utility used by Windows 95 to support numerous telecommunication programs, including HyperTerminal and Phone Dialer (discussed later in this chapter), and Dial-Up Networking (previously discussed in Chapter 6).

The Where I am section displays some of the data you provided in the previous dialog box and lets you change the name of what Windows 95 calls your Default Location. For example, you could highlight Default Location and type in Office to more specifically label your office computer's location. You can add more locations by clicking on the New button and typing another descriptive name, like this:

Having multiple locations was designed for the laptop or notebook user, so if you are using a desktop computer, you probably won't have much need to add multiple locations.

If you are dialing from a location outside of the United States, use The area code is text box for the city code. Omit any leading zeros.

The How I dial from this location section further defines the dialing parameters of a particular location. The first option provides numbers to access an outside line. Clicking on the Dial using Calling Card check box opens the Change Calling Card dialog box, described in the next section. The remaining two options in the section let you turn call waiting on or off with a given code, like *80, and select whether your phone is tone or pulse dialed.

USING A CALLING CARD

Windows 95 uses the Change Calling Card dialog box, shown in Figure 7–5, to store both the rules for dialing with a particular service, such as AT&T, as well as a possible calling card number. However, you can store dialing rules, as explained below, without a calling card number. Windows 95 provides some of the more popular telephone

Figure 7–5

Change Calling Card dialog box

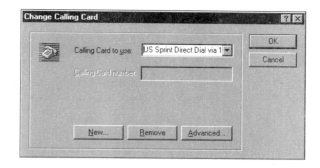

Figure 7–6

Dialing Rules dialog box

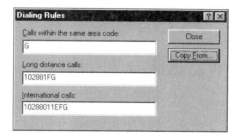

services and their dialing rules. You can use one of the built-in services or easily create your own either directly or by copying one of the services using the New and Advanced buttons at the bottom of the dialog box. The Advanced button opens the Dialing Rules dialog box, shown in Figure 7–6, in which you can enter the rules for dialing local, long distance, and international calls with the codes listed in Table 7–1.

For example, an international call placed using a Sprint calling card's 800 access number might look like 18008778000$T0011EFG$TH where

18008778000 is the Sprint access number

$ waits for the Sprint acknowledgment tone

T specifies that the digits which follow it are tone dialed

0 informs the carrier the call is to be billed to a calling card number

011 signifies an international call

E is a placeholder for the country code

F is a placeholder for the city code

G is a placeholder for the local number

$ waits for the Sprint acknowledgment tone

T specifies that the digits which follow it are tone dialed

H is a placeholder for the calling card number

Table 7–1.

*Calling
Card Codes*

Code	Description
ABCD	Special digits that will be dialed (tone dialing only)
E	Replaced by the country code
F	Replaced by the area code
G	Replaced by the local number
H	Replaced by the calling card number
T	Specifies that the following digits are tone dialed
P	Specifies that the following digits are pulse dialed
W	Waits for a second dial tone
0-9	Digits that will be dialed
,	Specifies a two-second pause (use multiple commas to increase the pause length)
* #	Digits that will be dialed (tone dialing only)
?	Causes a break in the dialing sequence for user input
!	Specifies a 1/2-second on-hook, 1/2-second off-hook flash
@	Specifies a ringback followed by five seconds of silence
$	Waits for a calling card "bong" sound

The actual phone number that's being dialed and that replaces the E, F, and G is entered or stored in the telecommunications program you are using, such as HyperTerminal or Phone Dialer, both covered later in this chapter.

When you are satisfied with your dialing location information, click on Close and OK as necessary to return to the Modem Properties dialog box. You are now ready to alter, if necessary, settings that directly affect your modem.

Setting Your Modem Properties

The Modem Properties dialog box, which you see in Figure 7–7, is opened by double-clicking on the Modems control panel. The list box and its associated three buttons display the modem(s) you have

Figure 7–7

Modem Properties dialog box

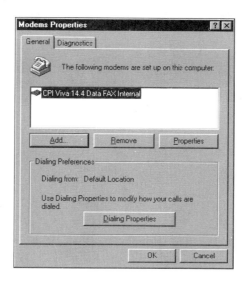

Figure 7–8

Properties dialog box for a particular modem

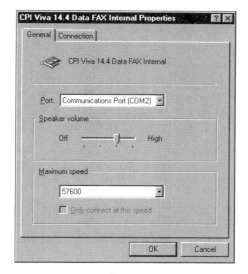

installed and give the opportunity to add additional units, remove those currently installed, or change their properties. Adding a modem opens the Modem Wizard, which was described earlier in this chapter. Removing a modem uninstalls it from Windows 95. To change a modem's properties, first highlight the name of the modem, then click on the Properties button. A two-tab Properties dialog box for that particular modem is displayed, as shown in Figure 7–8.

GENERAL TAB

The Port drop-down list box lists the communications (or serial) ports that are available for use. Make sure that the port displayed is the port that is being used by the modem (either plugged into or selected by the jumpers or switches on your modem). If they are not the same, you will receive an error message from Windows indicating that it cannot find a modem on the listed COM port.

The Speaker volume slider adjusts the volume of your dialing and other telecommunication sounds. With an internal modem the sounds are sometimes the only way to monitor the status of a connection. (I keep my volume louder so I can hear the connection being made and any error messages that are announced by the phone company.) External modems usually have a bank of LEDs (light emitting diodes) that let you monitor the progress of your transmit and receive signals.

The Maximum speed drop-down list box lets you choose the fastest speed you want your modem to try to transfer data. The numbers listed are in bits per second (bps) and are sometimes referred to as the baud rate of the modem. When describing a newer modem's speed, its baud rate and bps transfer rate are not the same. Newer modems use various compression schemes to increase the actual number of bits that are transmitted per second. For example, a 28,800-baud (often abbreviated 28.8) modem, through compression, can transmit up to 115,200 bps. You should select the fasted listed speed that your modem supports. If you find that you are having transmission errors, decrease the speed to the next lower setting.

Faster modem speeds generally coincide with enhanced international standards that make telecommunication more reliable and faster. These standards can be quite confusing to keep track of because there is nothing in the standard number that relates to its corresponding modem speed. Recent modem standards, associated speeds, and year introduced are listed in Table 7–2.

A number of 28.8 modems were manufactured prior to the V.34 standard being set. It is wise to not use these modems.

Compounding the confusion that surrounds modem nomenclature is that compression and error control standards are named with a similar format. For example, the Computer Peripherals Viva 14.4 Data/Fax modem, shown in the figures here, has a V.32bis transmission standard, a V.42 and MNP2-4 error control standards, and V.42bis and MNP5

Table 7–2.

Modem standards

Standard	Speed (uncompressed)	Year Introduced
V.22bis*	2400	1984
V.32	9600	1984
V.32bis	14,400	1991
V.34	28,800	1994

* The term bis (French for second) after the number indicates the standard is a revision to a previously established standard.

Figure 7–9

Connection tab for a specific modem

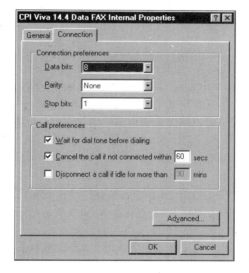

data compression standards. Fortunately, newer standards are backward compatible with older ones. A modem tries to establish a connection using its standards. If the modem on the other end doesn't support those standards, the sending modem will try using the next most recent set of standards.

CONNECTION TAB

The Connection tab, shown in Figure 7–9, allows you to set the defaults that are used when Windows telecommunication programs try to make a connection with another computer. Each connection can be further modified in the program to meet specific needs of the remote modem. The defaults in this tab establish a good overall baseline for most connections.

Figure 7–10

Advance Connection Settings dialog box

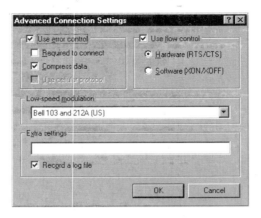

The Connection preferences section contains the three main parameters involved in making a connection: number of data bits, the type of parity used, and the number of stop bits. The most common configuration is 8-N-1, or 8 data bits, no parity, and 1 stop bit. This topic is explored in more detail in "HyperTerminal" later in this chapter.

The Call preferences section further customizes the nature of your outgoing calls. The Windows' default settings should work fine and need not be changed unless you have a specific need.

Clicking the Advanced button displays the Advanced Connection Settings dialog box, which you see in Figure 7–10.

If you are not having modem problems, you probably don't need to alter these settings. If you do change any of these settings, have your modem documentation available to verify your changes.

The Use error control section provides options that tell Windows 95 whether you want error control to be used for each connection, whether data compression is used, and, for cellular phone users, whether a cellular protocol is used.

The Use flow control section determines whether flow control is used and whether it is hardware or software controlled. Flow control determines the type of connection that is established between the telecommunication program and the modem. Check your modem documentation to determine whether flow control should be used, and if used, which type. Hardware control is generally preferable if the two modems that are communicating support it. You will often find that you will need to use software flow control.

The Low-speed modulation drop-down list of standards applies only to communicating with 300- and 1200-baud modems. There are different standards for domestic and overseas connections.

If you need to send any additional initialization data to your modem, you can type the data in the Extra settings text box. Be aware that any change to the initialization string is made to all connections you attempt. Changes are best made to a specific connection within a telecommunications program such as HyperTerminal. The Record a log file check box, when checked, creates a Modemlog.txt file in your Windows directory that maintains an audit trail of connection data, which comes in handy if you are having connection difficulties.

Using HyperTerminal

The Windows 95 solution to counter the "fear" sometimes associated with telecommunication is HyperTerminal, an easy-to-use, yet capable telecommunication package. HyperTerminal, as the Hyper- prefix implies, is a supercharging of Terminal, the program integral to Windows 3.x. More than just an upgraded Terminal with a few added whistles and bells, HyperTerminal takes full advantage of the Windows 95 32-bit architecture to provide more flexible and robust communication.

HyperTerminal has one major flaw: it cannot answer incoming calls. It can call other computers and can send and receive files, but if another computer calls you, HyperTerminal cannot answer.

Current users of programs designed for MS-DOS or Windows 3.x will appreciate the improved performance of their modems, especially at speeds exceeding 9600 baud, and better multitasking.

If you have a modem connected to your computer, you are ready to try out HyperTerminal. If you are modem-less, take the time to read through the remainder of this section to see why you might not want to be without one much longer.

Getting Started

HyperTerminal

You access HyperTerminal by opening the Start menu, selecting Programs, Accessories, and then clicking on HyperTerminal. The

Figure 7–11

HyperTerminal folder

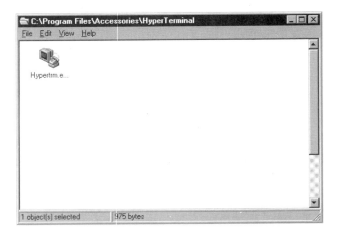

Figure 7–12

Connection Description dialog box

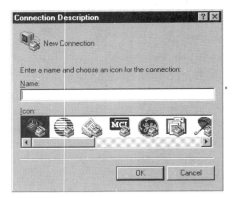

folder that opens contains the HyperTerminal icon as well as icons for each connection that you have established. If you haven't created a connection yet, the window only displays the HyperTerminal icon, shown in Figure 7–11.

SETTING UP A NEW CONNECTION

Double-clicking on the HyperTerminal icon gives you the opportunity to create a new connection through the Connection Description dialog box, as shown in Figure 7–12. This dialog box allows you to establish certain parameters you need to create a connection. HyperTerminal saves each connection as a file that can be displayed in a folder window like any other file, either as an icon or in a list.

A connection can be made to any computer connected with a modem to a phone line. That computer can be across town or around the world, and it can be to another PC like yours, to one that contains a BBS (or Bulletin Board Service), or to a computer that's part of an online service such as CompuServe, Prodigy, or a stock market quotation service.

For the purposes of learning about HyperTerminal, it is not necessary to have a connection that actually links with another computer, although it will certainly help illustrate HyperTerminal's capabilities. You can find many public (and free) BBS phone numbers in computer magazines and newspapers that service your local area. Also, many online services have free trial memberships you can log on to through an 800 number. Of course, if you don't have a modem installed, you won't be able to make a connection, but you can just plug in some information to see how HyperTerminal sets things up. Using whatever information you have available, set up a new connection with the following instructions:

 You can call (800)-848-8990 to establish an account with CompuServe, and use a local phone number to access it or the 800 number shown here.

1. Type a name (such as CompuServe) for your connection in the Name text box. This name will appear with the connection's icon in the HyperTerminal folder and in the title bar of HyperTerminal whenever the connection is active.

2. HyperTerminal provides a number of icon choices including many from well-known online services. Use the horizontal scroll bar to find one you like, click on it, and then choose OK. The Phone Number dialog box will open.

3. Use the Country code drop-down list box to establish the country you are calling, and type in the area code of the number in the Area code text box.

4. In the Phone number text box, type in the phone number of your connection without area code or special dialing prefixes, as shown in Figure 7–13.

5. Select the device (modem) you want to use from the Connect using drop-down list box. If your modem doesn't appear on the list, you should return to the previous sections on modem setup to ensure your modem is properly installed. Your completed dialog box should look similar to Figure 7–13 with the phone number of the service you are connecting to and your modem. Click on OK when you are satisfied with your settings.

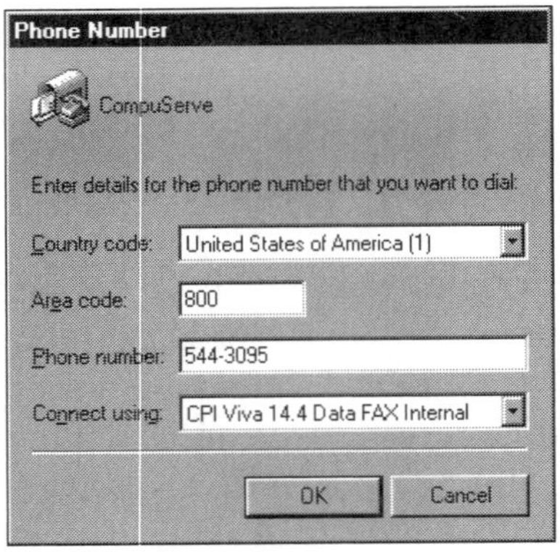

Figure 7–13

The Phone Number dialog box

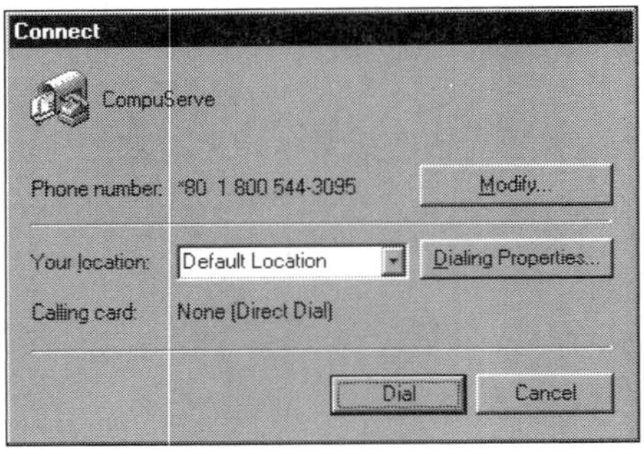

Figure 7–14

HyperTerminal Connect dialog box

At this point the Connect dialog box appears, as you can see in Figure 7–14, and you are ready to dial. If you need to change the phone number or add any special dialing instructions, you can use the Modify and Dialing Properties buttons to access dialog boxes to make the changes. The Dialing Properties dialog box, which you saw in Figure 7–4 and was discussed earlier in this chapter, lets you change your location to another location you may have set up and change the dialing parameters associated with that location. If you are dialing outside your area code, HyperTerminal will automatically provide the modem a 1 and the dialing area code you typed in the Phone Number dialog box. If you are dialing within your own area code and it's considered long distance, click on the Dial as a long distance call check box at the bottom of the Dialing Properties dialog box.

Before you actually dial and make a connection, spend a few more minutes reading the remainder of this section on HyperTerminal to see all that HyperTerminal can do for you. Cancel out of the dialog box(es) you may have on your screen until your screen looks like

Figure 7–15. This is the standard HyperTerminal window. Notice the name of your connection in the title bar. You will be prompted to save the connection before you exit HyperTerminal.

Navigating HyperTerminal

The HyperTerminal window contains the standard elements around its periphery including a title bar, menu bar, toolbar, and status bar. In the center, though, is the unique terminal window where the actual telecommunication takes place, and it contains such things as the AT commands used to establish modem synchronization or the latest stocks quotes from a retrieval service. Look at each of the window elements next.

MENUS

Four of the six menus—File, Edit, View, and Help—contain mainly standard Windows' options. The remaining two menus—Call and Transfer—are unique to HyperTerminal and provide the gateways to the key HyperTerminal operating features.

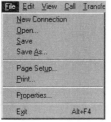

File menu   New Connection, the first option in the File menu shown on the left, displays the Connection Description dialog box that you saw earlier in the chapter in Figure 7–12. The second option, displays the Open dialog box, shown in Figure 7–16.

The Open dialog box shows the Windows 95 default location for the connection files, which is the HyperTerminal folder with the path of c:\Program Files\Accessories\HyperTerminal. The path is graphically displayed when you open the Look in drop-down list box. Toward the bottom of the dialog box is the Files of type drop-down list box, which defaults to the Session, or connection, files category. Each connection you create is given the .HT file extension when saved. The other file type available to open is Terminal files (.TRM), which are connections created using Terminal, the Windows 3.x telecommunication program. You can open each of your Terminal files in HyperTerminal and use the HyperTerminal features with them. HyperTerminal will prompt you to save the file when you exit. The .TRM file is then saved as a HyperTerminal (.HT) file and added to your collection of connections.

The Save and Save As options perform as they do in any other Windows program. Page Setup allows you to set up page layout parameters, such

Figure 7–15

*The Hyper-
Terminal window*

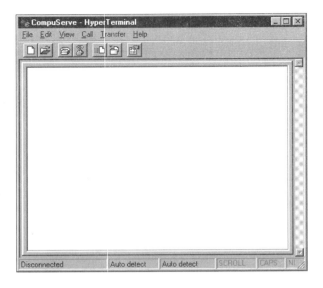

Figure 7–16

*HyperTerminal
file Open
dialog box*

as margins and orientation, and switch printers. The Print option lets you print multiple copies, select pages to be printed, and change properties related to your printer, such as resolution, how to print TrueType fonts, and other printer specific settings. HyperTerminal printing is covered in its own section later in this chapter.

Once you create a connection, you can modify specific attributes such as the number you are calling, using the File menu's Properties option. This opens the connection's Properties dialog box, shown in Figure 7–17.

In the Phone Number tab you can change the settings you established when you set up the new connection as well as open your modem's Properties dialog box by clicking on the Configure button.

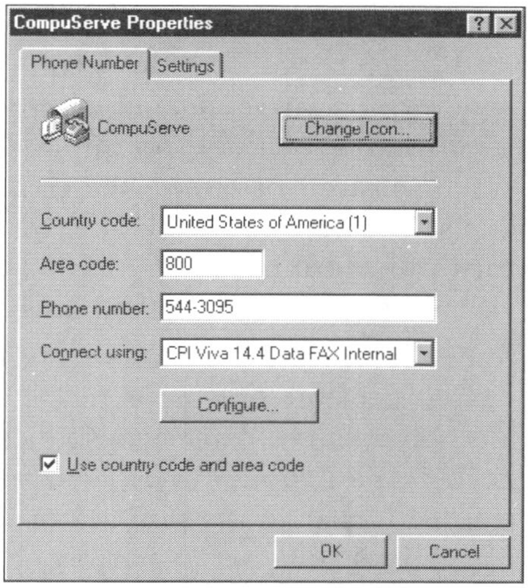

Figure 7–17

*A connection's
Properties
dialog box*

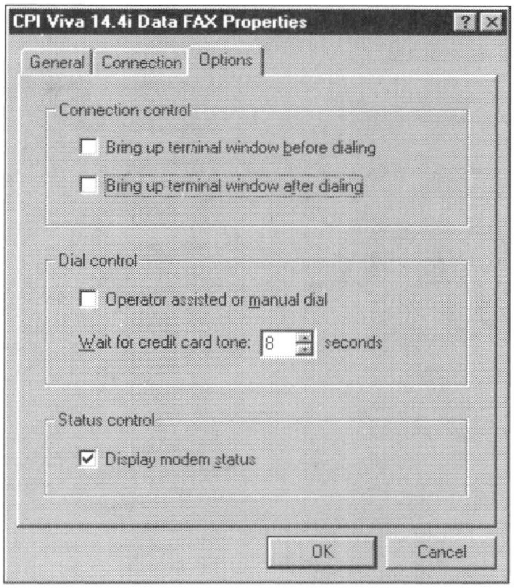

Figure 7–18

*Options tab for
a modem's
Properties
dialog box*

The General and Connection tabs in the modem's Properties dialog box were described in previous sections on modem setup. The Options tab lets you set up parameters specific to a connection. Figure 7–18 shows the Options settings for a connection to the CompuServe online service. These settings are what are normally used with most information services.

The Options tab settings let you to take manual control over modem dialing. The Connection control section allows typing commands directly to your modem. The first option lets you type modem commands before you dial; the second option doesn't display the terminal window or allow command input until after dialing. The Dial control section gives you the option of using operator-assisted or manual dialing instead of having the computer do the dialing. You can also adjust the time the computer waits to receive a tone from a credit card call. Turning on the Display modem status option gives you a visual progress check of the status of your connection.

Returning to the connection Properties dialog box, the Settings tab lets you change how your function ([F1] through [F12]), arrow, and [Ctrl] keys behave. You can also pick a terminal emulation (auto detect is your safest choice, unless you know a specific terminal you need to emulate), change the number of buffer lines, and turn sound on or off. The ASCII Setup button opens the ASCII Setup dialog box, shown next, that lets you establish settings for handling ASCII text and file transfers.

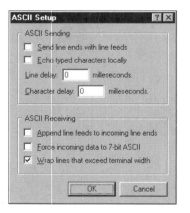

Edit menu   The Edit menu has three options. The Copy option allows you to copy selected text and graphics from the terminal windows to the clipboard. You can highlight text by clicking and dragging (the mouse pointer doesn't change to an I-beam when it is placed over text in the terminal window as it would in a text editor) or by pressing the [Shift] key and using the direction arrows. The Paste to Host option lets you copy the contents of the clipboard to the remote system to which you are connected. The third option in the Edit menu lets you select all items in the session, not only what appears in the terminal window.

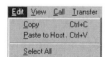

View menu   The View menu allows you to hide or display the toolbar and status bar, and to change the appearance of the text that appears in the terminal window.

Call menu   The two options on the Call menu allow you to start and end connections. The Connect option opens the Connection dialog box you've already seen. The Disconnect option breaks the modem-to-modem link, or in more familiar telephone terms, simply hangs up.

Transfer menu   The Transfer menu options are available after you have called a remote computer and established a link. The two options, Send File and Receive File, allow you to upload and download files from and to your computer. The Capture Text option creates a file of any incoming ASCII text. Send Text File transfers the text of an ASCII file to the remote computer. In this transfer the file is not transferred, just the text of the file appears on the remote computer's screen. Finally, Capture to Printer directly prints out any received ASCII text as it arrives on your computer.

Help menu   The Help menu is similar to most other Help menus. A single option Help Topics gets into HyperTerminal's help facility. The About HyperTerminal option provides copyright information concerning the company that developed HyperTerminal for Microsoft.

TOOLBAR

The toolbar provides quick access to the most commonly used menu options. Shown below, starting from the left, are the New and Open buttons, the Connect and Disconnect buttons, the Send and Receive File buttons, and the Properties and Help buttons. All of these buttons perform the same functions as their menu counterparts explained above.

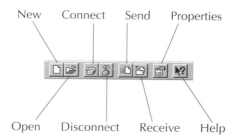

STATUS BAR

The status bar, located at the bottom of the window, provides useful information on many of HyperTerminal's features and settings. The status bar is divided into eight areas, as shown here:

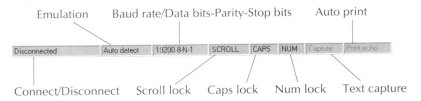

Maximize the HyperTerminal windows to view all of the status bar areas.

The first area on the left tells you whether you are connected or disconnected. The first area also can extend the full length of the status bar and provide a short description of the menu option you are pointing on. The second area in the status bar can display the type of terminal you are emulating, although normally it says Auto detect meaning that HyperTerminal will emulate the type of terminal the other computer is expecting. The third area gives useful data on the parameters set up to connect with another computer. The first number shown is the transfer speed in bits per second. The second component is a three-part term that identifies the number of data bits (4 through 8), whether parity is used (none, odd, even, mark, or space), and the number of stop bits (1, 1.5, or 2). For example, you might see 9600 8-N-1 in this area. Eight data bits, with no parity, and one stop bit is the most common configuration. The next three areas let you know if your (Scroll Lock), (Caps Lock), and (Num Lock) keys are toggled on or off. The final two areas, Capture and Print echo, become activated when you are capturing text to a file or to your printer.

TERMINAL WINDOW

The terminal window is where you see what is happening while you are connected. The window border defines essentially what you see on your monitor at a given instance. As more new data appears in the terminal window, previous data is still available, but it is scrolled up and out of the terminal window. You can access the unseen region by using the vertical scroll bar. When working with data in the terminal window, you can click the right mouse button anywhere in the window, and a popup menu will appear, as shown here:

The first six options are the same as regular menu options we've already discussed. The Snap option lets you expand the size of the terminal window to its maximum height and width.

Calling Another Computer

Now that you've taken a tour of HyperTerminal, it is time to try it out. First you'll connect with an online service and then connect with another PC.

USING AN ONLINE SERVICE

Even if you're not an experienced computer user, you have probably run across the names of the major online services including Compu-Serve, Prodigy, America Online, Genie, and now Microsoft Network. They offer an enormous range of services and topics including discussion groups, national weather reports, stock quotes, airline reservations, Internet access, and online shopping to name just a few. Although many of them provide additional software that you use to connect to them, you can still generally access them with any telecommunications program, such as HyperTerminal.

By following the next series of steps you'll log on to CompuServe using HyperTerminal. Without a CompuServe account (which you can get by calling the 800 number given earlier) you won't be able to log on, but the procedure is similar for other services or a BBS that you can use locally.

1. Using the Programs and then Accessories options of the Start menu, open HyperTerminal if it's not already running.

2.   Open the Connection Description dialog box, which is displayed automatically upon opening HyperTerminal if you do not have connections, or by double-clicking on the Hypertrm.exe icon, or if you are already in HyperTerminal, by opening the File menu and clicking on New Connection.

3.   Type a name for the connection you want to make (CompuServe), choose an icon (any icon is fine), and then click on OK.

4.   In the Phone Number dialog box that appears, type in the area code and seven-digit phone number (you can use your local phone number for CompuServe or use 800-848-8990 for which there is a CompuServe surcharge), and verify that your modem appears in the Connect using drop-down list box. Click on OK.

5.   You can now dial out in the Connect dialog box that is displayed, but you might want to check the Modify and Dialing Properties settings before you dial to make sure they are the way you want them. When you are ready, click on OK to return to the Connect dialog box.

6.   Click on Dial to begin the calling sequence.

You should hear a series of tones as the number is being dialed by the modem, the distinctive "whoosh" sound of a successful link, followed by silence. Often you will then see some sort of introductory message appearing in the terminal window. With CompuServe, you need to press Ctrl-C to which CompuServe responds by requesting your user identification and password, as shown in Figure 7–19. If these actions don't occur, double-check your settings and try again. A second failed attempt probably means your modem isn't properly installed.

Most online services (and BBSs) require a user identification number, or UserID, and password combination to log on. First time logons generally are prompted for some personal data and then are provided a temporary UserID and password for limited access. When you have provided the requested information, you are presented with a menu structure that allows you to navigate the particular service. CompuServe's main menu is shown in Figure 7–20.

From the main menu you are free (well, not really free unless you have an introductory access special; online services have a monthly flat fee, or an hourly fee, or a combination flat and hourly fee) to roam the offerings of the service. When you have completed your investigation of the service, sign off from the service. In CompuServe, type bye. You

Figure 7–19

CompuServe's logon screen

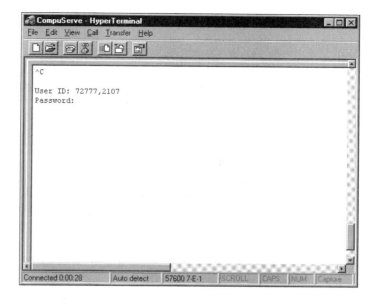

Figure 7–20

CompuServe's Main Menu

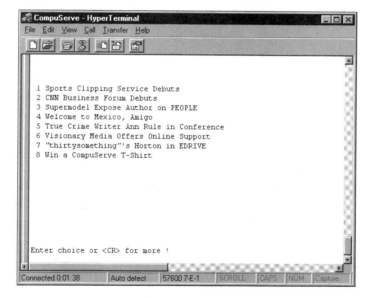

should see an acknowledgment of your leaving the service in the terminal window, and also the status bar Connect area will change to Disconnect. If you remain connected, manually disconnect by clicking on the Disconnect button (fourth from the left on the toolbar), or choose Call Disconnect.

Besides the ability to tap into repositories of information as just demonstrated, the other key capability of HyperTerminal is the sending and receiving of files and text. The next few sections cover the steps involved in these procedures. You will create a new connection identifying another desktop computer and see how easy it is to exchange information.

PREPARING FOR PC-TO-PC COMMUNICATIONS

Begin by asking a friend who has a modem-equipped computer and telecommunication software (other than HyperTerminal because HyperTerminal cannot receive a call) to set aside a few minutes to do some telecommunication with you. The ideal situation is for each of you to have two phone lines, one to send data and one available to talk through any problems. If you are limited to one phone line, it's not an insurmountable problem; you just have to communicate verbally what's going to happen before you begin the modem connection. Information that should be available to both parties includes the following:

- Each computer's phone number
- Each voice line phone number
- Protocol to be used (see Table 7–3)
- Modem speed (baud or bits per second)
- Number of data bits, parity mode, and number of stop bits (for example, 8-N-1)
- Path and name of the file(s) to be sent or received

The protocol used in data communications is a common set of instructions each modem uses to control the flow of transmitted and received data. HyperTerminal supports the six protocols listed in Table 7–3.

SENDING FILES

The first step in sending or receiving information is to make a connection.

1. Create a new connection using the procedures previously covered.

2. In the Connect dialog box, click on Dial to call the remote computer. After you hear the normal modem sounds, you will

Protocol	Description
Xmodem	Xmodem sends small blocks of data and uses a simple method of error correction. Xmodem is slower than most other protocols.
1K Xmodem	Derived from the Xmodem protocol, 1K Xmodem adds to the Xmodem protocol larger data blocks (1 KB instead of 128 bytes).
Ymodem	Another name for 1K Xmodem.
Ymodem-G	Derived from the Ymodem/1K Xmodem protocol, Ymodem-G adds hardware error control to the protocol. Modems that do not support hardware error control should use Ymodem instead.
Zmodem	A very reliable and fast protocol. The Zmodem protocol can send multiple files and automatically start file downloads (receiving) after you tell the remote computer to send a file.
Kermit	A rather slow, though flexible, protocol generally used by minicomputers and mainframes. Use faster protocols when the remote computer has them available.

Table 7–3.

Telecommunication protocols supported by HyperTerminal

see an acknowledgment of a successful connection appear in the status bar. You can now type messages back and forth between you and the other computer, as shown in Figure 7–21.

3. Click on the Send button (fifth from the left) or choose Transfer Send File to open the Send File dialog box shown here:

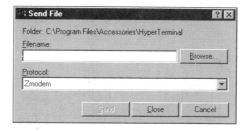

4. Supply the path and name of the file you want to send in the Filename text box, or use the Browse button to locate the file.

5. Choose a protocol for your transfer. Zmodem is generally your best choice unless the receiving party can't support it.

Figure 7–21

Desktop to desktop computer communication

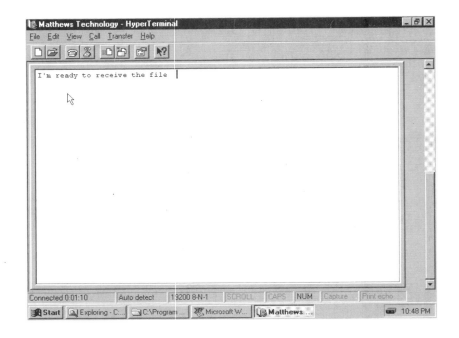

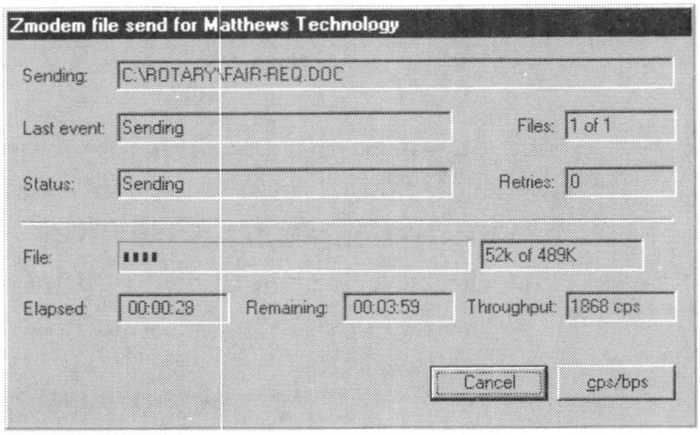

Figure 7–22

Sending file progress dialog box

6. Click on the Send button to start the transfer process.

   A dialog box that shows the progress of your file transfer is displayed, as in Figure 7–22.

7. When the file has been transferred, the progress dialog box closes, and you can disconnect by clicking on the Disconnect button.

RECEIVING FILES

As you read earlier, HyperTerminal cannot answer an incoming call. Therefore, you cannot connect with another computer whose sole telecommunication program is HyperTerminal. A common way to transfer files is for the sending party to call the receiving party and then send the file(s). To receive a file using HyperTerminal, you have to make the call, establish the connection, and then receive the file. This is not really a problem except that you shoulder all the toll charges if dialing long distance. Procedurally, it is almost identical to sending a file, as shown with these steps:

1. Use the same connection that you used to send a file, create a new one, or open another existing connection.

2. In the Connect dialog box, click on Dial to call the remote computer.

   After you make a successful connection, type any communication you need with the sending party.

3. Click on the Receive button (sixth from the left) or choose Transfer Receive File to open the Receive File dialog box, shown here:

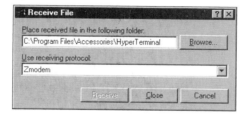

4. Supply the path where you want the receive file to be located.

5. Choose a protocol for your transfer.

   Timing is somewhat crucial here. The sending party should send the file just before you start the receive process. This is where it is very helpful to have two phone lines.

6. When you think the sending party has initiated the transfer process, click on the Receive button.

   A dialog box that shows the progress of your file transfer is displayed, as in Figure 7–23.

7. When the file has been completely transferred, the progress dialog box closes, and you can disconnect by clicking on the Disconnect button.

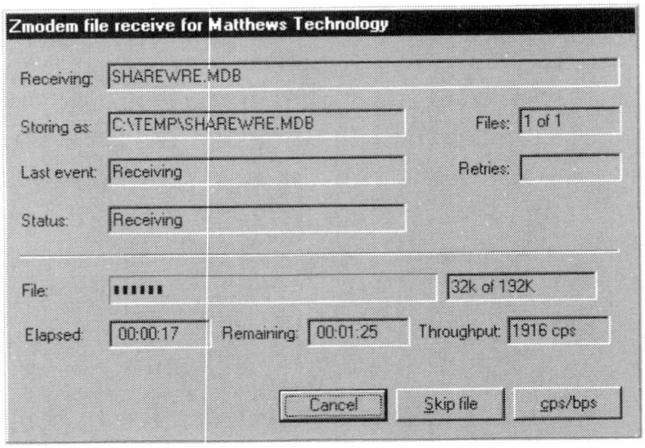

Figure 7–23

Receiving file progress dialog box

CAPTURING TEXT

It is often handy to have a copy of online data that usually just flashes by on your screen. Using HyperTerminal's text capture feature you can save the text that appears on your screen from a remote computer in an ASCII (.TXT) format. You can then open the file in a text editor (such as Notepad) and view, edit, or print it at your convenience. Follow these next few steps to see how easy this feature is to use.

1. Captured text is appended to the end of any existing .TXT file. HyperTerminal has a default file called Capture.txt. If you don't want to use the default file, create one now using WordPad. From the Start menu click on Programs, Accessories, and WordPad. From the File menu choose Save As, enter the path and filename you want to use, and choose Text Only in the Save as type drop-down list box. Close WordPad.

2. Make your connection with the remote computer.

3. From the Transfer menu, click on Capture Text. The Capture Text dialog box will open as shown here:

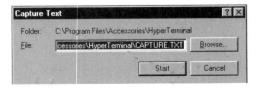

4. If you do not want to use the default file, either type a path and filename in the File text box, or use the Browse button to locate a file to which you can append the captured text. Click on Start.

You can control when to stop, pause, or resume capturing text once you start. The Transfer menu Capture Text option changes to produce a submenu when text capturing is activated, as shown here:

Capture.txt

To see the results of text capturing, you should be able to double-click on the Capture.txt icon in the HyperTerminal folder if you used the default file for capturing. If you used some other file name with a .TXT extension, you can also double-click on it to see it.

SENDING A TEXT FILE

Just as sending a file is the opposite of receiving a file, sending a text file is the reverse of capturing text to a file. You send a text (.TXT) file from your computer, and the text appears on the receiving party's screen, as if it were being typed very fast. This is what appears on your own screen when you access an online service or BBS. The remote computer opens a file that contains the logon and introductory information and sends it to your computer. As with any HyperTerminal data transfer, you first must set up a connection with the remote computer. Once you have established a connection, you can send a text file with these steps:

1. Click on the Transfer menu Send Text File option. The Send Text File dialog box appears, as you can see in Figure 7–24.

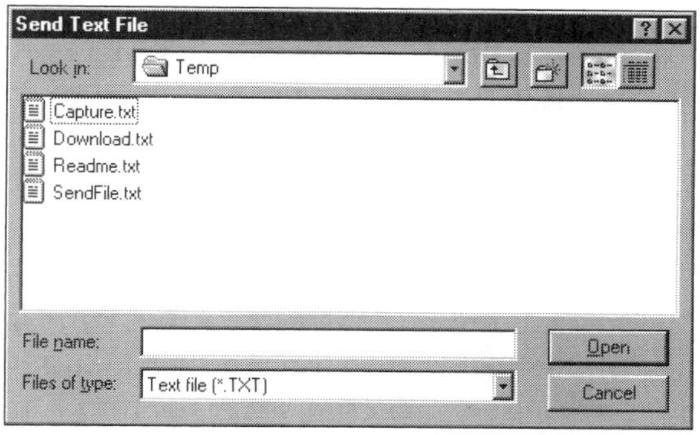

Figure 7–24

Send Text File dialog box

2. Locate the file you want to send using the Look in drop-down list box to locate the correct folder. Click on the file, and its name will appear in the File name text box. Click on Open.

   The text in the file will appear simultaneously in your terminal window and on the receiving party's screen.

3. When the end of the file appears in the terminal window, hang up by clicking on the Disconnect button.

Printing

There are three different routes you can take to print data that comes to your computer:

- For a file that was transferred to your computer or a file that was created by capturing ASCII text, use an appropriate program such as WordPad or NotePad.

- For information that is in your terminal window, use the Print Setup and Print options of the File menu to format and print it.

- For ASCII text as it is being received, use the Capture to Printer option in the Transfer menu.

To format data that is in the terminal window, use the Page Setup option in the File menu to change the size, orientation, margins, and printer paper source of your printed information, as shown in Figure 7–25. As you change a setting, the sample document dynamically adjusts to show the effect of your action. The Printer button, located at the bottom of the dialog box, opens up a secondary dialog box where you can change printers and adjust printer properties.

Figure 7–26 shows the Print dialog box, opened by choosing File Print. Standard printing options are available, including choice of printer/properties, an option of printing to a file, range of data to print, number of copies, and an option to collate or not.

If you know in advance you want to print everything that will eventually appear in the terminal window, you can use the Transfer menu option Capture to Printer. This option is a toggle, meaning it will remain on or off until you click on it again. A check mark appears to the left of the option when it is turned on. When activated, all data coming to your computer is sent to your printer as it arrives. There are

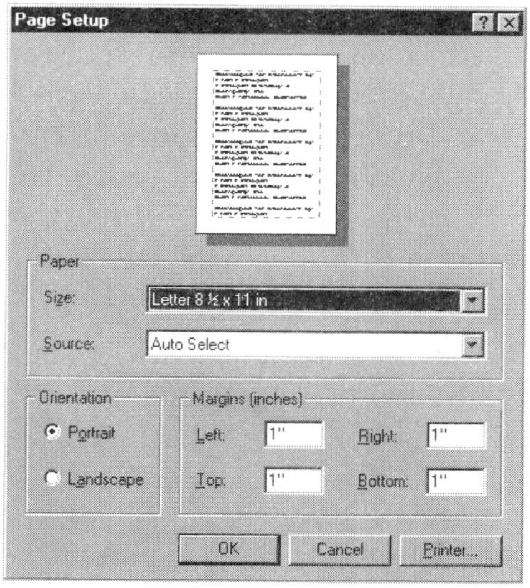

Figure 7–25

*Page Setup
dialog box*

Figure 7–26

Print dialog box

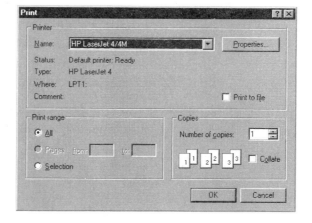

two things you need to set up before this option can work properly. First, make sure your Page Setup specifications from the File menu are correct, and secondly, ensure your printer is turned on and is online.

Using Phone Dialer

The Phone Dialer applet is another new feature in Windows 95 that combines the capabilities of a computer and a telephone. Although a phone dialer is nothing new, Windows 95 has given it a number of advanced features (including conference calling, logging, speed dialing, and handling call waiting) that haven't been commonly available. To see how Phone Dialer can further make your computer a complete communications center, double-click on the Phone Dialer icon located in the Start menu, Programs, Accessories list.

Dialer.exe

The Phone Dialer closely resembles the dialing face of many desktop telephones, as you can see in Figure 7–27. You can use the Phone Dialer to dial a local, long distance, or international phone number in one of the following ways:

- With the Phone Dialer as the active window, type the number on your keyboard. The number will appear in the Number to dial drop-down list box, and you need only to click on Dial to initiate the call.

- Open the Number to dial drop-down list box and select a recently dialed number and then click on Dial.

- Click on the applicable letters or numerals of the alphanumeric keypad. The results of each mouse click appear in the Number to dial text box. Click on Dial to initiate the call.

- Click on a Speed dial button. The number you assigned to a particular button appears in the Number to dial text box, and then Phone Dialer initiates the call.

The Speed dial buttons are set up by choosing Speed Dial from the Edit menu. The Edit Speed Dial dialog box opens, as shown in Figure 7–28. You can also click on a blank button to open the Program Speed Dial dialog box, which limits editing to a single button

Figure 7–27

The Phone Dialer

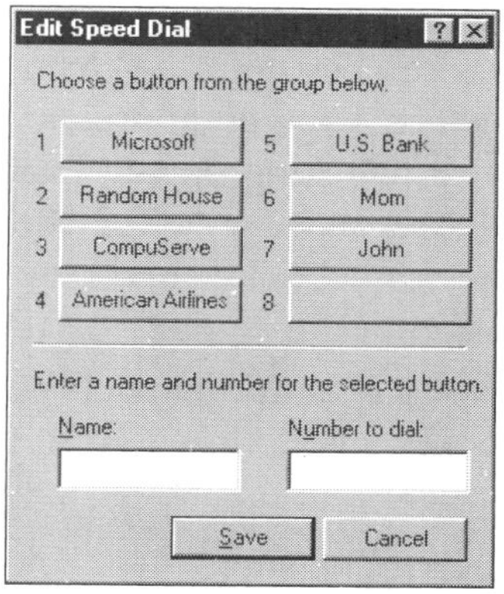

Figure 7–28

*The Edit Speed
Dial dialog box*

and provides the same text boxes as the Edit Speed Dial dialog box
for naming the button and assigning a number to be dialed.

You can assign your most frequently used phone numbers to the
Speed Dial buttons by simply clicking on a button and typing in a
name for the button and then the number to be dialed. Click on Save
after entering all that you want to enter.

Menus

Three of the four Phone Dialer menus—File, Edit, and Help—contain mainly options with which you are familiar. The first option in
the Tools menu, Connect Using, opens a dialog box of the same
name, as shown here:

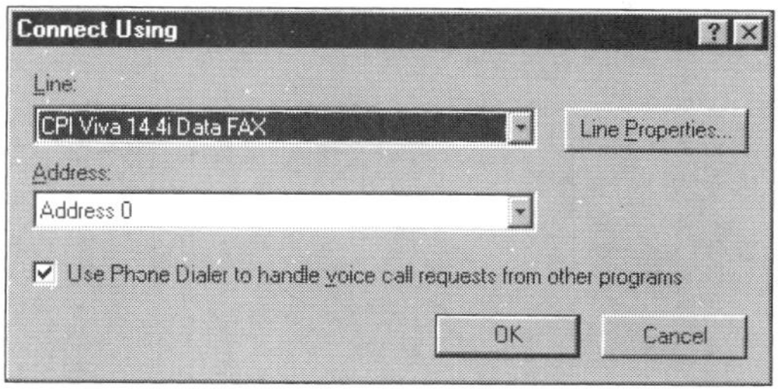

Windows 95 provides the capability to handle multiple connections
that are voice and/or data lines. A listing of all the lines you have set
up is provided by the Line drop-down list box. This listing corresponds
to the number of devices you have installed. For the majority of users

who have a single modem and one line, the default line and its associated address need not be changed. If you have more than one modem installed in your computer, you can choose on which line to make your call. Clicking on the Line Properties button opens the modem Properties dialog box for the modem that is selected in the Line drop-down list box. This is the same dialog box that is used to change the properties of an installed modem.

The Tools menu Dialing Properties option opens the same Dialing Properties dialog box used in modem setup. The final option, Show Log, opens the Call Log dialog box, which keeps a record of your incoming and outgoing calls from Phone Dialer, as shown next. You can choose to log incoming, outgoing, both, or neither category of calls using Options from the Log menu.

Finally, the Call Log dialog box gives you the dialing option of selecting a call in the log and choosing Dial from the Log menu.

Though this chapter has covered a lot of material in the world of telecommunications, it has just scratched the surface of what Windows 95 is capable of handling. The next chapter, "Using Microsoft Exchange for Mail and FAX," explores how the communications center of Windows 95, Microsoft Exchange, integrates the many mailing systems available to you.

Using Microsoft Exchange for Mail and Fax

Modern personal computers are no longer confined to the physical dimensions of the case that lies on or next to your desk. The computer of the 90s is a part of a larger network of computers encompassing not only a local area network but also all of the information services and remote computers you can reach with telecommunications. With the Microsoft Exchange, Windows 95 provides a *Grand Central Station* for all of the messaging and faxing needs you have with this larger network.

Microsoft Exchange is a universal front-end that lets you create, send, receive, forward, and save messages to and from a number of sources using the Inbox. Windows 95, by itself, can send and receive messages over a LAN with other Windows 95 users, as well as use telecommunications with the Microsoft Network online service, CompuServe, and Microsoft At Work Fax. Other e-mail services using the Exchange, including those over the Internet, are available with the optional Windows 95 Plus Pack and third-party vendors.

Besides providing an extremely functional and flexible user interface for managing messages, the Exchange also incorporates the Windows 95 mail system, which allows the members of a workgroup to use e-mail among themselves. The full version of Microsoft Mail, of which Windows 95 Mail is a subset, can cross workgroup boundaries through its postoffice to communicate with other workgroups in the organization. The Windows 95 postoffice (or workgroup mail center) can only provide mail services within its own workgroup. As part of the Windows 95 extendibility program, you can upgrade the postoffice to the capabilities of a full-version postoffice by purchasing the Microsoft Mail Server software.

Before you set up the Exchange, there are several decisions that you should make. The first two concern Microsoft Mail. You need to decide whether you will be using Microsoft Mail to send and receive messages. If you will, you also need to determine which computer in the workgroup will be the postoffice. The Exchange cannot be fully set up on your computer until you know where the postoffice will be. Therefore, the first step is to establish a postoffice. If that has already been done by someone else or you are not planning on using Microsoft Mail, skip ahead to *Setting Up the Exchange* later in this chapter. Also, if you are upgrading a computer that had a Windows for Workgroups postoffice, the workgroup postoffice has been converted to a Windows 95 postoffice.

Setting Up and Managing a Postoffice

There are a few considerations to keep in mind before you select a computer to be your workgroup postoffice. Foremost, the postoffice computer should have ample CPU, memory, and disk-space resources to handle this additional burden. You do not want to use the slowest computer in the workgroup to be the postoffice. Secondly, the postoffice must be open (the postoffice computer turned on) whenever users might want to send and receive mail. Lastly, someone has to perform the administration of the postoffice, which for a large workgroup can turn into a significant task. Once you have settled these details, you are ready to begin setting up the postoffice.

Setting Up a Postoffice

Start the process of setting up a postoffice by opening the Microsoft Mail Postoffice control panel with the following steps:

Microsoft Mail
Postoffice

1. Open the Start menu, choose Settings Control Panel, and after the Control Panel opens, double-click on the Microsoft Mail Postoffice icon. The Workgroup Postoffice Admin dialog box

Figure 8–1

The opening Workgroup Postoffice dialog box

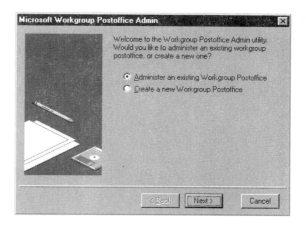

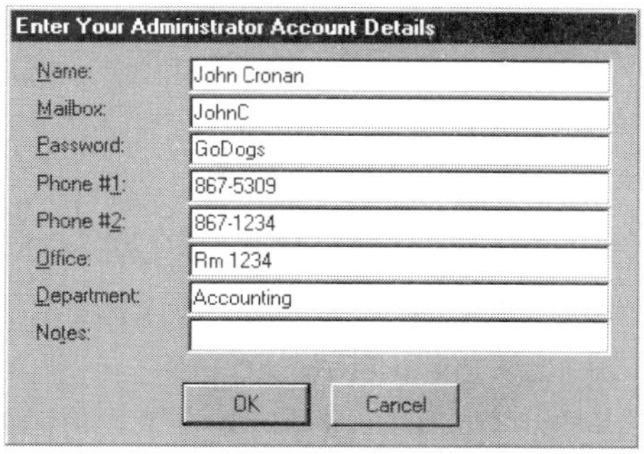

Figure 8–2

Establishing the administrator's account details

opens, as shown in Figure 8–1. The two options in the dialog box let you administer an existing postoffice or create a new one.

2.   Choose the second option, Create a new Workgroup Post-office, and click on Next. The second Admin dialog box opens and suggests a default location for the postoffice files. Unless you have a specific reason to change the location, accept the default location. Click on Next twice to confirm your location.

3.   The Enter Your Administrator Account Details dialog box opens with a suggested mailbox name and generic password. Edit these two text boxes to your liking and supply data for as many of the remaining fields as you feel necessary, as shown in Figure 8–2. The data that you supply will be available to others in your workgroup, so there might be some informa-tion you do not want to enter.

 Make sure you record the mailbox name and password that are displayed in the Enter Your Administrator Account Details dialog box before you click on OK. You will need these two personal identification items the next time you attempt to access the workgroup account.

4. Click on OK. A message box opens to let you know you must share the directory where the postoffice is located so other users can access it. Click on OK to finish the procedure.

Sharing resources, such as the postoffice directory, was covered in Chapter 6; however, there are a few points worth reviewing. In the Sharing tab of the Properties dialog box for the postoffice directory, provide a descriptive name for your workgroup in the Comment text box. Also, ensure Full Access is granted to allow all users in your workgroup access to the postoffice's mail. If you want to add a level of security to mail access, choose Depends on Password and enter a password in the Full Access Password text box.

Managing the Postoffice

The postoffice administrator's duties include adding and removing workgroup members, changing user information such as forgotten passwords or new phone numbers, and backing up the postoffice files.

The postoffice is accessed from the Microsoft Mail Postoffice control panel, which you open as you did above in creating the postoffice. Once the control panel is open, you can access the administrative functions with the following steps:

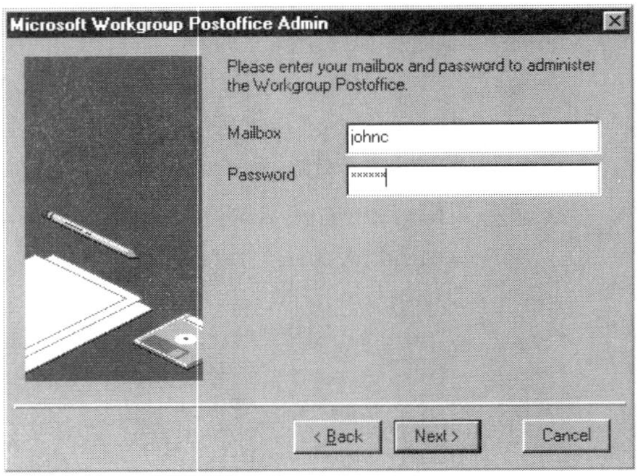

Figure 8–3

Logging on as the account administrator

![Microsoft Workgroup Postoffice Admin dialog box. Please enter your mailbox and password to administer the Workgroup Postoffice. Mailbox: johnc, Password: *****. Buttons: < Back, Next >, Cancel]

1. Choose the first option, Administer an existing Workgroup Postoffice, and click on Next.

2. Verify the postoffice location, and click on Next to open the administrator's logon screen, shown in Figure 8–3. Enter your password and click on Next.

3. The Postoffice Manager dialog box opens, as you can see in Figure 8–4. New users are added, established users are removed, and user data is changed by selecting the user's name and clicking on the Details button. A details dialog box, shown next, identical to the administrator's personal data dialog box, lets the administrator assign the user a mailbox name, password, and enter other contact information.

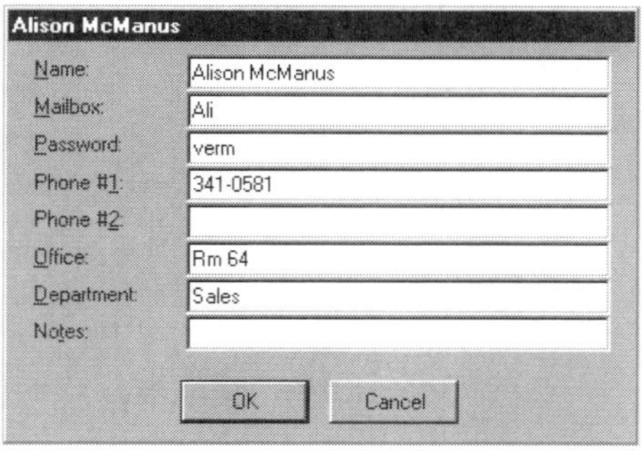

Alison McManus

Name:	Alison McManus
Mailbox:	Ali
Password:	verm
Phone #1:	341-0581
Phone #2:	
Office:	Rm 64
Department:	Sales
Notes:	

OK   Cancel

Tip   Before you have new users try to connect to the workgroup postoffice, create new user accounts for them. They won't be able to log on until they have accounts established. Prior planning will save them some frustration and save you from being bombarded with requests for assistance.

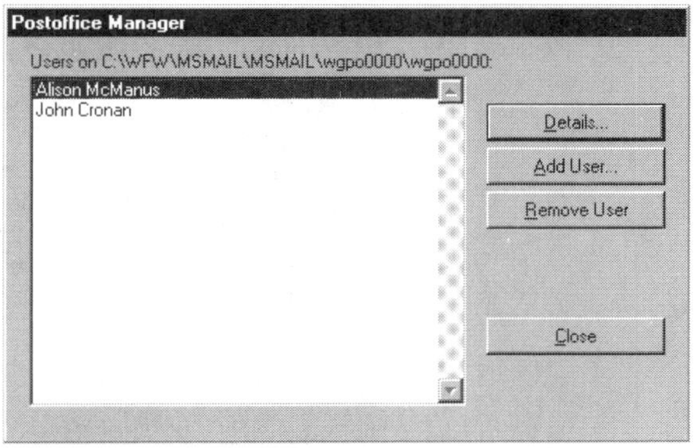

Figure 8–4

The Postoffice Manager dialog box

Postoffice Manager

Users on C:\WFW\MSMAIL\MSMAIL\wgpo0000\wgpo0000:

Alison McManus
John Cronan

Details...
Add User...
Remove User

Close

4. Click on OK in any open user dialog box, and click on Close in the Postoffice Manager dialog box to finish.

Setting Up the Exchange

Inbox.exc

Before you can explore the Exchange, you have to ensure it's properly installed on your hard disk. Microsoft Exchange is installed during your setup of Windows 95. If your desktop has an icon for the Exchange Inbox, you have the Exchange installed. If not, you need to install it with the next few steps:

Add/Remove Programs

1. Open the Start menu and choose Settings Control Panel. Double-click on the Add/Remove Programs control panel.

2. Click on the Windows Setup tab of the Add/Remove Programs Properties dialog box, and then click on the check box next to the Microsoft Exchange component, as shown in Figure 8–5.

3. Click on the Details button to view the subcomponents of the Exchange that will be installed unless you clear their respective check boxes (shown in Figure 8–6). When you have selected the subcomponents that you want installed with the Exchange, click on OK.

Figure 8–5

Turning on the Microsoft Exchange component to be added to your system

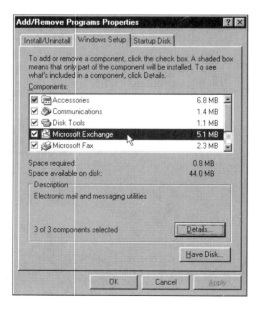

Figure 8–6

Choosing which Exchange subcomponent(s) to install

4.   Click on OK to begin the installation process. Have your Windows 95 CD-ROM or disks available to be put in their drive when requested by the setup routine.

Using Profiles

To use the Microsoft Exchange you need to create a profile, or controlling file, for the Exchange. The profile contains information such as the messaging service(s) to be used, mailbox and password names, type of connection used, and server location. If you access multiple mail services such as Microsoft Mail, Internet Mail, and Compu-Serve, a singular profile provides a convenient way to log on to all services using the information required for each. However, there is a penalty for combining several messaging services into one profile (see the following Caution). A common situation for a single user to use multiple profiles is on a laptop or notebook computer. When at the office, the portable computer is connected to the mail server via a LAN connection, and when on the road, remote access is used. Multiple users of the same computer that access messaging services each require at least one profile for their own particular needs.

When you open the Exchange, it attempts to log on consecutively to all of the messaging services listed in its startup profile and to retrieve messages. Depending on how many messaging services are in the profile, the type of connection (LAN or dial-up), and the size and number

of messages, a lot of time and computer resources can be used. You might consider creating more than one profile: a startup profile to handle your highest-volume messaging, and separate profiles to cover less often used and dial-up services.

You can choose which profile the Exchange uses in two ways: from the Mail and Fax control panel or when you start up the Exchange. Both of these methods are discussed in upcoming sections. Unfortunately, you cannot switch profiles once you have opened the Exchange. You must close the Exchange and then reopen it with the new profile.

Microsoft Services Setup

The first time you open the Exchange, the Inbox Setup Wizard starts and walks you through creating your first profile. Do that next.

1. Double-click on the desktop Inbox icon, or open the Start menu and choose Programs Microsoft Exchange. The first dialog box of the Inbox Setup Wizard opens, as shown in Figure 8–7. The wizard assumes you haven't used the Exchange before, so continue by clicking on Next.

    The second dialog box presents a list of services with which the Exchange has the capability of interchanging messages, as shown in Figure 8–8. (Your list may not include Internet Mail; see the next Note.)

Your list of services will include Internet Mail only if you have installed Microsoft Plus! for Windows 95.

Figure 8–7

Opening dialog box of the Exchange Setup Wizard

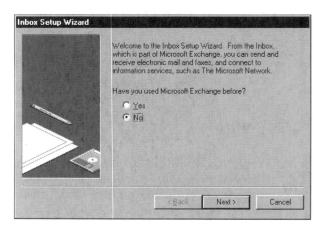

Figure 8–8

Choosing which information services to have available in the Exchange

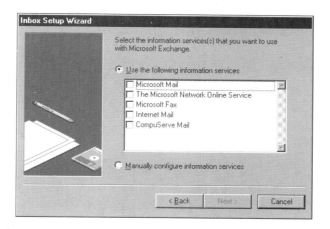

2. Choose the service(s) that you have an immediate need to use. You can easily add others to the same profile or create multiple profiles as the need arises using the Mail and Fax control panel. The Manually configure information services option, below the information services list box, should only be chosen by advanced users who have software drivers available to change or add a particular service.

In the next series of steps you'll configure three of the possible services: Microsoft Mail, Microsoft Network, and Microsoft Fax. You can set up additional connections to Internet Mail, CompuServe Mail, and other messaging providers depending on your needs and the software you have available. Although each type of connection (LAN or dial-up) is mentioned in this chapter, the type of connection illustrated to access a particular service may not be the same as you use. However, the procedures to set up either type of connection are similar. Skip over any steps that do not pertain to you. Here are the steps to configure the three information services:

1. Click on Next, and a dialog box asks for the location of your Microsoft Mail postoffice. Verify the location on your system or the computer on which it is located, and click on Next.

2. Select your name from the list of Microsoft Mail users, click on Next, supply your password in the dialog box that follows, and then click on Next again.

3. The next service to set up is The Microsoft Network, shown in Figure 8–9. There is nothing to enter or choose here, so after reading the text, click on Next.

Figure 8–9

Microsoft Network dialog box

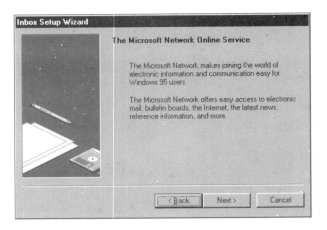

Figure 8–10

Configuring Microsoft Fax

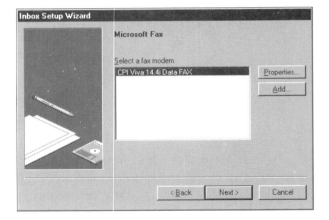

4. Microsoft Fax is next, and the first task is to select a modem, as shown in Figure 8–10. If the correct fax modem is not shown, click on Add. If you add a device, you can choose from a dedicated fax modem or one that serves the network. Click on Next when you are ready.

5. The next dialog box you see lets you choose how to answer incoming fax calls. Unless you have a dedicated fax line, the default manual method is best, so as to not interfere with voice or data usage on the same line. Click on Next after making your choice.

6. Verify your name, location, and add your fax number in the Microsoft Fax dialog box shown in Figure 8–11. When you are done, click on Next.

Figure 8–11

Second Microsoft Fax configuration dialog box

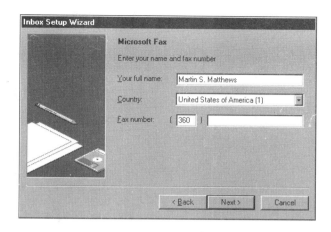

7. The final Inbox Setup Wizard dialog box tells you are done and lists the information services you now have available. Click on Finish to complete the process. The Choose Profile dialog box will open asking you to select the profile you want to use in opening the Inbox. For now choose Cancel. You'll come back in a moment and restart the Exchange Inbox.

You can change the Exchange profile you have just created to add or remove services, further configure the services you currently have set up, or add additional profiles through the Mail and Fax control panel. The next few sections describe how you can customize the three components that were initially set up in your profile.

Mail and Fax Control Panel

The Mail and Fax control panel allows you to add, remove, or make changes to your Microsoft Exchange profiles. Double-clicking on the Mail and Fax control panel opens the default profile Properties dialog box and displays its three tabs, as shown in Figure 8–12. The initial default profile name is Microsoft Exchange Settings, which appears in the title bar.

The list box at the top of the Services tab contains all of the components in the profile. By selecting an information service you can choose many attributes that relate to how a particular service is used by the Exchange.

Choosing the Add button lets you add any additional service that Windows 95 recognizes, by either choosing from those currently installed or by installing with the Have Disk button, as shown here:

You can find out a lot about a service by selecting it and clicking on the About button. The About Information Service dialog box for Microsoft Mail is shown next. Each information service is comprised of one or more dynamic link libraries (.DDLs) which are listed in the File Names list box. Other pertinent data specific to each .DLL is also provided.

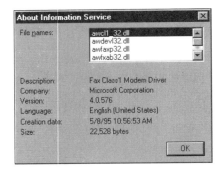

Information services that are no longer needed in a profile can be removed by using the Remove button.

The Copy button in the Exchange Settings Properties dialog box allows you to copy any selected information service from one profile into another. The About button displays the same data about a service that was displayed through the Add dialog box. The Show Profiles button displays the General tab of the Microsoft Exchange Profiles dialog box, shown in Figure 8–13. This is the place to add and remove profiles, and to establish which profile the Exchange starts with. The Properties button in the Microsoft Exchange Profiles dialog box opens the Properties dialog box (Figure 8–12) for a selected profile.

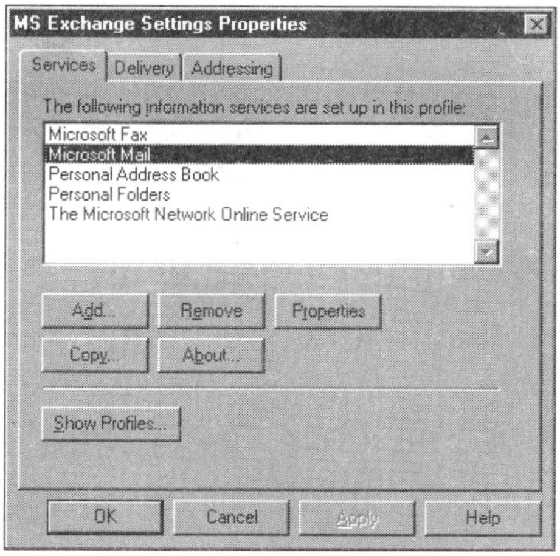

Figure 8–12

A profile's properties dialog box

Figure 8–13

General tab showing all available profiles

Do that now to return to the Microsoft Exchange Settings Properties dialog box. Each information service's properties are accessed by selecting the service and clicking on the Properties button. Select Microsoft Mail, and click on the Properties button.

Microsoft Mail Properties

The Microsoft Mail properties dialog box, shown in Figure 8–14, holds several tabs that allow you to configure Microsoft Mail for either a LAN or a dial-in connection.

Figure 8–14

*Configuring
Microsoft Mail
properties*

CONNECTION TAB

When you first began the process of setting up the Exchange, the wizard asked you for your workgroup postoffice location. That same address appears in the Enter the path to your postoffice text box. From here you can change its location if, for example, the postoffice is moved to another computer.

The option buttons let you choose the manner in which you connect to your mail server. The first option applies when you have both LAN and dial-in needs. The Exchange senses when you are connected to the LAN; otherwise it assumes a dial-in connection. The next two options specifically connect via a LAN or through a dial-in connection. The Offline option allows you to compose messages when you are not connected using either method. Any sent mail is temporarily held in an Exchange folder called the Outbox. When you do connect to your mail server, any mail in the Outbox is then transferred.

LOGON TAB

The Logon tab, shown in Figure 8–15, displays your mailbox name and password. Your password is masked to keep unauthorized persons from reading it. If you want your password automatically entered so you don't have to type it, click on the applicable check box. If you want to change your password, click on the Change

Figure 8–15

Microsoft Mail's Logon tab

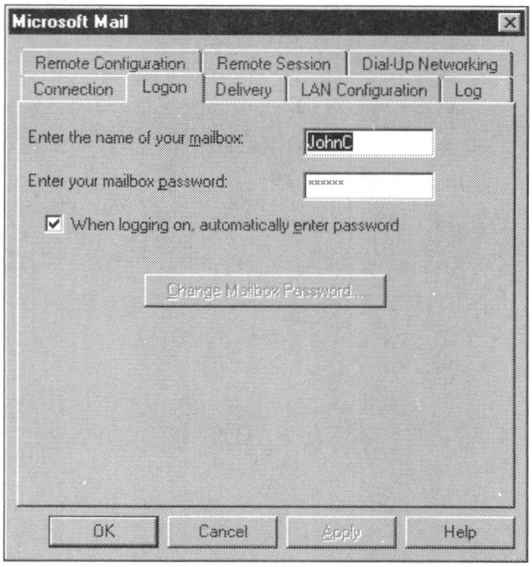

Figure 8–16

Microsoft Mail's Delivery tab

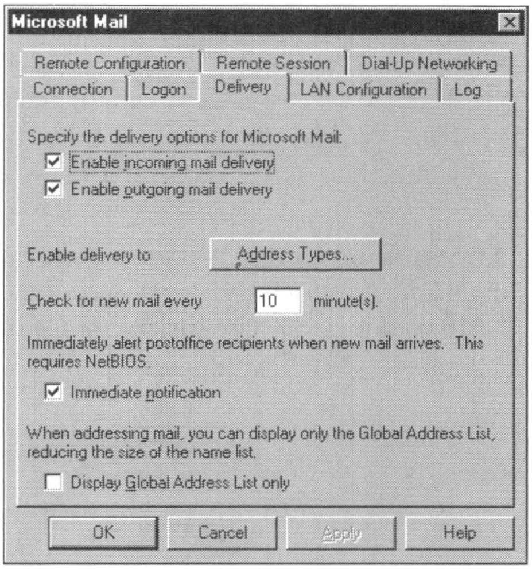

Mailbox Password button. The button is dimmed, or unavailable, unless you already have the Exchange open (and have therefore entered the correct password).

DELIVERY TAB

You have a lot of control over how your mail is transferred to and from your mailbox through the Delivery tab, shown in Figure 8–16. The two check boxes at the top of the dialog box let you turn off either incoming or outgoing mail. The Address types button opens a list box that allows you to enable or disable delivery to various addresses. You can choose the interval when the Exchange checks the server for new mail. Checking for mail requires some processing effort, and much like autosaving a document in a word processor, too short of an interval can become counterproductive. The final two check boxes provide opportunities for immediate notification of high priority messages and narrowing the field of names that appear when addressing messages.

LAN CONFIGURATION TAB

Figure 8–17 shows three options that apply only when you are connected to the postoffice via a LAN. The first check box, Use Remote Preview, lets you look at the headers of your messages prior to downloading the entire message queue. Both this option and the next can also be chosen from the Exchange Tools menu. The second check box, Use local copy, lets you choose a personal address list that resides on your computer instead of the larger list that is maintained at the postoffice. The final check box, Use external delivery agent, runs a program that may speed up a slow LAN.

 **The options in the LAN Configuration tab are primarily designed for dial-up connections. Although you can activate them for use with a LAN connection, the default state is for them to be off.**

Figure 8–17

*Microsoft Mail's
LAN
Configuration tab*

Microsoft Mail

Remote Configuration | Remote Session | Dial-Up Networking
Connection | Logon | Delivery | LAN Configuration | Log

These options apply only when this computer is on the LAN.

If you don't want to automatically transfer all mail, you can use Remote Mail on the Tools menu to move, copy, or delete items.

☐ Use Remote Mail

You can use a local copy of the postoffice address list instead of the copy on the server.

☐ Use local copy

You can use an external delivery agent to manage mail delivery. If you are on a slow LAN, this may speed up delivery.

☐ Use external delivery agent

OK　Cancel　Apply　Help

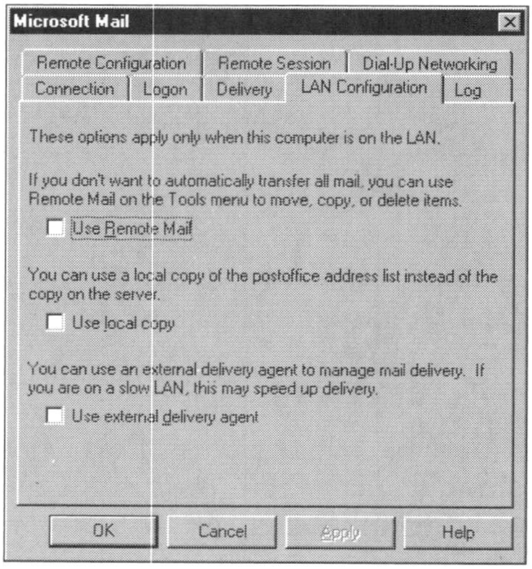

Figure 8–18

Microsoft Mail's Dial-up Network tab

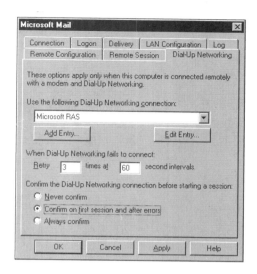

The final four tabs deal specifically with dial-up, or remote, connections.

LOG TAB

The Log tab determines whether you want to create a log of significant events for dial-up connections and where it's located. A history log can often aid in trouble-shooting attempts.

DIAL-UP NETWORKING TAB

The Dial-up Networking tab, shown in Figure 8–18, allows you to select a remote connection to link with your postoffice. If you click on the Add Entry button, the Make a New Connection wizard opens and guides you through setting up a remote connection. Changes to existing connections are made using the Edit Entry button. The next two sections in the dialog box allow you to choose the number of retry attempts and the interval for a failed connection, and the level of confirmation for your remote session. A remote session is the period of time that you are actually connected to the postoffice with your modem.

REMOTE SESSION TAB

Figure 8–19 shows the Remote Session tab where the most specific remote features are available. The first check box lets you choose whether you want the remote connection to take place every time

Figure 8–19

Microsoft
Mail's Remote
Session tab

you start the Exchange. If you click on this check box, the remote session remains connected until you close the Exchange. The next section of the tab provides three different ways to automatically terminate the remote session. The first check box, After retrieving item headers, is used in conjunction with the Use Remote Preview check box in the Remote Configuration tab, described next. Clicking on the Schedule Mail Delivery button opens the Remote Scheduled Sessions dialog box, which lets you create up to 16 different schedules for hands-off connection. Clicking on the Add button opens the Add Scheduled Session dialog box, shown here:

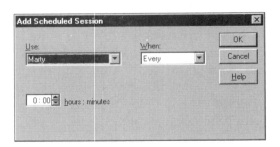

You can choose which remote connection to use and whether to connect at a specified interval, weekly at a specific time, or just once at a specific time.

REMOTE CONFIGURATION TAB

The last tab in this dialog box is identical to the LAN Configuration tab, described earlier in this section, except the check boxes pertain to remote connections. The one difference between the two tabs is that for LAN connections all the check boxes are off by default; they are all turned on by default for remote connections.

Microsoft Fax Properties

The faxing program included in Windows 95 offers many of the capabilities associated with full-featured third-party software. The real strength of Microsoft Fax is its ability to integrate faxes with your other messages in the Exchange. In the Exchange your faxes have access to a broad range of viewing and file management choices. But first you should review the Microsoft Fax properties and see how they can best serve your needs.

As with Microsoft Mail, the Microsoft Fax properties are accessed from the profile's Properties dialog box. Select Microsoft Fax from the list of information services, and click on the Properties button.

MESSAGE TAB

The Microsoft Fax Properties dialog box opens with the Message tab displayed, as shown in Figure 8–20. The Time to Send section allows you to choose when to send a fax. You can take advantage of cheaper toll rates by choosing the Discount rates option and clicking on the Set button. The Set Discount Rates dialog box, shown next, lets you adjust the dialing time bracket to match discount periods.

The Message format section provides three options that determine whether the text in the faxes you send can be edited for subsequent

Figure 8–20

*Microsoft Fax's
Message tab*

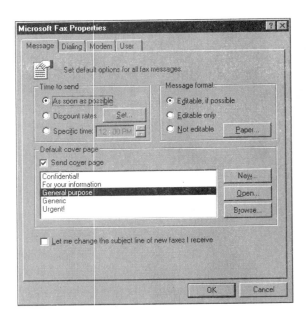

uses. Only recipients that use Microsoft Fax have automatic editing ability with Microsoft Fax senders without the use of third-party optical character recognition (OCR) software. The first option, Editable if possible, covers all situations without the chance of fax nondelivery. If you choose the second option, Editable only, faxes will not be received by non-Microsoft Fax users. The last option sends a fax in the conventional format, which requires OCR software to convert the graphic text images into an editable format. The Paper button opens the Message Format dialog box, shown below, which gives options for the paper size of the fax message and any attached documents, as well as their resolution and orientation.

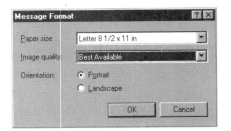

 Change the resolution of toll faxes to a lower dpi to shorten the transmission time and save on long distance charges.

Figure 8–21

*Fax Cover
Page Editor*

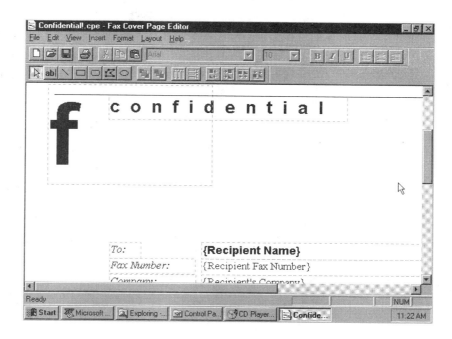

The Default cover page section lets you choose whether you want to send a cover page and lists available covers you can use. The three buttons let you create a new cover or open and edit an existing one using the Fax Cover Page Editor, shown in Figure 8–21. Using the editor is covered later in this chapter. Checking the Let me change the subject line of new faxes I receive check box causes new faxes to be received as attachments to Windows 95 mail messages. You can then edit the fax subject line, so the message header that appears in the Exchange is more descriptive.

DIALING TAB

Figure 8–22 shows the properties that determine how you dial a fax transmission. The I'm dialing from group lets you check which dialing location you currently have selected. The Dialing Properties button opens up the same dialog box that was used in Chapter 7 to set up a modem and HyperTerminal. The Toll Prefixes button opens the Toll Prefixes dialog box where you specify which calls within your area code are long distance. The Retries section determines how many dialing attempts are made and at what interval.

Figure 8–22

Microsoft Fax dialing tab

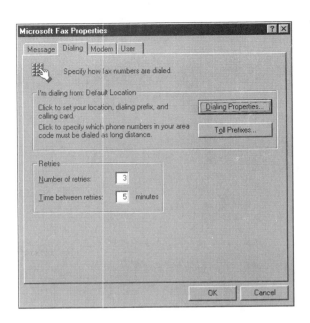

MODEM TAB

The Modem tab, shown in Figure 8–23, lets you choose a fax modem from those you have installed and change its properties, set it as the default, remove it, or add a new one. Clicking on the Available fax modems section's Properties button opens the Fax Modem Properties dialog box, shown here:

The Answer mode section lets you choose how your fax modem answers incoming fax calls. The first option sets the fax modem to answer after a certain number of rings. This option should only be

Figure 8–23

*Microsoft Fax
Modem tab*

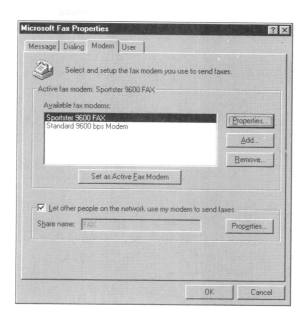

used on lines that predominately handle fax transmissions. The second option, conversely, is best suited for lines that share voice and fax. When Microsoft Fax senses an incoming fax, it sends a notification, so you can choose to answer it. The last option is self-explanatory. The other two sections let you adjust speaker volume and specify how outgoing faxes are called. Clicking on the Advanced button opens a dialog box of the same name, shown next. You should consider disabling high-speed transmission and error control if you experience reliability problems in your faxing.

The Enable MR compression check box, when checked, uses compression to send and receive faxes. A slight gain in speed might be offset by a greater sensitivity to transmission interference. The Use Class 2 if available check box specifies that fax modems use only Class 2 if they have the capability to use both the older standard Class 1 and the newer standard Class 2. If you are having problems sending and receiving faxes, try using this option. Be aware that turning on this option will prevent you from sending or receiving editable faxes and using error correction. The Reject pages received with errors check box provides four levels of tolerance that reject pages received with errors. The lower the tolerance the more likely pages will be rejected.

Returning to the Modem tab, clicking on the check box next to Let other people on the network... allows you to share your fax modem across the network and activates the Share name text box, so you can provide a share name. Click on the Properties button to finalize the sharing process.

USER TAB

Figure 8–24 shows representative entries made in the User tab. When you design a fax cover page you can enter codes that automatically include data from the User tab such as your name, business, address, and phone numbers.

Figure 8–24

Microsoft Fax User tab

The Microsoft Network Properties

The last information service in the profile set up here is the Microsoft Network (MSN). Select The Microsoft Network Online Service in the profile Properties dialog box, and click on the Properties button. The Microsoft Network dialog box opens, as shown in Figure 8–25. The Transport tab lets you choose how you want messages brought in from MSN. The first option copies messages in their entirety to the Exchange whenever you log on to MSN but does not disconnect. The second option downloads headers and disconnects. After you have reviewed the headers, you can then use Remote Preview to download the messages you want to see. The third option downloads messages when connected to MSN and then disconnects, so you can read them offline without any connection costs.

The option in the Address Book tab shown in Figure 8–26, Connect to MSN to check names, specifies whether you want to connect to

Figure 8–25

Microsoft Network dialog box

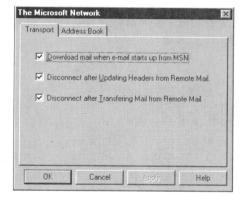

Figure 8–26

Address Book tab

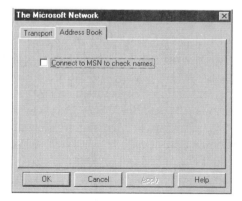

Figure 8-27

*Organizing
incoming and
outgoing messages
and faxes*

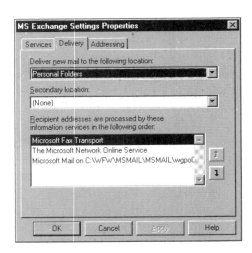

MSN to verify addresses. If you leave the check box unchecked, you can work offline while composing messages. Connecting to The Microsoft Network is covered in Chapter 9.

There are two remaining tabs in the profile's Properties dialog box: Delivery and Addressing.

Delivery Tab

Figure 8-27 shows the options that determine where your incoming messages are received and the order in which outgoing items are sent. Incoming messages are sent to personal folders that are set up for the Exchange.

Addressing Tab

In the Addressing Tab, shown in Figure 8-28, you determine in what order your address books are searched, which address book keeps personal addresses, and which address books are checked (and in what order) when you send a message. You can add or remove address books or lists. Selecting a book or list and clicking on the Properties button allows you to see additional information concerning that particular address file, as shown in Figure 8-29.

Next, see how the Exchange can be used to create and manage your electronic messages and online faxes.

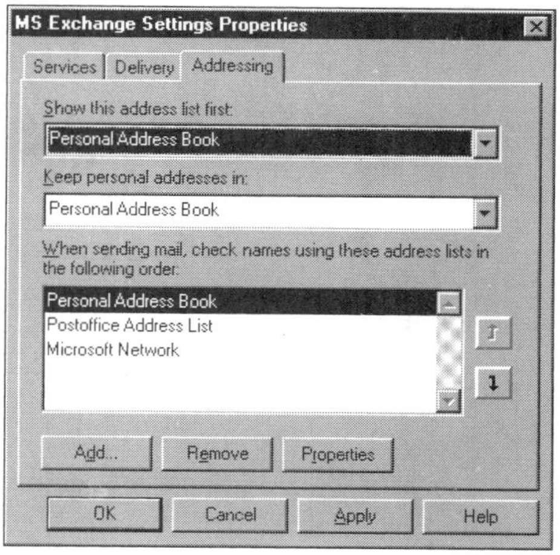

Figure 8-28

Addressing tab

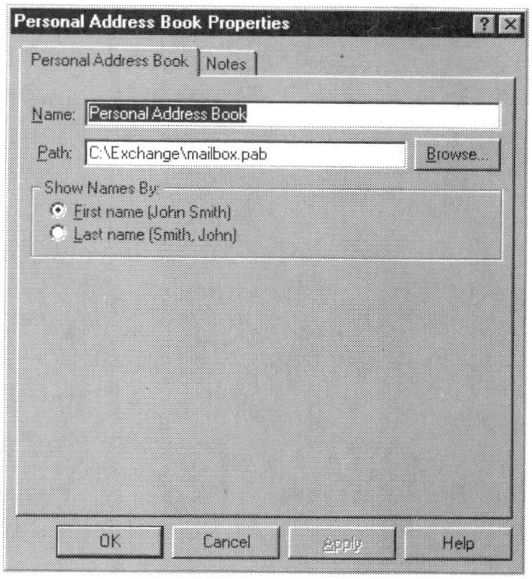

Figure 8-29

Address Book (or list) Properties dialog box

Microsoft Mail

This section uses Microsoft Mail to demonstrate the capabilities of the Exchange to send, receive, and organize messages. If you use a messaging service other than Microsoft Mail, some features might work differently and appear different from those in this section, but the underlying principles are the same.

The Exchange is opened by double-clicking on the Inbox icon on the desktop, or opening the Start menu and choosing Programs Microsoft

Figure 8–30

Exchange Viewer window in its two-pane view

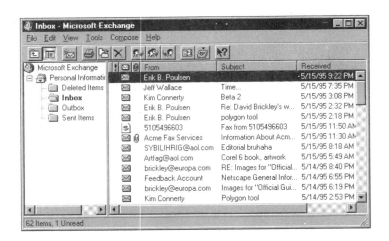

Exchange. You may first be asked which profile you want to use. If so, choose the profile with Microsoft Mail. Depending on how you set up your messaging service to connect when the Exchange opens, you might have a delay while the Exchange dials up a connection or goes out on the LAN to retrieve messages that are at the postoffice. When a connection is completed, the Exchange Viewer window opens, as shown in Figure 8–30. The Viewer looks similar to the Explorer, with a two-pane view containing a folder (or directory) structure on the left, the contents of the active folder on the right, and supporting menus and toolbar.

Outgoing Mail

There are several ways to send a message. You can compose a new message, reply to a received message, or forward to new recipients either received or self-composed messages. The Exchange provides a multi-use form for creating messages that offers a wide variety of options for sending mail. To see that form, click on the New Message button (second button from the left on the toolbar), or choose New Message from the Compose menu, or double-click on an existing message. The sending form appears, as shown in Figure 8–31.

As you can see from the array of menu and toolbar choices, creating a message in the Exchange is not limited by a shortage of features or formatting possibilities. To get a feel for all the features that are

Figure 8–31

Exchange form to create a new message

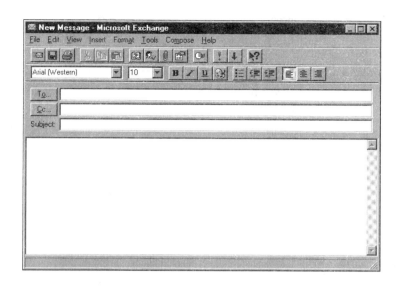

available, the next several sections describe the menu options and their uses. Many of these options are also available from the Viewer menus and perform the same function.

FILE MENU

The File menu options, shown on the left, allow you to perform standard file maintenance tasks on messages. The Send option does as its name implies; it sends the current message to its named recipients. The Save option saves a copy of whatever information you have in the New Message form and displays it as a message in the currently open Viewer folder. Choosing the Save As option opens a dialog box of the same name that lets you save a message in formats that word processors and text editors support: .TXT, .RTF, or .MSG. The .RTF format is the preferred choice because it retains formatting attributes. Figure 8–32 shows an example of how a .RTF-saved message appears in WordPad. The Move and Copy options in the File menu let you transfer a message to other folders, which is discussed in the *Organizing Messages* section later in this chapter. The Print, Delete, and Close options perform standard Windows operations. Clicking on Properties opens the current message Properties dialog box, as shown in Figure 8–33. Besides providing details of the message, you can set sending parameters, such as the level of importance and whether you want receipt notification.

Figure 8–32

*.RTF-formatted
message opened in
WordPad*

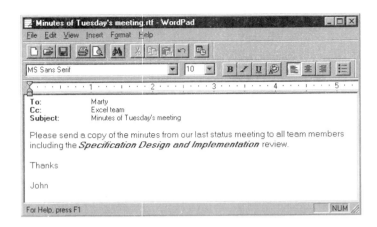

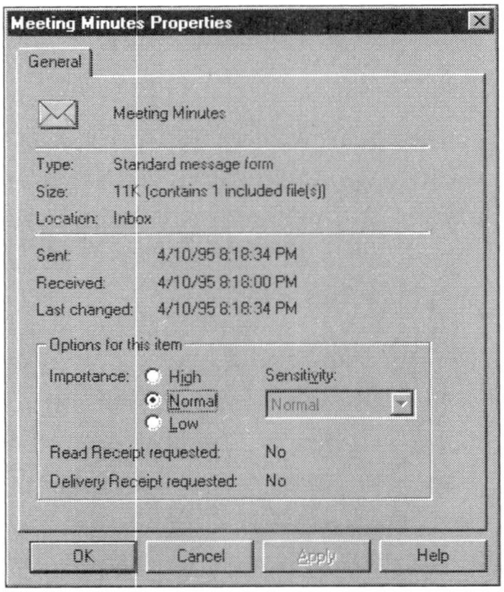

Figure 8–33

*Message
Properties
dialog box*

EDIT MENU

The Edit menu shown next has many familiar options such as Undo, Cut, Copy, Paste, Select All, Find, and Replace. The Paste Special option allows you to insert the contents of the Clipboard, in several formats, into a message. You can then open the message using the source of the paste, such as Microsoft Word 6.0. Alternatively, you can create an OLE (object linking and embedding) link from the source text or picture, so any changes made to the source are automatically reflected in the saved message. The Links option lets you manage any links you create. See Chapter 12 for more information on using OLE. The AutoText option provides a quick means to insert frequently used words, phrases, or even paragraphs.

VIEW MENU

The View menu shown below allows you to selectively display the toolbars and status bar. When sending a message, you need to have addressees, so by default you have displayed the most commonly used send boxes, To and Cc (carbon copy). You can choose to add a Bcc (blind carbon copy) box, whose recipients are hidden to all other recipients. When working on a saved message, the Previous and Next buttons are available to easily open other messages in the same folder.

INSERT MENU

The three options in the Insert menu, shown on the left, allow you to attach files, saved messages, and new or existing objects such as charts or pictures. The Insert Files and Messages dialog boxes are similar to standard browsers. Each dialog box also provides a button to switch quickly between the two types of documents and options to insert the document as text or as a file, as shown in Figure 8–34. The Insert Object dialog box lets you embed OLE graphic objects you create or have saved as files. Saved files and messages can also be linked.

Figure 8–34

*Insert Message
dialog box*

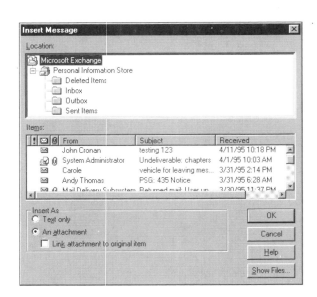

Figure 8–34

*Insert Message
dialog box*

FORMAT MENU

The two Format menu options, shown on the left, open dialog boxes that provide several formatting features that rival those found in many word processors. For quicker access use the formatting toolbar, shown next.

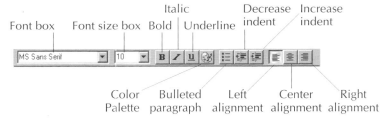

TOOLS MENU

The Tools menu shown below contains options that support addressing, customizing the standard toolbar, and changing properties for the information services in the current profile. The Address Book option opens the Address Book dialog box, shown in Figure 8–35, with your default address book displayed.

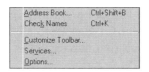

Tip

You determine which address book opens by default by opening the Mail and Fax control panel, selecting the applicable profile, and opening the Addressing tab. Choose an address book in the Show this address book first drop-down list box.

Within the Address Book dialog box, you can change address books, quickly find names by typing them or using the scroll bar, choose recipients by selecting their name and clicking on the applicable sending category—To, Cc, or Bcc (when activated). The New button lets you add to your personal address book new entries that use other e-mail providers such as MSN or the Internet. Details about a person are available from the Properties button, which opens that individual's Properties dialog box, shown in Figure 8–36. Clicking on the Add

Figure 8–35

Address Book dialog box

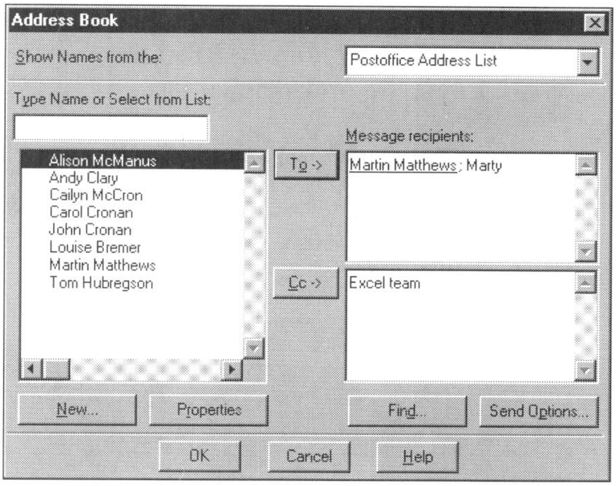

Figure 8–36

Personal data on an individual from the Postoffice Address List

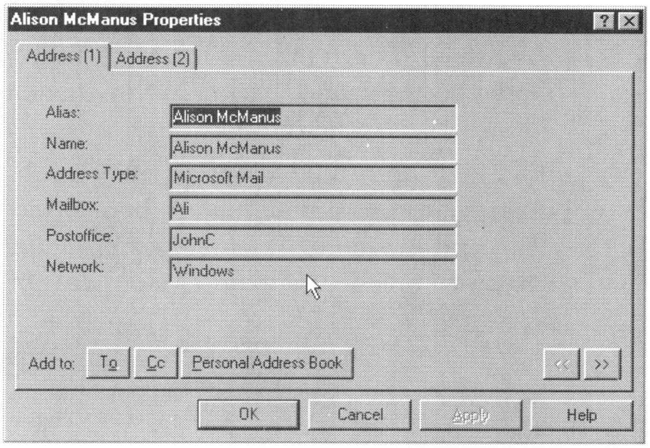

to: Personal Address Book button is the easiest way to add members to your personal address book from an administrator-controlled address book, such as Microsoft Mail or MSN.

Back in the Tools menu, another addressing-related option is Check Names, which checks the names listed in the sending boxes against available address books to ensure the names are listed. If a name is not listed (usually the alias is misspelled), a dialog box opens, notifying you of the discrepancy and allowing you to change it.

You can modify the standard toolbar to display several different buttons from those that appear by default. Clicking on the Customize Toolbar option opens a dialog box of the same name, shown next. You can easily add or remove buttons to display those actions you use most by clicking on the button in the right list before which you want the new button to appear, and then clicking on the new button in the left list. For example, in the next illustration, clicking on Add will place the Delete button immediately after Edit-Paste and to the left of the separating space.

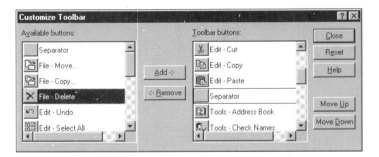

The Services option opens a dialog box that lists the information services in the current profile and allows you to make the same changes to the list as you can in the Mail and Fax control panel's profile Properties dialog box, discussed earlier in this chapter. Using the Services option is a much faster way to modify your profile once you are in the Exchange.

The final option, Options, opens a multitabbed dialog box, as shown next, that consolidates many mail options scattered throughout the Mail and Fax control panel and also adds some new capabilities. You can customize many mailing attributes from this one location.

COMPOSE MENU

The Compose menu shown below has options to create a New Mes-sage to Reply to the Sender or All recipients on received messages, and to Forward messages to recipients who were not on the original distribution.

HELP MENU

The Help menu, shown next, provides online help assistance for the information services in the current profile. Dial-up services will have help available after you connect to them and are not listed in this menu.

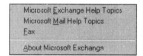

Sending, Replying to, and Forwarding Mail

To illustrate the Microsoft Exchange, look at a typical mailing scenario where a message is sent, replied to, and then forwarded. Refer to the foregoing section on menu options if you need to review the specifics of a particular option or dialog box.

SENDING A MESSAGE

If you don't have the Exchange open, open it now from either its desktop icon or the Start menu, and then use the following instructions to create and send a message:

1. Open the New Message form by clicking on the New Message button on the toolbar.

2. Type in the To and Cc recipients, or open the Address Book by clicking on the To or Cc buttons. Entries taken from an address book or checked in the address book show up underlined.

Separate multiple recipients in the To, Cc, and Bcc boxes with a semicolon.

3. Add any text to the message and then insert a file, message, or object from the Insert menu or by clicking on the Insert File button (the paper clip). The recipient(s) Inbox will display a small paper clip in the message header whenever there is an attachment.

4. Notify the recipient(s) that this is a high-priority message by clicking on the Importance: High button. A red exclamation point will appear in their Inbox in the message header.

5. To let yourself know the recipient(s) have read your message, click on the Read Receipt button.

Your message should look similar to Figure 8–37. When you are satisfied with your own message, click on the Send button.

OPENING AND REPLYING TO MESSAGES

Messages arrive in your Inbox folder when you open the Exchange and periodically thereafter as long as the Exchange is active on your computer. You are notified of new arrivals by an icon appearing next to the Taskbar's clock.

Unread (or unopened) messages appear with their headers in bold in the Viewer. After you have read (or opened) a message, the header returns to a normal style. You can bold or unbold message headers

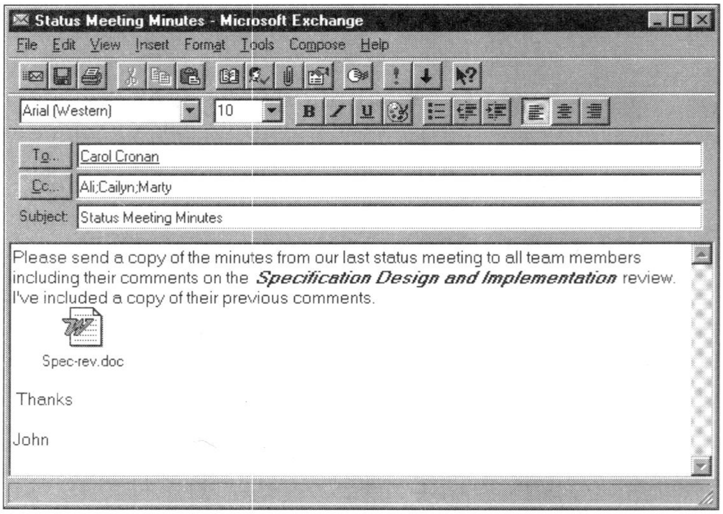

Figure 8–37

Outgoing message example

Figure 8–38

Opened message

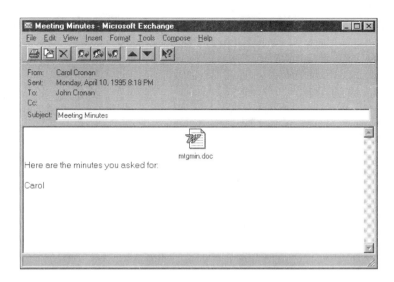

using the applicable Mark as... options in the Edit menu. Open a message using one of the following methods:

- Double-click on a message header.
- Select the header, and choose Open from the Inbox File menu.
- Right-click on the header to open a popup menu, shown on the left, and select Open.

The message opens in a window similar to the send form. An example message is shown in Figure 8–38. This form offers a set of buttons that accommodates tasks you can perform with messages, tasks such as printing and opening any previous or following messages in the current folder.

Clicking on an attached file icon and then choosing File Object from the Edit menu opens a secondary menu that allows you to open the file in its associated program such as Word or 1-2-3; print the file; quickly display the file; save the file using a browser; or rename the file. Choose to reply to the sender or all the original recipients by choosing the applicable Compose menu option or toolbar button. The reply form opens looking similar to Figure 8–39.

You can reply to messages directly from the Viewer by right-clicking on the message header and choosing the reply option you want from the popup menu.

Figure 8–39

A reply window showing the original and reply messages

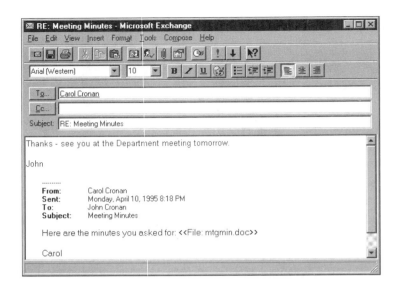

The original message is repeated with space above it for your reply message. If you're using the default Windows color scheme, the reply text appears in blue. You can also add additional To and Cc recipients. Click on the Send button when your message and any attached documents or objects are completed.

FORWARDING MESSAGES

Forwarding is similar to replying except you send messages to recipients who were not on the original distribution. Any composed or received message in a messaging folder can be forwarded. Messages can be forwarded directly from the Inbox Viewer or from an opened message form in the same manner as a replied message. The forwarding message is displayed in the sending form text area with space above it for any forwarding comments, as shown in Figure 8–40. The toolbars appear as they do for new messages, including the Forward button, as you can see next.

Managing Messages

The real power of the Exchange lies in its organizational features. You can store messages and faxes in cascading folders, sort messages by their message header categories, change which columns of header information to see, and list only specific messages through a find browser.

Figure 8–40

Message and comments ready for forwarding

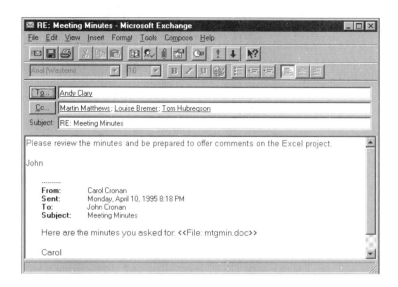

STORING MESSAGES

The Exchange folders and messages within those folders are saved in a personal information store. The personal information store is a file with the .PST extension that contains a database of all your messaging information. The personal information store file is analogous to the .MMF file used in Windows for Workgroups. Upon upgrading to Windows 95, .MMF files are converted to the .PST format and are available for use. The personal information file is named Mailbox.pst and is located in your Exchange folder.

When backing up critical files, include Mailbox.pst. To quickly locate your personal information store open the Start menu, choose Find, Files or Folders, and search for the file named Mailbox.pst.

Within the personal information store, the Exchange creates four folders: Deleted Items, Inbox, Outbox, and Sent Items. These serve most immediate needs. However, as your inventory of messages grows, you may want to clear out the Inbox and move the messages into more meaningful locations. New folders are created by selecting the folder one level above the level of the new folder. Choose New Folder from the File menu, and give it a name. You can create sub-levels of folders just as you do in the Explorer.

Messages are easily moved from one folder to another by dragging them from one pane of the Viewer to the other. Pressing the Ctrl key

Figure 8–41

Several levels of personal folders

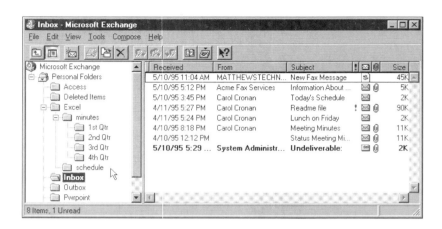

as you drag them copies the message. You can also use Move and Copy options found on the File menu or the popup menu opened by right-clicking on a message. Figure 8–41 shows several levels of added folders.

VIEWING MESSAGES

Since messages are part of a database (your personal information store), you can view them in a number of different arrangements: according to column headings, several layers of more specific categories or groups, and ascending and descending order. Finally, you can find messages that fit a set of parameters you choose. The View and Tools menus contain options that allow you to customize how you view your messages and faxes.

Organizing Columns The View menu Columns option lets you choose the header columns that appear on the right pane of the Viewer. Figure 8–42 shows the Columns dialog box with lists of available and shown columns. Each column's width is displayed when it is selected in the Show the following columns list to let you know approximately how much space that column is using.

Change the width of a column by pointing on the intersection to the right of a column, wait for the mouse pointer to change into a cross, and then drag left to decrease or drag right to increase the column size.

Grouping Messages The View menu Group By option lets you group messages in the current folder by any of the columns listed in

Figure 8–42

Customizing the columns displayed in the Viewer

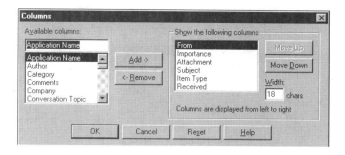

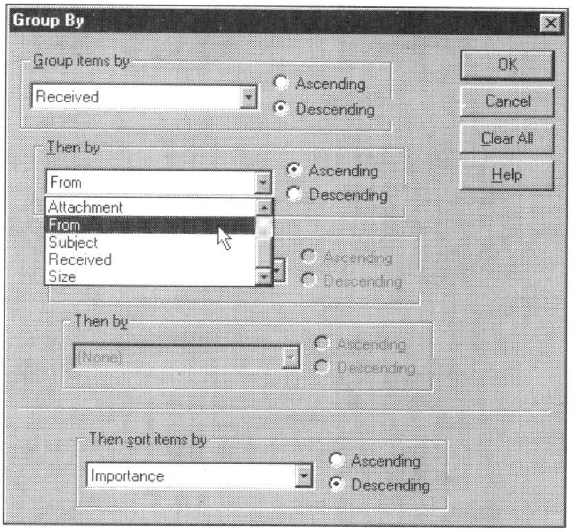

Figure 8–43

The Group By dialog box

the Group items by drop-down list box, as you can see in Figure 8–43. This lets you combine, for example, all messages from a particular sender. The adjacent option buttons, for this header, default to an ascending order for the messages within this group. You can subgroup the messages into three more levels and then sort subsequently after that. An example of grouping by sender, importance, whether there is an attached file, and when received is shown in Figure 8–44. Notice that each group level can be expanded or contracted by clicking on the plus or minus sign.

Sorting Messages The View menu Sorting option provides a quick way to list all files in a folder by specific categories, that is, by the current column headers. You may need to clear any groupings you have set up in the Group By dialog box before you can effectively sort the messages in the folder.

Figure 8–44

*Grouping
by sender,
importance,
attached files,
and when received*

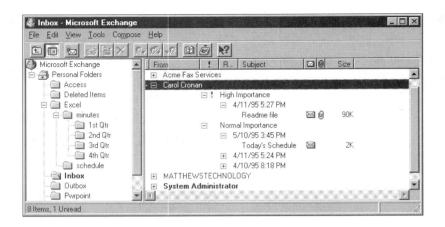

Finding Messages   Finding messages with the Tools menu Find option offers the most precise manner to see a specific message. Much like a query in database terminology, finding just lists those items that meet the criteria you establish. The Find dialog box, shown next, provides text and check boxes to enter your search parameters. The Advanced button opens another dialog box that provides even more specific searching opportunities.

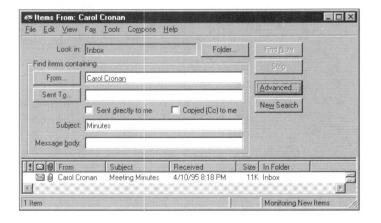

Microsoft Fax

Microsoft Fax is the faxing capability included with Windows 95, and it integrates nicely with the messaging scheme provided by the

Exchange. In fact, the two vehicles, messaging and faxing, share many common tools such as addressing. Microsoft Fax takes full advantage of the Windows 95 architecture to provide the following features:

- Send faxes from a number of points within Windows 95 or your applications
- Send editable text to other computers that use Microsoft Fax
- Share a fax modem throughout a network
- View faxes quickly as either thumbnails or full pages through the Fax Viewer
- Create custom cover pages with the Fax Cover Page Editor
- Send sensitive documents securely using advanced encryption techniques

Sending Faxes

You are never more than a mouse click or two away from being able to send a fax. If you followed the steps earlier in this chapter to set up profiles, you may have already established some faxing properties that affect how your faxes are sent. You can return to the Microsoft Fax Properties dialog box through the Mail and Fax control panel or from the Exchange Viewer. In the Viewer, choose Microsoft Fax Tools from the Tools menu, and click on Options.

The next three sections describe the different ways to start the Compose New Fax wizard, which walks you through sending a fax. The ways are from the Exchange, from the Explorer, and from an application.

SENDING A FAX FROM THE EXCHANGE

You can send a message and attached files as a fax from the Exchange (Inbox) Viewer by using the following steps:

1. From the Viewer choose New Fax from the Compose menu to open the Compose New Fax wizard. Determine if you need to change your dialing properties, and then click on Next.

2. The second dialog box opens as shown in Figure 8–45. Type in the recipient's name and fax number, or select them from an address book. Faxes can be sent to multiple recipients by clicking on the Add to List button after the original recipient's

Figure 8–45

Entering fax destination information

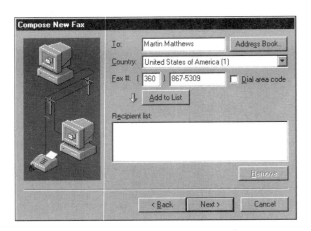

name and number is entered and then repeating the process. Click on Next when you are done.

3. Decide if you want a cover page, and if so, select it from the list. Creating cover pages is covered later in this chapter. Clicking on the Options button provides a dialog box of more sending choices that you saw earlier in this chapter as Figure 8–20. Click on Next.

4. The next dialog box provides text boxes for the fax subject and cover page notes. The subject appears in the recipients Inbox when the fax arrives. After you type in your text, click on Next.

5. The next dialog box gives you the opportunity to attach files to your fax. Any attached file(s) will print out along with the cover page and notes. Choose Next to arrive at the final dialog box. Click on Finish to send the fax.

After a short delay, you'll hear the number being dialed, and a new icon will appear next to the Status bar's clock to let you know faxing is in progress. You will be kept informed of the status of your transmission throughout its transfer in the Microsoft Fax Status dialog box.

SENDING A FAX FROM THE EXPLORER

The Explorer offers two ways to send a fax. In the first method you create a shortcut icon on your desktop by dragging the Microsoft Fax icon from the Printers windows to your desktop. Next, simply drag a

Figure 8–46

Dragging a file to be faxed from the Explorer to the desktop

file from the Explorer to the Microsoft Fax shortcut icon on your desktop, shown in Figure 8–46. The program associated with the file type opens the document and then subsequently opens the Compose New Fax wizard. Alternatively, you can right-click on a file in the Explorer and choose Send To in the popup menu and then Fax Recipient to open the Compose New Fax wizard.

SENDING A FAX FROM A PROGRAM

You have two choices to send a fax when working in a program such as a word processor. Programs that conform to the Windows 95 MAPI messaging interface can open the Compose New Fax wizard when you choose Microsoft Fax as a printer. Instead of printing to a physical printer, the document is *printed* to the wizard. Also, you can open the Start menu from the Taskbar, then choose Programs, Send To, and Fax Recipient from the secondary menu.

CREATING COVER PAGES

Microsoft Fax provides a short list of five commonly used cover page formats to get you up and going: Urgent, Confidential, General Purpose, Generic, and For Your Information. If you find reasons to

Figure 8–47

*For Your
Information fax
cover sheet*

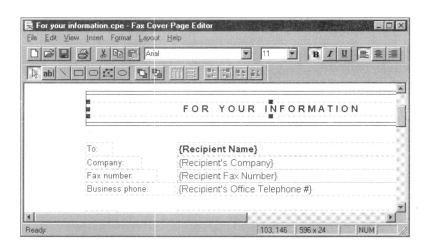

modify them or create your own, the Fax Cover Page Editor provides ample features to add text, graphics, and address book information. To open the editor, click on the Start menu; choose Program, Accessories, and then Fax Cover Page Editor. Figure 8–47 shows the editor with the For Your Information sample displayed.

The Fax Cover Page Editor offers a wide range of drawing and editing tools to make changes a simple process. If you are familiar with desktop publishing and drawing programs such as Microsoft Publisher, you will find the design techniques very similar. Besides creating your own text and graphics with the available buttons on the toolbars, you can insert objects and special fields that import address book information. Each of the fields within braces (curly brackets) are keyed to text boxes in your address books. By choosing from the Insert menu the three categories of address book data—Recipient, Sender, and Message—you can merge already stored information on your cover sheet. Experiment with the provided formats, and save any designs so they will be available when you next open the Compose New Fax wizard.

Receiving Faxes

To receive a fax you must have started the Microsoft Exchange by double-clicking on the Inbox or by selecting it from the Start Programs menu. The fax icon (a miniature fax machine) will appear next to the clock in the Taskbar. When you see that icon, if your modem is connected and turned on, you are ready to receive a fax. In the Fax

Figure 8–48

Newly arrived fax displayed in the Exchange Inbox

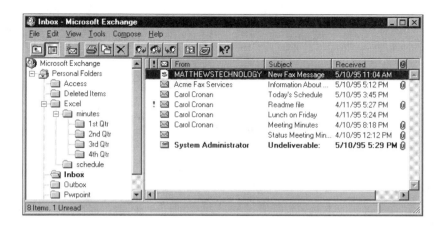

Properties dialog box you made the choice of how you wanted Microsoft Fax to answer an incoming call: after a set number of rings, manually, or not answer. You don't need to perform any action if you chose the first or third option. If you chose Manually, the Microsoft Fax Status dialog box appears when an incoming call is received, as shown next. You can then choose to accept the call if you are expecting a fax or to hang up Microsoft Fax and accept the voice call. You can open the Microsoft Fax Status box at any time by clicking on the fax icon next to the Taskbar clock.

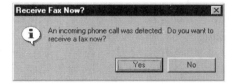

Incoming faxes appear in the Exchange Inbox along with any other messages you might have, as shown in Figure 8–48. Now you can view editable messages and print them as you would any message.

Faxes that arrive in noneditable format are opened in the Fax Viewer, shown in Figure 8–49. You can view faxes one page at a time or with all pages in small thumbnails. The thumbnails allow you to determine which page(s) you want to see in more detail.

Besides receiving a fax from another user, you can request a fax from the growing number of fax service companies that provide information such as software support and promotional material. Clicking on

Figure 8–49

Opened fax in the Fax Viewer

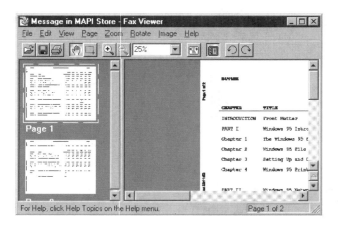

the Exchange Tools menu, choosing Microsoft Fax Tools and then Request a Fax opens the Request a Fax wizard. The wizard guides you through the steps to retrieve available documents or to type in a specific document name and its password, if applicable.

Sharing

There are two components to a shared fax modem: the fax server whose computer contains the fax modem, and the fax clients who use the services of the shared fax modem as if it were their own. You set up the fax server from the Modem tab in the Microsoft Fax Properties dialog box, provide a share name in the text box of the same name, and set additional sharing properties by clicking on the Properties button. Any client desiring to use the fax server also needs to open the Modem tab (on their own computer) and use the following steps:

1.   Click on the Add button, and choose Network fax server in the Add a Fax Modem dialog box. Click on OK.

2.   In the Connect To Network Fax Server dialog box, type in the shared path to the network fax server. This will look like \\Computer name.

3.   Back in the Modem tab, select Network Fax Server, and click on Set as Active Fax Modem.

Send faxes as described in the previous section, *Sending Faxes.* Incoming faxes arrive at the fax server's Inbox and are then routed as standard mail messages.

Security

There are two types of security encryption methods available to send secure faxes:

- Password-protected
- Key encrypted

Faxes must be in an editable format (a text or word processing format) to use these security measures. Password-protected faxes are assigned a password by the sender. The receiver must supply the same password to open the fax. Key encrypted faxes involve exchanging software *keys* with the recipients to ensure only the sender and recipient(s) are eligible to open the fax. Key encryption is set up from the Exchange Tools menu's Microsoft Fax Tools option. Clicking on Advanced Security in the secondary menu opens the Advanced Fax Security dialog box where you can create a key set.

Security features, password or key, are activated through the Options button in the Compose New Fax wizard (below the section where you choose whether to attach a cover page). Clicking on the Security button in the Send Options for this Message dialog box opens the Message Security Options dialog box, shown in Figure 8–50. From here you can choose whether to activate a particular security measure.

Figure 8–50

Choosing a particular security measure

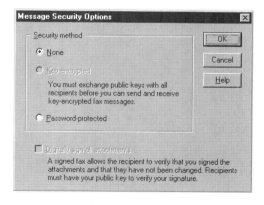

The Microsoft Network and Online Services

O f all the uses for a modem, online services are the most far-reaching. *Online services*, or *information services*, provide a connection using your computer and modem that allows you not only to get a lot of information but also to perform many functions such as mail exchange, chatting with others, shopping, trading stock, and making airplane reservations. For that reason, the term *online services* is preferred to *information services*.

An online service combines information with communication. Its information side is hard to imagine. Most online services provide access to vast amounts of information including a number of international libraries; encyclopedias; extensive databases of reference material for finance, law, literature, medicine, and science; and online access to many publications, journals, and newspapers. You have already seen in Chapter 8 how you can use an online service as a postoffice through which you can send and receive mail to transfer both messages and files. Equally important are the many specialized *forums* where you can send and receive messages and files on a particular topic as well as read and *download* (copy from the service to your computer) those messages and files placed in the forum by others. A good example of forums are those that provide customer support for computer hardware and software.

You've probably heard of several online services. One of the oldest, and now by far the largest, is CompuServe Information Service. Others include America Online (AOL), Genie, Prodigy, and the new Microsoft Network. In all of these cases one company owns all of the computers and receiving communications equipment and makes all of the decisions on what to offer and how to offer it. One online service (and it's arguable whether it fits that term) is the Internet. The Internet is a network of literally thousands of independent organizations (companies, universities, and governmental units) tied together with high-speed communications lines, each of which owns one or more computers with associated communications equipment, and each deciding what they are going to offer and how they will offer it.

In this chapter you'll explore the Microsoft Network and the Internet as examples of online services. You'll see how to get started using a service, how to get around (*navigate*) in them, and how to get the most use of them.

The Microsoft Network Online Service

The Microsoft Network (MSN) is the newest online service, making its debut with Windows 95. It therefore makes full use of the Windows 95 graphical user interface and takes advantage of the multitasking and multithreaded design provided in Windows 95. This allows MSN to carry out several tasks at the same time and to have a look and feel similar to other parts of Windows 95. MSN's offerings, though, are very similar to CompuServe, AOL, and other online services, including the following:

- **Bulletin boards**, where you can exchange messages and files on a particular subject

- **Chat rooms**, where you can *talk* via your keyboard with other people currently signed on to MSN or observe ongoing conversations

- **Electronic mail**, which you can send and receive with other MSN members as well as anyone connected to the Internet

- **File libraries**, where you can download articles, graphics, programs, and product support information to your own computer

- **Information services**, where you can get news, sports, weather, and product information
- **Internet access**, where you can send and receive mail, participate in newsgroups, and browse the World Wide Web
- **Microsoft Information**, where you can get both new product information as well as support on products you currently have

Also, like other online services, MSN offers worldwide access with local phone numbers in 40 countries covering a large part of the population. In the United States, almost 100 percent of the population can connect via a local phone number. Payment for MSN services in the United States is by means of one of four credit cards (Visa, MasterCard, American Express, and Discover) whose number you enter at the time you sign up for MSN.

Signing Up for MSN

In order to use MSN you must sign up by giving Microsoft your name, address, your phone number, and a credit card number to pay for the service. Also, you need to find out what phone number your computer will call to connect to the service. (Initially you use an 800 number, but once signed up for MSN, you must use a phone number in your local area.) If you choose to install the Microsoft Network, you can sign up by double-clicking on the MSN icon on your desktop.

First, you must have a modem and phone line connected to your computer, and you must have set up the modem either during Windows 95 Setup or through the Modems control panel (see "Setting Up a Modem" in Chapter 7). If you did not install the MSN software when you set up Windows 95, you can use the Add/Remove Programs control panel and select the Windows Setup tab, click on The Microsoft Network so a check mark appears in the check box (as shown in Figure 9–1) and then click on OK.

With a modem and MSN software installed on your computer and the modem connected to a phone line, you are ready to sign up for the service. You'll need a credit card number and expiration date, and a user name and password that you'll want to use. Use these instructions now to sign up for MSN.

The Microsoft Network

1. Double-click on the Microsoft Network desktop icon. The opening MSN window will appear, as shown in Figure 9–2.

Figure 9–1

Installing the Microsoft Network

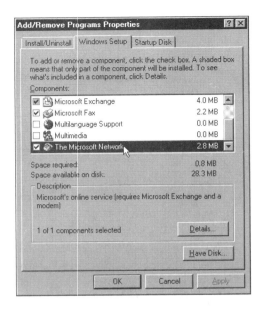

Figure 9–2

The opening Microsoft Network window

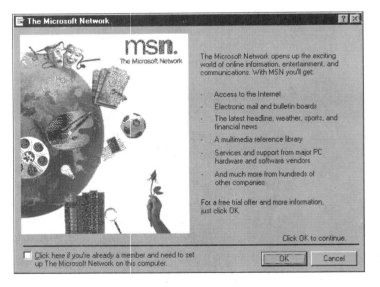

2.   Click on OK, enter your area code and the first three digits of your phone number, click on OK a second time, and then click on Connect. MSN will dial its 800 number; get the latest software, product information, and phone numbers; and then disconnect. The initial MSN sign-up window will appear, as you can see in Figure 9–3.

Figure 9–3

Initial Microsoft Network sign-up window

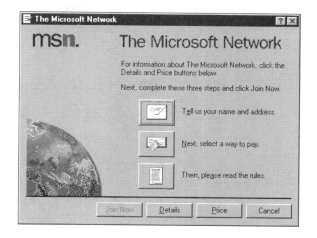

Figure 9–4

MSN's name and address entry window

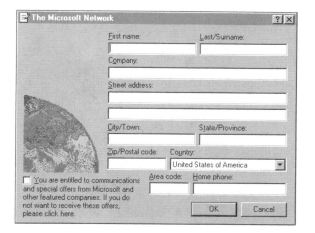

3. First click on the Details and then the Price buttons to learn more about MSN, especially what it costs. When you are done looking at the information, and if you still want to go ahead, click on the top button to enter your name and address. A data entry window similar to Figure 9–4 opens.

4. Enter all of the information requested and then click on OK. Back at the initial sign-up window, click on the middle button to select a way to pay. A second data entry window will open, like you see in Figure 9–5.

5. Select the method that you want to use to pay for your MSN services, enter the necessary information, and click on OK.

Figure 9–5

MSN's method of payment entry window

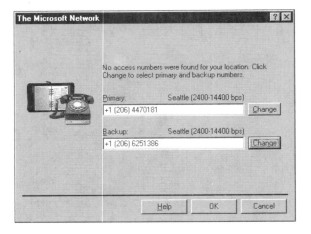

Figure 9–6

Phone number selection dialog box

When you return to the initial sign-up window, click on the bottom button and read the membership agreement. If you wish to proceed, click on I Agree; if not, click on I Don't Agree.

6. Back at the initial sign-up window, if you are proceeding, click on Join Now; otherwise, click on Cancel. With a go-ahead you will be shown primary and backup phone numbers for your location in a selection dialog box that looks like Figure 9–6.

7. If the phone numbers do not look like the best choices to you, or if you are not shown any numbers, you can choose new ones by clicking on Change and selecting the country, state or region, and access number that is correct for you. Then click on OK and, if necessary, repeat the process for the backup

phone number. When you are done, click on OK to complete the phone number selection.

8. Click on Connect, and MSN will then use the primary phone number to connect you to the service. Upon being connected, you will be asked to enter a member ID name and a password. Your member ID can be anything you want it to be as long as it is unique. Your password also can be anything you want it to be as long as it is at least eight characters long and no more than 16. When you are done, click on OK and then on Finish when you see the congratulatory message. That completes the installation.

The Microsoft Network Environment

The Microsoft Network has many unfamiliar objects and features. The purpose of this section is to look at many of the MSN objects and determine their function. First, though, look at how you will normally sign on.

SIGNING ON TO MSN

When you first double-clicked on the MSN desktop icon, you got the window you saw in Figure 9–2 that began the process of signing you up for MSN. After you have completed the sign-up process, when you double-click on the MSN icon, you get the Sign In dialog box, shown in Figure 9–7. This dialog box contains the member ID and the password that you set during sign-up. The member ID stays in the dialog box from one session to another, although you can change it to another

Figure 9–7

MSN Sign In dialog box

Figure 9–8

*Connection
Settings
dialog box*

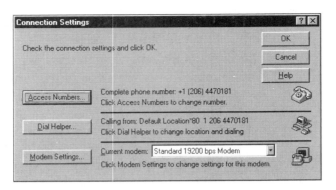

ID at any time. The default for the password is that you enter it each time. You can, if you wish, click on Remember my password, and you will not have to enter it each time (see the Caution in this section).

 **If others use your computer and might possibly sign on to MSN when you don't want them to, do not activate Remember my password.**

The Settings button opens the Connection Settings dialog box, shown in Figure 9–8. Here you can change the MSN access number using a dialog box similar to what you used when you originally signed up. Also, you can change the dialing codes you need to use, as well as your modem settings, using the same dialog boxes you saw in Chapter 7.

 Back in the Sign In dialog box, strange as it may seem, you use the Connect button to connect to MSN. When you successfully do that, you will see the MSN Central window, shown in Figure 9–9. From MSN Central, all of MSN opens up to you, as you'll see in the next section. Just in case the MSN Central window is not enough to tell you that you are online with MSN, two icons appear in the Taskbar next to the clock, as shown on the left. The first is the standard modem icon to tell you the modem is functioning, and the second is the MSN icon that tells you are online. If you have mail waiting for you, you will first see a message box telling you so and asking if you want to open your Inbox, like this:

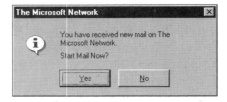

Figure 9–9

MSN Central window

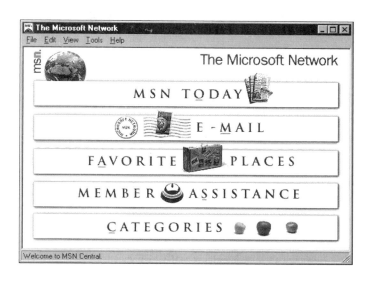

Figure 9–10

The Microsoft Network Address Book

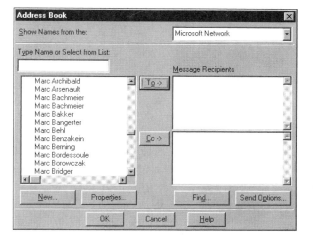

Note

To receive mail from MSN you must have MSN in your active Exchange profile. See Chapter 8 on how to do this.

If you click on Yes in the mail waiting message box, your Inbox will open and display your mail. If you do not see your mail appear, open the Tools menu in the Inbox, and click on Remote Mail and The Microsoft Network. With your Inbox open, you can do everything you can do with the mail system, as you saw in Chapter 8. One thing is different: if you create a new message and click on the To button, the MSN Address book will be available, showing everybody who has an MSN account, as you can see in Figure 9–10.

 The Exchange Address Book shows all of the people who have MSN accounts.

USING MSN CENTRAL

The MSN Central window provides a central transfer point to go from one area of MSN to another. It has five buttons that allow you to quickly get to the major areas of MSN. These buttons open the following areas:

- **MSN Today** opens the online viewer, where you can see and access current topics and a calendar of events.

- **E-Mail** opens your Inbox window, which allows you to send and receive e-mail.

- **Favorite Places** opens a folder where you can place and then quickly access services and folders that are important to you.

- **Member Assistance** opens a folder containing folders, files, and services related to member assistance.

- **Categories** opens a folder containing other folders on major topics in which people are interested; each folder contains other folders on subtopics as well as files and services related to each topic.

In the above descriptions, the phrase "files, folders, and services" is repeatedly used. Files and folders are the standard Windows files and folders. *Folders* contain other objects including other folders, files, and services. *Files* are objects that you download to your computer or display in WordPad or other word processors. *Services*, on the other hand, refer to a set of objects that are unique to MSN. Services include the following:

- **Forums,** which are really folders that contain one or more bulletin boards, chat rooms, file libraries, suggestions boxes, and possibly additional folders, all related to a particular topic

- **Bulletin boards**, where you can post and read messages; also called *BBS*s for bulletin board services

- **Chat rooms,** where you can carry on a live conversation using your keyboard

- **Kiosks,** where general read-only information is posted for you to read; normally the information describes the forum, its rules, and its manager

- **File library**, where you find and download files to your computer
- **Suggestion box**, a specialized, sometimes write-only, bulletin board where you can post suggestions about the forum

The MSN Central includes what on the surface looks to be a fairly standard set of menus. Within the menus, though, there are a number of unique options. These same menus and options are used throughout MSN

File Menu The File menu, shown below on the left for the MSN Central and on the right for subsidiary folders, provides the unique options of adding the selected item to the Favorite Places folder, and of signing into or out of MSN.

Edit Menu The unique option in the MSN Edit menu, shown below on the left for the MSN Central and on the right for subsidiary folders, is Go to, which allows you to jump to the MSN Central window, the Favorite Places window, or other locations. If you select Other Location, the Go To Service dialog box opens where you can type a Go word to transfer to a particular area or service. For example, if you type CompGame you will directly open the Computer Games forum in the Computers and Software category. You can find the Go word for a service by right-clicking on the service and opening the Properties dialog box, an example of which you can see in Figure 9–11.

Figure 9–11

*Properties dialog
box for a service
showing the
Go word*

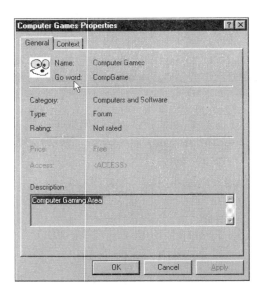

 You can find the Go word for a service by right-clicking on the service and opening the Properties dialog box.

View Menu The View menu, shown below on the left for the MSN Central and on the right for subsidiary folders, has several unique options in MSN.

The Options option of the View menu in the MSN Central or in subsidiary folders opens the Options for The Microsoft Network dialog box, shown next. This lets you set several options that determine how MSN will operate. The automatic disconnect time is important, because if you forget to sign off of MSN and leave your computer, you could run up a large bill without meaning to. Showing MSN Today takes extra time while you are bringing up MSN, so you may not want to show it.

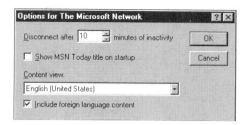

 Set the disconnect time to a fairly short time so that if you forget to sign off, you won't run up too large a bill.

Tools Menu The Tools menu, shown next, is the same for both the MSN Central and the subsidiary folders. All of its options are unique and important.

The Find option opens a submenu that is the same as the Tools, Find option in the Explorer. This allows you to find files and folders on your computer, find computers on the network, and find items on MSN. The Password option opens the Change Your Password dialog box, shown in Figure 9–12. In order to change your password, you must first correctly enter your current password and then type a new password twice.

Figure 9–12

Change Your Password dialog box

The Billing option opens the submenu shown on the left. The Payment Method option in the submenu opens a dialog box where you can elect to change either your name and address or your payment method. These, in turn, open the same dialog boxes that you used to originally sign up for the Microsoft Network (shown in Figures 9–4 and 9–5).

The Summary of Charges option in the Billing submenu opens your Online Statement, similar to the one in Figure 9–13. To fill in the statement, click on Get Details, select the period you want to see, and click on OK.

The Subscriptions option in the Billing submenu opens the Subscriptions tab of the Online Statement, as shown in Figure 9–14. This shows and allows you to change the subscription plan and any special credits that are the basis of your current billing. If you click on the plan, you'll see a description of it. You may be able to change to other plans by clicking on Change.

The File Transfer Status option of the Tools menu opens the File Transfer Status window, shown in Figure 9–15. This allows you to manage the queue of files that you are transferring to your computer. Through the File menu and toolbar in this window you can pause and restart the transfer process, you can remove a file from the queue, and you can tell MSN to complete the transfer process and

Figure 9–13

Online Statement showing current charges

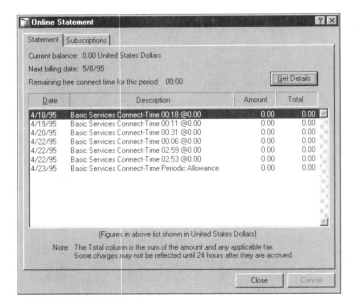

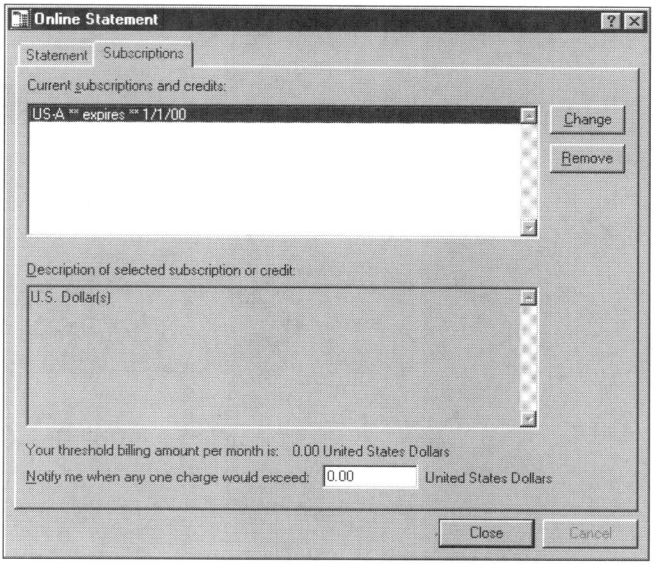

Figure 9–14

Subscriptions tab of the Online Statement

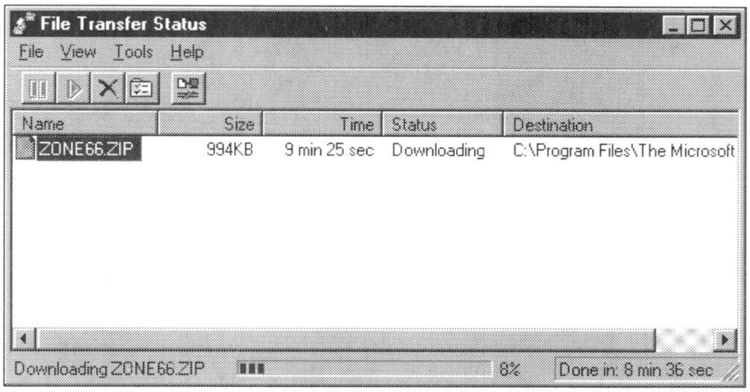

Figure 9–15

File Transfer Status window

then automatically disconnect. If you click on the second from the right button in the toolbar while in the File Transfer Status window, you will open the Options dialog box, which you can see in Figure 9–16. Here you can hold files in the queue until you ready to download them, automatically decompress compressed files, and delete compressed files after decompressing them. Most importantly, the File Transfer Options dialog box is the place you can identify the folder on your computer where, by default, downloaded files are placed. This location starts out as `C:\Program Files\The Microsoft Network\Transferred Files`. You can change it to any folder you wish.

Figure 9–16

File Transfer Options dialog box

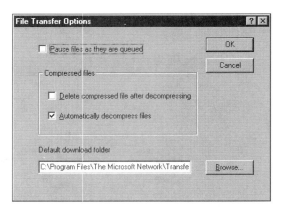

The Connection Settings option of the Tools menu opens the same Connection Settings dialog box that you saw while going over the sign in process (see Figure 9–9).

Help Menu The Help menu, shown below, is the same for both the MSN Central and the subsidiary folders. Its only unique option, Member Support Numbers, provides worldwide phone numbers to support the users of MSN.

Toolbar buttons The toolbar, shown below, that is used in all MSN subsidiary folders and is similar to that in the MSN Central, has four unique buttons. The purpose of each of these is shown in Table 9–1:

Exploring the Microsoft Network

Take a few minutes now and explore a small part of what the Microsoft Network contains. In the process, you'll see how the various services operate and how to make best use of them. Start by clicking on the Categories button in the MSN Central. The Categories windows will open, as you see in Figure 9–17. Here you see the categories of information and services that are available on MSN. Double-click on one of the categories, for example, Computers and Software. The

Button	Purpose
⌂	Go to the MSN Central window
✳	Go to the Favorite Places window
⇤	Sign off of the Microsoft Network
⊞	Add to your Favorite Places folder

Table 9–1.
MSN unique toolbar buttons

Figure 9–17
The Categories window

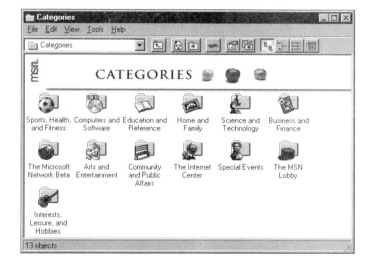

window for that category will open, as shown in 9–18. Double-click on a folder, which at this level is probably a forum. For example, Computer Games, which doesn't use the folder icon, is still a forum, as you can see when its window opens similar to what is shown in Figure 9–19. The Computer Games window shows each of the normal services in a forum. These services are described next.

SUBSIDIARY FOLDERS

Related
Internet
Newsgroups

Subsidiary folders may contain anything a folder can contain including any of the services, files, and of course more folders.

BULLETIN BOARDS

Most bulletin boards, or BBSs, are subdivided into specific topics. For example, if you double-click on the Computer Games BBS, a window

Figure 9–18

*A particular
category window*

Figure 9–19

A forum window

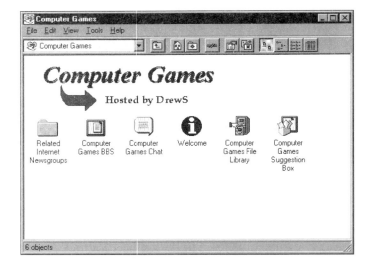

Computer
Games BBS

opens showing you a list of subjects related to computer games. If you then double-click on a subject, you get a list of posted messages showing their subject and author, as you can see in Figure 9–20. By double-clicking on a message, you can open and read it in a message window (shown in Figure 9–21) which is very similar to the Exchange message window. Once a message is open, you can store a copy of it on your computer by choosing Save As from the File menu and selecting a path and file name from the browser. You can also reply to

Figure 9–20

Bulletin board service

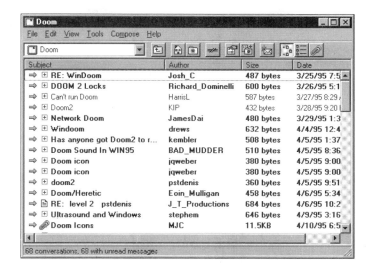

Figure 9–21

Bulletin board message

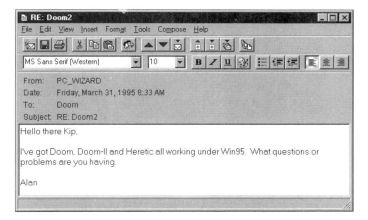

the message on the BBS, create a new message that you want to post, or go to other adjoining messages in this BBS.

When you create a new BBS message (by clicking on the New Message button or selecting New Message from the Compose menu, typing the message, and clicking on the Post button or selecting Post Message from the File menu), you add another *message* to the BBS. When you reply to a message, you add to a *conversation* in which all replies are hidden behind the original message. You can tell that a message has one or more replies because its icon will have a plus sign in it. If you click on the icon, you will see the first reply; if you hold down (Shift) while you click on the icon, you will open all replies.

Figure 9–22

Search form for searching MSN

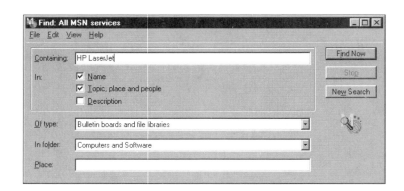

You can expand an entire BBS conversation by holding down Shift **while clicking on the icon for the lead message in the conversation.**

To help you find information in a BBS or a file library, you can sort the information in ascending order by clicking on the button at the top of the column you want to sort (Subject, Author, Size, and Date; see Figure 9–20). Also, you can search one particular BBS folder or all services in MSN using the Find option, either from the Start menu or from a Tools menu. For example, if you wanted to search for HP LaserJet in all BBSs and file libraries in the Computers and Software category, you would fill in a search request like the one shown in Figure 9–22.

CHAT ROOMS

The chat room window has three panes, as you can see in Figure 9–23. The largest pane in the upper left shows the conversation as it takes place. The smaller window at the bottom shows what you type. When you are ready, you can post what you type by clicking on Send. If you are not sure how to get started, watch for a while and see how others are doing it, then jump in and say hi, ask a question, or offer a comment. The window on the right shows the people who are currently signed on to the chat session (*spectators*). The rightmost three buttons on the toolbar are unique to a chat room and have the functions described in Table 9–2.

To change your own Member Properties entry, open E-Mail from MSN Central, choose Address book from the Tools menu, click on the magnifying glass button to bring up Find, enter your ID name, and

Figure 9–23

*Chat room
window*

Table 9–2

*Unique
Chat room
toolbar buttons*

Icon	Name	Function
	Show Spectators	Turns off spectators in the spectators pane in special read-only chat sessions where there is a panel discussion
	Member Properties	Opens the Member Properties dialog box with additional information about the selected spectator, as shown in Figure 9–24
	Ignore Spectator	Turns off messages from the selected spectator

**click OK. When your name is displayed, right-click on it and choose
Properties. Note that the date of birth should be in the format
MM/DD/YY.**

The chat window also has several unique menu options. The File menu
allows you to save the chat session you have observed with the Save
History and Save History As options (the latter to rename it). The View
menu allows you to turn on or off the showing of spectators and the
ignoring of spectators. The Tools menu allows you to select all the
members, to invert that selection, to designate selected members as spectators or participants, and to open the Chat Options dialog box, shown
in Figure 9–24. In the Chat Options dialog box you can turn on or off
the display of people coming to and going from the chat room, automatically save the chat history, and insert blank lines between messages.

Figure 9–24

Chat Options dialog box

Figure 9–25

A kiosk's text file in Word for Windows

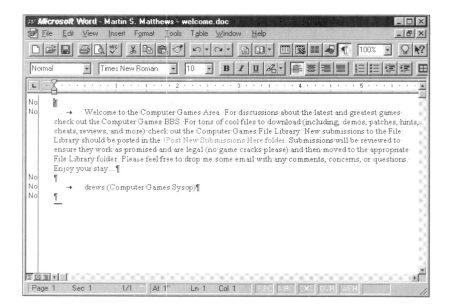

INFORMATION KIOSKS

Welcome

An information kiosk is a text file that, when you double-click on it, is downloaded to your computer and causes WordPad or another word processing program to load and display the file, as shown in Figure 9–25. If this does not work for you (for example, you see a message that the file is being downloaded, but then nothing is displayed) the file's type is not properly associated with either WordPad or another word processing program. Files to be downloaded, as discussed here (not BBS attachments), are files with either .DOC or .RTF extensions. Use the instructions in Chapter 2 (see "Associating Files") to associate these file types with the word processor of your choice.

When you are done reading the contents of a kiosk, close the word processing program, and you will be back in MSN. When you do that, though, the files are not saved unless you do it *before* you close the word processor.

FILE LIBRARY

Computer
Games File
Library

A file library is a special, read-only BBS, as you can see in Figure 9–26. Most of the messages in a file library contain attached files, as shown in Figure 9–27, which you can download to your computer using one of the techniques described in the next section. You can

Figure 9–26

*File library form
of a BBS*

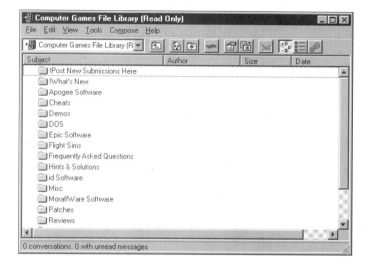

Figure 9–27

*Downloadable
files attached
to a message*

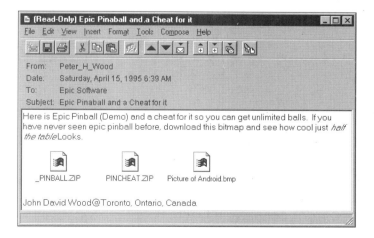

upload files to some libraries by attaching them to a message that is a reply to a message with the subject !Post New Submissions Here, which you can see in Figure 9–26.

Downloading Files   There are several ways to download files depending on what you want do with them. If you want to download a file and immediately load it into a program to read or use, then you can do one of the following: (In this case, the file will not be saved on your computer unless you separately do so in the program you use to open it.)

- Double-click on the file.
- Right-click on the file, choose File Object, and select Open.
- Click on the file, open the Edit menu, choose File Object, and click on Open.

If you want to download a file and immediately save it as a file on your computer, then you can use one of the following techniques: (In this case, the file will be saved on your computer, and you must take separate steps to load and use it.)

- Open the message, open the File menu, choose Save As, select Attachments, click on the file you want downloaded, and click on OK.
- Right-click on the file, choose File Object, and select Download.
- Click on the file, open the Edit menu, choose File Object, and click on Download.
- Click on the file, open the Edit menu, choose File Object, click on Properties to see the file's properties (size, download time, and price) before downloading, and then click on Download.

 Unless you specify otherwise, the files you download and save on your computer will be saved by default in the C:\Program Files\The Microsoft Network\Transferred Files folder.

When you download a file, the File Transfer Status window opens. You read about this window in the earlier section "Tools Menu" and can see it in Figure 9–16.

Figure 9–28

Suggestion box BBS

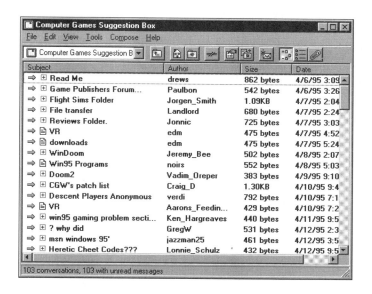

SUGGESTION BOX

Computer
Games
Suggestion
Box

A suggestion box is a special form of a BBS, as you can see in Figure 9–28. In some cases, as that in Figure 9–28, you can read and reply to other people's suggestions. In other cases, as in the MSN Suggestions, it is write-only, and you cannot see or reply to suggestions from others.

There are a number of areas of MSN that have not been discussed. One of them, accessing the Internet, will be discussed in a moment. Of the rest, you should be able to use the descriptions of the MSN window components, and your knowledge of BBSs, chat rooms, and file libraries to find your way around. It is a fascinating place and worth your time to explore. Begin by exploring Member Assistance from the MSN Central to see the many forms of help that are available in MSN.

Using the Internet

If you think that MSN is a large collection of information and services, the Internet makes MSN seem insignificant and the problem of finding what you want many times more difficult. The Internet is a collection of computer networks (a network of networks) that literally spans the globe. It is many different entities—governments, universities, companies, and individuals—that have interconnected themselves with high-speed communications lines for the purpose of sharing information and communicating. The Internet is also, in a sense, the huge collection of information that is available from all the sources that are connected to it.

There are at least three ways that you can use the Internet from Windows 95: from the Microsoft Network you can use Internet mail and you can read Internet newsgroups; from the Microsoft Exchange you can use Internet mail; and by using Dial-Up Networking you can open an Internet connection and start programs that access the Internet. If you use MSN, you need nothing more than Windows 95, a modem, and an MSN account. If you use either of the other two ways of accessing the Internet, you need an account with an Internet provider, and you need additional software.

Accessing the Internet from MSN

The Microsoft Network provides an easy way to access the Internet if what you want to do is exchange messages over it and read Internet newsgroups. (It may be that, by the time you read this, MSN may offer other Internet services such as browsing the World Wide Web.) Using MSN also saves you a lot of setting up, as you'll see in the discussion on the other ways to access the Internet.

EXCHANGING MESSAGES OVER THE INTERNET

Exchanging messages over the Internet is a simple matter with MSN. If someone wants to send you an Internet message through your MSN account, all they need to do is address it to

memberID@msn.com

where *memberID*, of course, is your unique MSN member ID that you use to sign on to MSN. If that is done, when you next sign on to MSN, you'll see a message that you have mail waiting. Simply click on E-Mail in the MSN Central to open the Microsoft Exchange Inbox, and you'll see your new mail messages at the top of the list, as shown in Figure 9–29. If you double-click on a new message, it will open and you can read it.

To send a message to someone on the Internet, start a new message from the Exchange Inbox window (see Chapter 8), and put their Internet address in the To area, as you can see in Figure 9–30.

Figure 9–29

Exchange Inbox showing new messages

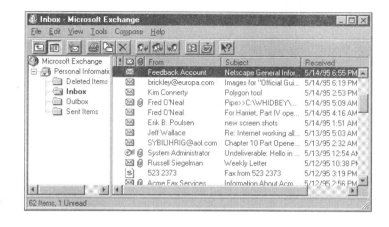

Figure 9–30

Sending a message on the Internet

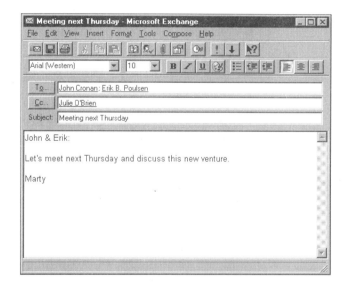

Then complete the message and click on the Send button in the toolbar. Your recipient's Internet mail box should get the message in a short time.

 You cannot attach files to messages being sent over the Internet using MSN.

 Messages sent over the Internet and over MSN itself are not as fast as they are on your LAN.

READING INTERNET NEWSGROUPS

Internet newsgroups (also called USENET) are a large collection of BBSs that are organized into a hierarchical structure with seven *official* and a large number of unofficial top-level categories. Each of these categories are then broken down into a great many sub-categories. For example, one newsgroup is `rec.arts.movies.reviews`. The top level category is `rec` for recreation. The rest of the name then forms the structure to get to movie reviews. The seven official top-level categories are as follows:

- **comp** for computer topics
- **misc** for miscellaneous topics
- **news** for Internet news topics
- **rec** for recreational topics
- **sci** for science topics
- **soc** for social topics and for socializing
- **talk** for general discussion topics

MSN carries all seven of these categories in a folder labeled Usenet Newsgroups. In addition MSN has a large number of regional, international, and other newsgroups in a folder; and finally, MSN has a folder of other popular newsgroups.

At the time this was written, you could only read Internet newsgroups (you could not post to them), and only some of the great many newsgroups were available.

The Internet Center

To open the Internet newsgroups, open Categories from the MSN Central, and then double-click on The Internet Center icon. From The Internet Center forum, double-click on Newsgroups, and then double-click on Usenet Newsgroups. The Usenet Newsgroups window will open, as shown in Figure 9–31. From here double-click on a category to open a window of subcategories. If you pick one, you'll finally see the actual message listings in the familiar MSN BBS window, like that in Figure 9–32. The only difference from a normal MSN BBS window is that currently the Internet Newsgroups window is read-only; you cannot make postings to them. Like any BBS, you can sort (ascending only) the messages by subject, author, date, and size by clicking on the appropriate title button above the list. You can also use the Start menu or Tools menu Find command to search MSN for a newsgroup topic.

Figure 9–31

Usenet Newsgroups

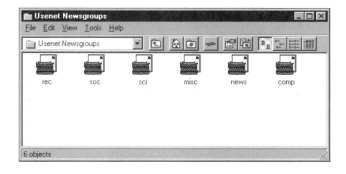

Figure 9–32

A particular newsgroup's messages

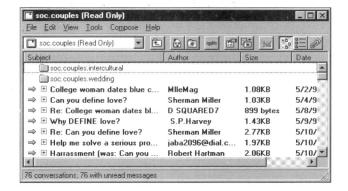

Newsgroup messages may contain language and content that you find objectionable and that you may not want your children to see. The Internet is uncensored, and a great deal of material gets posted each day, both good and bad. It is each individual's prerogative to judge what they will read and what they will let their children read.

Directly Using the Internet

Sending and receiving Internet mail directly removes a middleman and allows you to attach files to your messages. If you want an Internet account for other purposes, it is probably advantageous for you to directly use Internet mail. To do this, besides a modem and a phone line, you need a PPP (point-to-point protocol) account with an *Internet provider* (a company that provides telecommunications access to the Internet), and you need Internet mail software.

The Microsoft Plus! For Windows 95 software package includes an Internet mail package that integrates with the Microsoft Exchange and uses similarly designed windows, dialog boxes, and menus. You should be able to get Microsoft Plus! directly from Microsoft or from a local supplier; see the literature that came with Windows 95. This book will describe using Microsoft's Internet Mail package and will assume that is what you are using.

To use Microsoft's Internet Mail, your Internet provider must provide a PPP (point-to-point protocol) account and must be running a POP3 mail server.

Your Internet provider may be a network server to which you are already connected with a LAN, in which case you need to search no further. Ask your network administrator if this is true. Otherwise, shop for an Internet provider that is within your local phoning area, as you would shop for anything else that has long-term importance for you—look in newspapers, probably the business section; ask people whose opinions you trust; call several providers and compare prices, services, and staying power; choose one and sign up. Once you have decided on a provider, get the following information from the provider that you will need to use the Internet:

1. Your user name
2. Your password
3. The provider's domain name
4. The phone number you are to use to dial into the provider or a LAN communications link
5. The provider's DNS server IP address
6. The authentication technique used by the provider (do they use a terminal window?)

If you are dialing in to a provider, you will also need:

7. Your IP address
8. An IP subnet mask
9. The provider's gateway IP address
10. Whether you use your provider's domain name or their IP address as the name of the provider's mail server
11. Whether you use your regular user name and password for access to your mailbox

Your Internet address is *usename@domainname*. You will see in the next section where to use all of this information. Your provider should readily have it all and be helpful in how to use it.

SETTING UP INTERNET MAIL

Setting up Internet mail is one of the more complex chores in Windows 95, but some of it you may have already done. Assuming that your modem is already set up and running, you have four tasks to perform:

1. Install dial-up networking (which you may have done in Chapter 6).
2. Set up TCP/IP networking protocol.
3. Set up a dial-up networking account.
4. Set up an Internet mail profile.

If you do not have dial-up networking already installed, go back to Chapter 6 and install it now. Then read each of the following three sections to carry out the other tasks.

Setting Up a TCP/IP Networking Protocol TCP/IP, you may remember from Chapter 5, stands for Transmission Control Protocol/Internet Protocol. It is the rules two computers use to exchange information with each other over the Internet. Therefore your computer must be using that protocol to connect to the Internet. If you have set up a LAN, you are probably using either NetBEUI or IPX/SPX for your networking protocol, but not TCP/IP (it is not as good for LANs). The following steps will guide you through the setup of TCP/IP for dial-up networking (you must have Dial-Up Networking installed first—you should see a folder by that name in My Computer).

1. Open the Start menu, choose Settings Control Panel, and after the Control Panel opens, double-click on the Network icon.
2. Click on Add, click on Protocol, and click on Add again. This will open the Select Network Protocol dialog box, shown in Figure 9–33.
3. Click on Microsoft in the left column, on TCP/IP in the right column, and click on OK. This brings you back to the Network dialog box where you should see TCP/IP bound to both Dial-Up Adapter and to your LAN adapter if you have one.

Figure 9–33

*Select Network
Protocol dialog box*

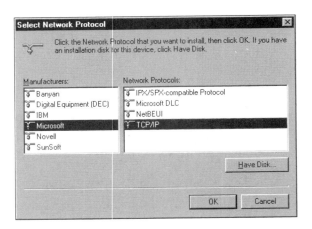

4. If you are going to connect to the Internet through dial-up networking and not your LAN, you probably do not want TCP/IP bound to your LAN adapter, and you need to make doubly sure it is bound to your dial-up adapter. Use these substeps for that purpose:

    a. In the Network dialog box, click on the protocol line showing TCP/IP being bound to your LAN adapter, and then click on Remove, like this:

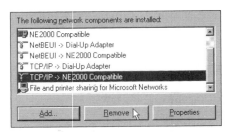

    b. Click on Dial-Up Adapter (not the TCP/IP protocol) in the Network dialog box, and then click on Properties. The Dial-Up Adapter Properties dialog box should open.

    c. Click on the Bindings tab, and you should see a check mark next to TCP/IP, as shown next. If not, click on the check box and then on OK. You'll be returned to the Network dialog box.

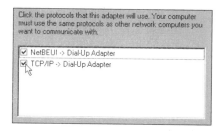

If you use dial-up networking for connecting to your LAN or to another Windows 95 computer, you will have other protocols bound to your dial-up adapter, as you see above.

5. Click on the TCP/IP protocol bound to your dial-up adapter and then on Properties. The TCP/IP Properties dialog box will open, as shown in Figure 9–34.

6. If necessary, click on the IP Address tab; then if your Internet provider gave you an IP address, click on Specify an IP address, and type the address with periods or decimal points where your provider indicated they should be. If your provider did not give you an IP address, make sure Obtain an IP address automatically is checked.

Figure 9–34

TCP/IP Properties dialog box

7. If your provider gave you a subnet mask, enter that in the space provided; otherwise, leave it blank and click on the DNS Configuration tab. (If you come back to this dialog box after closing it, you will see the Subnet Mask field filled in with `255.255.255.0`, which is fine).

8. Click on Enable DNS, enter your user name in the Host text box and the provider's domain name in the Domain text box. Then type the provider's server IP number in the DNS Server Search Order text box, click on Add, type the provider's domain name in the Domain Suffix Search Order text box, and click on Add a second time. Your DNS Configuration tab should look like what you see in Figure 9–35, but with your settings.

9. If your provider gave you a gateway IP address, click on the Gateway tab, enter the IP address in the New gateway text box, and click on Add.

10. The WINS Configuration tab should have Disable WINS Resolution selected; the Advanced tab should show None under Property; and Bindings should show Client for Microsoft Networks checked but File and printer sharing for Microsoft Networks not checked.

Figure 9–35

DNS Configuration

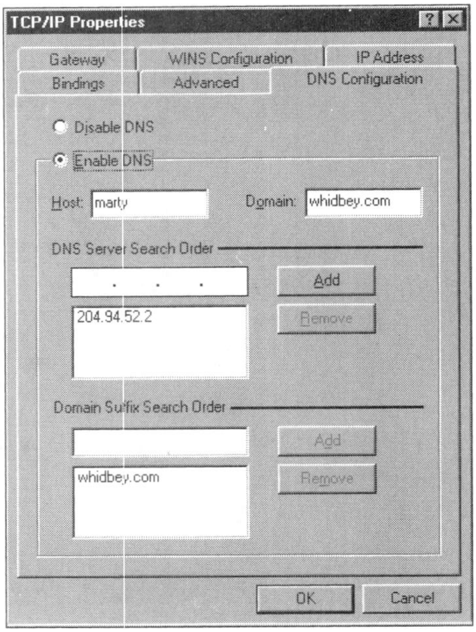

11. Click on OK to close the TCP/IP Properties dialog box, click on OK again to close the Network dialog box, and select Yes in answer to the question `Do you want to restart your computer now?`

If you leave File and printer sharing for Microsoft Networks checked in the Bindings tab of the TCP/IP dialog box, there is a faint chance that someone could get into your computer while you are connected to the Internet. Since there is no reason to bind this service to TCP/IP if you are using it only for the Internet, it is best not to have it available for that protocol.

Setting Up a Dial-Up Networking Connection The next task is to set up a dial-up network connection. Use the following steps for that purpose:

1. Open My Computer, and double-click on the Dial-Up Networking folder. If you have not set up a dial-up networking connection before, the Make New Connection Wizard will open. Otherwise, double-click on Make New Connection, and the Wizard will then open.

2. Type your provider's name, make sure your modem is properly specified, and then click on Configure. Your modem Properties dialog box will open.

3. Make sure that everything is properly set up for your modem. If your provider said that you needed to use a terminal window to log on, it can't be automatic, so click on the Options tab, and click on Bring up terminal window after dialing, as shown next. Then click on OK to close the Modem Properties dialog box and on Next to continue with the Make New Connection Wizard.

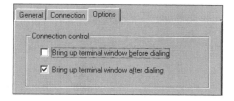

4. Type the area code (if you need to use it) and the phone number that the provider told you to use to connect to the Internet, and click on Next. Click on Finish to complete the new connection.

When the wizard closes, your Dial-Up Networking window will look something like this:

Next, set up the properties for your new Internet connection.

1. Right-click on the Internet connection, and choose Properties from the popup menu that appears. The connection's properties dialog box will open, as shown in Figure 9–36. The settings should be as you have already set them. The same is true about the Configure button, which shows your modem settings.

2. Click on the Server Type. The settings should be as shown in Figure 9–37. The Type of Dial-Up Server must be PPP:..., Internet, and you should have only the TCP/IP protocol checked.

3. Click on TCP/IP Settings. This opens the TCP/IP dialog box, which contains information similar to that entered in the Network TCP/IP dialog box, but for some reason, this

Figure 9–36

Internet connection Properties dialog box

Figure 9–37

Server Types dialog box

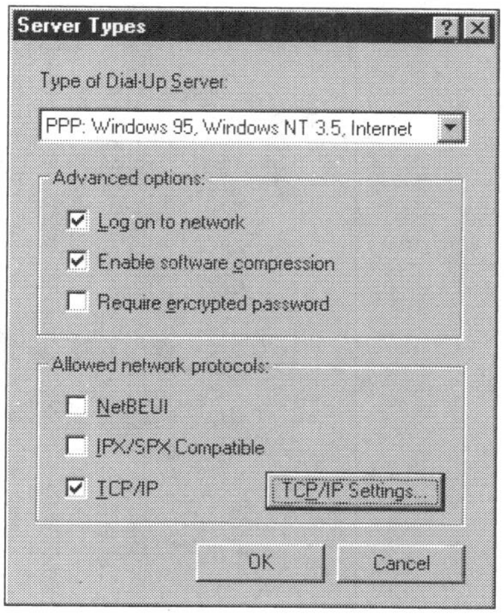

Figure 9–38

Dial-Up connection's TCP/IP settings

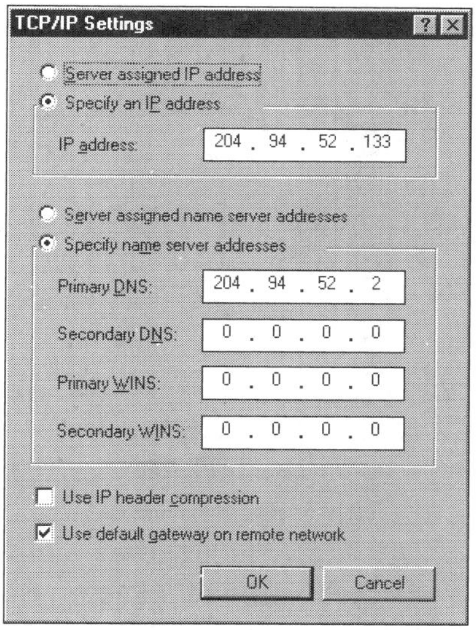

information is not carried over to the Server Type TCP/IP dialog box. If your provider gave you an IP address, click on Specify an IP address, and enter that address. Click on Specify name server address, and enter your provider's IP address as the Primary DNS. If necessary, click on Use IP header compression to turn it off, and then click on Use default gateway on remote network to turn it on. When you are done, your TCP/IP Settings dialog box should look like Figure 9–38, except with your IP addresses.

Figure 9–39

Terminal window

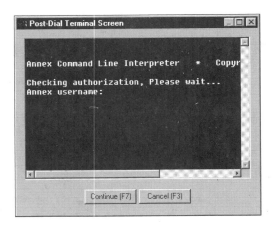

 If you leave IP header compression on, it can cause your Internet connection not to work even if you get connected.

Finally, try out your new Internet connection.

1. Double-click on your new connection icon. A dialog box should appear with your user name and the provider's phone number filled in. Type in your password, and if you don't want to type it each time, click on Save password. Then click on Connect.

2. You should see a Connecting Status box appear and then the terminal window open, as shown in Figure 9–39. Type in your user ID, password, and PPP as requested. Then click on Continue or press F7. The terminal window will disappear, and the Connected message box will appear. You should also see the modem icon in the Taskbar next to the clock. Click on Details, and your message box should look like this:

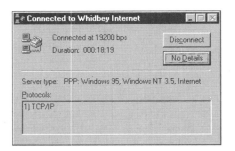

Now that you are connected, you can start and run any Windows-based Internet application, such as NetScape or Mosaic. For now, though, you have one last task to set up Internet Mail, so click on Disconnect.

Setting Up Internet Mail and Its Profile   The final task is to set up Internet mail itself and its Mail and Fax Profile. Use the next set of steps to do that.

1. Follow the instructions that came with Microsoft Plus! Internet Mail to install it on your computer with Windows 95.

2. Then open the Control Panel again, and double-click on Mail and Fax. The Mail and Fax dialog box will open.

You have a choice of setting up Internet mail as an independent profile or as part of the MS Exchange profile. While you are still testing everything, it is best to set up an independent profile, so you have only one service at a time to worry about. You can then add Internet to the Exchange profile later.

3. Click on Show Profiles and then on Add. The Inbox Setup Wizard will appear. Click on Use the following information services and select only Internet mail. Click on Next.

4. Type Internet as the Profile Name and click on Next.

5. Click on Modem as the method to use to connect to the Internet and then click on Next.

6. Select the dial-up connection you made above for connecting to the Internet and click on Next.

7. Depending on whether your provider told you to use their domain name or their IP address as the mail server name, select the appropriate item, enter the name or number and click on Next.

8. At least initially, click on Automatic to automatically download all new mail, and then click on Next.

9. Type in your Internet mail address in the form `username@domainname` and click on Next.

10. Unless your provider told you differently, type in your user name and your password, and click on Next. Assuming you want to use the Exchange's default address book and folders setup, click on Next twice again.

11. Assuming that you do not want to wait for the extra time to start the Exchange every time you start your computer, select Do not add Inbox to the StartUp group and click on Next.

12. You are done, so click on Finish. You should see Internet in the list of Exchange profiles. Click on Close.

You can now send and receive Internet messages through the Microsoft Exchange. Try it by double-clicking on the Inbox and selecting Internet as the profile to use. You will hear the modem dialing; see the terminal window appear; enter your user name, password, and click on Continue; see the connected message; and finally, see the Inbox open with your Internet mail. Try sending mail using the instructions in Chapter 8.

If your Internet mail is not working, go back to your Internet provider and review all of the items that you should be getting from him or her, and then very carefully review all of the installation steps. Your problem is most likely a semantic one between what your provider calls something, how it is described here, and what the dialog box says it is. Hopefully the instructions here help clarify that.

USING THE INTERNET CONNECTION

Although Internet mail is a very important aspect of the Internet, there is a great deal more to the Internet than just e-mail. All of it has to do with finding and accessing information. Among the functions that you can perform on the Internet are the following:

- Locating an individual's address on the Internet with *Whois* programs
- Locating information on the Internet with *Gopher* programs
- Accessing and transferring files across the Internet with *FTP* programs
- Browsing and accessing graphically displayed information with *Web Browsers* such as Mosaic and Netscape

Of the four functions, FTP, which stand for *file transfer protocol*, is probably the most valuable, because it allows you to download other programs. On the CD that is included with this book, you will find the program Wftp32.exe, which is an excellent 32-bit FTP that runs with the Windows 95 Internet dial-up connection. Most Windows-based Internet programs use a standard set of functions called the

Windows Sockets Library, or *WINSOCK* for short. If you see that a program uses the Windows Sockets Library or is WINSOCK compliant, you know that it will run with the Windows 95 Internet dial-up connection. See Chapter 14 for more information about Ws_ftp32.exe and other Internet related programs included on the *Windows 95 Power Tools* CD.

To run any WINSOCK Internet programs, such as Wftp32 or Netscape, you start your Internet dial-up connection, and when you see the Connected message shown earlier, start the program that performs the function you want to use. For example, to use Wftp32, use the following steps:

1. Open My Computer and the Dial-Up Networking folder and double-click on your Internet dial-up connection. (If you use the Internet very much, you may want to put a shortcut to your connection on the Start menu or the desktop to speed up this process.)

2. Click on Connect, and if necessary, enter your user name, password, and PPP in the terminal window.

3. When you see the message that you are connected, locate and start (double-click on) Wftp32.exe. You'll see the WFTP32 window open and then the Session Profile dialog box on top of it, as you can see in Figure 9–40.

4. Select a site to which you want to connect. For example, to get the latest version of the Mosaic web browser, you would select Mosaic and click on OK. This will connect you to ftp.NCSA.uiuc.edu (National Center for Supercomputer Applications at the University of Illinois Urbana-Champaign

Figure 9–40

*WS_FTP32
Session Profile
dialog box*

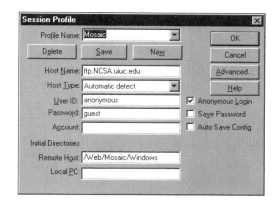

Figure 9–41

WS_FTP32 connected to the National Center for Supercomputer Applications at the University of Illinois

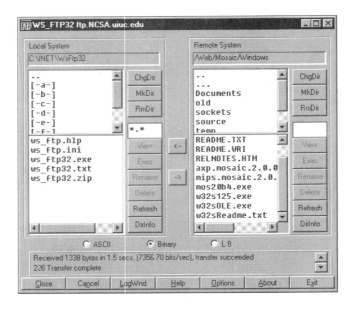

campus) in the directory that holds the latest copy, as shown in Figure 9–41.

Version 1.4 of Wincim, the Windows CompuServe Information Manager, can use a Windows Sockets connection to the Internet to access CompuServe. This can save you a long distance phone call if you have a local Internet provider and a long distance CompuServe number.

This chapter has just barely opened the door to the Internet. With Windows 95 and the many WINSOCK tools available, you have a very powerful and easy to use means to explore it.

PART IV

Windows 95 Multimedia and Accessories

You probably bought Windows 95 as an operating system—*to handle tasks that are generally considered part of an operating system. Windows 95 also provides many additional programs that perform functions that are not classically part of an operating system. You have already seen such programs in the communications and messaging area, discussed in Part III. Part IV continues that discussion, examining multimedia and then the many accessories, or applets (little applications) that come with Windows 95.*

The multimedia area is really a combination of true operating system functions that provide support for audio and video software and hardware, as well as several programs that implement multimedia functions, such as the CDPlayer and MediaPlayer. Chapter 10 will cover both aspects of Windows 95 multimedia.

Chapter 11 will look at all of the Windows 95 accessories not discussed elsewhere in this book. These include the Calculator, Character Map, Direct Cable Connection, NotePad, Paint, and WordPad, as well as the games.

Using Multimedia

Multimedia is the frosting on the Windows 95 cake! Anyone who has used a computer-based encyclopedia with multimedia will agree; anyone who has played a computer game with multimedia will agree; anyone who has spent a day in front of a computer with an audio CD playing will agree. You can use a computer without multimedia and perform the vast majority of tasks you need to accomplish, but with multimedia these tasks become much more pleasant and fun. Multimedia is CD-quality digital audio and full-motion video integrated into your programs on your desktop (or laptop) computer. It is looking up *Louis Armstrong* in a computerized encyclopedia and seeing a film clip with sound of him playing his trumpet, as shown in Figure 10–1 (sorry you can't also hear it); it is seeing a film clip with sound of a tax expert giving you advice in the middle of your tax preparation package (Figure 10–2); it is greatly enhanced audio and video in such games as Myst (Figure 10–3).

Windows 95 provides built-in support and many enhancements for multimedia. These include the ability to record and play back high-quality digital audio; to play back digital video more smoothly in a larger viewing area; to compress and decompress audio and video files with several built-in choices of compression schemes (codecs); and to support other applications in capturing and recording full-motion video. Windows 95's 32-bit, multitasking, multithreaded architecture lends itself to providing higher-quality, smoother running, more realistic multimedia sequences.

Figure 10–1

Louis Armstrong playing his trumpet, from Encarta

Figure 10–2

Marshall Loeb in TurboTax Multimedia

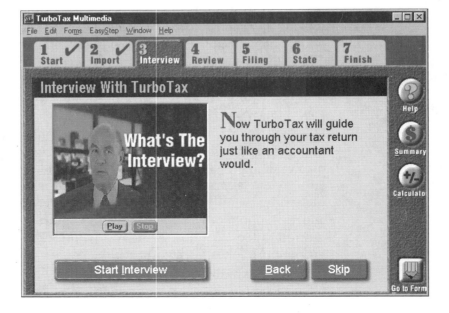

Figure 10–3

Myst, the game

In this chapter you'll review what hardware and software are necessary for multimedia and see how to install it. You will then examine the multimedia accessories that are available in Windows 95. Finally, you will learn how to use codecs with multimedia files and how to assign sound clips to events on your computer.

What Is Needed for Multimedia?

There are many different degrees to which you can implement multimedia. At a minimum you need a computer with a 486 or higher processor; floppy and hard disks (160 MB or more); a keyboard, VGA monitor (640 x 480 pixels), and video adapter; and 4 MB of memory. To this you must add a sound card, speakers, and a CD-ROM disk drive. In such a system you will be able to read a multimedia CD and play back digital audio and video clips. In a minimum system, the video image will be small and may be jerky; there will be pauses as new segments are loaded off the disk; and the audio will be of lower quality.

To improve on the minimum system, you do not have to go to the opposite extreme on any component. Rather, upgrade all components evenly and to a lesser degree. The following components represent a reasonably balanced system:

- 486 processor, 66 MHz
- 8 MB of memory
- PCI (or VESA) local-bus disk and video controllers
- SVGA (800 x 600) 16-bit monitor running with at least 256 colors
- Double-speed (2x) multisession CD-ROM drive
- 16-bit sound card with MIDI support

Of the above components, the local-bus video controller probably gives you the greatest benefit; local-bus performance is approximately ten times that of an ISA-bus system. A faster processor will probably not buy you much improvement in multimedia. On the other hand, going to 24-bit video with more than 256 colors will significantly improve the playback of video sequences. After local-bus and improved video, the next thing to improve is memory, followed by a quad speed (4x) CD-ROM drive.

Installing Multimedia Cards

Much of what was said in Chapter 5 about setting up network adapter cards applies here to installing multimedia cards. Multimedia cards require that several settings be made on the cards, so that they properly communicate and work in harmony with the rest of your computer. 16-bit sound cards typically have the following settings:

- I/O port addresses for
  a. Game port (fixed at 200h–20Fh)
  b. Audio interface (variable, 220h–233h is typical)
  c. MIDI interface (variable, 330h–331h is typical)
  d. FM music synthesizer (fixed at 388h–38Fh)
- Interrupt request line (IRQ) (variable with 5 or 7 typical)
- Direct memory address (DMA) channel for
  a. 8-bit data (variable, channel 1 is typical)
  b. 16-bit data (variable, channel 5 is typical)

If your sound card also has a CD-ROM controller on it, there may be additional settings. If your CD-ROM uses its own controller, the controller may have settings. These settings must be made so they do not conflict with other devices in your computer. Of particular concern are SCSI-disk controllers (possibly used for a CD-ROM drive), which, by default, tend to use the same I/O port address as a sound card's MIDI interface and the same high DMA channel. To determine which resources are currently used and which are currently available, open the System control panel, and from the Device Manager tab, print the System summary report. This report lists the IRQ, I/O port address, upper memory, and DMA channel used by every device in your computer. From this you can determine what resources are available for the multimedia card. Also, consult Tables 5–2 and 5–3 in the "Setting Up Network Adapter Cards" section of Chapter 5. These tables show typical IRQ and I/O port address assignments. Table 10–1 below shows the same information for DMA channels.

Watch out for I/O port address and DMA channel conflicts between SCSI-disk controllers and 16-bit sound cards.

Based on the System summary report and on the tables, you will be able to make the appropriate settings on your card(s). When that is done, install the card in your computer, being careful of static electricity, and run Add New Hardware from the Control Panel, as you read about in Chapters 5 and 7.

Table 10–1.
DMA channels and their normal use

DMA Channel	Standard or Typical Use
0	May be available
1	May be available, may be used by a sound card
2	Standard floppy-disk controller
3	May be available
4	Direct memory access controller
5	May be used by a SCSI controller or a sound card
6	May be available
7	May be available

Figure 10–4

Adding the multimedia components of Windows 95

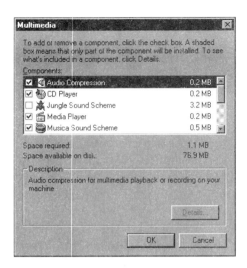

With the hardware configured and installed, install the multimedia components of Windows 95 with the following steps:

1. Double-click on Add/Remove Programs in the Control Panel to open the Add/Remove Programs Properties dialog box.

2. Click on the Windows Setup tab, and scroll the list until you see Multimedia.

3. Double-click on Multimedia to open the list of multimedia components, as you can see in Figure 10–4.

4. Select (make sure the check box has a mark in it) the multimedia components you need or want.

    The Windows multimedia components include three types of objects: software multimedia tools, including CD Player, Media Player, Sound Recorder, and Volume Control; audio and video compression techniques; and various schemes for assigning sounds to computer events, such as opening a window or getting a warning message. There is a significant size variation among the sound schemes, so if you have limited disk space, you'll want to consider these carefully. On the other hand, you will probably want all of the software devices.

5. When you have selected the components you want, click on OK twice to have them installed.

With your hardware installed, you are ready to set up and try some of the multimedia accessories included with Windows 95.

Using Windows 95 Multimedia Accessories

The Windows 95 multimedia accessories include CD Player, Media Player, Sound Recorder, and Volume Control. These represent some good, if basic, means to explore primarily audio multimedia. Look at each of these tools next.

Using the CD Player

The CD Player allows you to control and play audio CDs. Unless you are in the music business, this is something that you will do purely for pleasure. For those of us who spend most of our lives in front of a computer, though, it is a great enhancement to those lives!

Cdplayer.exe

The easiest way to start the CD Player is to simply insert an audio CD in your CD-ROM drive; after a brief time, the CD Player will start automatically and play the audio CD. You can also start it by opening the Start menu and choosing Programs, Accessories, Multimedia, and CD Player. When started, the CD Player dialog box opens, as you can see in Figure 10–5.

If you do not want to play a CD automatically when you insert it in the drive, hold down Shift **when you insert the audio CD.**

The CD Player has a primary set of controls, described in Table 10–2, that are much like a mechanical CD or tape player. The toolbar buttons, described in Table 10–3, and the menus add functionality not found in many mechanical CD players.

One of the best features of the CD Player is the Play List, shown in Figure 10–6, where you can select the tracks you want to play and the order in

Figure 10–5

*CD Player
dialog box*

CD Player

Disc View Options Help

[11] 01:22

Artist: New Artist   <D:>
Title: New Title
Track: Track 11   <11>

Total Play: 75:57 m:s   Track: 05:31 m:s

Table 10–2.

CD Player controls

Button	Name	Description
▶	Play	Starts playing the audio CD in the drive
❙❙	Pause	Pauses playing the audio CD in the drive
■	Stop	Stops playing the audio CD in the drive
◄◄	Previous Track	Goes to the beginning of the current track, or if already there, to the beginning of the previous track
◄◄	Skip Backwards	Goes back one second on current track
►►	Skip Forwards	Goes forward one second on current track
►►❙	Next Track	Goes to the beginning of the next track
▲	Eject	Ejects the CD from the drive

Table 10–3.

CD Player toolbar buttons

Button	Name	Description
📝	Edit play list	Opens the list of tracks for editing (see Figure 10–6)
🕒	Track time elapsed	Displays in the digital panel below the toolbar the time elapsed playing the current track
🕒	Track time remaining	Displays in the digital panel the remaining time to complete playing the current track
🕒	Disk time remaining	Displays in the digital panel the remaining time to complete playing the entire disk
⇅	Random track order	At the end of a track, the next track to play is randomly selected
↻	Continuous play	At the end of the last track, the player starts over at the beginning of the first track
☰	Intro play	Plays the first ten seconds of each track

which you want to play them. You can also enter the artist, title, and the description of each track, and this information will be stored for you and appear the next time you insert that particular CD. Use the following instructions to select specific tracks in the order you want them played:

Figure 10–6

*List of tracks
to be played*

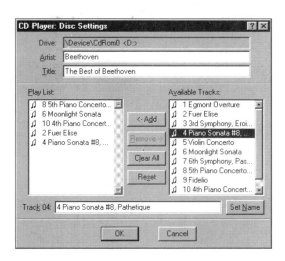

1.   Open the Play List either by clicking on the Edit Play List
      button on the left of the toolbar or by choosing Edit Play List
      in the Disc menu.

2.   Click on Clear All to clear the Play List.

3.   If you wish, you can enter the name of the artist, the title of
      the CD, and the description of each track.

**When you are entering the track descriptions, if you press
Enter at the end of each entry, you will both set the name and
be ready to enter a new name. If you click on Set name, you
will have to separately highlight the old name to replace it.**

4.   Double-click on the tracks in the right column in the order
      you want them played. You may click on the same track mul-
      tiple times if you want that track repeated.

5.   When the Play List is the way you want it, click on OK to
      close the dialog box, and then click on Play to begin playing
      your list of tracks.

If you do take the time to enter your CD titles and track descriptions,
you will get a very informative display of what you are currently playing, as you can see in Figure 10–7.

The digital display shows the track currently being played and one of
three times: the elapsed time in the current track, the time remaining
in the current track, the time remaining on the disk (which does not
show the current track number). In both cases in which the remaining

Figure 10–7

CD Player with artist, title, and track information

time is displayed, the figure has angle brackets on either end of it, as shown at the beginning of this paragraph. When you minimize the CD Player, the Taskbar entry, if it is large enough, will still show the track and time, also shown on the left. You can control which time is displayed from both the View menu and the toolbar.

Tip   If the Taskbar area is too small to see the digital display, move the mouse pointer to the task. You will see a popup display with the track and time.

The Preferences option in the Options menu opens the Preferences dialog box, shown next. Most of the entries are self-explanatory, except possibly the Intro play length, which is the length of time that the beginning of each track is played when the Intro Play button is pressed. This can be from 5 to 15 seconds with 10 seconds being the default.

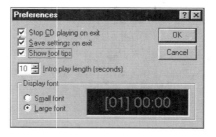

Using the Media Player

The Media Player allows you to play video movie clips in the Video for Windows format (.AVI extension), waveform audio clips in the .WAV format, MIDI sound clips in either .MID or .RMI formats, and audio

Figure 10–8

Video file being played with the Media player

Figure 10–9

Media Player Options dialog box

Mplayer.exe

CDs. If you look in the Media folder within the Windows folder on your hard disk, or in the \Funstuff\Videos folder on the Windows 95 CD-ROM, you will find a number of these files to try out. For example, the Goodtime.avi video clip is shown being played in Figure 10–8. The Media Player provides a wide sampling of multimedia capabilities. Try out a number of the files in the mentioned folders to see this for yourself.

You can start the Media Player either by double-clicking on a media file (.AVI, .WAV, .MID, or .RMI), or by opening the Start menu and choosing Programs, Accessories, Multimedia, and Media Player. The controls in the Media Player are similar to the CD Player controls, as described in Table 10–4. Options in the Edit menu provides further controls, as shown in Figure 10–9. Several of the settings in the

Figure 10–10

Video Properties dialog box

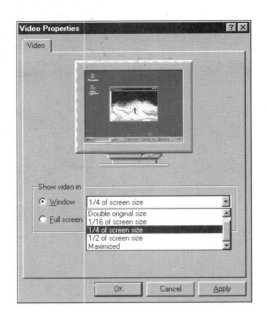

Table 10–4.

Media Player controls

Button	Name	Description
▶	Start	Starts the playing of the current media clip
■	Stop	Stops the playing of the current media clip
▲	Eject	Ejects the CD in the drive
◄◄	Previous Mark	Backs up and begins playing at the previous mark, either set by you or naturally occurring, like a track on a CD
◄◄	Rewind	Backs up a small increment and begins playing
►►	Fast Forward	Jumps forward a small increment and begins playing
►►|	Next Mark	Jumps forward and begins playing at the next mark, either set by you or naturally occurring
▼	Start Selection	Sets a mark to begin a selection you want to define
▲	End Selection	Sets a mark to end a selection you are defining

Options dialog box determine how media clips that are embedded in a document are handled. The Play in client document allows you to double-click on an audio or video file in, say, a Word for Windows document, and have it played. This is discussed later in this chapter under "Linking and Embedding Media Clips." The Selection option of the Edit menu allows you to define a specific selection of a media clip. The Device menu allows you to select a type of device, open a folder of those devices, and then set the properties for that kind of device. For example, for video devices you can set the screen size for playback, as shown in Figure 10–10.

The Media Player Start button becomes a Pause button once you have started playing a clip.

Using the Sound Recorder

The Sound Recorder allows you to digitally record sounds from a number of sources including microphones, CDs, MIDI devices (keyboards and synthesizers), and other audio devices like tape drives. The recordings are saved as .WAV waveform files, which can be attached to computer events and embedded in other documents (see related sections at the end of this chapter).

Sndrec32.exe

You start the Sound Recorder by opening the Start menu and choosing Programs, Accessories, Multimedia, and Sound Recorder. The Sound Recorder is a very simple device with controls similar to a mechanical tape recorder, as you can see in Figure 10–11, and as described in Table 10–5. You can use Insert File and Mix File from the Edit menu to replace or blend into the recording existing .WAV files. One interesting result of this is that you can mix several .WAV files in the \Windows\Media folder or place them one after the other to create a unique sound recording. You can also create some interesting special effects by increasing or decreasing the volume and/or speed of, or adding an echo to, the playback of a sound clip.

Figure 10–11

Sound Recorder

Table 10–5.

Sound Recorder controls

Button	Name	Description
◄◄	Seek to start	Returns to the beginning of the clip
►►	Seek to End	Goes to the end of the clip
►	Play	Plays the current clip (either what was recorded or what has been opened)
■	Stop	Stops playing or recording
●	Record	Starts recording

Figure 10–12

Volume controls

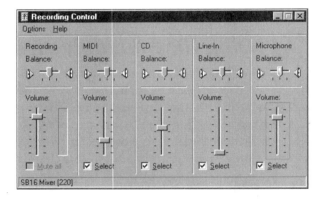

Using the Volume Controls

The volume controls, shown in Figure 10–12, allow you to set the volume and balance and, thereby, to mix four or five different audio inputs and an overall audio output. The volume controls are used in conjunction with the other Windows 95 multimedia tools, especially the Sound Recorder.

Sndvol32.exe

You open the volume controls by opening the Start menu and choosing Programs, Accessories, Multimedia, Volume Control. You can adjust the volume of a particular device by dragging the volume slider up to increase the volume or down to reduce the volume. From the Properties option in the Options menu, you can determine if the volume controls are for recording or playback, the mixing device you are using, and the volume controls you want to have available, as you can see in Figure 10–13.

Figure 10–13

*Volume Control
Properties
dialog box*

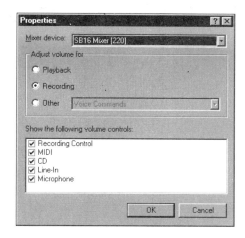

Multimedia Control Panel

Multimedia

The Multimedia control panel, which is shown in Figure 10–14, provides the central point for all multimedia settings, although the second through the fourth tabs also are available in the Media Player Devices menu. The Audio tab allows you to choose the devices you will use for audio recording and playback, what the volume level for each will be, and the recording quality you want to use. The Audio tab is also where you can turn on or off the volume control icon in the notification area on the right of the Taskbar. When this is turned on, a small speaker appears in the notification area, as shown on the left. If you click on the icon, a popup volume control opens that allows you raise or lower the volume as well as mute it (turn it off altogether), as you can see next.

The Video tab allows you to adjust the size of the video image; the MIDI tab allows you to configure the MIDI output and start the MIDI Instrument Installation Wizard; the CD Music tab allows you to specify the drive letter of the CD-ROM drive and the volume for the headphone jack; and the Advanced tab lets you change the properties of your installed multimedia devices, described next.

Figure 10–14

Multimedia control panel

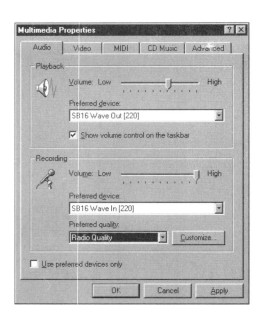

Multimedia Device Drivers

The Advanced tab, shown in Figure 10–15, provides access to the multimedia device drivers that you have installed. This tab lists all the available categories of multimedia devices. For those categories that have a driver installed, there is a plus sign to the left of them. If you click on the plus sign, the category will open and provide a description of the driver that is installed for that category. If you double-click on a driver or select it and click on Properties, you will get the Properties dialog box for the driver, such as that shown in Figure 10–16. For the most part these dialog boxes simply allow you to turn the drivers on or off, and the Settings button only tells you the copyright and version information. Two of the primary entries in the Advanced tab of the Multimedia Properties dialog box are for audio and video compression. This subject will be covered in detail in a moment.

The Media Control Devices entry in the Advanced tab represents a special class of device drivers that implement the Media Control Interface (MCI) for specific devices. MCI provides a common set of commands like Play, Pause, and Stop that can be applied to a wide variety of devices such as VCRs, CD players, and laser-disk players. The detail entries under Media Control Devices, as shown

Figure 10–15

*Advanced tab of
the Multimedia
control panel*

Figure 10–16

*Properties dialog
box for a
device driver*

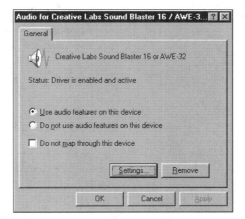

next, represent all those that are available in Windows 95 and not
necessarily those for installed devices.

Using Audio and Video Compression

When you digitize audio and video material, a very large amount of disk space is needed. For example, a little more than an hour's worth of music can fit on a CD-ROM that is equivalent to about 640 MB, and the same amount of space will hold only a little more than two minutes of video! Also, color video requires a data stream of more than 5 MB per second, and the newest and fastest 6x CD-ROM drives provide only 900 KB per second. For these reasons audio and video compression have become very important to computer multimedia and a major asset of Windows 95, which includes alternative schemes, called *Codecs*, for compressing and decompressing digital audio and video. These codecs are shown in Figure 10–17 and are described in Tables 10–6 and 10–7.

Table 10–6.

Audio codecs in Windows 95

Codec	Description
CCITT G.711, A-Law, u-Law	Consultative Committee for International Telephone and Telegraph standards for compressing and decompressing telephone conversations in North America. Provides a 2-to-1 compression ratio.
DSP Group TrueSpeech	High-quality voice compression, although it should not be used for other than voice. Cannot be compressed in real time, so you must temporarily store the uncompressed audio. Can be decompressed in real time. Good for audio notes in a text document, and for voice mail.
GSM 6.10 Audio	European Telecommunications Standards Groupe SpÈcial Mobile recommendation. Uses real-time compression with good voice quality. Developed for cellular phones.
IMA ADPCM	Interactive Multimedia Association's standard for 4-to-1 compression of 16-bit .WAV files. Provides real-time compression, primarily of music, without much loss in fidelity. (ADPCM stands for adaptive-differential pulse code modulation, a form of compression.)
Microsoft ADPCM	An early codec originally used with most .WAV files and now generally replaced by either TrueSpeech for voice or IMA ADPCM for music.
Microsoft PCM Converter	Used to convert 16-bit .WAV files so they can be played with 8-bit sound cards. Used whenever a sound clip is beyond your card's capabilities.

Figure 10–17

Windows 95 audio and video codecs

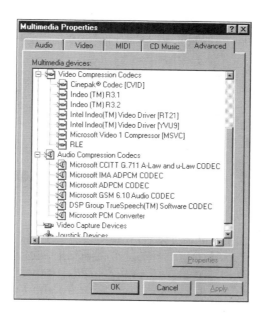

Table 10–7.

Video codecs in Windows 95

Codec	Description
Cinepak	Provides high-quality playback but at an extreme cost of more than 12 hours of compression time for ten minutes of finished video. Normally used in high-quality CD-ROM titles.
Indeo R3.1 and R3.2	Intel developed video codec that provides almost the quality of Cinepak but with real-time compression. Release 3.2 is the latest and offers a common codec between the Apple Macintosh and Windows.
RLE	Meant for use with simple bitmapped images and will not work well with detailed photographs and motion pictures. (RLE stands for run length encoding.)
Video 1	Microsoft developed codec that provides very efficient (low-cpu usage) moderate-quality compression of full-motion video and higher-quality compression of detailed photographs.

Codecs are selected and applied at the time an audio or video clip is saved on a disk. You can see that by looking at the Sound Recorder, choosing Save As from the File menu, and then clicking on the Change button at the bottom of the dialog box. This opens the

Sound Selection dialog box. If you open the Format drop-down list box, you'll see the list of audio codecs, as you can see here:

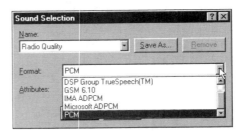

The video codecs in Windows 95 are for decompressing and playing video clips. To compress a video image you must have a video capture board, which in most cases includes hardware capability for compression. Intel, for example, sells an inexpensive video capture board with Indeo compression built into the board. If you get a video capture card that uses a codec not included with Windows 95, for example either Motion JPEG or MPEG (MPEG is superior for motion pictures), use the Add New Hardware Wizard to install the card, and you will be asked to select the codec you want to install.

When you play back a media clip, the codec used to store the clip will be identified and correctly applied as the clip is playing. Besides video codecs included with Windows 95, Apple's QuickTime 2.0 for Windows provides excellent performance and a good balance between the resources required and the resulting quality. A number of experts believe that QuickTime is the preferred video codec. Most products that use QuickTime include a QuickTime for Windows player on the disk.

Assigning Sound Clips to Events

Sounds

Windows 95 includes the capability to assign sounds to various computer events, such as the opening of a menu, the appearance of a message, maximizing a window, arrival of mail, and exiting Windows. You can access this capability through the Sounds control panel, which open the Sounds Properties dialog box, shown in Figure 10–18. You can use this dialog box in two ways. First, you can use the Schemes drop-down list box in the bottom of the dialog box to select a prefabricated scheme of assigning sounds to events.

Figure 10–18

*Sounds Properties
dialog box*

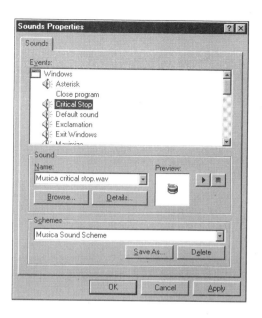

Secondly, you can select an event in the top list. If the event has a loud speaker next to it, a sound has been assigned to it. You can hear that sound by pressing the right-pointing arrow in the middle right of the dialog box. If you want to assign a different sound, you can open the Name drop-down list box and select a different sound, or you can use the Browse button and look for other sounds on your disk. When you have created a new scheme, you may save it by clicking on Save As.

Using Windows 95 Accessories

Windows 95 provides some accessory software with its standard product offerings.

- **Calculator** provides arithmetic, statistical, and scientific tools for performing calculations.

- **Character Map** allows you to select and copy special characters not available from the keyboard in order to insert them into documents.

- **Direct Cable Connection** establishes a connection between two computers linked by direct cable.

- **Games** is a folder containing three Windows 95 games: FreeCell, Minesweeper, and Solitaire. (A fourth, Hearts, is discussed in Chapter 6.)

- **NotePad** is a text editor, useful for editing ASCII text and program code.

- **Paint** is a drawing and graphics program that allows you to import or create art which can be exported to word processing or other applications.

- **WordPad** is a capable word processor that also can be used to examine and work with files of nonstandard formats, such as program code.

373

Figure 11–1

Calculator window, standard view

Calculator

The Windows 95 Calculator accessory assists you with arithmetic, statistical, and scientific calculations. It is accessed by opening the Start menu and selecting Programs, Accessories, and then Calculator. The Calculator window has two display modes: one for standard calculations, as shown in Figure 11–1, and one for statistical and scientific calculations. The original default is for the Standard window to be displayed. After that, the mode last used will be displayed when you open the Calculator.

The Calculator Window

Regardless of the display mode, the Calculator window has only two menus besides the Help menu: Edit and View.

- **The Edit Menu** contains the normal Copy and Paste operations that copy numbers into and from the Clipboard.
- **The View Menu** contains two options: Standard and Scientific. If you select Standard, the calculator shown in Figure 11–1 will be displayed. Use it to perform the arithmetic operations. If you select Scientific, the calculator shown in Figure 11–2 will be displayed. Use it to perform scientific and statistical operations.

At the top of the Calculator, you have the calculator display area where numbers are entered and results are displayed. Below the display area is a row of option buttons. On the left, the buttons establish the number system to be used:

Figure 11–2

Calculator window, scientific view

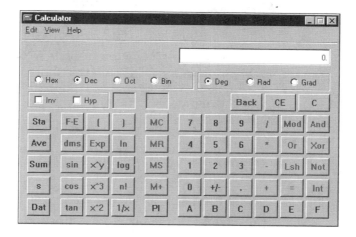

- **Hex** for hexadecimal numbers. When Hex is selected, the lettered buttons (A, B, C, D, E, F) on the lower right of the calculator become available and are used to enter the hexidecimal numbers.

- **Dec** for decimal numbers.

- **Oct** for octal numbers. Only numbers 0 through 7 are available with this option.

- **Bin** for binary numbers. Only the numbers 0 and 1 are available.

Hex, Dec, Oct, and Bin are very useful for converting a number in one system, or base, to another. Simply enter the number, say, in decimal, and then click the button for the system to which you want to convert.

On the right, the option buttons set trigonometric input defaults. When the numbering system is decimal, the buttons are:

- **Deg** for degrees. Keyboard shortcut is F2

- **Rad** for radians. Keyboard shortcut is F6.

- **Grad** for gradients. Keyboard shortcut is F4.

When the numbering system is hexadecimal, octal or binary, the option buttons become these:

- **Dword** displays the 32-bit representation of the number in the calculator display area. The keyboard shortcut is F2.

- **Word** displays the lower 16 bits of the number in the calculator display area. The keyboard shortcut is $\boxed{\text{F3}}$.

- **Byte** displays the lower 8 bits of the number in the calculator display area. The keyboard shortcut is $\boxed{\text{F4}}$.

Below the number systems are check boxes that set defaults for scientific and statistical calculations:

- **Inv** sets an inverse function. It can be used with sin, cos, tan, PI, log, Ave, Sum, s, and certain other scientific functions. The keyboard shortcut is $\boxed{\text{I}}$. The inverse function is turned off when a calculation is complete.

- **Hyp** sets the hyperbolic function. It is used with sin, cos, and tan. The hyperbolic function is turned off when a calculation is complete. The keyboard shortcut is $\boxed{\text{H}}$.

In both Standard and Scientific modes, you have these keys available to you on the Calculator:

- **Back** ($\boxed{\leftarrow\text{Backspace}}$ on the keyboard) deletes a single digit.
- **CE** ($\boxed{\text{Del}}$ on the keyboard) erases the last entry.
- **C** ($\boxed{\text{Esc}}$ on the keyboard) clears the calculations totally.
- **MC** clears the calculator's memory.
- **MR** recalls a number from memory.
- **MS** stores a number into memory, overwriting any other contents.
- **M+** adds a number to the contents of memory.
- $\boxed{\text{Num Lock}}$ on the keyboard allows you to use the keypad for entering numbers.

For statistical calculations, you have these buttons available:

- **Sta** displays the Statistics Box where statistical numbers are stored. The keyboard shortcut is $\boxed{\text{Ctrl}}$-$\boxed{\text{S}}$.

- **Ave** calculates the average of the numbers in the Statistics Box. You can calculate the mean of the squares with Inv and then Ave. The keyboard shortcut is $\boxed{\text{Ctrl}}$-$\boxed{\text{A}}$.

- **Sum** calculates the sum of the numbers in the Statistics Box. You can use the sum of the squares with Inv and then Sum. The keyboard shortcut is $\boxed{\text{Ctrl}}$-$\boxed{\text{T}}$.

- **s** calculates the standard deviation where *n*-1 is the population parameter. Use Inv then s to calculate the standard deviation with population parameter as *n*. You must click on Sta first before this button is available. The keyboard shortcut is Ctrl-D.

- **Dat** places a number in the Statistics Box. You must click on Sta first before this button is available. The keyboard shortcut is Insert.

For scientific calculations, you have many functions available. To get a description of any button that you may not know, click on it with the right mouse button. A What's This label will pop up. Click on it, and a description of the button will be displayed.

Performing Arithmetic Calculations

The Standard view Calculator (see Figure 11–1) performs the following arithmetic functions: addition (+), subtraction (-), division (/), multiplication (*), square root (sqrt), percentages (%), and number reciprocal (1/x). Follow these steps to enter an arithmetic function:

 **To find out what a key is used for, click on it with the right mouse button, and then click on the What's This label.**

1. Enter the first number of the function.

2. Click on the operator: / to divide, * to multiply, - to subtract, + to add, sqrt for square root, % for percentages, or 1/x for reciprocals.

3. Enter the next number and operator, and continue entering until you have finished.

4. Click on = to complete the calculation.

Using the Calculator's Memory

To store a number temporarily while you are performing other calculations, follow these steps:

1. To store a number into memory, calculate it first and then click on MS.

2. To add other numbers to it, click on M+.

3. To subtract a number in the display from one in memory, click on +/- to make the display number negative, and click on M+.

4. To look at the result, or enter the result in the Calculator Display area, click on MR.

5. When you are ready, clear the memory by clicking on MC.

 **Clicking on MS is the same as clicking on MC and then M+.**

Performing Statistical Calculations

Statistical functions, available in the Scientific view, provide average, sum, and standard deviation functions. Follow these steps to enter a statistical function:

1. If necessary, click on Scientific in the View menu. The Calculator view will change to include the statistical functions.

2. Enter your first number into the calculator display area.

3. Click on Sta to open the Statistics Box where data is stored. The Statistics Box will be displayed, as shown in Figure 11–3.

Four buttons now become available:

- RET returns to the Scientific Calculator view.
- LOAD loads the number selected in the Statistics Box into the Calculator display area.
- CD, Clear Digits, removes the selected number from the Statistics Box.
- CAD, Clear All Digits, clears all numbers in the Statistics Box.

4. Click on Dat to enter the data into the Statistics Box. The Statistics Box will disappear.

Figure 11–3

Statistics Box

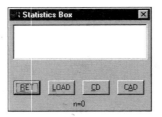

5. Continue to enter the rest of the numbers, clicking on Dat after each entry.

6. To see what is in the Statistics Box, click on Sta. To return to the regular Calculator, click on RET.

7. Click on one of the statistical operators to complete the function. The result will appear in the Calculator display area.

Performing Scientific Calculations

Scientific calculations, such as those using logarithms, can be performed in this mode. To find out what a button does, click on it with the right mouse button, and a What's This label will be displayed. Click on the label, and you'll see the explanation of the button. Follow these steps to perform a scientific calculation:

1. Click on Scientific in the View menu. The Scientific mode will be displayed.

2. If needed, choose a number system: hexadecimal, decimal, octal, or binary.

3. Enter your first number and click on an operator.

4. Continue to enter numbers and operators as needed.

5. Click on = for the result.

Character Map

Character Map

Character Map provides access to all characters in a given font, including characters unavailable from the keyboard. You can select characters to copy and then insert them into documents.

You access the Character Map by opening the Start menu and selecting Programs, Accessories, and then Character Map. The Character Map will be displayed, as seen in Figure 11–4.

Character Map Window

The Character Map window contains on the upper left a drop-down list box listing the fonts available. To the right of the Font list, is the Characters to copy entry box. To the right of it are three buttons:

Figure 11–4

Character Map window

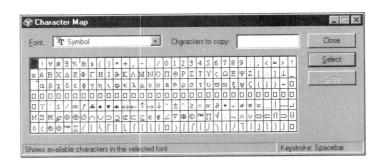

- **Close** closes the Character Map window.
- **Select** selects a character and places it in the Characters to copy box.

You can also select a character and place it in the Characters to copy box by double-clicking on it.

- **Copy** places the highlighted contents of the Characters to copy box into the Clipboard where it can be pasted to a document.

Below the Font and Characters to copy boxes are the characters in the designated font.

Using the Character Map

Follow these steps to select and then copy characters for inserting into another document:

1. Create the document into which you want the special characters inserted.

2. Open the Start menu and select Programs, Accessories, and then Character Map.

3. Click on the down arrow on the Font drop-down list box, and select the font you want.

4. Find the characters you want copied, and double-click on each. You can also select them, and then click on Select.

When you click on a character, the status bar will display the keystrokes needed to produce it.

5. When all the characters from all the fonts you want are in the Characters to copy box, click on Copy.

6. Close the Character Map accessory, and bring up the document.

7. In the Edit menu click on Paste. The copied characters will be inserted into the document.

 **By placing your pointer on a character and holding down the mouse button, you will see an enlargement of the character, as shown here:**

Direct Cable Connection

Direct Cable
Connection

Direct Cable Connection establishes a connection between you and another computer so that you can share folders, even if you are not networked. It is primarily used to connect portable and desktop computers.

 **You can gain access to networks if the computer with which you have a direct cable connection is connected to a network.**

Access Direct Cable Connection by opening the Start menu and selecting Programs, Accessories, and then Direct Cable Connection. (If it is not on your menu, you will need to install it using the Add/Remove Programs control panel.) The Direct Cable Connection Wizard will be displayed, as shown in Figure 11–5.

Follow these steps to install your direct cable connection:

1. Open the Direct Cable Connection, if necessary. The Direct Cable Connection Wizard will lead you through the installation.

2. Select between connecting as a Host computer, where others will access your resources, and connecting as a Guest, where you will access resources on another computer. Then, click on Next.

3. Select the port to be used. If you must install a new port, click on Install New Ports, and follow the directions. Attach

Figure 11–5

Direct Cable Connection Wizard

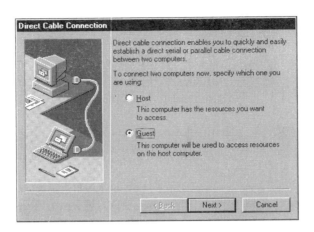

a serial or parallel cable to each computer and click on Next when you are finished.

4. To complete the installation, click on Finish. (If you are installing as a Host, you also may want to click on Use password protection to protect others from casually accessing your resources.)

 **To successfully use the direct cable connection, both the Host and Guest computers must install using Direct Cable Connection.**

Games

Windows 95 comes with at least four games: FreeCell, Hearts (discussed in Chapter 6), Minesweeper, and Solitaire. Here's a brief discription of each and how you get started playing.

FreeCell

Freecell.exe

FreeCell is an engaging game that can become addictive! Similar to Solitaire, it is more a game of strategy than one of chance. Follow these steps to begin the play:

1. Bring up the game by opening the Start menu and selecting Programs, Accessories, Games, and then FreeCell. The game board will be displayed.

Figure 11–6

FreeCell game board

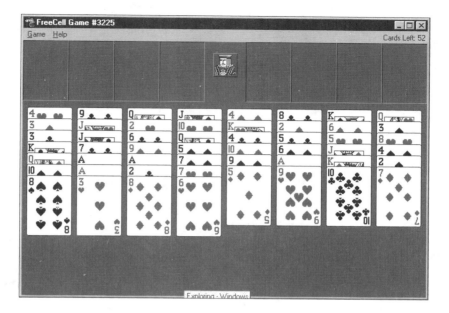

2. Open the Game menu and select New Game. The game board will be filled with columns of cards and eight empty cells along the top, as shown in Figure 11–6.

The four empty cells on the left of the "king" are free cells to be used for storing cards temporarily. The cells to the right are to hold cards of a given suit, from the ace up. The object of the game is to get all cards into the cells on the right. To do that you arrange cards at the bottom in sequence by number, color alternating. So you will place a black six on a red seven, for example, using the free cells as needed to get to the numbers you need.

3. Double-click on aces to place them in the cells to the upper right, and on all other cards to place them in the free cells.

4. Click on cards to select them, and then move the pointer to where you want to place the cards, and click there. The cards, if possible, will be moved.

Minesweeper

Minesweeper

Minesweeper is a game of chance where you try to accumulate points by not encountering mines. Follow these steps to get started:

Figure 11–7

Minesweeper game board

1. Bring up the game by opening the Start menu and selecting Programs, Accessories, Games, and then Minesweeper. The game board will be displayed, as seen in Figure 11–7.

   You will see a mine counter displayed on the upper left of the game board, a timer on the upper right, a reset button (smiley face) between the two, and empty squares. The object of the game is to find the mines in the squares as quickly as possible without actually clicking on them. As you click on a square, you will see either a number or a mine. The number tells you how many mines are contained in the eight squares surrounding the clicked-on square. You mark the suspected mines with the right mouse button. Once you actually click on a mine, the game ends.

2. To restart the game, open the Game menu and select New, or click on the smiley reset button.

You can set the difficulty of the game from the Game menu. The more difficult the level, the more squares are displayed.

Solitaire

Solitaire is a game of both chance and strategy. Similar to FreeCell, the object of the game is to end up with the deck of cards arranged in suits from the ace up to the king. Follow these steps to get started:

1. Open the Start menu and select Programs, Accessories, Games, and then Solitaire. The game board will be displayed, as seen in Figure 11–8.

Figure 11–8

*Solitaire
game board*

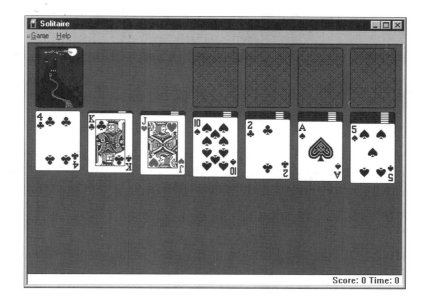

You will see a row of seven groups of downturned cards with
the top card turned up. In the upper left, a downturned stack
of cards is waiting to be clicked on. In the upper right are
four empty cells where you will place the cards, beginning
with the aces. Here are some tips:

- Double-click on the aces to begin a suit run.
- Drag any immediately numbered cards onto the next
  highest number of a different color. For example, you
  might drag a red four onto a black five.
- When all possible card sequences are made, click on the
  stack of cards in the upper left of the game board to get
  another possibility. If it fits in a card sequence, drag it to
  the position.
- Drag kings to the empty spaces on the board created by
  dragging cards onto others to start a mixed sequential run.
- Choose a different card back for your deck by selecting
  Deck from the Game menu.
- By selecting Options from the Game menu, you can
  choose to draw every third card or every card (the default),
  score using the Vegas method or the Standard method
  (the default).

2. When you want a new game, click on Deal in the Game menu.

3. When you are finished with the game, click on Exit in the Game menu, or click on the Close button in the upper right corner of the window.

Notepad

Notepad

Notepad is a simple editor to use with ASCII text and program code. It contains a few special features, such as enabling you to look at the contents of the Clipboard, and to create a log of events, as explained shortly.

You access Notepad by opening the Start menu and selecting Programs, Accessories, and then Notepad. The Notepad window will open, as shown in Figure 11–9.

The Notepad Window

The Notepad window contains three menus (in addition to Help) with many features common to folders which have been described in earlier chapters. The unique features are explained here.

THE FILE MENU

The File menu contains one unique option: Page Setup. Page Setup, when selected, displays a dialog box where you can customize your

Figure 11–9

Notepad window

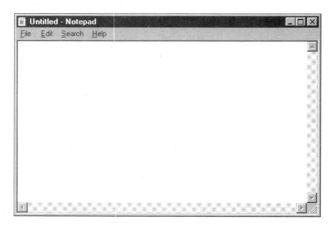

page setup, including paper size and source; orientation of portrait (tall) or landscape (wide); top, bottom, left, and right margins; and header and footer text. As you adjust the page setup options, a display of the page is reflected on the right of the dialog box. By clicking on Printer, you can change the printer and its properties.

THE EDIT MENU

The Edit menu contains two features that need some explanation:

- **Time/Date** inserts the time and date into the document where the pointer is positioned.

- **Word Wrap** acts as a switch to turn word wrap on and off. When word wrap is turned on, the lines end at the edge of the screen, continuing on the next line, so that you can see the contents. Word wrap does not affect the way the document will print; it is useful for editing on the screen.

THE SEARCH MENU

The Search menu contains two fairly common features for finding text:

- **Find** displays a dialog box where a string of characters for which you want to search, is entered in the text box (See Figure 11–10). You can specify whether the search is to be conducted Up the document (backwards towards the beginning) or Down (forward towards the end). If case is important, check Match case.

- **Find Next** repeats the previous Find. The shortcut key for Find Next is F3 .

You can create a log for recording events by typing .LOG on the top left margin of a document and then saving it. Each time you open the document, Notepad will append the time and date to its end, so you can begin typing with this information already entered.

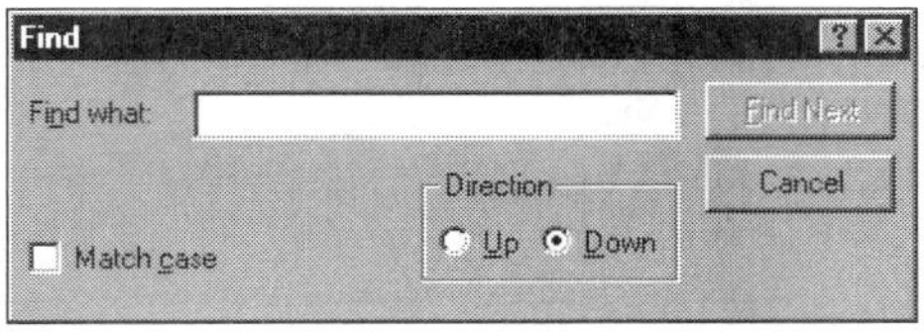

Figure 11–10

Find dialog box

Find		? X
Find what:		Find Next
	Direction	Cancel
☐ Match case	○ Up ● Down	

Paint

Paint

Paint is a drawing program that comes with Windows 95. With it you can draw colorful shapes and lines, including text and graphics. Paint allows you to create logos, brochures, graphics for other documents, and even backgrounds for the desktop.

You start Paint by opening the Start menu and selecting Programs, Accessories, and Paint. The Paint window is then displayed, as shown in Figure 11–11.

The Paint window will initially be named "untitled" in the title bar. It contains six menus on the menu bar. Its toolbox appears on the left of the drawing area, and a color palette is displayed beneath it.

The Menus

The six menus contain options for working with your art objects. File concerns the files and how to work at that level. Edit allows you to manipulate the object itself. View gives you options for how your screen will be displayed. Image presents some powerful options for enhancing the art object. Options allows you to set defaults and preferences for

Figure 11–11

Paint window

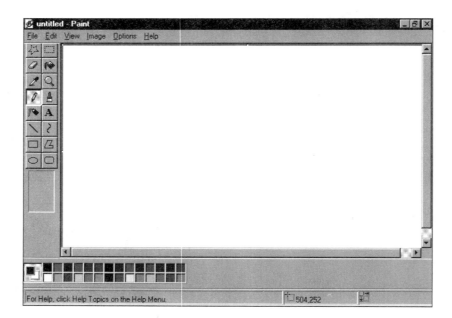

colors and image transparency. Finally, Help offers you online assistance to the Paint application.

THE FILE MENU

The File menu contains many standard options and a couple that are specifically intended for Paint (See Figure 11–12). The options and their descriptions are as follows:

- **New** allows you to create a new art object. When you click on New, a fresh screen will be displayed.
- **Open** retrieves an existing bitmap object from disk.
- **Save** saves the active object to the current disk locations.
- **Save As** saves the active object to the file and folder that you designate. You can change the name or save it in a new location with this option.
- **Print Preview** allows you to see the object as it will be printed. When you select this option, you have additional buttons available:
  - **Print** sends the displayed object to the printer.
  - **Next Page** displays the next page of the art document.
  - **Prev Page** displays the page before this one.
  - **Two Page** displays an odd- and even-numbered page together, as you would see in a book.
  - **Zoom In** enlarges the object. You can also zoom in when the pointer is a small magnifying glass, by clicking on the part of the object you want to enlarge. (See Figure 11–13.)

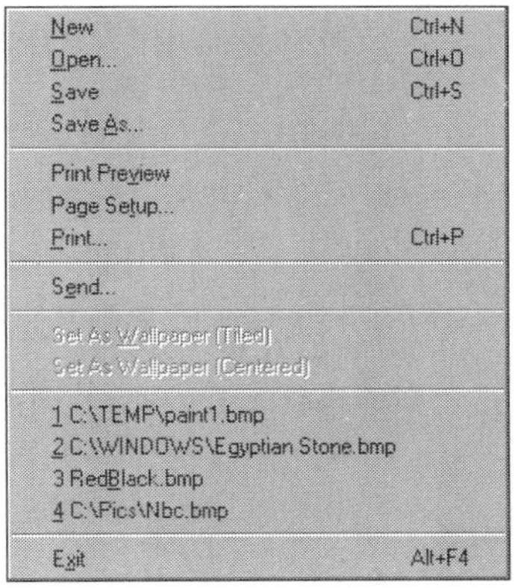

Figure 11–12

File menu for Paint

New	Ctrl+N
Open...	Ctrl+O
Save	Ctrl+S
Save As...	
Print Preview	
Page Setup...	
Print...	Ctrl+P
Send...	
Set As Wallpaper (Tiled)	
Set As Wallpaper (Centered)	
1 C:\TEMP\paint1.bmp	
2 C:\WINDOWS\Egyptian Stone.bmp	
3 RedBlack.bmp	
4 C:\Pics\Nbc.bmp	
Exit	Alt+F4

Figure 11–13

Zoom In window

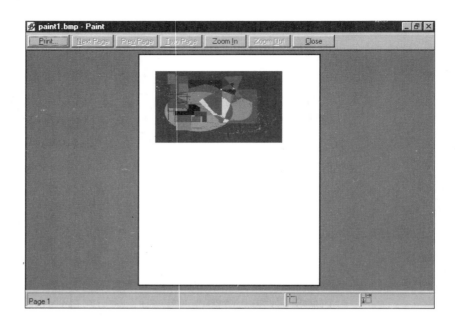

- **Zoom Out** reduces the object back to its original size. You can also just click on the object to reduce it.

- **Close** closes the Print Preview, returning you to the Paint drawing screen.

■ **Page Setup** displays a dialog box where you can set the page specifications. You specify the Paper Size, Paper Source, orientation (Portrait or Landscape), and set the margins for Left, Right, Top, and Bottom. The image of the page on the top of the dialog box will reflect your changes. By clicking on the Printer button, you can also change the printer or its properties.

■ **Print** sends the object to the printer. You may change the printer, number of copies to print, or print just a range of pages or a selected section of the object.

■ **Send** allows you to send the object to another computer. When you select this option, Microsoft Exchange is loaded (after you choose the profile to use, if you have more than one) and the New Message dialog box is displayed where you enter the name of the person to whom you're sending the object, add any message to accompany the attached object file, and then click on the Send icon.

- **Set As Wallpaper (Tiled)** allows you to create a background wallpaper design which will be repeated in a tiled manner. This is suitable for smaller designs that can be repeated to form a pattern. The object name, when saved in the \Windows folder, is entered into the Wallpaper designs available.

- **Set As Wallpaper (Centered)** creates a background wallpaper design that is centered on the screen. This is appropriate for larger designs which are not suited for tiled displays. The object name, when saved in the \Windows folder, is entered into the wallpaper designs available.

You must save your file before it can be used as desktop wallpaper.

- *Object Filenames* of previous objects you have recently created or worked on will be displayed. By clicking on its name, an object will be opened automatically for you.

THE EDIT MENU

The Edit menu presents options for working with the art object. Here are the options (See Figure 11–14):

- **Undo** reverses, or undoes, the previous action. You can undo up to three times.
- **Repeat** repeats the previous actions.
- **Cut** deletes the selected part of an object and places it on the Clipboard.
- **Copy** duplicates the selected part of an object and places it on the Clipboard.

Figure 11–14

The Edit menu

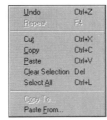

- **Paste** places the contents of the Clipboard onto the drawing area where the pointer is positioned.

- **Clear Selection** clears a selected part of the screen. You must first use the Free-Form Select or Select tools to enclose the portion of the drawing you want to clear.

- **Select All** selects all parts of an object and all objects in the drawing area.

- **Copy To** allows you to copy the selected objects to a file. A dialog box will be displayed where you can enter the path and filename.

- **Paste From** allows you to insert a file. A dialog box will be displayed where you can enter the path and filename to be pasted.

THE VIEW MENU

The View menu, seen in Figure 11–15, determines whether you can see the toolbox, color box, and status bar. It also controls the size of the image and whether it is seen as a bitmap, and if text is being used, whether the text toolbar is displayed. These are the options:

- **Tool Box** displays the toolbox on the left of the screen.

- **Color Box** displays the color palette below the drawing area.

- **Status Bar** displays the status bar beneath the color box. It displays tool box functions as the individual buttons are clicked on and describes menu items.

- **Zoom** displays a submenu of five options for viewing a variety of images of the object (See Figure 11–16):

Figure 11–15

View menu

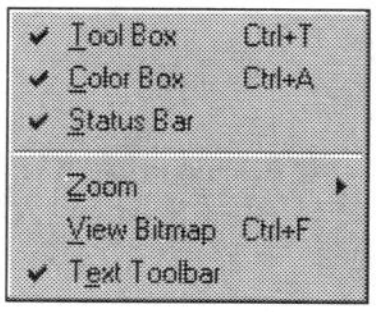

✔ Tool Box	Ctrl+T
✔ Color Box	Ctrl+A
✔ Status Bar	
Zoom	▶
View Bitmap	Ctrl+F
✔ Text Toolbar	

Figure 11–16

Zoom Submenu

Normal Size	Ctrl+PgUp
Large Size	Ctrl+PgDn
Custom...	
Show Grid	Ctrl+G
Show Thumbnail	

- ▨ **Normal Size** displays the object at its normal size. This option is usually chosen after viewing the image at an enlarged size.
- ▨ **Large Size** enlarges the object.
- ▨ **Custom** allows you to define the view you want. You can Zoom to 100 percent, 200 percent, 400 percent, 600 percent, or 800 percent of the object's normal size.
- ▨ **Show Grid**, available in enlarged view, displays a grid over the object, so that you can make your work more accurate and precise.
- ▨ **Show Thumbnail**, available in enlarged view, displays a small thumbnail display of the object on the screen. You can see the results on the whole object as you manipulate a small part of it.

- ■ **View Bitmap** displays a full screen view of the object. Click on the screen to return to the normal view.

- ■ **Text Toolbar**, which is displayed when the Text tool is selected, allows you to choose font, size, and bold, underline, or italics styles.

THE IMAGE MENU

The Image Menu, seen in Figure 11–17, provides features which enable you to produce some dramatic enhancements of your art. You can flip or rotate selected objects, stretch or skew them, invert colors, or change the attributes of your overall drawing, such as its width. Here are the options:

- ■ **Flip/Rotate** allows you to flip or rotate a selected part of your object. When you select this, the Flip and Rotate dialog box is displayed, which allows you to flip horizontal, flip vertical, or rotate by angle (which can be 90, 180, or 270 degrees).

- ■ **Stretch/Skew** displays a Stretch and Skew dialog box shown in Figure 11–18, which allows you to stretch vertically or

Figure 11–17

Image menu

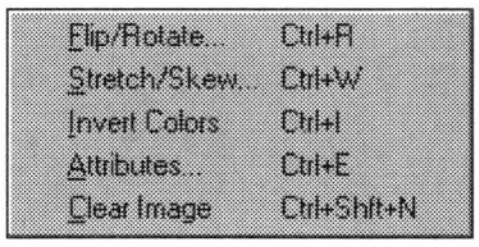

Flip/Rotate...	Ctrl+R
Stretch/Skew...	Ctrl+W
Invert Colors	Ctrl+I
Attributes...	Ctrl+E
Clear Image	Ctrl+Shft+N

Figure 11–18

*Stretch and Skew
dialog box*

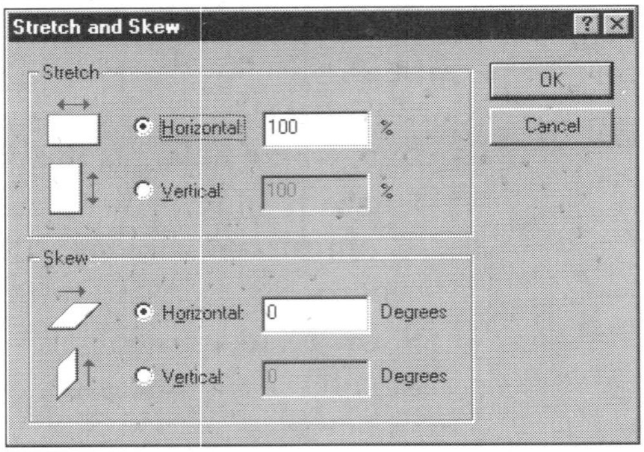

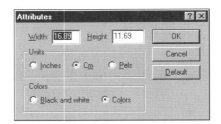

Figure 11–19

*Attributes
dialog box*

horizontally a selected object. You can also skew vertically or horizontally a selected object.

■ **Invert Colors** causes colors to be displayed in their complements.

■ **Attributes** allows you to change the overall attributes of the drawing: its width and height, units of measurements (between inches, centimeters, and pels or pixels), and whether it is in black and white or color. If you click on the Default button, the attributes are returned to their default settings, seen in Figure 11–19.

■ **Clear Image** clears the current image from the screen. You can Undo it, but if you first perform three other actions without saving it, the drawing will be lost.

THE OPTIONS MENU

The Options menu allows you to work with colors more precisely, getting the exact combinations that you want. Here are the options:

■ **Edit Colors** displays a dialog box so that you can see the basic colors available and create custom colors if none meet your requirements. To create a custom color, click on a basic color

Figure 11–20

Edit Colors expanded for defining custom colors

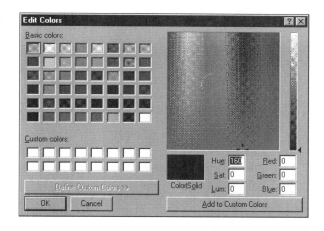

that seems close to it, and then click on Define Custom Colors. The dialog box will be expanded to include a color matrix and alternative ways of controlling the color (See Figure 11–20). You can establish a color either by setting the hue, saturation, or luminosity of a color; by setting the amount of red, green, or blue; or by clicking on the color in the color matrix. The numeric entry boxes may have these values:

- **Hue** is a numeric value associated with colors where 0 is red, 60 is yellow, 120 is green, 180 is cyan, 200 is magenta, and 240 is blue. By changing the hue, you change the reds, greens, and blues.
- **Sat** measures the amount of saturation for the color, up to a maximum of 240.
- **Lum** measures the brightness of the color.
- **Red** indicates the amount of red in the color.
- **Green** indicates the amount of green in the color.
- **Blue** indicates the amount of blue in the color.

By dragging the mouse across the color matrix, you can see the colors displayed. The settings below the matrix are set to correspond. This may be an easier way for you to create the color you want.

- **Get Colors** allows you to get colors from another computer, disk, or folder.
- **Save Colors** saves a selected color to disk.

- **Draw Opaque** switches your drawings from opaque to transparent by clicking on this option. An opaque drawing covers the underlying drawing, while transparent drawings allow the underlying drawing to show through.

THE HELP MENU

The Help menu provides two options: Help Topics, which provide both systemwide help and help specific to Paint; and About Paint, which gives you memory, resource usage, copyright, and product release information.

The Tool Box

The Paint Toolbox displays the tools available for creating and changing your drawings, using lines, shapes, text, and colors. By placing the pointer over a toolbox button, you'll see two clues as to what the button does. The status bar, beneath the color box describes its function and a popup label appears displaying its name.

 Beneath the tool box, a blank rectangular area contains optional choices for some of the buttons. For example, if you choose Magnifier, a selection of magnifying strengths will be displayed. If you choose the Rounded Rectangle, as shown here, choices varying the border and transparency of the box will be displayed:

You may choose these tools from the toolbox:

- **Free-Form Select** selects an area by allowing you to draw a line around an irregularly shaped area. Click on the icon, and drag the pointer around the area to select it. A selection box will replace your Free-Form Select drawing.

- **Select** creates a rectangularly shaped selection box. Click on the icon, and then drag the pointer diagonally across the area to be selected.

- **Eraser/Color Eraser** erases part of a drawing, both color and lines, as you move the eraser tool over it. Click on the Eraser icon, choose an eraser size from the area beneath the toolbox, and drag the eraser over the part of the drawing to be erased.

 The area created by Eraser can be filled with color.

■ **Fill With Color** fills an enclosed area with color. Click on the Fill With Color icon, place the pointer with the end of the poured liquid icon in the area to be filled, and click the mouse.

 **If there is a break in the enclosed area, the color will leak outside the lines.**

 ■ **Pick Color** duplicates a color in one area and transfers it to another. Click on the Pick Color icon, click on the object in the drawing whose color is to be duplicated (the tool changes to Fill With Color), click on the object or area where you want the color transferred.

 **To see if you have selected the right color to be copied, look beneath the tool box. A color will flash as you click the Pick Color on an object to select the color. If you wanted another color, repeat the procedure.**

 ■ **Magnifier** enlarges a defined area. Click on the magnifier icon. The pointer will become a rectangular box which you use to define the area to be enlarged. Click on the area to be enlarged, then click on a power choice beneath the toolbox. To change the magnification, click on the Magnifier icon, then click on a power choice again. To return to normal size you can either select 1X from the power choices or click the Magnifier icon on the drawing.

 **To see a part of the drawing hidden because it is too large for the screen, use the scroll bars.**

 ■ **Pencil** draws a line. Click on the Pencil icon, click on a color from the color box, and draw the shape you want.

 ■ **Brush** draws lines of varying shapes and widths. Click on the Brush icon, select the shape and width from beneath the toolbox, click on the color the line is to be, and draw the shape.

 ■ **Airbrush** draws groupings of dots, or splotches, on the drawing. Click on the Airbrush icon, select the size of splotch you want from beneath the toolbox, click on the color of the splotch, and drag the pointer or click on the drawing to effect the airbrushed look.

Figure 11–21

Text box woith
Fonts toolbox

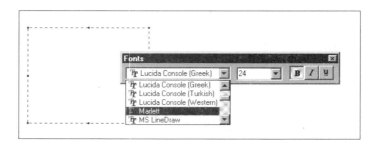

- **Text** types text onto a drawing. Click on the Text icon, click on the color for the text, and create a text box by dragging the pointer where you want text to be inserted. In the Fonts toolbox that appears (see Figure 11–21), click on the font, size, and style (bold, italic, underline). Click within the text box and type.

If you want the text box to contain no background colors, click on the top image beneath the toolbox. If you want to type directly onto the drawing, select the bottom image.

- **Line** draws a straight line. Click on the Line icon, click on the color for the line, click on the beginning point of the line, drag the pointer to an end point, click once to anchor the line before continuing, or release your mouse button to end the line altogether.

- **Curve** draws a curved line between two points. Click on Curve, click on a color, click on the beginning point of the curve, drag the line to the ending point, click once to anchor the line before continuing. To create a curve, click beside the line anywhere and drag. Click twice to end the line.

To create a teardrop, click on the Curve icon, click on a beginning point, click on a point twice the size of the teardrop to form a straight line, and click on a point in the direction the teardrop is to form. The line bends in two to form the teardrop.

- **Rectangle** draws a box. Click on Rectangle, click on a color, place the pointer at the upper-left corner of the rectangle, drag it diagonally down to the lower right. Below the toolbox select a box: rectangle with border and background showing through; rectangle with border and fill; rectangle with no border and fill.

- **Polygon** draws straight lines connecting in various shapes and angles. Click on the Polygon icon, and select a color.

From beneath the toolbox, choose between a shape with border and background showing through; shape with border and fill; shape with no border and fill. Place the pointer at the beginning point of the shape, and draw the first line segment by dragging the pointer. Release the mouse, place the pointer where the second line segment is to end, click the mouse button, and continue clicking for the line segments until the drawing is complete. Click twice to end the drawing.

- **Ellipse** creates an elliptical shape. Click on the Ellipse icon and select a color. From beneath the toolbox choose between a transparent shape with a border; a shape with a border and fill; a shape with no border and fill. Place the pointer in the upper left of the ellipse, and drag the pointer diagonally to the lower right.

By pressing [Shift] **while you drag the pointer, you will force a perfect circle to be drawn.**

- **Rounded Rectangle** operates like Rectangle; however, the corners of the rectangular shape are curved rather than squared.

The Color Box

The color box, located at the bottom of the drawing area, displays the available colors. You select a color by clicking on it. The foreground color is displayed in the top square on the left. The background color is displayed on the square beneath the foreground one. Select the foreground color with the left mouse button, and the background color with the right mouse button. The procedure for using the color box is to first select the tool, then the tool shape, if applicable, and finally, the color. The line or shape will be drawn in the color selected.

To create your own colors, select Edit Colors from the Options menu. The dialog box displayed is explained above in "The Options Menu" section.

WordPad

WordPad is a simple but capable word processor which can directly read both Word 6.0 and Windows Write files as well as Rich text and ASCII files. It is accessible by opening the Start menu and selecting Programs, Accessories, and then WordPad.

Figure 11–22

*WordPad window
with its menus,
toolbar, and
format bar*

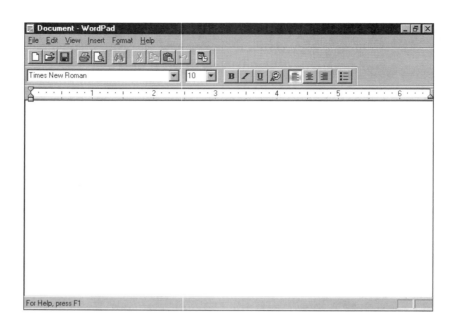

Figure 11–22

*WordPad window
with its menus,
toolbar, and
format bar*

The WordPad Window

When you open WordPad, the window, seen in Figure 11–22, contains five menus plus Help. These menus contain some unique items along with the common folder options described in earlier chapters. Below the menus are a toolbar and format bar containing buttons for many commands, an optional ruler, and, finally, the word processing area. Beneath the text area is the status bar, which is where messages and command descriptions are displayed.

THE FILE MENU

The File menu contains commands for dealing with files. It is where you create new files, open existing ones, save, and print files. Most of these commands are common to all File folder menus. However, this File menu also contains these special options:

- **Print Preview** displays the document as it will be printed (see Figure 11–23). You can check the pagination, margins, and page breaks plus other specifics, before the pages are printed. When you select Print Preview, you'll see a different set of buttons on the toolbar:

  - **Print** sends the document to the printer.

Figure 11–23

Print preview screen

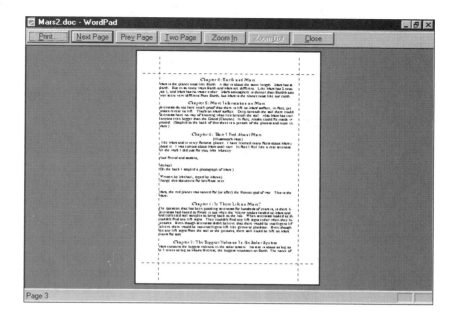

- ▨ **Next Page** and **Prev Page** display the next and previous pages.

- ▨ **Two Page** displays two pages so that you can see pages as in a book.

- ▨ **Zoom In** enlarges the part of the document where the pointer is clicked.

- ▨ **Zoom Out** reduces the size again.

- ▨ **Close** returns to the normal word processing screen.

- ■ **Page Setup** displays a dialog box for setting paper size and source, orientation (portrait or landscape), and margins. You can also change the printer from this dialog box.

THE EDIT MENU

The Edit menu contains these options which allow you to manipulate the text in word processing documents:

- ■ **Paste Special** copies linked or embedded information from the Clipboard into a document. When you select Paste Special, a dialog box gives you the option to link or embed the information.

- **Find** searches for a character string. To find whole words, select Match whole word only; otherwise, you will find all embedded occurrences of the string as well. If capitalization is important, click on Match case.

- **Find Next** repeats the previous Find command.

- **Replace** replaces one sequence of characters with another. You specify the search criteria in Find what. You specify the replacement value in Replace with. As in Find, you can Match whole word only and Match case. When a find is made, you have the option of Replace to replace that one occurrence, Replace All to replace all occurrences, or Find Next to ignore the find and continue searching for the next occurrence.

- **Links** automatically or manually updates any linked objects in WordPad and allows you to open the program which has created the linked object, so that you can edit the original. The changes will be reflected in the linked object.

- **Object Properties** displays the Package Properties of the object. It provides the type of object, size and location on the General tab. The View tab contains Display as editable information or Display as icon properties. You can change the icon here, and depending on the object, you may see Scale properties as well. The Link tab is similar to the Links option described above.

- **Object** allows you to edit a linked object. When you select Object, you can then either edit or open the object. The creating program will be started so the object can be edited. Once the object is selected, this option may change to be more explicit. For example, if you have selected a sound file to edit, Object changes to Media Clip Object with appropriate options of Play, Edit, or Open.

To return to WordPad once the object has been edited, click outside the object. To return to WordPad if you clicked on any command other than Edit, select Exit and Return to filename from the File menu.

THE VIEW MENU

The View menu contains five options for varying the screen display:

- **Toolbar**, when selected, displays the top toolbar.

- **Format Bar**, when selected, displays the format bar beneath the toolbar.

- **Ruler**, when selected, displays the ruler. You can set tabs and margins on the ruler by clicking on it to indicate where you want a tab placed. You can drag margin settings and tabs to different locations on the ruler.

- **Status Bar**, when selected, displays the status bar which displays command messages and statuses, and descriptions of commands.

- **Options** displays a dialog box, see in Figure 11–24, for establishing defaults for a document being edited. The Options dialog box has six tabs, although four of them are identical:

  - **Options** tab allows you to set the units of measurement for the document, in inches, points, centimeters, or picas. You can cause a word at a time to be selected, as you begin to drag the pointer over a word, by selecting Automatic word selection. If you leave it unchecked, dragging the pointer will select character by character.

  - **Text, Rich Text, Word 6**, and **Write** tabs allow you to set Word Wrap options and toolbar displays for each type of text. For Word wrap, you can choose between No wrap; Wrap to window, where the screen determines when the line wraps to the next line; and Wrap to ruler where the margins determine when the line wraps. As in the View menu, you can also set the defaults for each type of text (Word 6, Rich Text, Text, or Write) for displaying the toolbar, format bar, ruler, and status bar.

  - **Embedded** contains the same options as the other text tabs, except it contains no option for displaying the status

Figure 11–24

Options dialog box

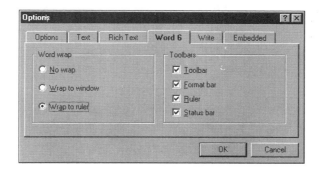

bar. This is because you will be editing in the embedded object's creating application.

THE INSERT MENU

The Insert menu provides options for inserting the time and date or another object:

- **Date and Time** inserts the time and date where the pointer is positioned. You can choose between various date formats when you click on the option.

- **Object** displays an Insert Object dialog box. In it you can choose whether the object to be inserted will be created new from a selected application, or whether it will be created from an existing file. Click on Display As Icon to display the inserted object as an icon rather than what it is, as an image, for example.

  Once you click on Created New and an object type, the screen will become the application to create that type of object. For example, if you insert a sound file, the Media Player application will be displayed. If you insert a bitmap image, Paint will be loaded, as shown in Figure 11–25. You create the object using the tools on the loaded screen. When

Figure 11–25

*Creating a
bitmap image
from Word
loads Paint*

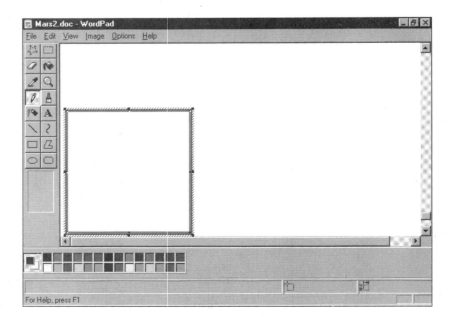

you are finished, click outside the box containing the object, and WordPad will return.

If you select Create from File, you will be able to enter the path and filename of the file to be inserted. Browse is available if you need it. To create a linked file, click on Link. This will create an address reference only in the document so that modifications are done in the original and reflected in the document. If you don't select Link, the object will be embedded within the document. In this case, it exists as a separate object that can be modified. Click on Display As Icon to display the inserted object as an icon rather than as an image.

FORMAT MENU

The Format menu provides options that vary the format style of the sentence or paragraph:

- **Font** displays a dialog box so that you can select a font, font style, size, and whether special effects of strikeout and underline are used.

- **Bullet Style** places a bullet where the pointer is placed and allows you to create an outline type of style. When you press Return, another bullet begins the next line.

- **Paragraph** allows you to set left, right and first line indentations, and an alignment of left, right or center. Figure 11–26 shows the Paragraph dialog box.

- **Tabs** displays a dialog box for setting or clearing tabs. You remove existing tabs by clicking on Clear All. Set new tabs by typing a tab stop in the Tab stop position text box, then clicking on Set. You can clear individual tabs by selecting them and clicking on Clear.

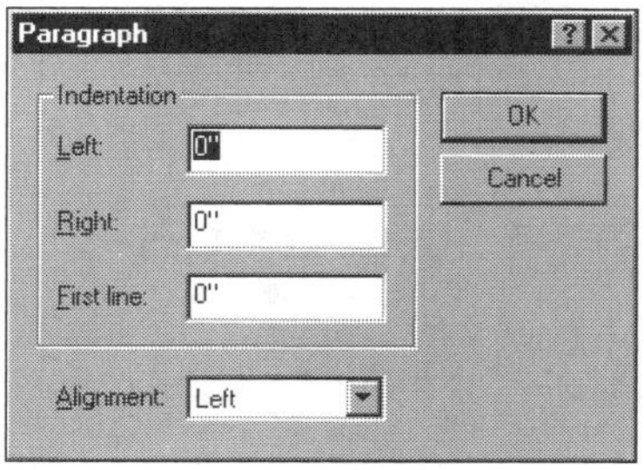

Figure 11–26

Paragraph dialog box

THE TOOLBARS

There are two toolbars to help you work more easily and efficiently. Table 11–1 describes the buttons in the topmost toolbar, and Table 11–2 shows the buttons in the Format Bar. Most of these toolbar buttons duplicate options in the menus, but they are accessed by simply clicking on the button.

Table 11–1.

Toolbar buttons

Button	Name	Description
	New, Open, Save	New creates a new document; Open retrieves an existing document; Save saves the active document to disk
	Print, Print Preview	Print sends a document to the printer; Print Preview displays the current document page on the screen as it will be printed
	Find	Find searches for characters matching the criteria you specify
	Cut, Copy, Paste	Cut deletes text; Copy duplicates text; Paste inserts cut or copied text from Clipboard into document
	Undo	Cancels or undoes the last action
	Date /Time	Inserts the date and time into the document

Table 11–2.

Format Bar controls

Control/Button and Name	Description
Font, Size	Allow you to change the font and its size for selected text
Bold, Italics, Underline	Make the selected text boldface, italics, or underlined
Color	Lets you specify color for selected text
Align Left, Center, Align Right	Align the selected text to the left, center, or right
Bullets	Places bullets at the beginning of the paragraph

PART V

Windows 95 Advanced Topics

One of the beauties of Windows 95 is that it can satisfy the needs of many different types of users, from the beginner to the systems expert. Part V addresses two areas that are more of interest to system professionals than they are to new users. Yet these areas of system management and using DOS are every bit as well addressed by Windows 95 as is the user interface.

Chapter 12 discusses system management and the optimizing of Windows 95. It looks at how you implement Windows 95 in an organization and how to use the tools in Windows 95 to manage that task. Chapter 12 also looks at the optimization questions and how Windows 95 itself and its tools answer those questions.

Chapter 13 covers the running of DOS programs under Windows 95 and the use of the Windows 95 command language. The chapter looks at the ways to run even the most stubborn DOS programs and then describes the many commands available and the different ways of running them.

System Management and Optimizing Windows 95

indows 95 has an unusual dual personality. It offers both a very easy and intuitive end-user environment, and at the same time it is an excellent environment for a system or network administrator to manage. In the first eleven chapters of this book you have seen the great end-user environment provided by Windows 95. In this chapter you'll see that Windows 95 is an equally great administrative environment. The chapter is broken into two major areas, system management and optimization.

System Management

System Management is one of those terms that sound great, but it has such a broad scope that it is difficult to know what it means. In this context, *system management* refers to the continuing control of who is using what on the computers in an organization and how are they doing it. Windows 95 includes many features that address system management. Among these are several layers of security measures, the use of system policies, the provision for remote administration of networked workstations, and the use of the system registry.

Security Measures

Effective computer security protects a computer from unauthorized use or access, as well as provides easy access and unhindered use to those that are authorized. Windows 95 has been designed to accomplish both objectives in the following ways:

- Windows 95 provides two different types of security: *share-level* security that specifies the type of access that is available to specific resources on the computer such as disks, printers, and folders; and *user-level* security that specifies the access rights of each individual using the system.

- Windows 95 provides multiple levels of security that may be used as necessary; this includes the Windows 95 logon, program access, network access, computer access, resource (printer or disk) access, and individual folder access.

- Windows 95 provides for a password list, or caching, which allows the Windows 95 logon password to open a list of passwords that are automatically used to provide access to other resources and multiple networks.

- Windows 95 provides for the use of either simple passwords or the establishment of policies that require longer alphanumeric (harder to break) passwords.

- Windows 95 provides for the remote use of a password editor to change a user password list.

Obviously the security measures taken in a large client-server network are significantly more stringent than those on a small peer-to-peer network or on a stand-alone computer. The client-server software (either Windows NT or Novell NetWare) controls many of the security measures, and although handled well in the Windows 95 client, it is beyond the scope of this book. Here we'll focus on security measures that can be implemented on peer-to-peer and stand-alone systems.

 **User-level security requires that a list of user passwords and permissions be kept on either a Windows NT or NetWare server and is not available in peer-to-peer networking.**

USING PASSWORDS

In Windows 95 passwords can be assigned to the following events or resources:

- Windows logon
- Computer (screen saver) access
- Printer and disk access
- Program access
- Individual folder access
- Remote administration permission

Each of these passwords is applied under different circumstances and is changed in a different place, as described in the next sections. In addition to these six areas, there is another area where you can possibly run into passwords: when signing on to a network to which you are not normally connected. Since this area is outside of Windows 95, it is not discussed further.

Windows Logon Password The password request that you see when you first start up Windows 95 is the lock in the front door of Windows 95. The password that you use in response to this request is the primary logon password. If you choose, it can not only let you into Windows 95, it can also open a password list that will automatically supply the passwords that you need for network, program, and resource usage. The password list is discussed later in this chapter.

Passwords

The logon password is set either during Windows 95 setup or in the Passwords control panel, shown in Figure 12–1. By clicking on Change Windows Password, you open the following dialog box:

Change Windows Password	? X
Old password:	[ ]	OK
New password:	[ ]	Cancel
Confirm new password:	[ ]	

To change the Windows logon password, you must enter the existing, or Old, password and then enter the New password twice to confirm it. If you have never entered a password since installing Windows 95, the default password is the absence of any password (called a *null*), and you simply press [←Enter] or click on OK to use it. In the Change Windows Password dialog box, if you have not previously entered a password, you can press [←Enter] or [Tab] or click on New Password to "enter" a null password. If you don't want to use a Windows logon

Figure 12–1

*Password
Properties
dialog box*

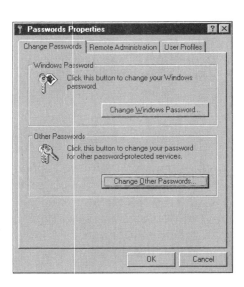

password, you can change it to a null by pressing ⏎Enter in the New password field and in the confirmation field.

Computer Access Password When you step away from your computer while you are inside Windows, someone could come up, use your computer, and potentially do something you don't want done. To prevent this, Windows 95 has a password attached to the screen saver. The password prevents clearing the screen and activating the keyboard, so it prevents using the computer. When you have the screen saver active, it puts a screen saving (and potentially energy saving if your monitor has this feature) pattern on the screen if you have not used the keyboard or mouse for a set period of time. Without the password, if you press a key or move the mouse, the screen saver pattern will disappear. With password protection turned on and the screen saver active, when you press a key or move the mouse, you are asked to enter a password. If you do not enter the correct one, the screen saver pattern continues to cover the screen, and you can't do anything with the keyboard except enter the password.

To activate the screen saver and turn on its password, use the following steps:

Display

1. Open the Control Panel and double-click on the Display icon.

2. When the Display Properties dialog box opens, click on the Screen Saver tab to open the dialog box shown in Figure 12–2.

Figure 12–2

*Screen Saver tab
in the Display
Properties
dialog box*

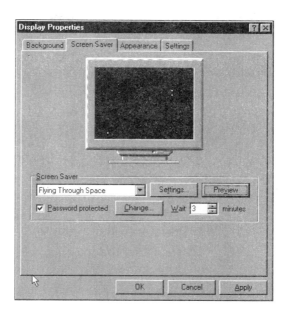

3. Select a screen saver other than None, and click on the Password protected check box.

4. Click on Change; enter the password you want to use, first in the New password text box and then in the confirmation text box; and click on OK.

5. Set the Wait time to a time that is right for you, and then click on OK again.

Once you have turned on the screen saver and its password, then, after waiting the set amount of time, the screen saver will appear. When you press a key or move the mouse, the password request will appear as you can see here:

When you set the time after which the screen saver will activate, you have two opposing considerations: if you set it too short, the screen saver will activate every time to take a sip of coffee; if you set it too long, you may have to wait longer than you want before leaving your desk. One way to prevent this is to make a shortcut for your preferred screen saver, and place it on your desktop or even attach a hotkey to it. This way you can activate the screen saver by either double-clicking on it or pressing the hotkey. Use the following instructions to create the shortcut and a hotkey:

1. In the Explorer\Windows\System folder select the Details view, and then click on Type in the heading above the list of files to sort the list by type.

2. Scroll down the list of files to find the Screen Saver files, and select the one you want to use.

3. Right-click on the file, select Create Shortcut, and then drag the shortcut to the desktop.

4. Right-click on the screen saver shortcut icon, select Properties, and click on the Shortcut tab.

5. Click in the Shortcut key text box, and press a key you want to use as the hotkey to start the screen saver. If you press a function key (F1 – F12), you can use that key alone. If you press any normal alphanumeric key (A–Z and 0–9), you'll get Ctrl + Alt + the key you pressed. Most of the functions keys are used elsewhere, so the safest approach is to use the Ctrl + Alt + a key combination. When you have selected a key, click on OK.

You now have on your desktop a screen saver icon that you can click on at anytime, as well as a hotkey you can press, to start a screen saver and protect your system if you step away from your computer.

Printer and Disk Access Password In a network environment, if you share your disks and printer, you may then want to control who has access to them. In Chapter 6, you may remember that when you share a resource you can set a password in several different ways. As a quick reminder, review the following steps for setting a password, first for a shared disk drive, and then for a shared printer.

1. Right-click on a disk drive in either My Computer or the Explorer, and choose Sharing in the popup menu that appears. The Sharing tab of the disk's Properties dialog box opens, as you can see in Figure 12–3.

2. Choose an Access Type. If it is Read-Only or Full access, you can enter a password for that type. If the Access Type is

Figure 12–3

Sharing tab of a disk's Properties dialog box

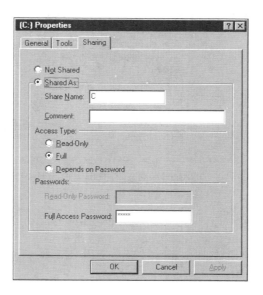

Depends on Password, you can enter a different password for each type. This allows you to give different people different access.

If a user is already accessing your resources when you set a password for those resources, the user will not be affected by the password change until he or she exits from and returns to Windows and tries once more to access your resources.

To set a password for a shared printer, use these steps:

1. From My Computer, the Explorer, or the Start menu Settings option, open the Printers folder, and right-click on the printer you want to share.

2. Choose Sharing from the popup menu that appears. The Sharing tab of the printer's Properties dialog box will open, as shown in Figure 12–4.

3. Click on Shared As; enter a Share Name, optionally a Comment, and a Password twice, first in the dialog box and then in the confirmation dialog box.

If you try to use either a disk or a printer that has been password protected, you'll be asked for the password, as shown next.

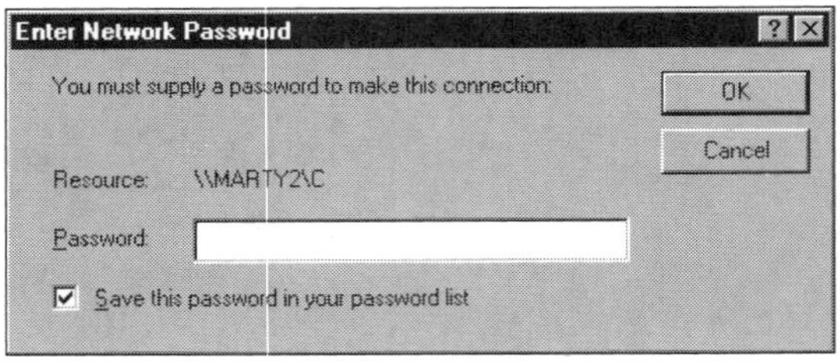

Enter Network Password

You must supply a password to make this connection:

Resource: \\MARTY2\C

Password: [   ]

☑ Save this password in your password list

OK

Cancel

If you save the password in your password list by clicking on the check box of that name, you will not have to enter the password again unless the owner changes the password.

If you have mapped another computer's drive to your computer, and the password has changed, you will not be able to access the drive without remapping it with the new password. See Chapter 6 on how to map a network drive.

Microsoft Mail
Postoffice

Program Access The use of passwords in programs is completely dependent on the program. The one program within Windows 95 with password protection is Microsoft Mail. The Microsoft Mail postoffice administrator must set the password with the following steps:

1.   Open the Microsoft Mail Postoffice from the Control Panel. The Microsoft Workgroup Postoffice Admin wizard will open

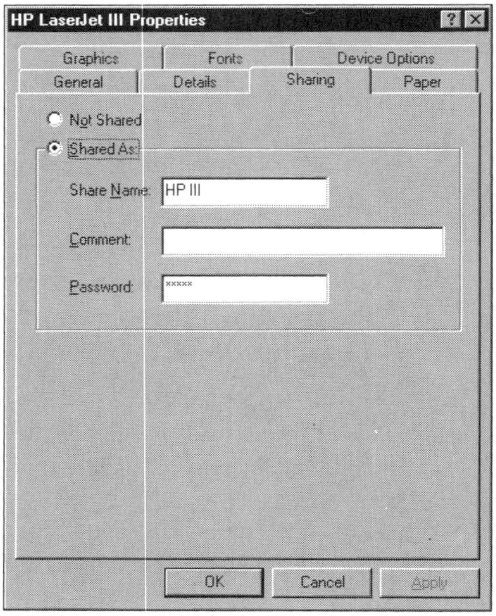

Figure 12–4

Sharing tab of a printer's Properties dialog box

HP LaserJet III Properties

| Graphics | | Fonts | | Device Options |
| General | Details | Sharing | Paper |

○ Not Shared

◉ Shared As:

Share Name: [HP III   ]

Comment: [   ]

Password: [*****   ]

OK   Cancel   Apply

Figure 12–5

Changing the password for a postoffice mail box

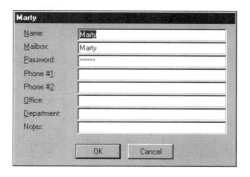

and ask if you want to administer an existing postoffice or create a new one. Leave the default of Administer an existing Workgroup Postoffice, and click on Next.

2. The path to the existing postoffice will be shown. You can change it, Browse for another postoffice, or leave it alone. When you are ready, click on Next.

3. The administrator is then asked for her or his password. (This is set when the postoffice is set up. It can be changed with a later step in the setup.) After entering the correct password, click on Next.

4. You can then identify the postoffice user whose password you want to change. (Here is where you can identify the administrator and change his or her password.) The mailbox holder's information box will open, as shown in Figure 12–5.

5. After changing the password, which does not require a confirmation, click on OK and then Close.

After a password has been set for Microsoft Mail, when you try to use it, you will be stopped and asked for the password, as shown next. By clicking on Remember password, you will not have to reenter the password in the future.

Figure 12–6

*Folder Properties
dialog box
showing the folder
is shared via the
disk's being shared*

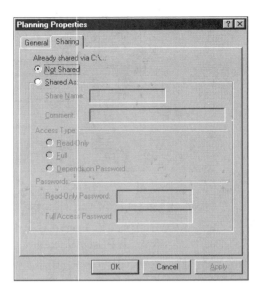

If you are also using the Exchange mail folders, you will also be asked for that password, which can be saved.

Folder Access Password Although you can password protect disks, you can also go one level further down and password protect folders, although you must turn *off* disk sharing for folder sharing to take affect. Sharing and password protecting a folder requires the same steps as sharing a disk except that you right-click on a folder instead of a disk. When you open the Properties dialog box, if the folder is already shared via the disk, you are told that, as you can see in Figure 12–6.

Disk sharing takes precedence over folder sharing, so if your disk is shared, all the folders are automatically shared under the disk's password.

With either Novell NetWare or Windows NT you can assign passwords to individual files, although you cannot do that in Windows 95.

Remote Administration Permission Password In a network environment it is sometimes desirable to have an administrator remotely (from another computer) manage all the computers in a workgroup or on the network. To do that, permission must be granted on each computer to allow the remote administration of that computer. Use the following steps to accomplish that:

Figure 12–7

*Remote
Administration
permission tab*

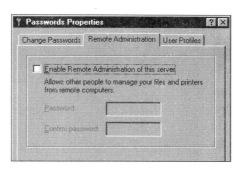

1. From the Control Panel double-click on Passwords to open the Passwords Properties dialog box.

2. Click on the Remote Administration tab to open the dialog box shown in Figure 12–7.

3. Click on Enable Remote Administration of this server, and enter and confirm the password to be used.

PASSWORD LIST

When someone has a number of passwords to remember, he or she tends to write them down and even post them on the front of their computer or monitor. To solve the problems of too many passwords, Windows 95 has a password list, or cache, that stores the passwords for the following items:

- Shared disks, printers, and folders on computers running Windows 95 and accessed by the computer with the password list

- Password protected programs

- Windows NT logon password and NetWare user IDs and passwords

When you log on, your logon password automatically opens the password list and provides the passwords as you access the resources. You can control whether a password is stored in the list by selecting, or not, the Save this password in your password list check box, as you can see in Figure 12–8.

There is no way to see all the passwords in your password list, but you can see the items controlled by passwords in the list in the Password List Editor, shown in Figure 12–9 and discussed later in this chapter

Figure 12–8

When you enter a network password, you can save it in your password list

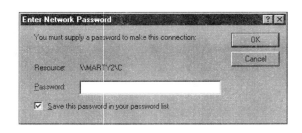

Figure 12–9

Password List Editor

under "Remote Administration." The password list can be turned off using the System Policy Editor, also described later in this chapter.

USER PROFILES

Another way of controlling the use of a computer or computers on a network is through user profiles. User profiles are a set of specifications, which can be unique to each user who signs on to the computer, that specifies how the computer will look and behave. User profiles provide for the following:

- Multiple users on a single computer, each with a different set of specifications

- A user accessing several computers with his or her own unique specifications

- A network administrator enforcing a standard set of specifications for all computers in a workgroup to better support inexperienced users

Figure 12–10

User profiles folder structure for two users

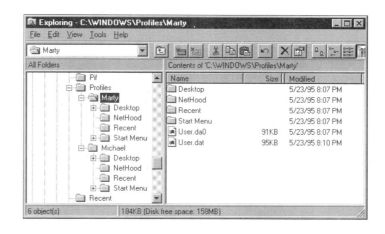

User profiles cover most of what you can customize in Windows 95, including the desktop background, the font used, the icons and shortcuts on the desktop, the contents of the Start menu, network connections, and program settings. The files and folders that represent the profile of a given user are stored in a folder for that user in the \Windows\Profiles folder. The files and folders include the User.dat Registry file (see the discussion of the Registry later in this chapter), a backup Registry file User.da0, and four folders that hold the contents of the desktop, the Network Neighborhood, the Start menu, and recent documents you have directly started. Figure 12–10 shows a Profiles folder for two users, Marty and Michael. In a client-server network environment, the contents of the Profiles folder is stored on the server and downloaded when a user signs on to a computer. That way the user can be on any computer in the workgroup and get their preferences.

Enabling User Profiles   User profiles are enabled through the User Profiles tab of the Passwords Properties dialog box, shown in Figure 12–11. In this dialog box tab, you can choose between all users using the same settings and each having her or his own settings. If you choose the latter, you can then choose to allow customization of two different sets of objects, as you can see in Figure 12–11. If you change the User Profiles tab and click on OK, you will be told that you need to restart Windows for the change to take effect. Click on Yes to make that happen.

If you want to disable user profiles, simply select the All users of this PC use the same preferences and desktop settings option, and the individual profiles will be eliminated.

Figure 12–11

*Enabling
User Profiles*

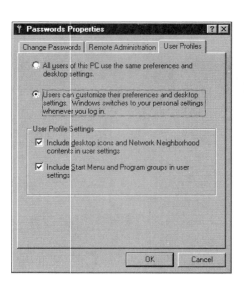

Using User Profiles The first time you log on to the computer after enabling user profiles, even though you have been using the computer for a long time, you will be told that

```
You have not logged on at this computer before. Would
you like this computer to retain your individual set-
tings for use when you log on here in the future?
```

If you answer Yes, a new profile will be created for you and stored in the \Windows\Profiles folder. Otherwise you will be logged on to the computer using the default user profile. If you have your own profile, any changes that you make to the desktop, the Start menu, or anything that is stored in the user portion of the Registry, which can include a lot of program customization, is stored in your profile and will appear when you next log on to that computer. At the same time, your changes will not affect other users who have their own profiles.

System Policies

System policies allow the central administration of a workgroup or network of PCs. Through system policies, the network administrator can control and easily change much of what the user sees and is able to do on his or her computer. This control extends to the look and contents of the desktop and the Start menu, the resources available on the network, the availability of Control Panel options, and many other functions that can be controlled only through system policies. System policies can also be used to establish certain password policies, such as the minimum length of passwords and whether passwords must contain both alpha and numeric information (thus making them harder to break).

System policies are established and maintained by the System Policy Editor. The System Policy Editor is a network tool and primarily a tool of larger networks. It creates a file named Config.pol that is stored on the network server and downloaded to individual computers where it replaces the User.dat and System.dat Registry files. Policies can be created for individual users by name, for specific computers by name, and for workgroups. Policies are also created for both default users and default computers. When a user logs on to a computer, the following steps take place:

1. The user's logon name is checked to see if it matches an individual user policy. If one exists, then it is downloaded and applied, and any group policies are ignored. If there is no user policy for the logon name, then the default user policy is downloaded and applied.

2. The logon name is checked for membership in a group. If one or more group memberships are found, then the applicable group policies are downloaded and applied.

3. The computer name is checked against specific computer policies, and if found, they are downloaded and applied. If no computer specific policies exist, then a default policy is used.

SETTING UP THE SYSTEM POLICY EDITOR

The System Policy Editor can substantially modify the look and operation of Windows 95. For that reason, it is not normally installed when installing Windows 95 and should be used with a reasonable amount of caution. The System Policy Editor is on the Windows 95 CD in the \Admin\Apptools\Poledit folder. Use the following steps to put the System Policy Editor on your hard disk:

1. Place the Windows 95 CD in its drive and close the Autorun program when it appears.

2. From the Explorer, locate the \Admin\Apptools\Poledit folder on the CD and drag it to the hard drive you want it on.

This will put the editor on your hard drive in the folder Poledit (you might want to rename the folder Policy Editor).

3.   Open the Poledit (or Policy Editor) folder and create a shortcut by dragging the Poledit.exe file to the \Windows\Start Menu\Programs\Accessories\System Tools folder.

 The System Policy Editor should be restricted to the use of network administrators and not installed or made available to most users.

USING THE SYSTEM POLICY EDITOR

Before actually applying the System Policy Editor, it is important to lay out a plan as to how the policies will be applied across a workgroup or network. In doing this, you first need to identify what groups, computers, and individuals need policies, and then what default policies are required for everyone else. Next you need to review the many options you can set when you establish a policy. You can best do that by looking at the Standard policy sample discussed shortly. Looking at the Standard policy sample allows you to see all the options and what Microsoft believes should be the default settings.

When you have developed a plan for how you will implement the system policies or have decided just to study what policies you can set, start the System Policy Editor, and look at the sample Standard policy provided by Microsoft with Windows 95 using the following steps:

1.   From the Start menu choose Programs, Accessories, System Tools, and click on System Policy Editor. The System Policy Editor will open.

2.   From the File menu, choose Open File, select the Windows 95 CD, choose \Admin\Reskit\Samples\Policies, and double-click on Standard.pol. Default User and Default Computer policies will appear in the editor, as you can see in Figure 12–12.

3.   Double-click on the Default User policy to open it. Click on several of the plus signs to open several of the entries, as shown in Figure 12–13.

Notice in Figure 12–13 that there are three types of check boxes, as follows:

■   **Empty** check boxes mean that the item will not be implemented, and if it was previously implemented, either by a policy or

Figure 12–12

System Policy Editor with default policies

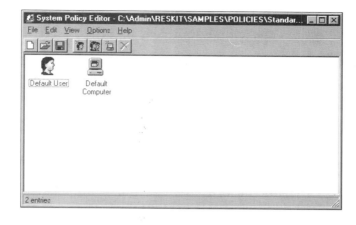

Figure 12–13

Default User Properties dialog box

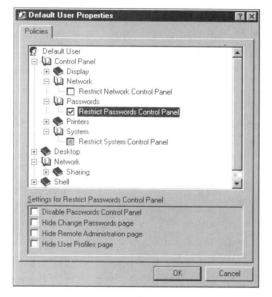

in the user's registry, it will be cleared (unimplemented) by an empty check box.

- **Checked** check boxes mean that the item will be implemented, and a group of settings will appear in the lower part of the dialog box for that item. This implementation will supersede any settings in the user's registry.

- **Grayed** check boxes mean that the policy makes no modification to the user's settings for this item. The user can set the item any way that she or he wishes.

The check boxes can be changed among the three states: empty, checked, and grayed, by repetitively clicking on the check box.

Be sure to leave a policy item grayed if you decide not to set that item. This will allow the user's settings to remain in effect, whereas if you clear the check box, it will clear the user's settings.

Go through both the Default User and Default Computer policies in the Standard.pol sample, seeing the recommended settings and considering the impact of the settings on your organization. Decide and document the settings that you want to make for the default users (the majority of your users) and default computer. Finally, decide if you have any special user, group, or computer needing their own policies—the system and/or network administrator(s), for example, should probably have a separate set of policies.

When you get ready to prepare your policies, you can either choose New from the System Policy Editor File menu or modify the Standard.pol, discussed above. In either case, it is important that the file be saved as Config.pol if you want it automatically downloaded at system startup. Both a new system policy and the Standard.pol sample start with default user and default computer policies. You should start with these and set the default policies for the majority of the workgroup. When you have finished with the default policies, you can add specific user, group, and computer policies by choosing those options in the Edit menu or by clicking the appropriate buttons in the tool bar as shown on the left (the fourth, fifth, and sixth buttons on the toolbar). When you open one of these policies, you will be asked to name it with a user, group, or computer name. The default and all specific policies are saved together in the same file, Config.pol.

In addition to setting system policies for a workgroup or an entire network, the System Policy Editor can be used to directly edit the Registry on a particular machine, as you will see later in this chapter under "Using the System Registry."

Remote Administration

Remote administration is the accessing of the administrative files in one computer from another—for example, the setting of passwords, profiles, and policies remotely. To use the remote administration facilities in Windows 95 you must be connected to a Windows NT or NetWare network and be using user-level security. Remote Administration must also be enabled in the Remote Administration tab of the Passwords Properties dialog boxes on each computer to be administered, as you saw above in the discussion on passwords. Finally, you must set up the Remote Registry services, which you can do with the following steps:

1. Open the Network control panel and click on Add. The Select Network Component Type dialog box will open.

2. Double-click on Service, and then, when the Select Network Service dialog box opens, click on Have Disk.

3. In the Install From Disk dialog box, click on Browse, select the path to the Windows 95 CD and the \Admin\Nettools\ Remotreg folder, and click on OK three times to close all the dialog boxes.

Once you have set up remote administration, there are five tools in Windows 95 that can be used. These and their functions are as follows:

- **System Policy Editor**, used to create and manage system policies and to edit a local Registry

- **Registry Editor**, used to edit a local Registry

- **Network Neighborhood**, used to manage the files systems including their structure and content

- **Net Watcher**, used to add and delete shared resources (printers and disks) and monitor their usage

- **System Monitor**, used to look for performance problems

To use one of the above tools, simply start the program, and then, for the System Policy Editor and System Monitor, select Connect from the File menu. For the Net Watcher, choose Select Server from the Administer menu, or for the Registry Editor, choose Connect Network Registry from the Registry menu. The Connect dialog box will appear, as shown next. Enter the name of the remote computer, and click on OK. You will be working on the remote computer.

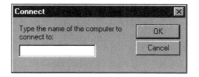

The System Policy Editor's system policy creating and management functions were described above under "System Policies." The System

Policy Editor registry editing function, as well as the Registry Editor's functions, are described later in this chapter under "Using the System Registry." The use of the Network Neighborhood and the Net Watcher were described in Chapter 7.

USING THE SYSTEM MONITOR

The System Monitor allows you to watch a number of different parameters that measure the activity and resource usage on a computer, either locally or remotely, as you can see in Figure 12–14. Start the System Monitor, and observe the operation of a remote computer with the following steps:

1. In the Start menu Run option, type **sysmon** and press ⏎Enter. The System Monitor will open.

2. Open the File menu, choose Connect, type the name of the computer to which you want to connect, and press ⏎Enter. You'll be viewing the remote computer.

3. To add parameters to the display, click on the Add button on the far left of the toolbar, select a category and an item, as shown in Figure 12–15, and click on OK.

4. You can change to a different type of display by clicking on the appropriate button in the toolbar. The bar chart is shown in Figure 12–16.

5. To change the color and/or scale of a parameter, click on the Edit button in the toolbar (third from the left), select the item

Figure 12–14

The System Monitor

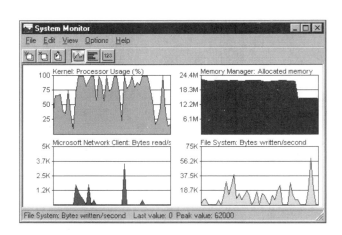

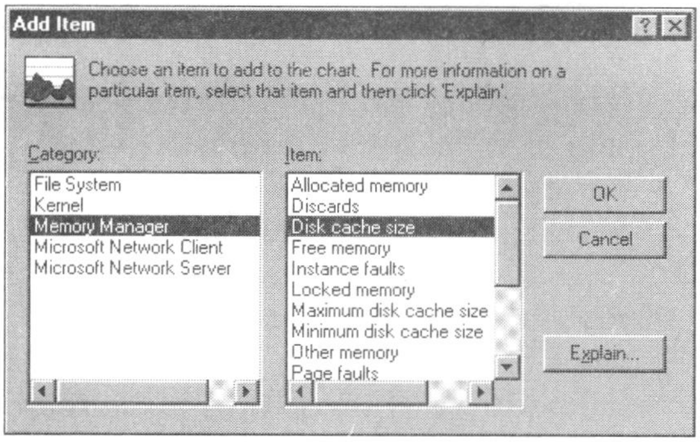

Figure 12–15

Adding an item to the System Monitor

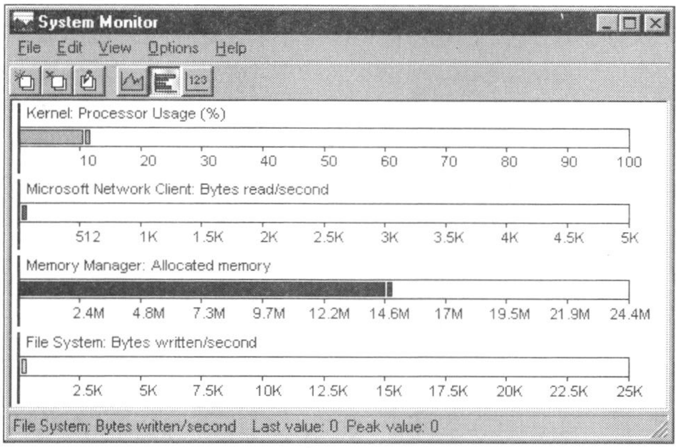

Figure 12–16

System monitor as a bar chart

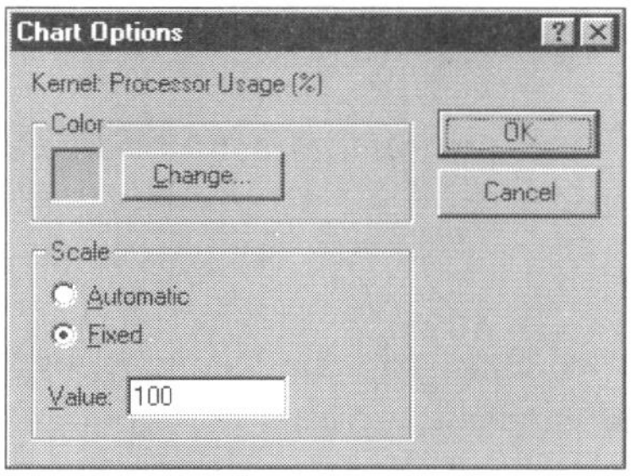

Figure 12–17

Chart Options dialog box

to be edited, and click on OK. The Chart Options dialog box will open, as you can see in Figure 12–17.

The System Monitor provides a very powerful tool for observing what is happening in your computer or another computer on your network.

Using the System Registry

The Registry is the central repository for all the configuration information in Windows 95. In earlier versions of Windows and DOS, a number of different files including Config.sys, Autoexec.bat, Win.ini and System.ini held similar, although much more limited, types of information. A smaller registry appeared in Windows 3.1, but the majority of the settings were still made in the .INI files. The .INI files, Autoexec.bat, and Config.sys are still in Windows 95, but only for backward compatibility with older programs and hardware. The Registry now contains all the information that Windows 95 needs to govern its operation, and all newer programs and hardware depend only on it.

The Registry is actually two different files, System.dat and User.dat, in the \Windows folder. (The .DAT files are hidden files, and to see them you must select Show all files in the Explorer's View menu Options dialog box.) Unlike the .INI files, the .DAT files are not text files and cannot be directly edited. The most common way to change the Registry is through the many settings in the Control Panel. In addition, as you read above, the System Policy Editor can both change the Registry directly or through policies that are created. Finally, Windows 95 has a program, the Registry Editor, that provides a very low-level form of directly editing the Registry.

When changing the Registry, you should first try to use the Control Panel, next the System Policy Editor, and only as a last resort use the Registry Editor. The Registry Editor allows you to directly change the Registry and does not check for syntax or semantic errors. With the Registry Editor it is possible to change the Registry in such a way that you cannot start Windows 95.

As a precaution against a bad Registry, Windows 95 maintains the backup registry files System.da0 and User.da0. It would not hurt for you to create a secondary backup before making any changes to the Registry.

Before changing the Registry, especially with the Registry Editor, protect your current settings by copying the .DAT files. You can quickly do that by selecting the two files in the Explorer, right-clicking on them, choosing Copy from the popup menu, right-clicking on any blank area on the right side of the Explorer window, and choosing Paste. Copies of the .DAT files will appear, like this:

Copy of USER.DAT	101KB	DAT File
Copy of SYSTEM.DAT	635KB	DAT File

Figure 12–18

The System Policy Editor with the local Registry

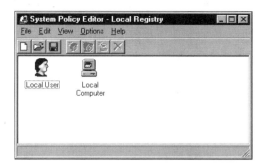

USING THE SYSTEM POLICY EDITOR

The System Policy Editor, as you learned above, can be used to directly edit your local Registry as well as create policies that are downloaded over the network and that replace the local Registry. Using the System Policy Editor to edit the local Registry provides the most comprehensive means to review and change your Registry. Use the following instructions to start the System Policy Editor and begin looking at your Registry (these instructions assume you have already gotten the System Policy Editor off the Windows 95 CD, as described above in "Setting Up the System Policy Editor"):

1. From the Start menu choose Programs, Accessories, System Tools, and click on System Policy Editor. The System Policy Editor will open.

2. From the File menu, choose Open Registry. The System Policy Editor opens, now displaying Local User and Local Computer (see Figure 12–18) instead of Default User and Default Computer as you saw above. The Local User and the Local Computer correspond to your User.dat and System.dat files.

3. Double-click on first the Local User and then the Local Computer icons to see the settings that are available and to make the changes that you want.

 The items in Local User and Local Computer only have two states, checked and empty, and don't have the grayed state of Default User and Default Computer.

USING THE REGISTRY EDITOR

The Registry Editor, or Regedit, provides the most detailed look at the registry and also the easiest one with which to do damage to the

Figure 12–19

The Registry Editor

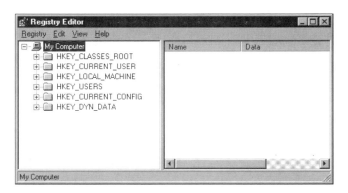

Registry. In Regedit you are literally looking at and potentially changing the Registry entries without any editing of whether those changes make any sense. Use these steps to open Regedit and look at your Registry:

1. From the Start menu, open the Run option, type **regedit**, and click on OK. The Registry Editor will open, as you can see in Figure 12–19.

2. Begin opening the Registry entries by clicking on the plus signs. You'll quickly see that there is a very detailed structure that does not easily lend itself to interpretation.

3. To change an entry, open it until you are at the lowest level, and then double-click on the Name in the right pane. The Edit String dialog box will appear, as shown here:

4. Edit the information in the Value data text box as needed. Remember, you must supply the validity checking of your changes.

THE REGISTRY STRUCTURE

The Registry is a complex hierarchical structure that has six key elements at its root. Each of the six key elements are in turn broken down into several other levels that finally result in a value that can be edited. In addition to editing the value, whole parts of the structure can be deleted (but do so with great caution!). The contents of each of the six key elements is as follows:

- **Hkey_Classes_Root** contains the information that associates a data file and its extension with a program file that can start and print the file.

- **Hkey_Current_User** contains the settings for a specific user. Included are both Windows preferences as well as program preferences. The Hkey_Current_User is a subset, or branch, of Hkey_Users representing the user currently logged on.

- **Hkey_Local_Machine** contains the specific configuration information for the computer on which Regedit is running. Included are the hardware that is installed, what resources (ports, IRQs, and memory) the hardware is using, and the software (drivers and other software) that is required for the hardware.

- **Hkey_Users** contains the information, both default and specific, about all users who can log on to the computer. Included are the default settings and preferences for both Windows and programs.

- **Hkey_Current_Config** contains the settings that are currently in place for the hardware in the computer on which Regedit is running. The Hkey_Current_Config is a subset or branch of Hkey_Local_Machine representing the current settings.

- **Hkey_Dyn_Data** contains dynamic information about the status and performance of the computer itself as well as most hardware components. Included is Plug and Play information (is a piece of hardware present?), any problems with the hardware, and performance indicators (CPU usage, bytes per second transferred, and so on).

The values at the bottom end of the hierarchy can be either alphanumeric strings, which are human readable, or hexadecimal or binary numbers, which are only computer readable (excluding one or two people with questionable human ancestry).

On the *Windows 95 Power Tools* CD there is a program called RegFind that will help you search the Registry for particular items and values. See Chapter 14 for a fuller definition and Chapter 15 for detailed documentation.

Optimizing Windows 95

In Windows 3.1 there were a number of fairly complex optimization issues that needed to be addressed, and it was difficult to know absolutely that you had the best configuration possible. Windows 95 significantly simplifies the optimization issues and gives reasonable assurance that you have achieved a good configuration. Windows 95 does this in three ways:

- Being a fully integrated 32-bit operating system, Windows 95 eliminates the DOS versus Windows questions and the using, or not, of 32-bit file and disk access.

- Such features as preemptive multitasking, a 32-bit kernel, and 32-bit device drivers provide improved system responsiveness, smoother background processing, improved system capacity, better memory management and process scheduling, improved resource management, and better overall performance—all of which reduce the need for optimization.

- Windows 95 has a number of self-tuning features that dynamically configure the system to Windows' current needs. This reduces the need for the user to perform these same functions. Among the self-tuning features are the following:

  - Dynamic disk, CD, and network caching in memory using VCACHE in which the cache can expand or contract as memory allows and needs demand. VCACHE is a 32-bit protected mode cache driver that replaces SmartDrive with a significantly improved caching algorithm for reading and writing information to and from a disk, CD, or the network. VCACHE relieves the user from having to specify the cache size and other SmartDrive settings.

  - Dynamic virtual-memory swap file that can expand and contract as memory needs demand. With a virtual memory swap file, some of the contents of memory that isn't currently being used can be swapped out to disk until it is needed. This frees up memory for other purposes. In Windows 3.x, the user had to decide between a temporary or a permanent swap file and determine how much disk space to allocate for that purpose. Windows 95 now makes those decisions for you, although you can override them if you wish (see the discussion later in the chapter).

■ Automatic system configuration decisions during Windows 95 setup that tailor Windows 95 to the hardware available and relieve the user from that task. For example, in a low-memory environment, background printing is turned off to conserve memory.

With all the automation and features in Windows 95, there are still optimization issues to consider, although if you were to ignore them you would still have a reasonably optimized system.

Windows 95 Optimization Tools

Windows 95 has several tools to assist you in the job of optimization. These are as follows:

■ **System Monitor**, as discussed above under "Using the System Monitor," lets you visually track system performance over time and from that tells you how your optimization efforts are going.

■ **Disk Defragmenter**, which was discussed in Chapter 2, optimizes your disk drive so that all the segments of a file are together on the disk. This needs to be run periodically to keep the disk at its best performance.

■ **Resource Meter**, shown in Figure 12–20, shows you how you are using the three resource stacks: System Resources, User Resources, and GDI (graphic device interface) Resources. As you run more programs, these resources will get used. In Windows 3.1 it was fairly easy to use up these resources and get an out of memory error message as a result even though you had a lot of regular memory free. You start the Resource Meter by opening the Start menu and choosing Programs, Accessories, System Tools, Resource Meter. You can also open Run, type **Rsrcmtr**, and press ⌐←Enter⌐.

Figure 12–20

Resource Meter

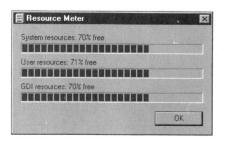

Figure 12–21

The amount of free memory available is shown in About Windows

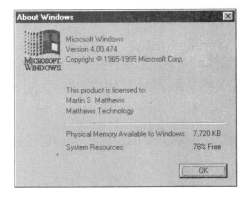

Figure 12–22

Device Manager within the System control panel

System

- **About Windows**, opened from the Help menu, tells you the amount of free memory that you have available as well as a summary of your System resources, as you can see in Figure 12–21.

- **System control panel** provides a large amount of information about the components of your computer, as shown in Figure 12–22. It is also the primary place where you can tune your file system, graphics, and virtual memory (see Figure 12–23). The System control panel is discussed further later in this chapter.

Figure 12–23

*Performance
tuning tab of
the System
control panel*

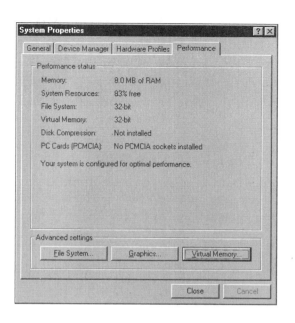

On the *Windows 95 Power Tools* CD there are several tools for working on system performance. Among these is Win, What, Where, which lets you track events over time. See Chapter 14 for a better description of this and other utilities on the CD.

System Optimization

The task of system optimization has three components: selecting and setting up hardware, decision making, and fine tuning.

HARDWARE CONSIDERATIONS

It may sound trite, but more, newer, and faster hardware will in fact run Windows 95 better. That has not always been the case with earlier operating systems. Some of the areas where Windows 95 performance can be improved with hardware are as follows:

- Windows 95 will run better on a 486 than on a 386 of the same clock speed due to the 486's 32-bit optimization.
- Windows 95 gives better video and disk performance with faster CPU and bus speed because the 32-bit drivers can use the faster speeds, whereas 16-bit drivers could not.

- Windows 95 performs better with more memory than did Windows 3.*x*, and with dynamic caching, Windows 95 does not need to be reconfigured when you add memory.

- Windows 95 provides improved printing performance with the newer bidirectional ECP (enhanced communications port) printer ports.

DECISION POINTERS

A part of achieving an optimized system is making wise decisions as you set up Windows 95. Here are some pointers related to decisions you will make in setting up a system:

- Use protected mode drivers whenever possible. Windows 95 .VXD 32-bit drivers replace .386 drivers that came with Windows 3.1 and provide considerable performance improvement.

Try running your system without the Autoexec.bat and Config.sys files. (Rename Autoexec.bat and Config.sys.) In this way you know that Windows 95 is using its own 32-bit protected mode drivers. If some piece of hardware or software requires that Config.sys or (less likely) Autoexec.bat to load a driver, keep the files to a minimum, and see if you can get 32-bit protected mode drivers for it.

- It is not necessarily true that DOS programs will run better in MS-DOS mode than they will in Windows. In MS-DOS mode, the DOS programs will *not* get the benefit of protected mode drivers, VCACHE, and 32-bit disk access, all of which can improve the performance of the program.

- Keep networking components to a minimum to both improve performance and reduce memory usage. Use only one networking client, either Microsoft or NetWare, but not both. Use only one network protocol: NetBEUI, IPX/SPX, or TCP/IP (see discussion in Chapter 5). Use as few network services as possible.

- Make the fewest possible changes to Windows 95 default settings in the performance area. During setup and during start-up, Windows 95 closely looks at your system, and based on that look it determines the best settings and configuration for your system to operate at its peak.

FINE TUNING

There are four areas where you can fine tune your system performance: in the file system, in graphics acceleration, in virtual memory usage, and in printing. It is highly likely that you do not need to do any fine tuning to get the best performance, and you may actually degrade it, but there are always exceptions. The key to fine tuning is to measure and track how you change the performance. The System Monitor is an excellent tool for observing how you are doing.

 **Keep a notebook with the computer in which you note the hardware installed, settings used, and the performance measures under various circumstances.**

 **Changing the performance-related settings can not only degrade performance, but it can cause your system to not operate properly.**

Tuning the file system, graphics acceleration, and virtual memory all begin by opening the System control panel and clicking on the Performance tab, which you saw in Figure 12–23.

Fine-Tuning the File System　By clicking on the File System button in the Performance tab of the System control panel you open the File System Properties dialog box, shown in Figure 12–24. Here you can select the role of the computer from among Desktop, Mobile, and Network server. This will be used to gauge the amount of memory to be dynamically allocated to disk caching.

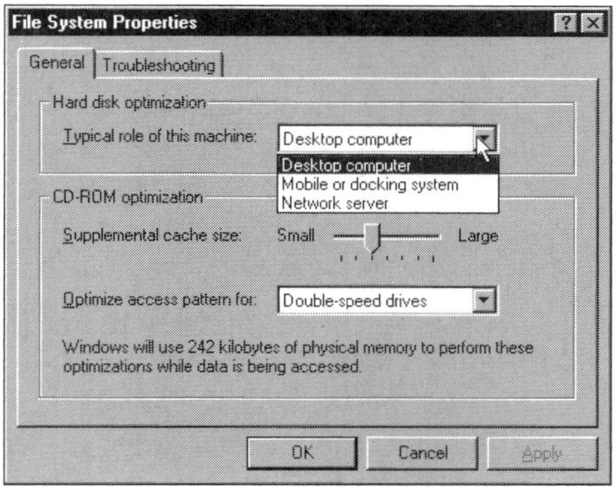

Figure 12–24

File System Properties

Figure 12–25

Troubleshooting tab

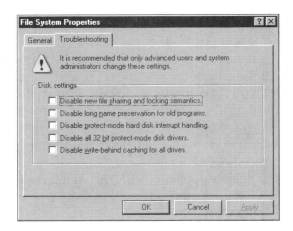

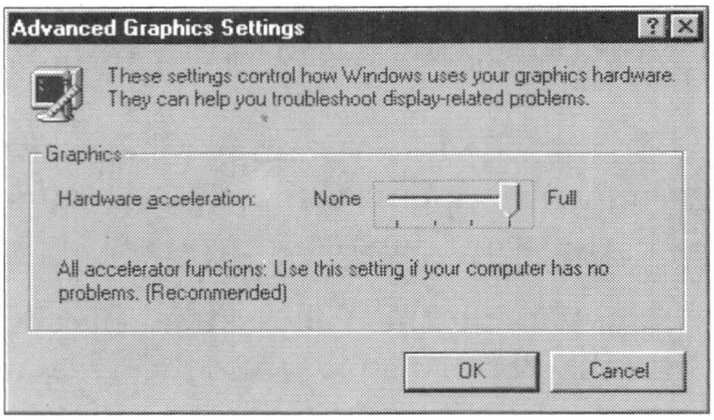

Figure 12–26

Advanced Graphics Settings

Since caching is dynamic, you cannot directly set aside memory for disk caching as you could in the Windows 3.*x* environment. This not only saves you the trouble but is a far more efficient use of your memory.

The CD-ROM optimization settings also provide a general framework that Windows 95 can use to determine the amount of cache memory to set aside for that purpose.

The Troubleshooting tab allows you to turn off various aspects of the file system for use in troubleshooting, as you can see in Figure 12–25. It is very strongly recommended that you fully consider the consequences of selecting any the troubleshooting items and that you turn them off as soon as possible after their use.

Graphics Acceleration Fine-Tuning The Performance tab's Advanced Graphics Settings, shown in Figure 12–26, determine how hard Windows pushes your graphics adapter. It is a trial-and-error type of setting: increase the speed until either you begin to see errors in your display or you are going as fast as possible.

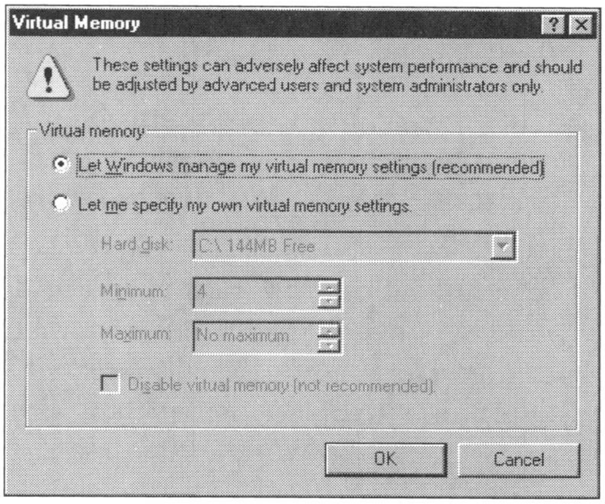

Figure 12–27

*Virtual
Memory settings*

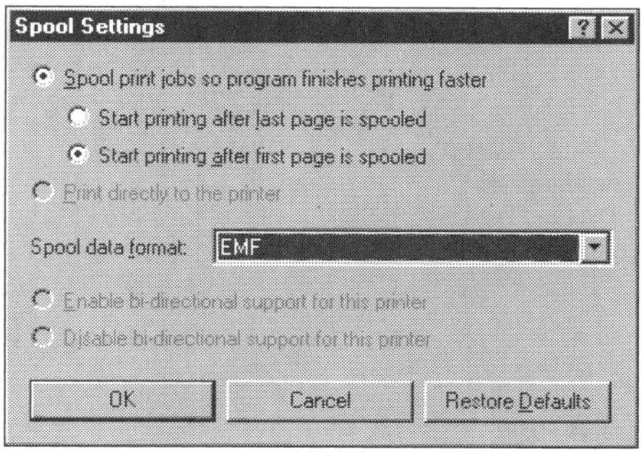

Figure 12–28

*Printer
spool settings*

Fine-Tuning Virtual Memory The Virtual memory dialog box allows you to determine if you want to override the Windows 95 dynamic virtual memory (swap file) allocation. If so, you can determine the disk drive to use and the minimum and maximum amounts of memory in megabytes to allocate to a swap file. If you change the disk, the best disk performance will be achieved by a very fast disk with little other usage. You can also disable virtual memory altogether, although that is strongly *not* recommended.

Fine-Tuning Printing In printing you can determine several elements of the spooling that will govern how fast the spooling will take place. These are set in the Spool Settings dialog box (shown in Figure 12–28), which you reach from the Details tab of the printer's Properties dialog box. The whole purpose of spooling is that you get back to your other work faster. If you start printing only after the last page is spooled, you'll get back to your other work faster, but the overall print time will be slower than if you begin printing after the first page has been spooled.

Unless you run into some problem, you want to use EMF (enhanced metafile format) for spooling. It is much more efficient with most printers. Also, if you have a bidirectional printer port and a printer that can use it, you definitely want to speed up printing.

The task of optimization is all but done for you in Windows 95, and unless you have unusual circumstances, there is little reason to change these automatically created settings. Your primary task is to determine if you are using 32-bit protected mode drivers.

Using DOS and the Windows 95 Command Language

Since Windows 95 has replaced both Windows 3.*x and* DOS 6.*x*, Windows 95 must now supply any needs that you have to use DOS. With all the capability and power in Windows, why would anyone want to use DOS? For many people, the answer is that they don't use DOS at all, and they are perfectly happy. For others, though, there are several compelling reasons to use DOS. Among these are the following:

- The user has a need (or desire) to run DOS programs, especially games, for which there isn't (or the person doesn't have) a Windows replacement.

- Certain tasks are easier in a DOS environment for long-time DOS users.

- Some debugging tasks require that you not be in Windows, so you must do them in DOS, or they are easier to perform in DOS.

For these reasons and probably others, DOS is alive and well within Windows 95. In this chapter you will explore Windows 95 DOS from two standpoints: running DOS programs and using the Windows 95 (DOS) command language.

Running DOS Programs

Most people who run DOS programs will be very pleasantly surprised at how easily and how well Windows 95 will run these same programs and at how many different ways there are to run them. You may find that your DOS programs run faster and better under Windows 95, even if the programs tell you they can't run under Windows. To run a DOS program you can

- Double-click on it
- Double-click on a shortcut to a DOS program with many options
- Use the Run option in the Start menu
- Open a DOS window, and start the program at the DOS prompt
- Boot to DOS, and start the program at the DOS prompt

For many DOS programs, you need to do nothing more than double-click on them from My Computer or from the Explorer. The programs run just as if they were a Windows program except that they run in a DOS window, as shown in Figure 13–1, or they run full screen. Normally, character-based programs run in a window, which you'll learn more about later in the chapter; and graphics programs run full-screen, which means that the Windows 95 Taskbar and all vestiges of Windows disappear from the screen, but Windows is still running in the background.

 **If a DOS program is running in either a DOS window or full-screen, you can switch to the other mode by pressing** Alt - ←Enter.

When a DOS program is started, the Apps.inf file, which comes with Windows 95, is automatically checked to see if there is an entry for that program. If there is, the settings in the Apps.inf file are used to run the program. If there is not an entry, the program is run using the default settings. If the default settings are not correct for the program, you can use a shortcut to start the program with custom settings, as you will see next.

Figure 13–1

DOS program running in a DOS window

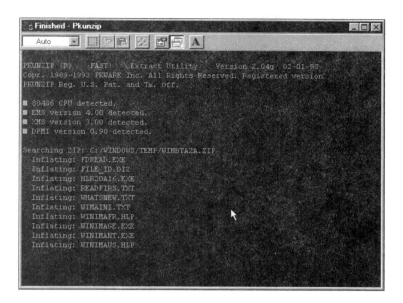

Shortcuts to DOS Programs

You can create a shortcut for a DOS program just as you can for a Windows program. For a DOS program, though, a shortcut can contain several special settings that allow you to determine how the program will run. For example, with a shortcut you can specify that the program be run in the following ways:

- In a window
- Full-screen
- In DOS mode
- Without detecting Windows
- By forcing Windows to shut down before running and restarting after quitting the program

You can create a shortcut to a DOS program in the usual ways: drag the program file from the Explorer or My Computer to another folder or the desktop; right-click on it and choose Create Shortcut; or select the program and choose Create Shortcut from the File menu. You can also create a shortcut for a DOS program by right-clicking on the program and choosing Properties. The Properties dialog box will open, as shown in Figure 13–2, with the settings that will be used for running that program. These settings are either the default settings,

Figure 13–2

A DOS program's Properties dialog box

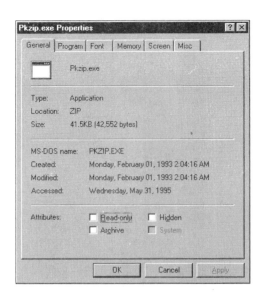

or those in the Apps.inf file. If you make any change to the settings, a shortcut is created in the current folder if you can write to it or in the \Windows\Pif folder if you can't.

The \Windows\Pif folder may confirm a suspicion you've had, that Windows 95 DOS shortcuts replace Windows 3.*x* .PIF files. When you installed Windows 95, any .PIF files that you had in the Windows directory were converted to shortcuts in the \Windows\Pif folder.

DOS SHORTCUT SETTINGS

A DOS file's Properties dialog box, similar to what you saw in Figure 13–2, is the same as the Properties dialog box for that file's shortcut. It has six tabs with the first tab primarily giving you information and allowing you to set the attributes. The meaning of the attributes are:

- **Read-only** means the file can be read and copied but it cannot be changed or deleted.

- **Archive** means the file has been changed since it was last backed up.

- **Hidden** means the file will not appear on a list of files unless the Show Hidden capability is turned on.

- **System** means the file is a system file used by Windows (or in the past by DOS) to run properly. By default, System files are not shown in file listings.

Figure 13–3

*DOS file
properties
Program tab*

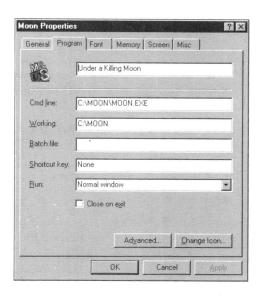

 The attributes should not be changed lightly—you should know the consequences before making a change.

Program Tab The Program tab, shown in Figure 13–3, provides the identity and how to run the DOS program. The top text box allows you to give the shortcut a name different than the DOS program, as was done in Figure 13–3. The other text boxes and controls have the following purposes:

- **Cmd line** must contain the full path and filename required to start the program.

- **Working** may contain the path and name of a folder to make current while running the program. (The program loads files from and saves files to this folder.)

- **Batch file** may contain the path and filename of a batch file you want to run before starting the program.

- **Shortcut key** may contain a set of keystrokes used to start the shortcut (click in the text box, and press the keys you want to use).

- **Run** allows you to start the program in a normal window (which may be full-screen; see Screen tab), in a maximized window, or minimized on the Taskbar.

- **Close on exit** automatically closes a program's window when it completes execution.

If you want to see any messages left by a DOS program when it completes execution, you do NOT want to select Close on exit.

Advanced Program Settings If you click on the Advanced button in the Program tab, the Advanced Program Settings dialog box will open, as shown in Figure 13–4. This dialog box allows you to select alternative ways to run a DOS program if it doesn't run in a normal Windows environment.

Sometimes when you run a DOS program under Windows, you'll get a message that it cannot run under Windows, as you can see in Figure 13–5. This message normally applies to running the program under Windows 3.*x* and often does not apply to Windows 95. To get around this, you can prevent the program from detecting Windows through

Figure 13–4

Advanced Programs Settings provides alternative ways of running DOS programs

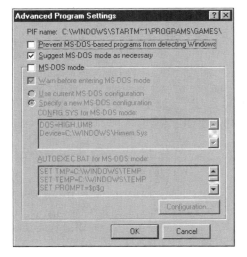

Figure 13–5

Spurious message that a program can't run under Windows

a check box in the Advanced Program Settings dialog box. In many cases, that's all it takes for the program to run.

If you are using Config.sys and Autoexec.bat files to start your system with Windows 95, it could be that you are loading real-mode drivers that are preventing your DOS program from running under Windows 95. If there is a possibility that real-mode drivers could be affecting you, try renaming your Autoexec.bat and Config.sys files, rebooting your computer so the changes to the files take effect, and then try starting the programs.

If your DOS program still does not run, the Advanced Program settings dialog box has one more option that is truly a last resort. This is MS-DOS mode (also called single-mode DOS) where you shut down Windows and reboot into DOS alone, run the program, and then when you are done, automatically restart, or reboot, Windows. This means that that you have to shut down all other programs, and more importantly, that the Windows 95 32-bit protected-mode drivers have to be shut down and the older real-mode DOS drivers used. You, therefore, will not have as much free memory nor the speed and efficiency of the newer drivers. The severity of this mode is indicated by the message that is presented when you try to start a program with the MS-DOS mode checked, as you can see here:

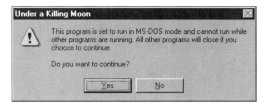

If you get tired of the MS-DOS warning message, you can turn it off by removing the check mark from Warn before entering MS-DOS mode. If you use MS-DOS mode, you can choose between using the current DOS Config.sys and Autoexec.bat files or specifying new ones in the Advanced Program Settings dialog box. With the latter selection, you can click on the Configuration button and use a check list to build these files, as shown in Figure 13–6. If you are not using Autoexec.bat and Config.sys files to run Windows 95, then this would be a good place to create them to run a recalcitrant DOS program.

Figure 13–6

*Check list
for creating
Autoexec.bat and
Config.sys files*

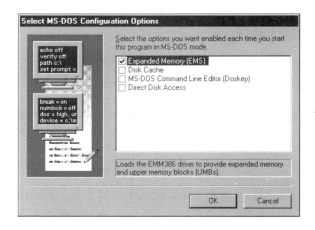

Figure 13–7

*Change Icon
dialog box*

Change Icon Option The Change Icon button in the Program tab of a DOS program's Properties dialog box opens the Change Icon dialog box, shown in Figure 13–7. This allows you to change the icon used with the shortcut to a DOS program on which you are working. You can pick an icon from the ones displayed, or you can click on the Browse button and display other file to search for icons. Many programs come with icons, but Windows 95 also supplies additional icons you can use in the following files: \Windows\Moricons.dll, \Windows\Systems\Pifmgr.dll, and \Windows\System\Iconlib.dll.

Font Tab The Font tab of a DOS program's Properties dialog box, which is shown in Figure 13–8, allows you to select the font size and type that you want to use if you run the program in a DOS window and not full-screen. This, of course, only applies to character-based programs and not graphics applications. When you select a font, you can see not only the font, but the size of the window to hold the standard 25 lines of 80 characters.

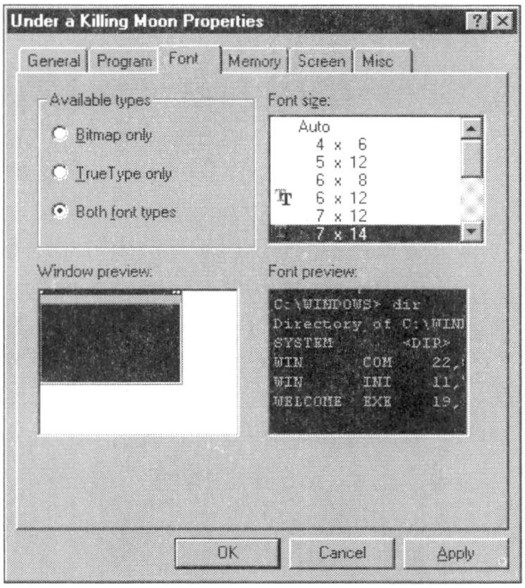

Figure 13–8

Font tab of a DOS program's Properties dialog box

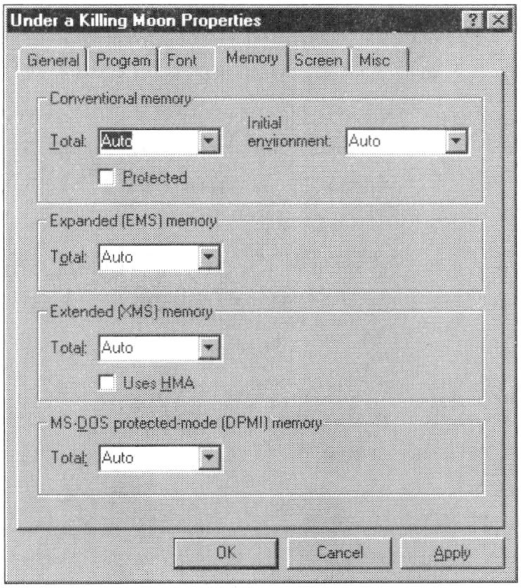

Figure 13–9

Memory tab of a DOS program's Properties dialog box

Memory Tab The Memory tab allows you to specify the amount of the various kinds of memory to allocate to running a DOS program, as you can see in Figure 13–9. For the vast majority of programs (DOS and otherwise) you want to let Windows 95 determine how memory should be allocated, so all of the settings should be left on Auto.

- **Conventional memory** is the first 640 KB of memory; it's also called base memory.

- **Expanded (EMS) memory** is an early attempt to provide memory greater than 1 MB and requires either a special memory card or a program to emulate Expanded memory in Extended memory. Windows 95 provides Expanded memory emulation as needed by DOS programs unless you have turned it off in your Config.sys file EMM386 command with a **noems** parameter. This Config.sys line and parameter are no longer needed with Windows 95 and should be removed, since Windows 95 only provides Expanded memory as it is needed and discontinues it when it isn't.

- **Extended (XMS) memory** is all memory in your computer above 1 MB (1,024 KB) and is the seamless extension of the first 1 MB.

- **Upper Memory Blocks (UMBs)** is the memory between 640 KB and 1 MB. It is used by ROM (read only memory), by drivers for various pieces of hardware, and by Windows 95.

- **High Memory Area (HMA)** is the first 64 KB of Extended memory. It is unique in that, unlike the remainder of Extended memory, DOS can directly address this area. It is normally used by drivers and MS-DOS itself. It is *not* a good idea to use this area for programs.

- **MS-DOS protected-mode (DPMI) memory** is a way for DOS programs to use Extended memory and is supported in Windows 95.

 **Under most circumstances you should not try to allocate memory either through Config.sys parameters or through the Memory tab.**

If you have a case where you believe that a manual allocation of memory is called for, you will need to use information supplied by the program's publisher to determine how much of what type of memory to allocate.

Screen Tab The Screen tab, which you can see in Figure 13–10, allows you to determine how the DOS program will use the screen. Here you can choose between full-screen and running in a window. If you choose to run in a window, you can choose its initial size, whether to display the toolbar, and whether to restore the previous window's settings when the DOS program is finished.

Figure 13–10

*Screen tab of a
DOS program's
Properties
dialog box*

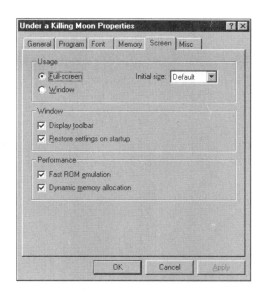

The Screen tab also provides two performance enhancing options. First, it allows you to emulate slower read-only memory (ROM) in faster RAM, thereby speeding up the program. Secondly, you can choose to use dynamic memory allocation to add and remove memory as a program needs it. Under normal circumstances, both of these boxes should be checked. If you run into problems writing to the screen, clear the check mark from Fast ROM emulation. If you find you are out of memory well into a program, you need to turn off Dynamic memory allocation.

Misc Tab The Misc tab of a DOS program's Properties dialog box, shown in Figure 13–11, allows you to specify a number of details about running your program. Under normal circumstances, the default settings of this tab should be used unless a particular problem appears. Then you can change the particular setting that addresses the problem. The settings and their purposes are as follows:

- **Allow screen saver** lets you inhibit the automatic startup of the screen saver by removing the check mark. The screen saver sometimes interferes with a DOS program.

- **Mouse, QuickEdit** lets you use the mouse to select text for cutting and copying. If this option is not checked, you must use Mark on the Edit submenu to select text.

Figure 13-11

Misc tab of a DOS program's Properties dialog box

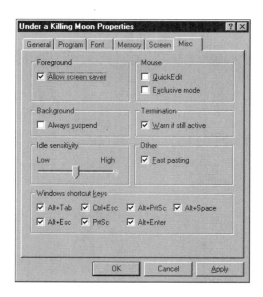

- **Mouse, Exclusive mode** prevents the mouse from being used as a Windows pointer and only allows its use in the DOS program.

- **Background, Always suspend** deallocates system resources (memory and CPU cycles) when the program is not active.

- **Termination, Warn if still active** gives you a warning message if you try to close a DOS window when the program is still active.

- **Idle sensitivity** lets you determine how long the program is to remain idle (no keyboard input) before reducing CPU resources. Lower sensitivity causes a longer wait, while higher sensitivity causes a shorter wait.

- **Other, Fast pasting** enables a faster method of pasting information into a document created by the program you are running. If pasting does not work, clear Fast pasting and try it again.

- **Windows shortcut keys** allows you to reserve keystrokes for Windows. A check mark beside a set of keystrokes means that Windows will intercept these keystrokes and act on them. If you clear the check mark, the keystrokes will be passed to the DOS program. See Table 1-1 in Chapter 1 for the meaning of the keystrokes in Windows.

The Run Option

Often when you run a DOS program, you want to add parameters or switches after the filename when you start the program. If the switches are the same each time you run the program, you can put these on the command line in the shortcut used to start the program. If the switches change each time you run the program, you need a place to type them. You can use the Start menu's Run option for this purpose. In the Run drop-down list box, you can type the full command, as shown here:

 If you repeat the same or similar commands in the Run option, open the drop-down list box to see recent commands you have entered, and either use them again or edit them for any changes.

The DOS Window

MS-DOS
Prompt

When a DOS program is run in a window, the window is automatically opened, and it is closed when you leave the program. If you want to interactively work in DOS, possibly run several programs or DOS commands, you can open a DOS window, such as that shown in Figure 13–12. You do that by opening the Start menu and selecting MS-DOS Prompt from the Programs option. If you use DOS a lot, you might want to make an additional shortcut and drag it to the desktop. You create an MS-DOS Prompt shortcut from the Command.com program in the \Windows folder. You can also start DOS from the Start menu by dragging Command.com there.

 Drag \Windows\Command.com to the Start menu to quickly start DOS from there.

The DOS window has a single menu, the System or Control menu, and, if you have it turned on, a toolbar. The menu, which is primarily

Figure 13–12

DOS window

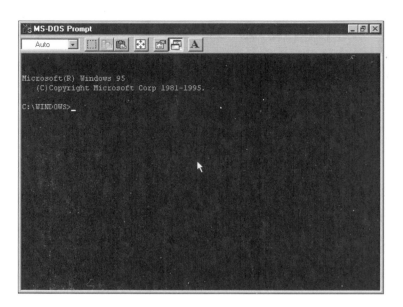

meant as a substitute for the mouse, is shown below and described in Table 13–1. The toolbar is described in Table 13–2.

You can open several DOS windows and paste between them using the Windows Clipboard. Each separate DOS window is an independent virtual machine (VM) with its own Command.com (command processor). This allows you to effectively multitask several DOS programs.

Booting to Old DOS

If all else fails and you cannot run a DOS program with any of the techniques discussed so far, you have one final option to try to run the program: rebooting the computer into your previous version of DOS. This is different than running in DOS mode, discussed above,

Table 13–1.

DOS Windows System Menu

Option	Description
Restore	Restores the window to its previous size when maximized
Move	Allows moving the window with the keyboard; press the arrow key(s) representing the direction you want to move
Size	Allows sizing the window with the keyboard; first press the arrow key(s) to indicate the side(s) to change, then press the arrow key(s) for the direction of the change
Minimize	Minimizes the window, so it becomes a task on the Taskbar
Maximize	Maximizes the window, so it fills the screen
Close	Closes the window
Edit	Provides the following edit commands:
Mark	Marks the current cursor location to begin and end a range
Copy	Copies the selected text to the Clipboard
Paste	Pastes the Clipboard contents to the current cursor position
Scroll	Scrolls the text in the DOS window
Toolbar	Turns the toolbar on and off
Properties	Opens the Properties dialog box

Table 13–2.

DOS Window Toolbar

Icon	Name	Description
7 x 12	Font	Allows you to select the size and type of font
	Mark	Allows selecting text with the mouse so the text can be copied or cut
	Copy	Copies selected (marked) text to the Clipboard
	Paste	Pastes the contents of the Clipboard at the current cursor location
	Full-Screen	Changes from running DOS in a window to running it full-screen
	Properties	Opens the Properties dialog box for the program in the window
	Background	Switches between exclusive foreground processing and background processing
A	Font	Opens the Font tab of the Properties dialog box

which is still Windows 95 DOS (DOS 7) with Windows pulled out of the picture. It is even different than shutting down and restarting in MS-DOS mode, which is the same as running in MS-DOS mode from Windows.

Booting into your old DOS requires interrupting and redirecting the startup process. You do that by pressing F8 *just before* you would otherwise see Starting Windows... When you press F8 at the correct time, you get a menu in which item 8 is Previous version of MS-DOS. By typing 8 and pressing ⏎Enter, you will start your previous DOS using the Config.sys and Autoexec.bat files that were in use prior to installing Windows 95. When Windows is running, these files are stored in the root folder as Config.dos and Autoexec.dos. If you wish, you can edit them in Windows for later use in starting your previous version of DOS.

When you are done using your previous version DOS, you must reboot normally to get back to Windows 95.

The Windows 95 Command Language

To create the Windows 95 command language, Microsoft has taken the old DOS command language, rewritten many of the commands to work with a 32-bit operating system, made several additions, and made a number of deletions. There are now six types of DOS commands:

- **Internal commands**, which are part of the DOS Command.com program and therefore can only run inside a DOS window where Command.com is running or in a batch file
- **External commands**, which are separate, independent programs and can be run directly from the Explorer or entered in the Run option or in a DOS window
- **Config.sys commands**, which are only used in creating or changing a Config.sys file
- **Batch commands**, which are only used in creating or changing a batch file
- **Network commands**, which are used to perform networking functions both before and after Windows starts
- **Internet commands**, which are used to perform various functions once you have established an Internet connection

The internal and external commands are now *native* commands that take advantage of the Windows 95 32-bit environment.

Using Commands

Windows 95 commands are normally typed at either the command prompt in a DOS window or in the Run option, or they are used in batch files. Most commands require parameters and/or switches after the command and have a specific order or *syntax* in which they must be typed. The command syntax has up to four parts, as follows:

- **Command Name**, which tells you what action is to be performed

- **Parameter**, which specifies the object on which the action is to be performed; if a command has two parameters, the first is the source (*from* object) and the second is the destination (*to* object)

- **Switch**, which selects alternative ways that a command operates; switches are preceded by either a forward slash (/) or a hyphen (-); if there are two or more switches, they are separated by a space and can be in any order

- **Value**, which provides information to a switch; values are preceded by either a colon (:) or an equal sign (=)

For example, the Copy command, shown below, has a command name of `copy`, an initial parameter (the source) of `c:\windows\general.txt`, a second parameter (the destination) of `a:\`, and two switches of `/v` and `/y`.

```
copy    c:\windows\general.txt    a:\    /v    /y
  |            |                    |      |     |
name      parameter 1          parameter 2   switches
```

A second example, the Format command, has a name of format, a single parameter of `a:`, and two switches (`/v` and `/f`) each with a value (`96 budget` and `1.44`).

```
format    a:    /v:96 budget    /f:1.44
  |       |       |        |       |     |
name  parameter  switch: value  switch: value
```

Figure 13–13

Copy command help listing

```
MS-DOS Prompt
7 x 12

C:\>copy /?
Copies one or more files to another location.

COPY [/A | /B] source [/A | /B] [+ source [/A | /B] [+ ...]] [destination
  [/A | /B]] [/V] [/Y | /-Y]

  source        Specifies the file or files to be copied.
  /A            Indicates an ASCII text file.
  /B            Indicates a binary file.
  destination   Specifies the directory and/or filename for the new file(s).
  /V            Verifies that new files are written correctly.
  /Y            Suppresses prompting to confirm you want to overwrite an
                existing destination file.
  /-Y           Causes prompting to confirm you want to overwrite an
                existing destination file.

The switch /Y may be preset in the COPYCMD environment variable.
This may be overridden with /-Y on the command line

To append files, specify a single file for destination, but multiple files
for source (using wildcards or file1+file2+file3 format).

C:\>
```

Figure 13–14

Format command help listing

```
MS-DOS Prompt
7 x 12

C:\>format /?
Formats a disk for use with MS-DOS.

FORMAT drive: [/V[:label]] [/Q] [/F:size] [/B | /S] [/C]
FORMAT drive: [/V[:label]] [/Q] [/T:tracks /N:sectors] [/B | /S] [/C]
FORMAT drive: [/V[:label]] [/Q] [/1] [/4] [/B | /S] [/C]
FORMAT drive: [/Q] [/1] [/4] [/8] [/B | /S] [/C]

  /V[:label]    Specifies the volume label.
  /Q            Performs a quick format.
  /F:size       Specifies the size of the floppy disk to format (such
                as 160, 180, 320, 360, 720, 1.2, 1.44, 2.88).
  /B            Allocates space on the formatted disk for system files.
  /S            Copies system files to the formatted disk.
  /T:tracks     Specifies the number of tracks per disk side.
  /N:sectors    Specifies the number of sectors per track.
  /1            Formats a single side of a floppy disk.
  /4            Formats a 5.25-inch 360K floppy disk in a high-density drive.
  /8            Formats eight sectors per track.
  /C            Tests clusters that are currently marked "bad."

C:\>
```

GETTING HELP WITH COMMANDS

You can determine what the *arguments* (parameters, switches, and/or values) are for a command by using online help in a DOS window—type the command followed by /?. For example, typing copy /? produces the information shown in Figure 13–13, and typing format /? produces the information shown in Figure 13–14.

ENTERING COMMANDS

There are several facilities that you can use in the entry of commands. These allow you to combine several commands, make the repetitive entry of commands easier, and control the processing of a command.

Symbol	Description
|	Pipes, or runs, the output of one command through another command to filter or arrange it
>	Redirects the output to a different device or file
>>	Appends the output to an existing file
| |	Runs the command after the symbol if the command before the symbol fails
&&	Runs the command after the symbol if the command before the symbol is successful
<	Redirects the input to be from a different device or file
&	Separates two commands on the same line
( )	Groups two or more commands
^	Allows the use of command symbols as text

Table 13–3.

Symbols Used to Combine Commands

Combining Several Commands If you want to combine several commands, say to pass information from one command to another, you can use the symbols shown in Table 13–3 to join the commands on a single command line with the effects described in the table.

If you want to use one of the command symbols in a command parameter, say a user name, you must precede the symbol with the control character (^). For example, the name Fish&Chips would be entered `Fish^&Chips.`

Examples of using command symbols are shown next. In the first example, the output of the Mem command is "piped," or filtered, through the More command, which breaks the output into screen or window-sized chunks. In the second example, the output of the Dir command, which is normally unsorted and sent to the screen, is piped through the Sort command and redirected to the printer on LPT1.

```
mem /c | more
dir | sort > lpt1
```

Aids in Command Entry If you have a number of commands to enter, typing the commands can become very laborious and repetitive. Windows 95 has several tools to reduce the severity of this problem.

Table 13–4.

Keystrokes Used for Editing with Doskey

Keystroke	Description
⬅ / ➡	Move nondestructively left or right within the command line
⬆ / ⬇	Place previous commands in the command buffer on the command line
Esc	Clears the command line
Del	Deletes the character above the cursor
F7	Displays a list of the previous commands in the command buffer
chars F8	Searches the command buffer for a command beginning with *chars*; if no characters are entered, F8 is the same as ⬆
F9	Allows you to enter the number of a command in the command buffer that you want to place on the command line

Among these are the Doskey command, special editing keys, and the tools in the DOS window.

The Doskey command allows you to do character editing on the command line and to reuse recent commands you have entered during the current DOS session. Doskey uses a *command buffer*, whose size you can establish (see Help for Doskey), to store recent commands. To use Doskey, simply type **doskey** at a command prompt. If you want it always available, you can put it in as the final entry of your Autoexec.bat file. With Doskey loaded you can use the keys in Table 13–4 to manipulate the current or previous commands you have entered in the current DOS session.

Doskey can also be used to create command-line macros and store them for the duration of a DOS session. See online Help for Doskey.

Command.com by itself has several editing keys defined, as shown in Table 13–5. You do not need to load Doskey to have these keys available, but they also work while Doskey is loaded.

The tools in the DOS window, Mark, Copy, and Paste, which you read about above, can be used to select, copy, and paste text on the command line.

Controlling the Processing of a Command You can use several keystrokes to pause or stop the processing of a command while it is executing. These keystrokes are as follows:

Table 13–5.

Keys Used for Editing on the Command Line

Keystroke	Description
F1	Places the most recent command back on the command line, one character at a time
F3	Places the most recent command back on the command line
←Backspace or ←	Deletes the character to the left of the cursor
Insert	Changes from the default overwrite mode to insert mode of editing

Ctrl+S or Pause	Pauses the execution of a command; press any other key to resume
Ctrl+C or Ctrl+Break	Stops the processing of a command

The effects of running commands cannot be undone.

Command Lists

The next six sections list the six types of Windows 95 commands. A final section lists the commands that were in MS-DOS 6.2*x* but are not in Windows 95.

INTERNAL COMMANDS

Internal commands are embedded in Command.com and are therefore only available at the prompt in a DOS window or when used in a batch file. Table 13–6 lists and describes the internal commands that are available in Windows 95.

EXTERNAL COMMANDS

External commands are separate programs that reside in the \Windows \Command folder. You can execute external commands directly by clicking on them in the Explorer, by typing them in the Run option, or by entering them at a command prompt. The external commands in Windows 95 are described in Table 13–7.

CONFIG.SYS COMMANDS

The commands shown in Table 13–8 are used exclusively in Config.sys files that are executed during startup to configure your system. With Windows 95 you may no longer need to use a Config.sys file.

Table 13–6.

Internal Commands

Command	Description
break	Turns on or off extended checking for Ctrl + C
cd or **chdir**	Changes the current directory or displays its name
chcp	Changes the active character set or displays its code page
cls	Clears the screen
copy	Copies files from a specified location to another
ctty	Changes the active terminal device
date	Displays the computer's date and allows you to change it
del or **erase**	Deletes the specified files
dir	Displays the files and subdirectories in the current or specified directory
exit	Quits DOS and returns to Windows
loadhigh or **lh**	Loads a program into upper memory
md or **mkdir**	Creates a directory or subdirectory
more	Allows you to view one screen at a time
path	Determines or displays the folders, or directories, that are searched for a program
prompt	Determines how the command prompt will look
rd or **rmdir**	Removes (deletes) a directory
ren or **rename**	Changes the name of file(s) that are specified
set	Sets, removes, or displays environmental variables
time	Sets or displays the computer's internal clock
type	Lists the contents of a text file
ver	Shows the version number of the operating system
verify	Verifies that files on two disks are the same
vol	Shows the volume label and serial number on a disk

Table 13–7.

External Commands

Command	Description
attrib	Changes or displays a file's attributes
chkdsk	Displays the status and fixes any errors on a disk (replaced by scandisk)
command	Opens a new DOS window with a command prompt
debug	Helps test and debug programs
defrag	Reorganizes a disk to group associated file segments in one area and thereby improves disk performance (this is a Windows utility)
deltree	Deletes all the files and folders that are in a folder, and then deletes the folder
diskcopy	Copies the contents of one floppy disk to another disk of the same size
doskey	Provides character editing on the command line, the reuse of previous commands, and the creation and use of command-line macros
drvspace	Compresses hard and floppy disk drives, and manages drives already compressed by either DriveSpace or DoubleSpace (this is a Windows utility)
edit	Starts an ASCII text editor, which can be used to create and edit such files as Config.sys and Autoexec.bat
extract	Decompresses .cab files on the Windows distribution disks
fc	Displays the differences between two files
fdisk	Prepares, at a low level, a hard disk for use with Windows 95 or MS-DOS (you must shut down Windows 95 to use this command)
find	Searches files for a specific text string
for	Goes through a set of files, running a command for each file in the set
format	Prepares, at a high level, a disk for use with Windows 95 or MS-DOS
keyb	Configures a keyboard for use with a specific language
label	Changes a disks volume label, or name
mem	Displays how memory is being used and how much is free

Table 13–7.

*External
Commands
(continued)*

mode	Displays the status of and configures the input and output devices on the computer
move	Moves and renames files and folders to specified locations
nlsfunc	Provides national language support (NLS) for specific countries
scandisk	Checks and repairs any damage found on disks and in the file system
setver	Reports a version number to programs requiring an earlier versions of DOS
smartdrv	Provides an older method of disk caching; replaced in Windows 95 (caution: do not use with Windows 95)
sort	Sorts and outputs data presented to it
start	Starts Windows-based programs at the command prompt
subst	Associates a drive letter with a path
sys	Copies hidden system files and Command.com to a disk so they can be used to start Windows 95
xcopy	Copies all the files (except hidden and system files) and folders in a folder

The Config.sys Device command can be used to load the standard device drivers described in Table 13–9.

BATCH FILE COMMANDS

Batch files contain a list of commands in an unformatted text file with an extension of .BAT or .CMD. When a batch file's filename is typed at a command prompt or in the Run option, or it is directly executed in the Explorer, the list of commands in the file are executed as if they had each been sequentially typed at the command prompt. Any of the internal or external commands can be included in a batch file. Additionally, the commands described in Table 13–10 provide for conditional processing in a batch file.

INTERNET COMMANDS

The Internet or TCP/IP commands in Table 13–11 allow you to interact and transfer information with non-PC computers, such as those running Unix. Once you have established a dial-up or network

Table 13–8.

Config. sys Commands

Command	Description
buffers	Allocates memory for a specified number of disk buffers
country	Enables use of country-specific conventions for sorting; for filename characters; and for displaying dates, times, and currency
device	Loads a device driver into memory (see device driver table below)
devicehigh	Loads a device driver into upper memory
dos	Loads part of the operating system into the upper memory area (UMA), the high memory area (HMA), or both
drivparm	Defines disk and tape drives parameters
fcbs	Specifies the number of file control blocks (FCBs) that can be open at the same time
files	Specifies the number of files that can be accessed at one time
include	Includes one configuration block in another
install	Starts a memory-resident program
lastdrive	Specifies the last drive letter that can be accessed
menucolor	Sets the background and text colors for a menu
menudefault	Specifies the default item on a menu and sets a value for timing out
menuitem	Defines up to nine menu items
numlock	Turns NUMLOCK on the numeric keypad on or off in a menu
rem	Prevents commands from running by making them remarks
shell	Identifies the path and filename of the command interpreter you want to use
stacks	Implements data stacks to handle hardware interrupts
submenu	Defines a menu item that, when selected, displays another menu
switches	Sets special options, so for example, an enhanced keyboard operates like the original PC keyboard

Table 13–9.

Standard Config. sys Device Drivers

Device driver	Description
display.sys	Enables the display of international character sets
driver.sys	Defines a logical drive that refers to a physical floppy drive
emm386.exe	Enables the use of expanded memory and the loading of real-mode device drivers in the upper-memory area
himem.sys	Manages extended memory, including the high-memory area (HMA), so that no two programs or device drivers use the same memory at the same time (this device driver must come before any commands that use extended memory)
keyboard.sys	Allows using a keyboard other than the standard U.S. QWERTY keyboard
mscdex.exe	Provides the basic driver support for CD-ROM drives

Table 13–10.

Batch File Commands

Command	Description
call	Calls a second batch program while keeping the first batch program running
choice	Displays a prompt for the user to make a choice and waits for the user to choose from among a set of keys
echo	Hides or displays the execution of a batch file or indicates whether echoing is on or off
goto	Transfers execution to a line in a batch file that is marked by a label
if	Tests a condition and executes a command if the condition is true
pause	Pauses the execution of a batch file and, while displaying a message, waits for any key to be pressed to continue
rem	Prevents commands from running by making them remarks
shift	Shifts the contents of replaceable parameters one parameter to the left

Table 13–11.

Internet Commands

Command	Description
arp	Modifies and displays the address translation tables for IP to Ethernet or Token Ring address resolution protocol
ftp	Transfers files between your computer and one running an FTP service; can be used either in a batch file or interactively
nbtstat	Displays your protocol statistics and TCP/IP connections using NetBIOS over TCP/IP
netstat	Displays your protocol statistics and TCP/IP connections.
ping	Verifies your connection to a remote host computer
route	Allows you to add, delete, modify, and print routes in a network routing table or to clear the entire table
tracert	Traces the route used to a given remote computer

connection, you can use these commands directly in the Explorer, in the Run Option, or in a DOS window. You can get help with the Internet commands by typing the command followed by -?. All of these commands except for FTP are used as diagnostic tools.

NETWORK COMMANDS

The network commands described in Table 13–12 allow you to start up, control, and shut down your network from DOS. You can use these commands in a batch file and from a command prompt, but some of the commands can only be used in real mode prior to starting Windows 95. Enter the commands with a space between net and the second word in the command. You can get help with the network commands by typing the command followed by /? or with **net help**.

DOS COMMANDS REMOVED FROM WINDOWS 95

The following DOS commands have been removed from a normal installation of Windows 95, although those commands with an asterisk can be accessed from the Windows 95 CD-ROM:

append, assign, backup, comp, dosshell, edlin*, ega.sys, expand*, fasthelp, fastopen, graftabl, graphics*, help, interlink, intersvr, join, loadfix, memcard, memmaker*, mirror, msav, msbackup,

Table 13–12.

Network Commands

Command	Description
net config	Displays the current network settings for your workstation
net diag	Displays diagnostic network information by running the Microsoft Network Diagnostic program
net init	Loads protocol and network adapter drivers but does not bind them to the Protocol Manager; for use in real mode only (bind the drivers using net start bind)
net logoff	Breaks your connection to the network resources to which you are connected; for use in real mode only and cannot be used with NetWare NCP servers
net logon	Logs you on as a member of a workgroup; for use in real mode only and cannot be used with NetWare NCP servers
net password	Changes your logon password; for use in real mode only and cannot be used with NetWare NCP servers (a special form, net password /domain:*name* or net password *server* can be used in a DOS window)
net print	Controls and displays the network print queue; cannot be used with NetWare NCP servers
net start	Initiates a network service or displays a list of current services; for use in real mode only
net stop	Terminates a network service; for use in real mode only
net time	Displays the time on or synchronizes your computer's clock with that on a server
net use	Connects to or disconnects from a shared resource, or displays information about resource connections
net ver	Displays the type and version number of the network redirector currently in use
net view	Displays a list of computers sharing resources or the resources being shared

msd*, power, print*, printer.sys, qbasic*, ramdrive.sys, recover, replace, restore*, romdrive.sys, share, smartmon, tree, undelete, unformat, vsafe.

PART VI

Windows 95 Power Tools Companion CD

One of the greatest bargains of all times is the software that is available simply for the asking. Of course, to ask for it, you must know about it. That is a two-sided problem: how do you find out about it, and how does the programmer tell you it's there. The answer is word of mouth, passing the word from one person to another. The grease that makes this go is that, if you like what you get, you contact the programmer and pay him or her for your continued use.

I have short-circuited that path a bit by searching for software that I call Power Tools, and then including the best of it on the CD-ROM that accompanies this book. I believe these programs merit your review if they fit a need you have. And if you agree that they are worthy of your continued use, I strongly encourage you to pay for them—that's what will keep new programs coming.

Chapters 14 and 15 describe the software on the CD. Chapter 14 summarizes each program and Chapter 15 contains their documentation.

Shareware and the Companion CD-ROM

The CD-ROM that accompanies this book contains a warehouse of software. All of these are truly power tools to enhance your use or enjoyment of Windows 95. It is software that comes from many different sources in different countries, including France, Switzerland, Canada, and the United States, and from big and little companies. All of the software, though, shares two important features:

- Each is a well-written program that deserves to be called a Power Tool.
- Each is being offered as either freeware or shareware.

Freeware is software that is offered free of charge, but there is no technical support, no printed manuals, and no upgrade policy. Although free, freeware may still be copyrighted, which means that the author retains the right to control distribution.

Shareware, in contrast, is not free. Shareware is provided free of charge for you to try and see if it is something you want to use on a recurring basis. If so, you are expected to pay a reasonable registration fee. In return, depending on the particular company, you may receive technical support, a printed manual, inexpensive upgrades, and other benefits.

In addition to what is in this book, if you look around on information services such as CompuServe, Microsoft Network, and America Online, as well as various local bulletin boards, you'll find a great amount of shareware available. This is one of the greatest bargains of all time. How many times have you had someone hand you a full-featured product and tell you to take it away with you and try it out on your own? And oh, by the way, if you happen to like the product, you might consider sending in a registration fee. Shareware works and is rapidly growing because people actually do that. I hope that if you find the software on the CD useful, you will register it and pay the fee.

Important! The software on the disk is offered AS IS, as it was received from the authors. Random House, Inc. and Martin Matthews, jointly and severally, make no warranty, either expressed or implied, as to the usability of the software or its fitness for a particular purpose; and they assume no liability for damages, direct or consequential, which may result from using the software or reliance on the documentation.

If you have trouble using any piece of software on the CD, you should contact the software's author (either company or individual) at the postal or e-mail address or phone number that is listed with the documentation in Chapter 15. If you have trouble contacting the author, you should contact the Association of Shareware Professionals (ASP), 545 Grover Road, Muskegon, MI 49442-9427, CompuServe 72050,1433; or contact the ASP Ombudsman at P.O. Box 5786, Bellevue, WA 98006, CompuServe 70007,3536.

Software on the CD-ROM

The software on the CD falls into five categories: graphics and multimedia software, Internet software, utility software, fonts, and games, as shown in Table 14–1.

Each of these products are described in more detail in the following sections. Further documentation on the software is provided in Chapter 15.

Table 14–1.

Software on the CD by category

Category	Name of Software	Author
Graphics	GrabIt Pro, V4.2	Software Excellence by Design Inc.
Graphics	Jasc Media Center, V2.01	JASC, Inc
Graphics	Paint Shop Pro, V3.0	JASC, Inc.
Graphics	Professional Capture Systems, V2.0	JASC, Inc.
Internet	MKS Enhanced Mosaic Web Browser	MKS, Inc.
Internet	Pping, V0.2	Intellisoft, Inc.
Internet	WFTP32, V2.01	Ipswitch, Inc.
Utility	File View for Windows, V1.3	Maze Computer Communications, Inc.
Utility	IconCalc, V1.01	David Feinleib
Utility	INIedit, V1.31	Kindel Systems
Utility	Mem, V1.21	David Feinleib
Utility	Print Switch, V1.06	David Feinleib
Utility	RegFind, V0.7	Intellisoft, Inc.
Utility	RipBAR V6.2 for Windows 95	SoftDesign
Utility	RipSPACE V3.0 for Windows 95	SoftDesign
Utility	Win, What, Where, V3.0	Basic Systems, Inc.
Utility	WinBatch 32, V5.1c	Wilson WindowWare, Inc.
Utility	WinClock, V4.0	David Feinleib
Utility	WinEdit 32, V5.1a	Wilson WindowWare, Inc.
Utility	WinImage, V2.1	Gilles Vollant
Utility	WinPrint, V1.53	Kindel Systems
Utility	Zip Manager, V5.2	Software Excellence by Design Inc.
Font	RRKeyFonts/PC	RoadRunner Computing
Game	Hop, V1.02	David Feinleib

Graphics and Multimedia Software

GRABIT PRO VERSION 4.2

GrabIt Pro is a screen capture program and a utility for working with other graphics programs. Using GrabIt Pro you can do the following:

- Capture either the Windows desktop or a selected window directly to the printer.
- Use image-scaling options to specify the exact size of your image. You also can select the "best fit to page" option which will size your image automatically for the best possible printout.
- Drag and drop bitmap and RLE files from the Explorer to Grabit Pro to open them.
- Automatically increment the capture names by one. Screen captures will start at Grab #-1 and increase from there.
- Click the right mouse button on any GrabIt Pro child window to access the following options: open a file, save a file, copy, paste, and print.
- Save the screen capture in inverted bitmap or RLE files.
- Change and set up different printers directly from the GrabIt Pro File menu.

GrabIt Pro is provided by Software Excellence by Design Inc., 14801 North 12th Street, Phoenix, AZ 85022, Voice: 602-375-9928, Fax: 602-375-9928, BBS: 602-375-9945, CIS: 72200,2276.

JASC MEDIA CENTER, VERSION 2.01

Jasc Media Center is designed to be your command center for multimedia file management and manipulation. It consists of all the necessary commands to manage your multimedia files. Jasc Media Center allows you to

- Organize your multimedia files into albums via thumbnails
- Arrange an album using drag and drop or one of many sort options
- Catalog your multimedia files using keywords and comments for future searches

- Scan for all the multimedia files on your system to hunt down those unneeded, space-wasting files
- View your images full-screen or in a configurable slide show
- Play .WAV, .MID, .AVI, .FLC, and .FLI files individually or with a configurable slide show
- Associate a .WAV file with images in a slide show, or play an audio CD in the background
- Configure Jasc Media Center to summon your favorite media file editors, even one for each file extension
- Print an entire album as a catalog or as individual images
- Utilize more than 35 different file formats
- Convert, move, copy, delete, or rename the original multimedia file

Multimedia files in an album may come from different folders and different drives. Special support for removable disks and CD ROMs allows you to track your files and have Jasc Media Center tell you which disk you need.

Jasc Media Center is provided by JASC, Inc., 10901 Red Circle Drive, Suite 340, Minnetonka, MN 55343, Voice: 612-930-9171, Fax: 612-930-9172, BBS: 612-930-3516, CIS: 76226,2652, Internet: jasc@winternet.com.

PAINT SHOP PRO, VERSION 3.0

Paint Shop Pro is a program that supports photo retouching, painting, and image format conversion. It allows you to do the following:

- **Painting** Choose from eight different brushes, or combine elements of the brushes to create a unique effect. A fill tool allows easy filling of large areas, and an undo brush allows mistakes to be easily corrected.
- **Photo Retouching** Work on existing images with the clone brush to duplicate any image areas. You can also use the push brush for easy touch-up, or enhance detail in small areas, and use the eyedropper to pick up and analyze a color from an image.
- **Image enhancement and editing** Flip, mirror, rotate, and crop images; add borders and frames; or resize and resample images.

- **Color enhancement** Alter the hue, saturation, lightness, and RGB levels. Also adjust the brightness, contrast, highlight, shadow, and midtone, if you like.
- **Image Browser** Visually search folders for easy to lose images.
- **Batch conversion** Convert large number of images from one format to another.

Paint Shop Pro provides image-viewing and printing functions to give you complete control over how your images appear. It also supports TWAIN-compliant scanners, as well as most image file formats.

Paint Shop Pro is provided by JASC, Inc., 10901 Red Circle Drive, Suite 340, Minnetonka, MN 55343, Voice: 612-930-9171, Fax: 612-930-9172, BBS: 612-930-3516, CIS: 76226,2652, Internet: jasc@winternet.com.

PROFESSIONAL CAPTURE SYSTEMS, VERSION 2.0

Professional Capture Systems is a combination of both Windows and DOS programs that provides screen capturing.

- The Windows program, JasCapture, allows capturing a defined area, a full screen, a window, or a client area. The capture can be sent to any combination of the Clipboard, printer, or disk, and can be saved in .BMP, .PCX, or .TIF formats.
- The DOS program, DosCapture, allows capturing standard and extended VGA-mode text screens and standard VGA-mode graphics screens. Captured screens are saved to .PCX graphics files.

Professional Capture Systems is provided by JASC, Inc., 10901 Red Circle Drive, Suite 340, Minnetonka, MN 55343, Voice: 612-930-9171, Fax: 612-930-9172, BBS: 612-930-3516, CIS: 76226,2652, Internet: jasc@winternet.com.

Internet software

MKS ENHANCED MOSAIC WEB BROWSER, VERSION 2.1

The MKS Enhanced Mosaic Web Browser makes it possible to read and display text and graphics in the same document and to easily move around the Internet. Users can quickly browse the resources of the World Wide Web to view hypertext pages on any topic of interest. The browser, which is a tool included with the MKS Internet Anywhere package, allows users access to the Internet functions of the Gopher, Archie and Veronica searches, and FTP file transfers.

The MKS Enhanced Mosaic Web Browser requires you to have a PPP Internet account with an Internet access provider.

 **The MKS Enhanced Mosaic Web Browser has a 30-day trial-use period after which the software will not operate. You must register with MKS at the address below to get a nonlimited version.**

The MKS Enhanced Mosaic Web Browser is provided by MKS, Inc., 185 Columbia Street West, Waterloo, ON, Canada N2L 5Z5, Voice: 519-883-3242, Fax: 519-884-8861, Internet: iasales@mks.com.

PPING, VERSION 0.2

Pping is a parallel ping utility for Windows NT and Windows 95. Pping is similar to the Ping program that comes with Windows 95. Ping sends an ICMP message to the remote machine and waits for a response. The output of Ping is verbose and needs some explanation to a lay person. Pping, on the other hand, gives a simple go/no-go type of response that is more suitable for checking if the remote machine is responding. Further, Pping accepts multiple remote machine names as well as wildcards for IP addresses.

Pping is provided by Intellisoft, Inc., Stoeckmattstr. 3, CH-5316 Leuggern, Switzerland, Voice: +41 56 455149, Fax: +41 56 455140, CIS: 100116,1001, Internet: raju@inso.pr.net.ch.

WFTP32, VERSION 2.01

WFTP32 is an Internet file transfer protocol (FTP) client that provides an intuitive means of transferring files between your computer and an FTP server on the Internet. It is both multithreaded and 32-bit and uses the TCP/IP Windows sockets that are in Windows 95. WFTP32 has the following features:

- Takes full advantage of Windows point-and-click capabilities
- Provides ease of use for the beginner, plus a full set of features for the power user
- Retains FTP server site profiles, user IDs, and passwords
- Provides multifile file transfer using standard Windows methods

WFTP32 has a expiration date of March 31, 1996 to encourage you to register the product. If you purchased this book after January 1, 1996, send a copy of your sales slip to Ipswitch at the address below, and they will send you another copy with a 90-day trial period.

WFTP32 is provided by Ipswitch, Inc., 81 Hartwell Ave., Lexington, MA 02173, Voice: 617-676-5700, Fax: 617-676-5710, CIS: 74777,3226, Internet: info@ipswitch.com.

Utility Software

FILE VIEW FOR WINDOWS, VERSION 1.3

File View for Windows allows you to browse file contents as text, either ASCII, hexadecimal dump for binary files, or raw text with no respect for line ends and other control characters that easily identify printable data in binary files. This program can configure, format, and display text to your specific needs. Some of the features are as follows:

- Stay on top of other windows for easy access
- Drag and drop files for easy viewing
- Registration in Windows registration database for easy file display and printing
- DDE support

File View is a utility program that is especially useful for Windows power users, programmers, and most casual users.

File View is provided by Maze Computer Communications, Inc., 269 Amethyst Way, Franklin Park, NJ 08823, Voice: 908-821-5412, Fax: 908-821-5412, CIS: 70152,1501.

ICONCALC, VERSION 1.01

IconCalc is a full-function calculator in an icon. It can stay in front of other programs, so that you can see/use it while you work. It includes the following features:

- Little memory required
- Context sensitive help
- Variety of color schemes from which to choose

IconCalc is provided by David Feinleib, 30 Hamilton Rd., #401, Arlington, MA 02174, Voice: 617-648-1457, Fax: 617-648-1561, CIS: 76516,20, Internet: 76516.20@compuserve.com.

INIEDIT, VERSION 1.31

INIedit is a quick, efficient way to edit Windows .INI files. A user interface makes it easy to change .INI file settings. Some features are as follows:

- Has a well-designed, easy-to-understand user interface
- Prints .INI files
- Allows editing of .INI files that are in folders other than the Windows folder
- Can be launched from other programs, allowing it to tightly integrate into larger solutions
- Is small and fast, written in tight C code
- Has thorough online help

INIedit is provided by Kindel Systems, 4522 194th Way N. E., Redmond, WA 98053, Voice: 206-868-9591, Fax: 206-868-9591, CIS: 71551,1455.

MEM, VERSION 1.21

Mem is a utility that displays the amount of free memory, the largest block of free memory, the percent of free system resources, and/or the amount of free disk space on drives that you select. Mem features include the following:

- Can sound an alarm when the disk space, free memory, or percent of free system resources goes below amounts that you specify (you can specify different amounts for each disk drive)
- Can stay in front of other programs so that you can see it while you work
- Has a variety of formatting and display options to make it easy to use and to read the numbers that are displayed

Mem is provided by David Feinleib, 30 Hamilton Rd., #401, Arlington, MA 02174, Voice: 617-648-1457, Fax: 617-648-1561, CIS: 76516,20, Internet: 76516.20@compuserve.com.

PRINT SWITCH, VERSION 1.06

The Print Switch program allows users that have a Hewlett Packard laser printer with a postscript cartridge to switch easily back and forth between HPPCL mode and postscript mode. It can also switch to HPPCL mode on startup. Print Switch automatically changes both the mode of the printer and the current printer driver.

> Print Switch is provided by David Feinleib, 30 Hamilton Rd., #401, Arlington, MA 02174, Voice: 617-648-1457, Fax: 617-648-1561, CIS: 76516,20, Internet: 76516.20@compuserve.com.

REGFIND, VERSION 0.7

RegFind is a utility for searching through a Windows 95 or Windows NT registry. It does not write to the registry and, therefore, should not cause any damage to it. It does not modify the registry in any way.

Among the uses for RegFind is that of searching for obsolete data. For example, if you change network names on a few nodes, you can search for old machine names, delete them from the registry, and thus speed up the performance when certain programs are started.

> RegFind is provided by Intellisoft, Inc., Stoeckmattstr. 3, CH-5316 Leuggern, Switzerland, Voice: +41 56 455149, Fax: +41 56 455140, CIS: 100116,1001, Internet: raju@inso.pr.net.ch.

RIPBAR VERSION 6.2 FOR WINDOWS 95

RipBAR is an program toolbar on which you can place programs and documents for easy launching. RipBAR also allows you to do command line launching, provides a drag-and-drop server, gives you memory and system information, provides Post-it–style notes, hot key support, and more in a package that remains unobtrusive on your screen. It is available for Windows, Windows 95, and Windows NT. RipBAR will allow you to do the following:

- Store programs and documents in a toolbar for easy launching.
- Use Drag and Drop to drop programs onto the bar, drop documents onto programs on the bar to view and edit them, and drop documents onto RipBAR's Print Tool for easy printing. You can also copy, as well as move, objects between groups.
- Group items and nest these groups. The unique tab interface makes access to any group (no matter how deeply nested) as easy as a mouse click.

- Use a variety of tools such as time and date display; memory, resource, performance, and disk space gauges; Post-it–style notes; and command line run tool.

- Use the Resource Tracker to monitor a program's use of resources so that you can track down those programs that don't clean up properly after themselves.

RipBAR is provided by SoftDesign, 28 Parkland, Point Claire Quebec, Canada H9R 2E8, CIS: 74777,2357, Internet: 74777.2357@compuserve.com.

RIPSPACE FOR WINDOWS 95

RipSPACE is a disk-space reporting tool. It analyzes a drive and the space consumed in each subfolder on it. With RipSPACE you'll be able to determine how much space is taken up by all the files connected with a program. RipSPACE allows you to define file types that are to be included in a file report. You can then determine how much total space is being taken up by a certain file type, such as bitmaps, dynamic link libraries, and executable files.

RipSPACE is provided by SoftDesign, 28 Parkland, Point Claire, Quebec, Canada H9R 2E8, CIS: 74777,2357, Internet: 74777.2357@compuserve.com.

WIN, WHAT, WHERE, VERSION 3.0

Win, What, Where is a multi-user time and usage monitor with project tracking for Windows. Its functions include the following features:

- A log of when a program was launched and how long it ran is kept.

- Multi-user capabilities allow you to gather usage information over the entire network; these tracking capabilities let you group activities based on a project.

- Keyboard and mouse tracking functions provide insights into how your users are using the mouse and keyboard, which is especially valuable information for ergonomists.

Win, What, Where won't get in the way. Load it and forget it. Your time and activities are automatically recorded.

Win, What, Where is provided by Basic Systems, Inc., 2103 West Canal Drive, Kennewick, WA 99336, Voice: 509-735-2386,

Fax: 509-735-1730, CIS: 70034,1341, Internet: 70034.1341@compuserve.com.

WINBATCH 32, VERSION 5.1C

WinBatch is a system utility programming language for Windows. Separate versions are available for Windows and for Windows NT or Windows 95. WinBatch manipulates the Windows interface, Windows programs, and network connections. It includes keystroke record and playback, and much more. It works from script files, so recorded events can be combined with advanced capabilities to automate operations impossible to record. WinBatch is often used to assemble reports, install software, automate testing, control processes, acquire data, and add efficiency to the Windows workstation. It has two components: a system control language called WIL (Windows Interace Language); and an interpreter that reads a text file written in the WIL language and performs the required manipulations. Some of the functions WinBatch can perform are:

- Solve numerous system management problems
- Run Windows and DOS programs
- Send keystrokes directly to programs
- Send menu items directly to Windows programs
- Rearrange, resize, hide, and close windows
- Run programs either concurrently or sequentially
- Display information to the user in various formats
- Prompt the user for any needed input
- Present scrollable file and folder lists
- Copy, move, delete, and rename files
- Read and write files directly
- Copy text to and from the Clipboard
- Perform string and arithmetic operations
- Make branching decisions based upon numerous factors
- Call dynamic link libraries
- Act as an OLE 2.0 Automation client

WinBatch is provided by Wilson WindowWare, Inc., 2701 California Ave. SW, #212, Seattle, WA 98116, Voice: 206-938-1740, Fax: 206-935-7129, CIS: 76702,1072, Internet: wwwtech@halcyon.com.

WINCLOCK, VERSION 4.0

WinClock is a digital clock for Windows that has the following features:

- Displays time and date in many different formats
- Has 25 alarms, which can be set for daily or only a specified date
- Displays the date in any of six languages
- Has a run program timer which runs programs at specified times
- Has an optional hourly "beep"
- Allows user to set date and time easily
- Optionally stays in front of other windows
- Remembers its position on the screen
- Has two stopwatches
- Has two countdown timers
- Allows the colon separating hours and minutes to be set to "blink"
- Has context sensitive help
- Has direct screen saver compatibility (auto-detect active screen saver)
- Has Cascade and Tile compatibility

Winclock is provided by David Feinleib, 30 Hamilton Rd., #401, Arlington, MA 02174, Voice: 617-648-1457, Fax: 617-648-1561, CIS: 76516,20, Internet: 76516.20@compuserve.com.

WINEDIT 32, VERSION 3.1A

WinEdit is an ASCII text editor, capable of editing numerous ASCII text files of almost unlimited sizes (limited only by available Windows memory). It is first and foremost a programmer's editor, with many features designed for creating and maintaining program source code, including Wilson's WinBatch files. Some of the things WinEdit can do are as follows:

- Build, debug, and run your programs directly from WinEdit with the ability to view any compiler errors or warnings and the corresponding source code
- Allow you to open numerous text files at once as an ASCII text editor

- Print half sized "two-up" pages side by side in landscape orientation
- Print header and footer text (document name, date and time, page number)
- Merge files together
- Word wrap your text to the size of the window

WinEdit is provided by Wilson WindowWare, Inc., 2701 California Ave. SW, #212, Seattle, WA 98116, Voice: 206-938-1740, Fax: 206-935-7129, CIS: 76702,1072, Internet: wwwtech@halcyon.com.

WINIMAGE, VERSION 2.1

WinImage (and WinImant, which is used with Windows 95 and Windows NT) is a disk image management utility. It can read, write, and format standard 360 KB, 720 KB, 1.2 MB, and 1.44 MB disks as well as the new 1.68 MB and DMF disks. The resulting image contains all floppy data including files, FAT, boot sector, folder, etc. WinImant supports long filenames (up to 255 characters).

WinImage makes an image of a floppy disk and writes an exact copy on another disk (similar to the DOS DiskCopy command). You can also read a floppy disk and write the image on a hard disk to copy many times to other floppy disks.

You can also build up a floppy disk image with WinImage. For example, if you want to output five files on a $3^1/2$-inch, 1.44-MB disk, you can create an empty 1.44-MB image and inject the five files into it. Then in one operation, you can format the floppy disk and write the image on it. In addition, you can do the following:

- Load an image by reading a floppy, or reading an image file, or creating an empty image
- Extract the files of an image onto any device—hard disk, network drive, or floppy disk
- Add files to the image, which can be copied onto a floppy with the *same* format, or saved in a file on the hard disk
- Combine several images in a chain operation, so when WinImage executes the batch, it repeats the sequence of the images

WinImage is provided by Gilles Vollant, 13, Rue François Mansart, 91540 Mennecy, France, Voice: 33-1-64 99 75 23, CIS: 100144,2636, Internet: 100144.2636@compuserve.com.

WINPRINT, VERSION 1.53

WinPrint makes printing ASCII or ANSI text files in Windows very simple. Text files can be dropped on WinPrint's minimized icon from the Explorer, and those files will print, formatted with headers and footers including the filename, date printed, date revised, and page numbers. It also allows the user to change options via a user interface. WinPrint's features include the following:

- Drag and drop files from the Explorer
- Print multiple pages on one piece of paper
- Complete control over all page formatting options, including headers and footers, margins, fonts, and page orientation
- Clean and elegant user interface
- Small and fast, written in tight C code
- Complete command line interface, which allows WinPrint to be called from other programs or solutions
- Configurations that can be saved, and multiple copies of WinPrint that can be run at the same time, each with its own configuration
- Thorough online help

WinPrint is provided by Kindel Systems, 4522 194th Way NE, Redmond, WA 98053, Voice: 206-868-9591, Fax: 206-868-9591, CIS: 71551,1455

ZIP MANAGER, VERSION 5.2 FOR WINDOWS 95

Zip Manager is a complete Windows-based archive file manager for Windows 95 and Windows NT. It allows you to create, extract, and manage compressed files in the .ZIP and .ARJ file compression formats, and it converts .ARC, .LZH, and .LHA file formats to .ZIP or .ARJ format. In addition Zip Manager lets you do the following:

- Open .ZIP and .ARJ files by double-clicking on them
- Use Windows multitasking with ZMZIP and ZMUNZIP programs

- Work in the foreground while compressing or uncompressing files in the background
- Use the right mouse button for access to the folder and archive windows
- Use macros to automate running
- Is compatible with Stacker, DoubleSpace, and DriveSpace

Zip Manager is provided by Software Excellence by Design Inc., 14801 North 12th Street, Phoenix, AZ 85022, Voice: 602-375-9928, Fax: 602-375-9928, BBS: 602-375-9945, CIS: 72200,2276

Fonts

RRKEYFONTS/PC

RRKeyFonts are fonts designed specifically for use in computer documentation. The shareware version includes a complete set of RRKeyCaps plus a sampler font containing characters from matching keyletter and Windows symbol font sets that you receive when you register your copy of RRKeyFonts. The typefaces include

- Plain 2-D characters that print well and are at standard body text sizes (10–12 points).
- All characters in all the keycap typefaces, which can be accessed in one or two keystrokes (one of which is Shift). Most of the keys are mapped mnemonically so you probably won't need a character map to remember which keycap is mapped to which key or what Alt number pad combination to use.
- The RRKeySampler typeface, a mixture of RRKeyLetters and RRWinSymbols designed to be used with this typeface for combinations like Ctrl-Y to produce a "Yes" button. Some other symbols are "No" button, Maximize, pull-down list, option button on, and so on.

RRKeyFonts/PC is provided by RoadRunner Computing, P.O. Box 21635, Baton Rouge, LA 70894, Voice: 504-928-0780, Fax: 504-928-0802, CIS: 76436,2426, Internet: 76436.2426@compuserve.com.

Games

HOP, VERSION 1.02

Hop is a Chinese Checkers-like game for Windows.

Hop is provided by David Feinleib, 30 Hamilton Rd., #401, Arlington, MA 02174, Voice: 617-648-1457, Fax: 617-648-1561, CIS: 76516,20, Internet: 76516.20@compuserve.com.

Documentation for the Companion CD-ROM

his chapter is a compendium of the documentation available for
the software on the *Windows 95 Power Tools* CD-ROM. Except
for some formatting and the most cursory of editing, this documentation is presented as it was received from the software authors. It is
also worthwhile to repeat the note from Chapter 14:

**Important! The software on the disk is offered AS IS, as it was received
from the authors. Random House, Inc. and Martin Matthews, jointly
and severably, make no warranty, either expressed or implied, as to the
usability of the software or its fitness for a particular purpose; and they
assume no liability for damages, direct or consequential, which may
result from using the software or reliance on the documentation.**

If you have trouble using any piece of software on the CD, you should
contact the software's author (either company or individual) at the
postal or e-mail address or phone number that is listed with the documentation in this chapter. If you have trouble contacting the author, you
should contact the Association of Shareware Professionals (ASP), 545
Grover Road, Muskegon, MI 49442-9427, CompuServe 72050,1433; or
contact the ASP Ombudsman at P.O. Box 5786, Bellevue, WA 98006,
CompuServe 70007,3536.

The documentation is presented in the order it appears in Table 14–1
in Chapter 14.

491

General Installation Notes

The *Windows 95 Power Tools* CD-ROM has a folder for each piece of software included. To work with a piece of software, use the following instructions:

1. Open the Explorer by opening the Start menu and choosing Programs, Windows Explorer.

2. Click on the plus sign next to your CD-ROM drive to open the folders under the CD-ROM.

3. Click on the folder for the piece of software you want to use, so its files are visible in the right-hand pane.

4. If the instructions say to use the Setup or Install program for that software, double-click on that program, and follow the instructions on the screen.

5. If you are to copy the software to your hard disk, use File, New, and Folder to create a new folder on your hard disk, and name it for the software. Press Ctrl-A to select the software on the CD, and then drag it to the new folder.

In the individual software folders on the CD, the software has been uncompressed and exists as it would on a hard disk. In the separate Zipped directory, the software is in its compressed state as an emergency backup. If, for some reason, the software in its named folder on the CD does not work, use the following steps:

 **The following steps are to be used ONLY if the software in its named folder on the CD does not work.**

1. Create a new folder on your hard disk for the software you want to use.

2. Copy the appropriate .ZIP file from the Zipped folder on the CD to the new folder on your hard disk.

3. Use Zip Manager included on this CD to unzip the files, or use PkUnzip 2.04g (which is available on most bulletin boards or from PKWare, Inc. 9025 N. Deerwood Drive, Brown Deer, WI 53223, Voice: 414-354-8699, Fax: 414-354-8559, BBS: 414-354-8670) to unzip (decompress) the file, and proceed as you would had you been able to use the original folder on the CD.

GrabIt Professional, Version 4.2

Copyright © 1990-1995 by Software Excellence By Design Inc. All Rights Reserved

14801 North 12th Street, Phoenix, AZ 85022, Voice: 602-375-9928,
Fax: 602-375-9928, BBS: 602-375-9945, CIS: 72200,2276

Type: Shareware
Registration Cost: $39.95
Crippled? Yes, won't capture directly to printer without registration

GrabIt Pro is a screen capture program and is also a utility for working with other graphics programs. We are providing it to help authors, programmers, and other technical people with a tool for writing documentation. We hope that you will take the time to register the shareware release of GrabIt Pro 4.2.

Installation Instructions and Help

The GrabIt Pro program files are in compressed format. You must run the GPSETUP program to expand them before the program can be used. The setup program will create a Start Menu Programs folder and add the program files and other important files to the folder.

INSTALLING AND RUNNING THE GPSETUP PROGRAM

After starting Windows and placing the *Windows 95 Power Tools* CD in its drive, use these instructons to install GrabIt Pro:

1. From the Windows 95 Taskbar, click on the Start button.
2. From the menu choose Run.
3. Enter the location of the GPSETUP program. If the CD-ROM drive is your D: drive, then you would enter: D:\GrabitPro\GPSETUP and press Enter or click on the OK button.
4. The GrabIt Pro setup dialog box will be displayed.
5. The edit field will display a suggested directory.
6. Press OK to accept the default directory or enter new destination directory, and press Enter or click on the OK button.
7. The setup program will create the directory for you and display the file installation progress dialog box.
8. When it has finished expanding and copying the files, it will create a new folder and add the folder to the Programs menu, accessible from the Start button on the Taskbar.

The User's Manual

The MANUAL.WRI file is the program user's manual. It has been carefully written and typeset in Windows Write format using Times New Roman 10-point font and formatted for a laser printer. All of the directions are written in an easy-to-follow, 1-2-3 step format. Please take the time to read the manual before calling for technical support. The documentation was written for GrabIt Pro for Windows NT version 3.5 which was recently released as Windows NT For Workstations. Any references in the manual to Windows NT apply to Windows 95.

New Features in Version 4.2

- Automatic Filename Incrementation during screen captures. This will make it much easier to track down a certain capture window during a session when you have captured 50 or more screens.
- A toolbar with Tool Tips test descriptions for each button. We would appreciate any help with button ideas for the Capture buttons. Depicting Window, Client, and Desktop capture in a button isn't an easy task!

Remember to Use the System Menu

Remember that when GrabIt Pro is minimized in the Windows 95 Taskbar, *all* of the capture commands are available from the system menu. Right-click on the GrabIt Pro button in the Taskbar, and the system menu will pop up. This allows you to capture images without having the GrabIt Pro window in your way. When you are done with a capture session, restore GrabIt Pro to its normal-size window by clicking on its button in the Taskbar. All of your captures will be ready to view with each capture in its own child window.

GrabIt Pro Procedures

The following are procedures for using the GrabIt Pro screen capture program.

CAPTURE AN ENTIRE WINDOW

Please Note: You can click anywhere on the capture dialog, not just on the capture icon, to begin a screen capture. This feature was provided so that you could have only a small portion of the capture dialog visible and still be able to capture a screen, instead of requiring you to click on the capture icon only.

1. Select Entire Window from the Grab menu or press Ctrl + W.
2. The Capture dialog box will be displayed.
3. Click on the capture icon, and *hold* the left mouse button down; the icon disappears, and the capture cursor is displayed.
4. Move the cursor to the title bar of the window you wish to capture.
5. Click on the title bar.
6. The window will be captured as soon as the left mouse button is released.
7. You can repeat this process as needed. Press Done to return to GrabIt Pro where you can review your screen captures.

CAPTURING THE WINDOW CLIENT AREA ONLY

You can click anywhere on the capture dialog, not just on the capture icon, to begin a screen capture. This feature was provided so that you could have only a small portion of the capture dialog visible and still be able to capture a screen, instead of requiring you to click on the capture icon only.

The client area of a window is that portion below the title bar and inside the border of the window. To capture the window client area only (no caption bar or border):

1. Select Client Area from the Grab menu or press Ctrl + C.
2. The Capture dialog box will be displayed.
3. Click on the capture icon, and *hold* the left mouse button down; the icon disappears, and the capture cursor is displayed.
4. Move the cursor to the client area of the window you wish to capture.
5. Click on the client area.
6. The client area will be captured as soon as the left mouse button is released.
7. You can repeat this process as needed. Press Done to return to GrabIt Pro where you can review your screen captures.

CAPTURING A SELECTED AREA OF THE SCREEN

This process is completely different in Windows NT than it is in Windows 3.1; please read the directions that follow carefully. You can mark and capture selected areas of GrabIt Pro child windows only. You *must* either open a file or perform the capture of a window, client area, or desktop before you can capture a selected area. Once you have done this, then follow the directions below. To capture a selected area of a GrabIt Pro child window:

1. Move the cursor to the upper left-hand corner of the area in the child window you want to capture.
2. Press and *hold* the left mouse button down. The cursor will change into the crosshair cursor.
3. As you move the mouse, you will see that the area you are marking is shown in inverse video.
4. When you have marked the area you wish to capture, release the left mouse button.
5. Your capture will be displayed in a new GrabIt Pro child window.

CAPTURING A MENU AND APPLICATION WINDOW WITH GRABIT PRO

There is only one way to do this under Windows NT. Follow the directions shown below.

To capture a menu and the application window at the same time:

1. Start the program that you want to capture.
2. Make sure that GrabIt Pro is running.

3. Switch to the other program, and select the menu you want to capture.

4. Press the Print Screen button.

5. The entire Windows desktop, including the application and its menu, are sent to the Clipboard.

6. Switch to GrabIt Pro, and choose Paste From Clipboard from the Edit menu.

7. Your application's screen and menu are displayed in a GrabIt Pro child window.

8. Now you can use the selected area capture of a GrabIt Pro child window to capture the menu portion of the screen. You will most likely need to use a paint program to clean up the area surrounding the menu for satisfactory results.

CAPTURING AN APPLICATION RUNNING FULL-SCREEN

1. Start the program that you want to capture, and then minimize it.

2. Make sure that GrabIt Pro is running.

3. Switch to the other program, and have it display the screen you want to capture.

4. Hold down the Alt key, and press the Tab key.

5. When the box in the middle of the screen reads GrabIt Pro, release the Alt key.

6. The GrabIt Pro window will now be displayed; choose Capture desktop from the menu.

7. Your applications screen will be captured.

CAPTURING A DOS SCREEN WITH GRABIT PRO

The client area of a window is that portion below the title bar and inside the border of the window.

1. Start your DOS application or a DOS Command Shell.

2. When the information you want to capture is displayed, press Alt + Enter.

3. This will put your DOS screen in a window.

4. Choose Grab Client Area from the main GrabIt Pro menu.

5. The Capture dialog box will be displayed.

6. Click on the capture icon, and *hold* the left mouse button down; the icon disappears, and the capture cursor is displayed.

7. Move the cursor to the client area of the DOS Window you wish to capture.

8. Click on the client area.

9. The client area will be captured as soon you release the left mouse button.

10. You can repeat this process as needed. Press Done to return to GrabIt Pro where you can review your screen captures.

If you are going to include your DOS screen capture in a document, we recommend that you save it as a monochrome bitmap and select the Invert check box. This will give you a very nice image with black text on a white background. By saving the image in monochrome format, you will conserve disk space.

Use the Invert option to save DOS screen captures as black on white for superior clarity when printed. This lends a look of professionalism to your documents.

CAPTURING THE ENTIRE WINDOWS DESKTOP

1. Select Desktop from the Grab menu or press Ctrl + D.
2. The GrabIt window will disappear.
3. The GrabIt window will reappear.
4. Your desktop grab will be displayed in a child window.

CAPTURING A WINDOW TO THE PRINTER

When you capture a window to the printer, your screen capture is also put into a GrabIt Pro window. This gives you confirmation of what exactly was sent to the printer. You can save this to disk as a digital representation of your print screen, or close it as needed. As noted elsewhere, these features are only available in the registered version of GrabIt Pro.

1. Select Entire Window from the Grab To Printer menu.
2. The Capture dialog box will be displayed.
3. Click on the capture icon, and *hold* the left mouse button down; the icon disappears, and the capture cursor is displayed.
4. Move the cursor to the title bar of the window you wish to capture.
5. Click on the title bar.
6. The window will be sent directly to the printer as soon as the left mouse button is released.
7. You can repeat this process as needed. Press Done to return to GrabIt Pro.

CAPTURING THE DESKTOP TO THE PRINTER

When you capture the Windows Desktop to the printer, your capture is also put into a GrabIt Pro window. This gives you confirmation of what exactly was sent to the printer. You can save this to disk as a digital representation of your print screen, or close it as needed. As noted elsewhere, these features are only available in the registered version of GrabIt Pro.

1. Select Window Desktop from the Grab To Printer menu.
2. The GrabIt window will disappear.
3. The GrabIt window will reappear.
4. Your desktop capture is sent directly to the printer.

CAPTURING SELECTED AREAS OF A GRABIT PRO CHILD WINDOW

You may want to capture only a portion of a previous GrabIt Pro screen capture, or a file opened from disk.

1. Move the cursor to the upper left-hand corner of the area in the child window you want to capture.

2. Press and *hold* the *left* mouse button down. The cursor will change into the crosshair cursor.

3. As you move the mouse, you will see that the area you are marking is shown in inverse video.

4. When you have marked the area you wish to capture, release the left mouse button.

5. Your capture will be displayed in a new GrabIt Pro child window.

OPENING AND VIEWING A BITMAP

To open a bitmap from disk, select File from the main menu and choose Open, or press CTRL + O. You can select a bitmap from the list box, enter the drive and path to the bitmap you wish to load, or use the directory list box to change to the directory where your bitmap is located and then select it from the list box. Pressing the Image Info button will show you the size and color format of the image currently selected in the list box.

SAVING A CAPTURED IMAGE TO DISK

Choose File Save from the main menu, or press CTRL + S; enter the filename of the bitmap in the edit field. You will need to enter the filename including the extension of either .BMP or .RLE. Since GrabIt Pro doesn't assume that every image you save will be a .BMP or .RLE file, it doesn't automatically add the file extension.

You can choose between various formats by selecting the Options button in the File Save dialog. The options are as follows:

Image Format	Color Options
Windows 3.x Bitmap	Monochrome/16 Colors/256 Colors/24-Bit Color/Inverse
OS/2 2.0 Bitmap	Monochrome/16 Colors/256 Colors/24-Bit Color/Inverse
RLE	16 Colors/256 Colors/24-Bit Color/Inverse

For users making screen shots for documentation and other presentations, you can convert on the fly your screen shots to monochrome by choosing the Monochrome option when saving your screen captures. The radio buttons are only functional for legitimate combinations of image and color options.

Important Information on Converting from Color to Monochrome When converting from 24-Bit or 256-Color images to monochrome, MAKE A TEST IMAGE FIRST! Some 256-color or higher drivers don't correctly support the standard Windows color palette. As a result, your image may be converted to solid black. This has been reported with several drivers, and we want you to be sure your driver works properly before you save an image and then find out it was destroyed by the graphics driver. You can safely convert 16-color bitmaps to monochrome when running a 16-color driver.

COPYING TO AND FROM THE CLIPBOARD

To copy text or graphics:

1. Select the area of the child window or the window you want to copy.
2. Choose Edit Copy or press Ctrl + Ins.
3. Choose Edit Paste or press Shift + Ins.
   OR...
   You can press the right mouse button for its menu.

PASTING TEXT OR GRAPHICS

1. Choose Edit Paste or press Shift + Ins. If the Clipboard is empty, you will receive an error message.
2. The pasted image will be displayed in its own child window. The title bar will say pasted and will list the size of your pasted image.
   OR...
   You can press the right mouse button for its menu.

PRINTING A SCREEN OR BITMAP AND USING THE IMAGE SCALING OPTIONS

Important! The scaling default is Best Fit To Page, so when you do a capture directly to the printer, you get the best possible result. If you enter x- and y-scaling options, they are NOT saved from one session to another. Since every image is different, it would not make sense to save individual image x and y numbers. If you capture the same screen many times, write down for future reference the x and y values that worked best for that image. Then you will have these figures ready the next time you capture the screen.

Option—Best Fit To Page Best Fit To Page will do exactly what its name implies. It examines the currently defined paper in your printer and tries to print an image that will best fit across the page. This is the default setting, and it works well on most screen printing jobs if the image is a window or desktop capture. As noted elsewhere, these features are only available in the registered version of GrabIt Pro.

Option—Stretch To Fill Page Select this option if you want to print an extremely large image, or want the image to fill the page regardless of size. As noted elsewhere, these features are only available in the registered version of GrabIt Pro.

Option—Scale the X- and Y-Axis for an Exact Image Size This is the most flexible option, but it will take some experimentation on your part. As shown in the graphic, the x and y coordinates start in the upper left-hand corner of the page. There is no set formula for scaling the image, but remember that the entire image will be sized to fit in the rectangle you specify. For example, if you enter 10 in both fields and print out a desktop capture, you will end up with a tiny printed image of the desktop. By the same token, if you specify a large area for an icon size image, it will be stretched to fit the area. As stated above, the only sure way to get the exact scaling for an image is to experiment with several different settings until the correct one is found for your image.

PRINTING A SCREEN CAPTURE OR BITMAP:

1. Select the window that contains the image you want to print.
2. Select Print from the File menu, or press Ctrl + P.
3. The image you selected will be printed.

Laser Printers With GrabIt Pro you can print a screen capture or portion of a screen capture immediately after you have captured it. In addition you can load from disk and print any Windows bitmap. GrabIt Pro will convert to shades of gray all of the colors it can to give you an accurate hard-copy representation of your captured screen. This gray scale dithering applies to Postscript and PCL laser printers only.

DRAG AND DROP FILES TO OPEN THEM

GrabIt Pro is a drag-and-drop client; this means that you can drag files from the Windows File Manager and drop them on the GrabIt Pro window to open them. You can drop as many files as you want, up to the point where your system runs out of resources available to open them. When this occurs, or if you drag and drop a file that isn't a bitmap, GrabIt Pro will inform you with the appropriate error message.

NTFS LONG FILENAME SUPPORT

GrabIt Pro supports the NT File System completely and will open and save files in both the new long filename format and the DOS 8.3 character filenames. Areas of the program that display file and directory names are horizontal scrolling, so that you can view the entire filename.

ACCELERATOR KEY REFERENCE

Listed below are all of the keyboard shortcut keys.

Action	Key Combination
Open a File	Ctrl + O
Save a File	Ctrl + S
Print a File	Ctrl + P
Copy a Graphic to the Clipboard	Ctrl + Insert
Paste a Graphic from the Clipboard	Shift + Insert
Capture the Entire Window	Ctrl + W
Capture the Client Area	Ctrl + C
Capture the Windows Desktop	Ctrl + D
Hide Window when Grabbing a Screen Shot	Ctrl + H

Technical Support

Before doing anything else, please call our BBS; we post patches and updates as needed to keep our software as functional and error free as possible. There is a good chance that the problem or question you have will be available via one of the online help bulletins or in the message base.

If you are having trouble with GrabIt, you have the following help options available to you.

Shareware Evaluation Users

There is no voice technical support available for shareware evaluation users.

1. You can get help by calling our BBS at 602-375-0531 (2400 Baud) or 602-375-9945 (9600 Baud). Leave a message with the sysop stating your problem. You will have an answer in a few days.

2. You can fax us with your problem at 602-375-9928. We will return your answer by fax only, so be sure to include your fax number with your tech support question.

3. You can leave a message in our CompuServe mailbox. Our CIS ID number is 72200,576.

Registered Users

You can use the options outlined above, and you can get direct phone help. Before you call for help, YOU MUST HAVE YOUR REGISTRATION NUMBER READY. It will be the first thing we will ask you for when you call.

The tech support phone number is 602-375-9928 and is available from 9:00 AM until 3:00 PM, Monday–Friday.

Jasc Media Center Version 2.01

Copyright © 1990-95 by JASC, Inc., All Rights Reserved

10901 Red Circle Drive, Suite 340, Minnetonka, MN 55343, Voice: 612-930-9171, Fax: 612-930-9172, BBS: 612-930-3516, CIS: 76226,2652, Internet: jasc@winternet.com

Type: Shareware
Registration Cost: $39.00
Crippled? No

Jasc Media Center allows you to easily manage your multimedia files. You can organize them into albums; use drag and drop to arrange the album; catalog the file using keywords and comments; scan the files for unneeded, space-wasting files; view and print the files; and much more.

Installing Jasc Media Center

Before you can use Jasc Media Center, you have to run the Jasc Media Center setup program from Windows, so it will work properly on your computer. You cannot just copy the files from the CD-ROM to your hard disk. The files on the CD are packed in a special way to save space. The setup program unpacks those files and builds them on your working disk.

1. Start Windows and place the CD-ROM in its drive.

2. Select Run from the Start Menu.

3. On the Command Line, type **d:\setup**, where *d:* is your CD-ROM drive.

4. Enter the drive and directory for the location where you want your Jasc Media Center files to be placed. It will suggest a drive and directory of C:\MEDIACNT.

    If you want the Jasc Media Center program files installed on a different drive or directory, just click the pointer to the right of the characters you want to change, backspace over the ones you want to erase, then type in the new designation.

5. Jasc Media Center Setup will unpack the necessary files and place them into your directory. The status of the operation will be displayed as the setup program does this work.

6. You will be asked if you would like to add Jasc Media Center to the program manager (Start Menu Programs folder in Windows 95). Select No if you do not want Jasc Media Center added to your program manager.

7. Select Yes to have the setup program automatically build a Jasc Media Center icon and add it to your program manager.

The setup program will notify you when the installation is complete.

The User's Manual

In order to keep the size of the shareware version of Jasc Media Center reasonable, no user's manual is provided. You will find that ALL menu items and associated dialog boxes, along with general information, is provided online using the HELP-INDEX menu option of the program.

When you purchase the licensed version of Jasc Media Center, you will receive the fully illustrated, perfect-bound User's Guide.

Technical Support

Technical support for Jasc Media Center can be obtained from:

■   USA: JASC, Inc. 10901 Red Circle Drive Suite 340 Minnetonka, MN 55343 USA, Voice: (612) 930-9171 (9 AM to 5 PM USA central time), Fax: (612) 930-3516 (24 hours), BBS: (612) 930-3516, Internet: jasc@winternet.com, CompuServe: JASC forum-GO JASC

- England: Digital Workshop First Floor, 8 West Bar Banbury, Oxon OX16 9RP England, Voice: (0295) 258335, Fax: (0295) 254590
- Japan: Personal Data Factory Shimoueki-cho 451-3, Isesaki-shi, Gunma-ken 372 Japan, Voice: 0270-21-1423

Distributing

You are encouraged to pass a copy of the shareware version of Jasc Media Center along to your friends for evaluation. If you do so, you must provide them with the entire set of Jasc Media Center shareware version files. These include the following:

SETUP.EXE, SETUP.INF, MC1.CMP, README.TXT, VENDOR.DOC, FILE_ID.DIZ, CDROM.TXT

If you intend to charge for distribution, you must adhere to the requirements of the VENDOR.DOC file.

Purchasing the Licensed Version

You may use the shareware version of Jasc Media Center for a 30-day trial period. If you would like to continue to use Jasc Media Center after the 30-day trial period, you are required to purchase the licensed version of Jasc Media Center.

When you purchase the licensed version of Jasc Media Center, you will receive a disk with the licensed version and the printed user's guide. Jasc Media Center may be purchased from a number of sources. You are free to purchase your copy from wherever you desire.

To obtain the listing of vendors and print an order form:

1. Start Jasc Media Center, and in the Shareware dialog box press the Help button.
2. Click the left mouse button on the vendor of your choice, and click the Print button in the Help System.

Paint Shop Pro, Version 3.0

Copyright © 1990-1995 JASC, Inc., All Rights Reserved

10901 Red Circle Drive, Suite 340, Minnetonka, MN 55343, Voice: 612-930-9171, Fax: 612-930-9172, BBS: 612-930-3516, CIS: 76226,2652, Internet: jasc@winternet.com

Type: Shareware
Registration Cost: $69.00
Crippled? No

Paint Shop Pro supports photo retouching, painting, and image format conversion.

Installing Paint Shop Pro

Before you can use Paint Shop Pro, you have to run the Paint Shop Pro setup program from Windows so it will work properly on your computer. You cannot just copy the files from the Paint Shop Pro disk to your hard disk. The files on the distribution disk are packed in a special way to save space. The setup program unpacks those files and builds them on your working disk.

1. Start Windows, and place the *Windows 95 Power Tools* CD-ROM in its drive.

2. Select Run from the Start Menu.

3. On the Command Line, type **d:\paintshoppro\setup**, where *d:* is your CD-ROM drive.

4. Enter the Drive and Directory. This is the location where you want your Paint Shop Pro files to be placed. It will suggest a drive and directory of C:\PSP.

   If you want the Paint Shop Pro program files installed on a different drive or directory, just click the pointer to the right of the characters you want to change, backspace over the ones you want to erase, then type in the new designation.

5. Paint Shop Pro Setup will unpack the necessary files and place them into your directory. The status of the operation will be displayed as the setup program does this work. If Paint Shop Pro came on more than one disk, during the unpacking of the disks you will be requested to insert the next disk.

6. You will be asked if you would like to add Paint Shop Pro to the program manager (Start Menu Programs folder in Windows 95).

   - Select No if you do not want Paint Shop Pro added to your program manager.
   - Select Yes to have the setup program automatically build a Paint Shop Pro icon and add it to your program manager.

7. The setup program will notify you when the installation is complete.

The User's Manual

In order to keep the size of the shareware version of Paint Shop Pro reasonable, no user's manual is provided. You will find that ALL menu items and associated dialog boxes, along with general information, is provided online using the HELP-CONTENTS menu option of the program.

When you purchase the licensed version of Paint Shop Pro, you will receive the fully illustrated, perfectbound User's Guide.

Paint Shop Pro Technical Support

Technical support for Paint Shop Pro can be obtained from:

- USA: JASC, Inc., 10901 Red Circle Drive, Suite 340, Minnetonka, MN 55343, Voice: (9 AM to 5 PM USA central time) (612) 930-9171, CIS: GO JASC
- England: Digital Workshop First Floor, 8 West Bar Banbury, Oxon OX16 9RP England, Voice: (0295) 258335, Fax: (0295) 254590
- Germany: Redaktionsburo Lakies Holger, Lakies Dobro 13, 29479 Jameln, Germany, Voice: (05864) 1328, Fax: (05864) 1312
- Japan: Personal Data Factory Shimoueki-cho 451-3, Isesaki-shi, Gunma-ken 372 Japan, Voice: 0270-21-1423

Distributing

You are encouraged to pass a copy of the shareware version of Paint Shop Pro along to your friends for evaluation. If you do so, you must provide them with the entire set of Paint Shop Pro shareware version files. These include:

SETUP.EXE, SETUP.INF, PSP1.CMP, README.TXT, VENDOR.DOC, FILE_ID.DIZ

If you intend to charge for distribution, you must adhere to the requirements of the VENDOR.DOC file.

Purchasing the Licensed Version

You may use the shareware version of Paint Shop Pro for a 30-day trial period. If you would like to continue to use Paint Shop Pro after the 30-day trial period, you are required to purchase the licensed version of Paint Shop Pro.

When you purchase the licensed version of Paint Shop Pro, you will receive disk(s) with the licensed version and the printed user's guide. Paint Shop Pro may be purchased from a number of sources. You are free to purchase your copy from wherever you desire. To obtain the listing of vendors, and print an order form:

1. Start Paint Shop Pro.
2. At the Shareware dialog box press the Help button.
3. Click the left mouse button on the vendor of your choice.
4. Click the Print button in the Help System.

Professional Capture Systems, Version 2.0

Copyright © 1990-1995 JASC, Inc., All Rights Reserved

10901 Red Circle Drive, Suite 340, Minnetonka, MN 55343, Voice: 612-930-9171, Fax: 612-930-9172, BBS: 612-930-3516, CIS: 76226,2652, Internet: jasc@winternet.com

Type: Shareware
Registration Cost: $39.00
Crippled? No

Professional Capture Systems allows you to capture a defined area, full screen, window, or client area. The capture can be sent to any combination of the clipboard, printer, and disk. It is saved using the formats .BMP, .PCX, or .TIF.

Installing Professional Capture Systems

Before you can use the Professional Capture Systems, you have to run the setup program from Windows, so it will work properly on your computer. Use the following instructions:

1. Start Windows and place the *Windows 95 Power Tools* CD-ROM in its drive.

2. Select Run from the Start Menu.

3. On the Command Line, type **d:\procapturesystems\setup**, where *d:* is your CD-ROM drive.

4. When you click on the OK Button, Windows will close the Run dialog box and load SETUP.EXE. The Professional Capture Systems Setup Screen will appear, then the setup program will prompt you to enter the drive and directory:

   ■ By default, the drive and directory for Professional Capture Systems are set to C:\PCS. If you want to install Professional Capture Systems somewhere else, type the drive and directory now.

   ■ When you're done, click on the OK Button, or press Enter. The setup program will install the files in the location you entered, and it will keep you posted on its progress.

5. Add Professional Capture Systems to Program Manager (Start Menu Programs folder in Windows 95).

   When it's done installing Professional Capture Systems' files, the setup program will ask if you want to add Professional Capture Systems to your Program Manager:

   ■ Select the No button to continue without adding it. See the next step below.

   ■ Select the Yes button to add Professional Capture Systems.

   If you choose to add Professional Capture Systems to your Program Manager, the setup program will prompt you to select a group.

   ■ By default, the setup program creates a new group entitled Professional Capture Systems. You can select a different group from the Group drop-down box.

   ■ Click on the drop down box to open it, click on the group that you want to select, then click on the OK Button.

6. When installation has been completed, you will receive a Completion prompt. To close the prompt, click on the OK Button, or press Enter.

The User's Manual

The user's manual is one of the files that will be unpacked and placed on your working disk when you run the Setup program. The file is PCS.TXT It is a text file.

When you purchase the licensed version of Professional Capture Systems, you will receive a fully illustrated, printed User's Guide.

Professional Capture Systems Technical Support

Technical support for Professional Capture Systems can be obtained from:

- USA: JASC, Inc., 10901 Red Circle Drive, Suite 340, Minnetonka, MN 55343, Voice: (612) 930-9171 (9 AM to 5 PM USA central time)
- England: Digital Workshop First Floor, 8 West Bar Banbury, Oxon OX16 9RP England, Voice: (0295) 258335 Fax: (0295) 254590

Distributing

You are encouraged to pass a copy of the shareware version of Professional Capture Systems along to your friends for evaluation. If you do so, you must provide them with the entire set of Professional Capture Systems shareware version files. These include:

SETUP.EXE, SETUP.INF, PCS1.CMP, README.TXT, VENDOR.DOC, FILEID.DIZ

MKS Enhanced Mosaic Web Browser, Version 2.1

Copyright © 1995 MKS, Inc., All Rights Reserved

185 Columbia St. West, Waterloo, Ont. N2L 5Z5, Canada, Voice: 519-883-3242 or 1-800-507-5777 (orders), Fax: 519-884-8861, Internet: iasales@mks.com

Type: Shareware
Registration Cost: $49.00
Crippled? Yes, limited to 30 days of use

Introduction

MKS Enhanced Mosaic Web Browser is one of the tools included with MKS Internet Anywhere, the solution for instant Internet access. With the MKS Enhanced Mosaic Web Browser, you can "surf the World Wide Web," or in other words, quickly browse the resources of the World Wide Web to view hypertext pages on any topic of interest. You can use it to access the Gopher, Archie, Veronica, and FTP facilities of the Internet.

The MKS Enhanced Mosaic Web Browser included with this book is operational for 30 days from the time of installation. When the 30 days are over, the software will no longer work, until you upgrade to the full version of MKS Internet Anywhere.

Upgrading to the Full Version

MKS offers readers of this book a special upgrade price of $49.00. To upgrade your software, contact MKS by phone, fax, or e-mail at the numbers above. Be sure to mention that you are a reader of the *Windows 95 Power Tools* book to receive the special upgrade price. When you upgrade your software, MKS will send the full version to you via mail. Included is 30 days of Technical Support and a 30-day money back guarantee.

Installing the MKS Enhanced Mosaic Web Browser

Instructions for installing and configuring your system are described below. Due to the requirements of Internet access, you must first obtain an account with an Internet access provider before you set up the software to make a connection. Here are the three main steps required to run the MKS Enhanced Mosaic Web Browser on Windows 95:

1. Obtain a connection to the Internet from an Internet access provider.
2. Install and configure the TCP/IP components of Windows 95.
3. Install and configure the MKS Enhanced Mosaic Web Browser.

STEP 1: OBTAIN AN INTERNET CONNECTION

What is an access provider? An access provider is a company or organization that provides you with an electronic connection to the Internet. Access providers are a necessary link—the Internet is not just out there for you to begin using; you need to connect with someone who is already connected to the Internet.

The best way to describe an access provider is to think of it as a "gateway." You establish a connection to an access provider to enter the Internet, and you leave the Internet by ending that connection. In fact, the term gateway is commonly used to describe the computers that serve your Internet requests.

The standard service for connecting to the Internet is TCP/IP, which stands for Transmission Control Protocol/Internet Protocol. Essentially, TCP/IP is the set of signals your modem sends to make it understandable by all other computers using the same protocol. To use Internet Anywhere on Windows 95 you require an account at an access provider who supplies TCP/IP service using PPP (Point-to-Point Protocol).

Arranging a connection to an access provider usually involves making a telephone call to the access provider and asking for a PPP account. After answering a few questions about your system and requirements, the provider gives you the information you need to configure your Internet Anywhere—login name, password, etc.

Once you know the provider satisfies your requirements, and you decide to use their services, there are several details you need to know about your account.

Often the provider will send you a piece of paper with all of the account details, by fax or postal mail. But many times the account details are given to you over the phone, so you need to make sure you get all of the necessary information. We recommend that you obtain the following details so you can reference them when you configure your connection with Windows 95 and MKS Internet Anywhere.

- The Internet provider's domain name
- Your login ID (a.k.a. username)
- Your password
- The provider's dial-up phone (modem) number
- The Default Gateway/IP Router IP address or domain name
- The Host/Peer IP address
- The SubNet mask
- The login script (send/expect sequence)
- The supported modem baud rates
- The parity, data bits and stop bits of the provider's modem

STEP 2: WINDOWS 95 SETUP

If you want to use the MKS Internet Anywhere demonstration software on Windows 95, you must install, configure, and run the Microsoft TCP/IP stack. To do this you must perform the following operations (in addition to installing and configuring Internet Anywhere):

1. Define your modem.
2. Install the Microsoft Dial-Up Adapter.
3. Install and configure the Microsoft TCP/IP stack.
4. Install and run the Dial-Up Networking application.

Chapter 9 of this book explains these steps in detail. Please see the applicable parts of that chapter.

STEP 3: MKS ENHANCED MOSAIC WEB BROWSER SETUP

There are two substeps to installing the MKS Enhanced Mosaic Web Browser software:

1. Installing the software.
2. Configuring the software.

Installing the Software The Setup program copies all the files needed to copy the MKS Enhanced Mosaic Web Browser onto your hard disk.

Note that the Setup program only copies the necessary files. Once you have the files on your computer, you need to configure a connection with an Internet access provider. In fact, the Setup program automatically starts the configuration process upon completion. The next section, "Configuring the Software," provides instructions for initially configuring your connection with an access provider.

To avoid any conflicts between the Setup program and other programs running on your computer, please shut down any programs you are currently running under Windows, except Windows itself, of course.

The first action you must take in the installation process is running the Setup program:

1.   Ensure the installation CD is in the CD-ROM drive.

2.   Click on the Start button from the Taskbar, and select the Run command. This prompts you to enter a command line.

3.   Type in the path and filename of the Internet Anywhere setup program, for example **d:\mksmosaic\setup** if *d:* is your CD-ROM drive, and click on **OK**.

The Setup program begins. After it initializes, you see a dialog box asking you to enter the directory where you want to install Internet Anywhere.

1.   Click on the OK button to accept the default installation directory.
     or
     Type in a different drive and directory name for installation.

2.   Click on the OK button.

When the Setup program finishes, you automatically begin the configuration process.

Configuring the Software   When the Setup program finishes, the configuration process, which is also known as the First Time Personalization process, automatically begins. This takes you through each stage of configuration step by step. Simply fill in the details in the dialog boxes that appear, based on information about your system and the details you receive from your Internet access provider.

When the First Time Personalization process is complete, you are ready to go. Simply double-click on the Internet Anywhere program icon, and your Internet journey begins.

Pping, Version 0.2

Copyright © 1994-95 by Raju Varhese, Intellisoft Inc., Switzerland, All Rights Reserved

Stoeckmattstr 3, CH-5316 Leuggern, Switzerland, Voice: +41 56 455149, Fax: +41 56 455140, CIS: 100116,1001, Internet: raju@inso.pr.net.ch

Type: Freeware
Crippled? No

Introduction

Pping is a multithreaded console utility for Windows NT and Windows 95. It is similar to the ping program that comes with Windows 95. Ping sends an ICMP message to the remote machine and waits for a response. The output of Ping is verbose and needs some explanation to a layperson. Pping, on the other hand, gives a simple go/no-go type of response that is more suitable for checking if the remote machine is responding. Further, Pping accepts multiple remote machine names as well as wildcards for IP addresses.

Pping has been tested with Windows NT 3.5 (build 807), Windows NT 3.51 (build 844), and Windows 95 beta 3 (build 347). The current version is 0.2, dated April 27, 1995.

Installing Pping

To install Pping, copy the files PPING.001 and PPING.EXE to an appropriate directory on your hard drive. You can also copy pping.txt to the same directory, if you like.

Usage

- The basic BNF syntax for invoking Pping is:

    Pping {control_arg} {address}

    This says that any number of control arguments may be followed by any number of addresses. Control arguments start with a / or - character.

- Permitted control arguments are:

    /report: [all | ok | error]

    Indicates what Pping should report. *All* causes successful and timed out messages to be reported. Ok says that only successful replies should be reported. Error indicates that only timed-out and errors are to be reported.

    /timeout: number_of_seconds

    By default Pping waits up to 5 seconds for a response. This control argument allows you to specify a more appropriate number for your network.

    /size: buffer_size_in_bytes

    By default a small message of 20 bytes is sent to each machine being pinged. This control argument allows the buffer size to be specified. The maximum size is 300 bytes; it silently sets it to 300 if the number you specify exceeds it.

    /times: number_of_messages_per_machine

    By default only one message will be sent to each machine that is being pinged. This control argument allows any number to be specified.

    /verbose

    This control argument will cause Pping to display additional information to be shown. Currently, the alternate address (dotted IP address or hostname) and the round-trip time (in milliseconds) are displayed. Note that round-trip times have an accuracy of a few milliseconds (~3 milliseconds on Windows 95, 10 on NT 3.5) and hence a value of 0 does not mean that it was instantaneous.

- Addresses may be a hostname (with or without domains) or an IP address in dotted decimal format. IP addresses can also have wildcards for specifying multiple machines with a comma or a dash for a range. The syntax for the IP address is:

```
numseq . numseq . numseq . numseq
```

where numseq is num [- num] [, numseq] and num is a decimal number between 0 and 255.

Examples

- To check if the machine NTBOX is running type: PPING NTBOX in a console window. It will display a line indicating if that machine has responded.

- Multiple machines can be checked by putting their names on the command line, as in PPING NTBOX1 NTBOX2 NTBOX3.

- Instead of names, one can also specify IP addresses in the dotted decimal format. Thus, PPING 195.234.67.89 will try to reach the machine with that IP address.

- One could check if all machines in that subnet are okay by giving 195.234.67.1-255. This will check all machines 195.234.67.1, 195.234.67.2, and so on until 195.234.67.255.

- Hostnames cannot have wildcards.

Contacting the Author

I would welcome any constructive criticism regarding the program, its usefulness to you, and any assorted ideas you have which might improve it. However, I cannot guarantee a response, and further, I cannot guarantee that I will fix bugs and/or incorporate your ideas into a future version.

Future Enhancement

This version is admittedly quite Spartan. I intend to extend it in a few ways when I get the time. When there are a lot of addresses to scan (around 2000), Pping does not wait for all threads to terminate. As this problem does not show up when the debugger is active, I have been unable to track down the cause of it. Hence, I would not use it if more than 1,500 machines are to be pinged. I strongly suspect that I'm hitting some limit in the OS.

Legalese

Pping is supplied "as is without warranty of any kind, either expressed or implied, including, but not limited to, the implied warranties of merchantability and fitness for a particular purpose. The entire risk as to the quality and performance of the program is with you. Should the program prove defective, you assume the cost of all necessary servicing, repair, or correction.

Miscellaneous

Pping uses ICMP.DLL that comes with the TCP/IP software for Windows 95 and NT. The executable, PPING.EXE, and the documentation file that you are reading are the only files that are supplied by me. Note that one thread is created for each address that it is to be pinged. If you ask it to scan 5,000 addresses, it can bring NT to its knees. Your paging file might not be big enough to handle it, and the machine may feel like molasses. Windows 95 is weaker in this respect: the mouse cursor may not be redrawn if Pping is busy doing its job. Caveat emptor.

WFTP32, Version 2.01

Copyright © 1994-95 by Ipswitch, Inc. All Rights Reserved

81 Hartwell Ave, Lexington, MA 02173, Voice: 617-676-5700, Fax: 617-676-5710, CIS: 74777,3226, Internet: info@ipswitch.com

Type: Shareware
Registration Cost: $45.00
Crippled? Yes, will cease to function on 3/31/96

WFTP32 is a standard File Transfer Protocol (FTP) client application for Windows Sockets. The user interface for this FTP client is designed with the novice FTP user in mind. Usage should be obvious. For more information on FTP please refer to the many different NETNEWS groups or one of the recent books on the Internet.

WFTP32 also provides for automatic downloads of files. See HLP file for information on Auto Transfer of Files.

Requirements

WFTP32 requires you to have a properly installed WINSOCK.DLL (in Windows 95) and requires Windows 3.1 or later.

Installation

1.　Create a directory for this program and copy WFTP32.EXE, WFTP.INI, WFTP32.HLP to that directory.

2. Put WFTP32 on your Programs Menu by using the Explorer and dragging the program into a folder under \Windows\Start Menu\Programs.

Valid Command Line Options

If you start WFTP32 from the Run dialog box, you can use the following command line options:

-i inifile (must be first in the line!)

-p profile_name (cannot be used with gets or puts!)

-ask (prompt for command line)

ftp://remotehost/pathname/filename [local:/pathname/filename] [-ascii]

file://remotehost/pathname/filename [local:/pathname/filename] [-ascii]

//remotehost/pathname/filename [local:/pathname/filename] [-ascii]

remotehost:/pathname/filename [local:/pathname/filename] [-ascii]

local:/pathname/filename //remotehost/pathname/filename [-ascii]

local:/pathname/filename remotehost:/pathname/filename [-ascii]

Problems, Bug Reports, and Suggestions

If you connect to a host that WFTP doesn't recognize (i.e. list boxes remain blank or are displayed incorrectly) try the following:

1. Try the different host types that are listed in the Options dialog box. (The change takes effect immediately; you do not need to change directories.)

2. If you can't find one that displays the directory correctly, then:
   a. Click on the LogWnd button, and save the message log to a file.
   b. Click on the remote side DirInfo button, and save the contents to a different file.
   c. Mail both files to support@ipswitch.com.

Send all bug reports, suggestions, etc. to support@ipswitch.com.

Program Information

THE INFORMATION AND CODE PROVIDED IS PROVIDED AS IS WITHOUT WARRANTY OF ANY KIND, EITHER EXPRESS OR IMPLIED, INCLUDING BUT NOT LIMITED TO THE IMPLIED WARRANTIES OF MERCHANTABILITY AND FITNESS FOR A PARTICULAR PURPOSE. IN NO EVENT SHALL IPSWITCH, INC. OR ITS SUPPLIERS BE LIABLE FOR ANY DAMAGES WHATSOEVER INCLUDING DIRECT, INDIRECT, INCIDENTAL, CONSEQUENTIAL, LOSS OF BUSINESS PROFITS OR SPECIAL DAMAGES, EVEN IF IPSWITCH, INC. OR ITS SUPPLIERS HAS BEEN ADVISED OF THE POSSIBILITY OF SUCH DAMAGES.

This program executable, help file, and related files may be distributed freely and may be used without fee by any individual until the expiration of the evaluation period. This version of WFTP32 is unsupported. To obtain a supported version, please contact Ipswitch, Inc. at info@ipswitch.com.

File View for Windows 95 and NT, Version 1.3

Copyright © 1990-1995 by Maze Computer Communications, Inc., All Rights Reserved

269 Amethyst Way, Franklin Park, NJ 08823, Voice: (908) 821-5412, Fax: 908-821-5412, CIS: 70152,1501

Type: Shareware
Registration Cost: $10.00
Crippled? No

File View for Windows, Version 1.3 allows you to view, browse, display, and print ASCII text files or hexadecimal dumps. It may be installed as menu option in Windows File Manager. Also, you can register it in the Windows Registration Database for both open and print; drag and drop files on it; customize display options to your needs; do text and hexadecimal searches; print files; copy to the Clipboard; and get extensive help in using File View.

Installing File View

File View can be installed as a Windows File Manager extension. When this is done, File Manager adds the File View FView! menu item to its menu bar. The drop down menu contains these options:

- Start Fview: starts File View if no instance is running or no instance responds to DDE requests.
- Options: displays the Options dialog box. See File Manager Extension Options for more details.
- Help: displays the File View help.
- About: displays the File View File Manager extension About box.
- User options: are menu items added by the user to start arbitrary program with this filename as parameter. See File Manager Extension Options for more details.

INSTALLATION

Use the following instruction to install File View on your hard drive:

1. Copy File View files FVIEW.EXE, FVIEW.HLP, FVIEWDLL.DLL, and MSVCRT20.DLL to a directory included in your PATH statement.

Continue with the next instructions to add File View to your File Manager menu:

2. Start Windows NotePad (open the Start menu and select Programs, Accessories, NotePad).

3. Open file WINFILE.INI in your Windows directory. It looks somewhat like this:

    [Settings]
    MinOnRun=1
    Replace=0
    LowerCase=1
    StatusBar=1
    Save Settings=0

4. Add the following paragraph at the end of file, if one does not exist:

    [AddOns]
    File Viewer=FviewDLL.DLL

5. Save the file and close NotePad. Close File Manager if it was started.

The File Manager will not load more that four extensions simultaneously. You may need to trade. If you decide to not to include FViewDLL as an extension, you can still use FView to conveniently browse files.

The most common errors made during installation of the FView File Manager extension are:

1. The name of the DLL is FViewDLL.DLL not FView.DLL!

2. Include the full path to FViewDLL.DLL, if it is not in your PATH.

How-To's, Usage Notes

- Quickly look at several files by using mouse (drag and drop) or using the keyboard (File View menu).

- Make File View the default program for .LST (or other) files by associating File View with file type .LST or by registering File View in Windows registration database.

- Keep File View from disappearing when other application becomes active by checking the View-Always on Top option.

- Mark a line for later reference by double-clicking on the line with the mouse or using F2.

- Select text for printing or Clipboard copying by clicking the left mouse button to select and clicking Shift + left button to extend selection.

- Print selected portion of the file by selecting the text and choosing File-Print-Selected Text.

- Find all occurrences of a string by using Find-MarkAll to tag all lines and locating them by pressing F2 (useful for finding errors in compiler listings).

- Continue searching at a line other than the top of the screen by clicking on the line after which you want to start searching, and then press F3.

- Continue searching at the next line by clicking on the selected line.

- See more data on the screen by using use Format-Font and choosing a smaller font.

- Display the entire length of very long lines by using Wrap option. Also, you can use Use Format-Options-Fixed Line Length option with very long line.

- See where lines actually end by using Format-Options-Show Background option.

- Stop a File View instance from opening other files by checking Ignore DDE item on File menu. Also, register without DDE support.

- Format print page by using Format-Options to change font, line and wrap options. Also, use File-Page Setup to select margins and page heading options.

- Start File View with the same formatting options every time by pressing Save in the Format-Options dialog box. Use command line options in the File Manager icon. Use command line options in the registration database.

- Integrate File View into other applications by using DDE commands to control File View.

- Start File View without opening a file by using -D switch on the command line, but enter no filename. Check Run Minimized box in Program Manager properties for the icon.

- Predefine titles for display and print by creating a file that contains only title lines. Open the title lines' file, set titles, and from the Format menu select Save Setup.

- Print report files by using the Eject on form feed option in the Page Setup dialog. Make sure that report page fits on the paper.

Advanced Topics

This section in the Help window describes more complicated aspects of using FView. It is intended for power users, network administrators, and all others who want or need to go one step further in understanding FView behavior and abilities.

Release Notes

Notes for version 1.3 of File Viewer:

- Selecting text with a mouse causes two-speed automatic scroll when the mouse pointer reaches the top or the bottom of the window.

- Menu structure has been realigned to accommodate new options and the current Windows application design recommendations.

- Most recently used files are listed in the File menu.

- Most recently used search strings are remembered and displayed in a drop-down list box.

- Search now correctly restarts at the top of the file after the bottom of the file has been reached.

- FVIEW.INI has a number of new administrative options.

- User-defined menu items have been added to the File Manager Extension.

- New command line switches have been added.

- Color choice dialog box has been added.

- Common dialog error 0xhhhh messages for Print & Print Setup has been addressed. This message may be displayed while selecting File/Print if the printer definition is invalid or has been changed while Fview was running. Simply select File/PrintSetup to select a printer.

- Screen zoom has been added. Use Ctrl-Z key combinations to zoom-in, zoom-out or reset zoom.

- Save/Load display setup profile has been added.

- File Manager Extension .DLL can now start an arbitrary program with the selected filename as parameter.

- In text mode FView will now display form feeds embedded in the file as horizontal dashed lines. Note that only form feeds at the start of a line are recognized as valid page ejects.

- This help file has been revised to reflect the new features.

- The Windows NT version is at this time source-level compatible with Windows 3.1 version but is compiled as native 32-bit WinNT application. Some #ifdef magic was necessary to make this happen. In future versions File View for Windows NT will support some NT specific features (long filenames, NTFS gimmicks, Unicode, etc.).

Registration

Users of File Viewer must accept this disclaimer of warranty:

FILE VIEWER IS SUPPLIED AS IS. THE AUTHOR DISCLAIMS ALL WARRANTIES, EXPRESSED OR IMPLIED, INCLUDING, WITHOUT LIMITATION, THE WARRANTIES OF MERCHANTABILITY AND OF FITNESS FOR ANY PURPOSE. THE AUTHOR ASSUMES NO LIABILITY FOR DAMAGES, DIRECT OR CONSEQUENTIAL, WHICH MAY RESULT FROM THE USE OF FILE VIEWER.

File Viewer is a shareware program and is provided at no charge to the user for evaluation. Feel free to share it with your friends, but please do not give it away altered or as part of another system. The essence of user-supported software is to provide personal computer users with quality software without high prices, and yet to provide incentive for programmers to continue to develop new products. If you find this program useful and find that you are using File Viewer and continue to use File Viewer after a reasonable trial period, you must make a registration payment to Maze Computer Communications. The registration fee will license one copy for use on any one computer at any one time. You must treat this software just like a book. An example is that this software may be used by any number of people and may be freely moved from one computer location to another, so long as there is no possibility of it being used at one location while it's being used at another—just as a book cannot be read by two different persons at the same time.

Commercial users of File Viewer must register and pay for their copies of File Viewer within 30 days of first use or their license is withdrawn. Site-license arrangements may be made by contacting Maze Computer Communications.

Anyone distributing File Viewer for any kind of remuneration must first contact Maze Computer Communications at the address above for authorization. This authorization will be automatically granted to distributors recognized by the (ASP) as adhering to its guidelines for shareware distributors, and such distributors may begin offering File Viewer immediately. (However Maze Computer Communications must still be advised, so that the distributor can be kept up-to-date with the latest version of File Viewer.).

You are encouraged to pass a copy of File Viewer along to your friends for evaluation. Please encourage them to register their copy if they find that they can use it.

This program does not have any printed documentation. All information on use and capabilities is included in the online help.

All registered users receive free technical support for 101 days from the date of registration. Also, all registered users receive a free upgrade to the next version of this program when that version becomes available. To report bugs, receive help and bug fixes please send a CompuServe message via CompuServe Mail to the number shown above or use normal mail, also shown above.

You can also register your copy of this program using CompuServe: type GO SWREG at any ! prompt and follow instructions.

Iconcalc, Version 1.01

Copyright © 1992-95 by David Feinleib, All Rights Reserved

30 Hamilton Rd., #401, Arlington, MA 02174, Voice: 617-648-1457, Fax: 617-648-1561, CIS: 76516,20, Internet: 76516.20@compuserve.com

Type: Shareware
Registration Cost: $12.00
Crippled? No

Introduction

IconCalc is a full-function calculator in an icon, for Microsoft Windows. It provides the following features:

- It can stay in front of other applications so that you can see/use it while you work.
- It takes up little memory.

- It has context sensitive help.
- It has a variety of color schemes from which to choose.

Requirements for Running IconCalc

- Microsoft Windows 3.0 or above
- IconCalc (ICONCALC.EXE, ICONCALC.HLP)

Running/Installing/Upgrading IconCalc

Please note that the following directions assume you are using a mouse. If you are not using a mouse, please refer to your Windows documentation for equivalent keystrokes.

INSTALLING ICONCALC

If you are upgrading from a previous version of IconCalc, you should copy this version of IconCalc to the same directory in which the old version is. Since configuration files of previous versions of IconCalc are not compatible with this version, the first time you run IconCalc you will see a message which tells you that your configuration file was created by a different version of IconCalc and that your preference settings have been reset to the default. You may want to change the settings back to your preferred settings.

1. Copy ICONCALC.EXE, DAFLIB.DLL, DAFLIB.HLP, and ICONCALC.HLP to your Windows directory or another directory of your choice. Note that you must copy ICONCALC.EXE, DAFLIB.DLL, DAFLIB.HLP, and ICONCALC.HLP to the same directory.

2. Do one of the following: (Note: Option d is highly recommended over a, b, and c.)
    a. Open the Start menu and choose Run. Type **iconcalc** (including the path) in the Open edit box and click OK. If you use this option, you will have to do this every time you want to run IconCalc.
    b. Drag ICONCALC.EXE to the \Windows\Start Menu\Programs \Accessories directory to create a shortcut there. You can then start IconCalc by opening the Start menu and choosing Programs, Accessories, Iconcalc.
    c. Drag ICONCALC.EXE to the \Windows\Start Menu\Programs \Startup directory to create a shortcut there. This option will automatically run IconCalc each time you run Windows.
    d. Do both b and c, which will automatically run IconCalc and allow you to run IconCalc easily if you close it.

IconCalc Options

To bring up a list of options, click once on the IconCalc system box. The options are as follows:

1. Help...This will bring up help about IconCalc and explain how to use context sensitive help. It will also display an index of all help available for IconCalc.

2. Preferences...This allows you to

    ■ Keep IconCalc in front of other applications
    ■ Have IconCalc beep when an operation button is selected
    ■ Have IconCalc beep when any button is selected
    ■ Change IconCalc's color scheme
    ■ Select the options you want and click on OK when you are done, or click Cancel to cancel the changes you have made

3. About... Displays information about IconCalc.

Getting Help

IconCalc help may be accessed in three ways:

1. Select help from the IconCalc system menu. This will display an index of all help available for IconCalc. It will also explain how to use IconCalc's context sensitive help.

2. You may access context sensitive help by clicking on one of the IconCalc system menu items, holding down the mouse button, and pressing F1.

3. You may access context sensitive help from most of IconCalc's dialog boxes by clicking on the Help button if one is displayed.

The Right Mouse Button

You must use the right mouse button to select buttons on the calculator; the left mouse button will bring up IconCalc's system menu. You may also use the numbers on the keyboard or the numeric keypad (NumLock must be on to use the numeric keypad) to enter numbers.

Moving IconCalc

To move IconCalc, click on IconCalc, and while holding the mouse button down, move IconCalc.

Closing IconCalc

Click once on the IconCalc system box, and then click on Close.

How to Contact Me

Comments and suggestions (and reports of problems) would be greatly appreciated. You can contact me at the address and number shown above.

How to Pay for and Register IconCalc

IconCalc is shareware. You may make copies of this program and give them to others as long as the documentation is provided with the program, both unaltered.

Please send $12 to receive a registration number which will disable the Shareware reminder message.

If you would like to receive IconCalc on disk, send an additional $3.00 for $5^1/4$-inch, $4.00 for $3^1/2$-inch disks. You will be able to receive support by BIX, CompuServe, FidoNet, or mail. Shipping to Canada is an additional $1.50. Shipping outside of North America is an additional $2.00. Please include your name, address, and current version number. (The version number may be found in the About Box.) See above for the address.

Site licenses, LAN licenses, and substantial quantity discounts are available.

Customization of IconCalc is available but is not included in the shareware registration fee. The fee charged for customization will depend on the amount and significance of the customization.

Thanks!

Thanks very much to Peter Kaminski for getting the icons "just right" and for coming up with the different color schemes.

Disclaimer

IconCalc is supplied as is. The author disclaims all warranties expressed or implied, including, without limitation, the warranties of merchantability and of fitness for any purpose. The author assumes no liability for damages, direct or consequential, which may result from the use of IconCalc.

INIedit Version 1.31

Copyright © 1990-95 by Charles E. Kindel, Jr., All Rights Reserved

Kindel Systems, 4522 194th Way NE, Redmond, WA 98053, Voice: 206-868-9591, Fax: 206-868-9591, CIS: 71551,1455

Type: Shareware
Registration Cost: $25.00
Crippled? No

Introduction

Most Microsoft Windows applications, and Windows itself, use .INI files to store configuration information. The Windows 3.0 and 3.1 documentation refers to these files as initialization files. The most famous of all .INI files is the WIN.INI file. If you have been using Windows for any length of time, you probably have, at the minimum, seen the contents of your WIN.INI file.

INIedit is a Windows 3 application designed to make modifying, viewing, and printing Windows .INI files easy. The application itself is composed of two files, INIEDIT.EXE and CTL3DV2.DLL. Both files are required in order for INIedit to operate.

INIedit was originally developed for Windows 3.x using the Microsoft Windows 3.0 Software Development Kit; the Microsoft C Compiler Version 6.0; and the Microsoft Macro Assembler Version 5.10. Version 1.31 was compiled with Microsoft Visual C++ 1.51. The documentation was produced using Microsoft Word For Windows, Version 6.0.

What Are .INI Files

In Windows 1.x and 2.x all applications and the system used WIN.INI to store configuration information. With the introduction of Windows 3.0 came "private" .INI files. Except for a few oddball applications all .INI files are stored in the directory in which Windows is installed. This directory is named \WINDOWS by default but may be different on your system. Also, all .INI files have the extension .INI, which is why they are called .INI files. .INI files have a specific format. There are sections, keynames, and values. A section is a group of keynames. Each keyname has associated with it a value. Sections are delimited by square brackets ([and]). Keynames are assigned a value using an equal sign (=). For example in the WIN.INI file there is a section titled "Windows," which is used to store information about your Windows setup. A typical [Windows] section might appear in the WIN.INI file as:

```
[Windows]
spooler=yes
run=
Beep=yes
NullPort=None
device=Apple LaserWriter II NTX,PSCRIPT,LPT2:
BorderWidth=4
Programs=pif exe com bat
MouseSpeed=1
load=clock.exe
```

If you look at the contents of your WINDOWS directory you will notice many .INI files (from DOS type **dir c:\windows*.ini**). Windows 3 applets like Control Panel and CardFile each have their own .INI files (CONTROL.INI and CARDFILE.INI respectively). Older Windows applications that were written for Windows 2.x still may store their data in the WIN.INI file. A good example of this is Word for Windows. Another .INI file that is very important to Windows 3.0 is the SYSTEM.INI file. SYSTEM.INI contains information about the Windows 3.0 system, such as the display driver and 386 Enhanced Mode Virtual Device Drivers. INIedit can be particularly helpful when editing the SYSTEM.INI file (but BE CAREFUL!). There is one catch, however, as the [386Enh] section of the SYSTEM.INI file breaks an important rule for .INI file formatting: it has many lines with the same keyname (device=) and different values. INIedit will not allow you to modify the [386Enh] section of SYSTEM.INI for this reason. If you must edit the [386Enh] section, use the Edit with NotePad feature of INIedit.

Installing and Running INIedit

Use the following instructions to install INIedit:

1. Copy the INIEDIT.EXE file to a directory in your path (many Windows 3 users have a directory called C:\WINAPPS).

2. Check to see if the file date of CTL3DV2.DLL is newer than the copy in your WINDOWS\SYSTEM directory (if any). If it is newer, copy it to your WINDOWS\SYSTEM directory.

3. Using Program Manager's File, New menu item, create Program Manager Item for INIedit.

4. To start INIedit, simply double-click on the INIedit icon.

Make sure the file CTL3DV2.DLL is in the WINDOWS\SYSTEM directory.

RUNNING INIEDIT

1. To start INIedit, follow the procedure you would for starting any Windows application. If you have created a Program Manager Item for INIedit, simply double-click on the icon. You can also double-click on INIEDIT.EXE from within File Manager or The MS-DOS Executive.

2. If you have not registered your copy of INIedit, you will be presented with two dialog boxes each time INIedit starts. The first dialog box provides information about registering INIedit. The second dialog box provides two edit controls in which you will enter your registration information (see Registration Information for more information on registration).

Once you enter your registration information, these two dialog boxes will not appear again.

Using INIedit

The main INIedit window has four areas of interest:

- The Menu Bar
- The INI filename dropdown combo box
- The Sections/Application Names box
- The Name = Value box

THE MENU BAR

The menu bar in INIedit has two top-level items on it: File and Help. Below are descriptions of each menu item:

- File, Open...

  Pops up a dialog box that allows you to select a .INI file that is not in your WINDOWS directory. Some applications choose to store their .INI files in their own directory. The INI filename combo box in the main window only contains files found in the WINDOWS directory.

- File, Edit With NotePad

  In some cases you may wish to view and/or edit the current .INI file with the NotePad editor. If you choose this menu item, NOTEPAD.EXE will be launched with the current .INI filename.

  INIedit does not allow you to edit the [386Enh] section of SYSTEM.INI due to the fact that this section is not in the standard Windows .INI file format. Use the File, Edit With NotePad menu item to launch NotePad when you wish to edit the [386Enh] section of SYSTEM.INI.

- File, Print

  Prints the current .INI file to the default system printer or the printer specified using the File, Printer Setup menu item.

- File, Printer Setup

  Pops up a dialog box that allows you to select and configure the printer you want INIedit to use when the File, Print menu item is selected.

- Help

  Opens online help and a dialog box that gives copyright information about INIedit. This dialog box also contains the version number of INIedit. When reporting bugs or requesting help, it is helpful to include these version numbers. Clicking on the icon in the main window has the same effect as this menu item.

THE INI FILENAME COMBO BOX

This combo box contains all .INI files that exist in your WINDOWS directory. When you select a file in this combo box, that file becomes the current .INI file. The Sections/Application Names list box is filled with all sections in the .INI file and the Keyname=Value list box is filled with all keynames and values found in the first section of the .INI file. All items are listed in alphabetical order.

THE SECTIONS/APPLICATIONS BOX

This box contains a list box with all of the sections in the current .INI file. You can add a new section using the Add button, or delete an existing section using the Remove button. When you highlight a section in this list box, the keynames and values found in that section will be listed in the Keyname=Value list box below. CAUTION: The Remove button is potentially dangerous! Once you remove a section with this button, that section and ALL of it's keynames and values are removed. Use with care!

THE KEYNAMES=VALUE BOX

This box contains a list box with all of the keynames and values found in the current section of the current .INI file.

- The Add button allows you to add a new keyname with value. Be careful that you do not add a keyname that already exists, or you will overwrite it.
- The Edit button allows you to edit the currently highlighted keyname and value. Double-clicking on a keyname has the same effect as pressing the Edit button.
- The Remove button will delete the current keyname = value line from the current .INI file.

Notice!

INIedit is DESIGNED to modify Windows Initialization files. CAUTION must be used whenever you modify WIN.INI or SYSTEM.INI. There is little chance that INIedit would corrupt one of these files, but it is possible that they could be modified incorrectly by the user.
THIS COULD CAUSE WINDOWS TO FAIL TO WORK or WORK INCORRECTLY, CAUSING LOSS OF DATA. BACK UP YOUR .INI FILES REGULARLY!
Program and Documentation Copyright © 1991-95, Charles E. Kindel, Jr. All Rights Reserved. Portions Copyright 1987-90 Microsoft Corporation. Windows, Windows 3.0, and Word For Windows are trademarks of Microsoft Corporation.

INIedit Files

Files included with INIedit are as follows:

INIEDIT.EXE	The main INIedit Windows Application
CTL3DV2.DLL	Windows DLL required by INIedit
README.TXT	This file
INIEDIT.HLP	INIedit Help File

 CTL3DV2.DLL must be copied into your WINDOWS\SYSTEM directory. You should only copy it there if its file date is newer than an already existing copy (or if there is no copy there). Once you have copied CTL3DV2.DLL to your WINDOWS\SYSTEM directory, you can remove all other copies from your system.

Technical Support

Technical support for INIedit is provided to registered users via electronic mail or by fax. If you are a registered user, you can contact the author for support on CompuServe. Send CompuServe mail to 71551,1455. Questions and suggestions can also be faxed to the author at (206)868-9591.

Registration

INIedit is not and has never been public domain software, nor is it free software. INIedit is a commercial application distributed as shareware. Nonlicensed users are granted a limited license (registration) to use INIedit on a 21-day trial basis for the purpose of determining whether INIedit is suitable for their needs. The use of INIedit, except for the initial 21-day trial, requires registration. The use of unlicensed (unregistered) copies of INIedit by any person, business, corporation, government agency or any other entity is strictly prohibited. A single-user license permits a user to use INIedit only on a single computer. Licensed users may use the program on different computers, but they may not use the program on more than one computer at the same time.

No one may modify or patch the INIedit executable and documentation files in any way, including but not limited to decompiling, disassembling, or otherwise reverse engineering the program.

A limited license is granted to copy and distribute INIedit only for the trial use of others, subject to the above limitations, and also the following:

1. INIedit must be copied in unmodified form, complete with the file containing this license information

2. The INIedit product consists of the following files: INIEDIT.EXE, CTL3DV2.DLL, README.TXT, and INIEDIT.HLP. All of these files must be copied in unmodified form.

3. INIedit may not be distributed in conjunction with any other product without a specific license to do so from Charles E. Kindel, Jr.

4. No fee, charge, or other compensation may be requested or accepted, except as authorized below:

    a. Operators of electronic bulletin board systems (sysops) may make INIedit available for downloading only as long as the above conditions are met. An overall or time-dependent charge for the use of the bulletin board system is permitted as long as there is not a specific charge for the download of INIedit.

    b. Vendors may charge a disk duplication and handling fee, which may not exceed ten dollars.

The single-user registration fee for INIedit 1.3 is $25 (US Dollars). Payment of this fee entitles you to:

- A registration number that will disable the startup shareware reminder windows contained within the program

- Free upgrade to all future shareware versions and a discount on future versions that are not distributed as shareware, if any

- Technical support via electronic mail

Diskettes containing the latest version of INIedit are available for $15. The most recent version of INIedit can always be found in the following places:

- The WINSHARE forum on CompuServe
- The Utilities forum on PC Magazine's PC MAGNET

Site licenses for INIedit are available. Contact the author for more information.

REGISTERING INIEDIT

INIedit may be registered in one of two ways:

1. Send a check for $25.00 (US Dollars) drawn on a U.S. bank made out to Charles E. Kindel, Jr. to the address above.

   Important points to remember when registering via mail:

   - The only forms of payment currently accepted are by check for United States dollars drawn on a United States bank (the cost of cashing a check drawn on an international bank is typically $25-$30, which is prohibitively expensive) or cash. If you do send a check drawn on a U.S. bank, but from an international branch, make sure the check clearly states where a U.S. branch of that bank is located.

   - You can print a registration form by selecting the registration form topic in WinHelp and using the File, Print... menu item. Using these forms makes processing orders much easier.

   - Make sure your name and address are clearly legible on the registration form and that you include a first and last name.

2. Log on to CompuServe, and type **go swreg**. This will take you to the Shareware Registration system. Your CompuServe bill will be charged for the registration fee, and your registration number will be sent to you via CompuServe Mail. INIedits SWREG ID is 547.

Mem, Version 1.21

Copyright © 1990-95 by David Feinleib, All Rights Reserved

30 Hamilton Rd., #401, Arlington, MA 02174, Voice: 617-648-1457, Fax: 617-648-1561, CIS: 76516,20, Internet: 76516.20@compuserve.com

Type: Shareware
Registration Cost: $10.00
Crippled? No

Introduction

Mem can display the amount of free memory, the largest block of free memory, the percent of free system resources, and/or the amount of free disk space on drives that you select. Mem can sound an alarm when the disk space, free memory, or percent of free system resources goes below amounts that you specify (a different amount may be specified for each disk drive). Mem can stay in front of other applications so that you can see it while you work. Mem has a variety of formatting and display options to make it easy to use the program and read the numbers that are displayed.

Requirements for Running Mem

- Microsoft Windows 3.0.
- Mem (MEM.EXE, MEM.HLP).

Running/Installing Mem

Please note that the following directions assume you are using a mouse. If you are not using a mouse, please refer to your Windows documentation for equivalent keystrokes.

1. Copy MEM.EXE to your Windows directory or another directory of your choice.

2. Do one of the following: (Note: Option d is highly recommended over a, b, and c.)

    a. Open the Start menu and choose Run. Type **mem** (including the path) in the Open edit box and click OK. If you use this option, you will have to do this every time you want to run Mem.

    b. Drag MEM.EXE to the \Windows\Start Menu\ Programs \Accessories directory to create a shortcut there. You can then start Mem by opening the Start menu and choosing Programs, Accessories, Mem.

    c. Drag MEM.EXE to the \Windows\Start Menu\ Programs\Startup directory to create a shortcut there. This option will automatically run Mem each time you run Windows. This option is especially useful if you are using Mem to help with software development or other situations in which you will need very often to see the amount of free memory or disk space.

    d. Do both B and C, which will automatically run Mem and allow you to run Mem easily if you close it.

Mem Options

To bring up a list of options, click once on the Mem system box.

1. Help... will bring up an index of help topics available for Mem using the Windows 3.0 help system.

2. Preferences... will display a dialog box from which you may select to display the amount of free memory, the largest block of free memory, the percent of free system resources and/or the amount of free disk space on drives that you select.

3. Display

    - Select Bring To Front to have Mem stay in front of other applications; if Bring To Front is not selected, Mem will not stay in front of other applications.
    - Selecting Commas will insert commas as appropriate.

- Selecting In Bytes will display all numbers in Bytes.
- Selecting In KB will display all numbers in KB.
- Selecting In MB will display all numbers in MB.

4. Notify When

- Selecting [Notify When] Free memory is below will cause Mem to sound an alarm if the amount of free memory goes below the number of bytes you specify in the edit box.
- You may select to have alarms go off for different drives when the amount of free space on a specified drive goes below the number of bytes specified in the edit box.
- You may set different amounts for each drive by selecting a drive, entering the number of bytes in the edit box, clicking [Notify When] Disk space on drive, using the scroll bar if necessary.
- Selecting [Notify When] Free System Resources goes below, will cause Mem to sound an alarm if the percent of free system resources goes below the percent that you specify in the edit box.
- If the alarm sounds, the Mem window will flash at the same time; to turn off the alarm, click on Mem to give it the focus.

5. Delay Between Updates. You may change the time between updates by entering the time you want between updates, in milliseconds, in the edit box. Mem will remember which options are selected so that the next time you run Mem, it will have the same options selected.

6. About... displays information about Mem.

Getting Help

Mem help may be accessed in three ways:

1. Select Help from the Mem system menu. This will display an index of all help available for Mem. It will also explain how to use Mem's context sensitive help.

2. You may access context sensitive help by clicking on one of the Mem system menu items, holding down the mouse button, and pressing F1.

3. You may access context sensitive help from most of Mem's dialog boxes by clicking on the Help button if one is displayed.

Minimizing Mem

If you want to cascade or tile the open windows, it is useful to minimize Mem, so that it does not get cascaded or tiled

- To do this, click on the system box, and select Minimize from the menu. Please note that Mem will take about one-half of a second to minimize itself since it saves its position on the screen before it is minimized.
- To restore Mem after you have minimized it, click once on the Mem icon, and then select Restore from the system menu.

Restoring Mem

After you have minimized Mem, you may restore it to its original size by one of two methods:

- Click once on the Mem icon, and then select Restore from the menu; or
- Double-click on the Mem icon.

Moving Mem

To move Mem, click on Mem, and while holding the mouse button down, drag Mem.

Closing Mem

To close Mem, do one of the following:

- Double-click on the Mem system box; or
- Click once on the Mem system box, and then click on Close.

How to Contact Me

Comments and suggestions (and reports of problems) would be greatly appreciated. You can contact me at the address or number shown above.

How to Pay for/Register Mem

Mem is shareware. You may make copies of this program and give them to others as long as the documentation is provided with the program, both unaltered.

Send $10 + $2.75 for $5^1/_4$-inch or $4.75 for $3^1/_2$-inch disks if you would like to register and receive the next version of Mem when it becomes available. Shipping to Canada is an additional $1.25; shipping outside of North America is an additional $3.25. In addition, you will receive support via BIX, CompuServe, FidoNet, or mail. Please include your name, address, and current version number. (The version number may be found in the About Box.). See above for the address. (Please specify disk size if appropriate.)

Site licenses, LAN licenses, and substantial quantity discounts are available. Customization of the Mem is available but is not included in the shareware registration fee. Please contact me for more information.

Thanks!

My thanks to Peter Kaminski for designing and drawing the Mem icon. Thanks to Bruce Wheelock and Paul Horner for their suggestions which contributed to the changes in this version 1.11. Thanks to Scott Dunn for the idea of adding the system resources option.

Error Messages

If you see the error message P1000 No system timers available Mem must use one of the Windows Timers, you should try closing another application, or closing Mem and running Mem again.

Liability

Mem is supplied as is. The author disclaims all warranties expressed or implied, including, without limitation, the warranties of merchantability and of fitness for any purpose. The author assumes no liability for damages, direct or consequential, which may result from the use of Mem.

Print Switch, Version 1.06

Copyright © 1991-95 by David A. Feinleib, All Rights Reserved

30 Hamilton Rd, #401, Arlington, MA 02174, Voice: 617-648-1457, Fax: 617-648-1561, CIS: 76516,20

Type: Shareware
Registration Cost: $19.00
Crippled? No

Introduction

The Print Switch program allows those users that have a Hewlett Packard laser printer with a postscript cartridge to switch easily back and forth between HPPCL mode and postscript mode. It can also switch to HPPCL mode on startup.

Print Switch automatically changes both the mode of the printer and the current printer driver.

Using Print Switch

To use the Print Switch program, place PSWITCH.EXE in your \Windows\Start Menu\Programs\StartUp folder. This will cause Print Switch to be loaded automatically every time you start Windows.

CHANGING THE PRINTER MODE

There are several ways to change the printer mode. The easiest way is simply to double-click on the Print Switch icon while the program is running. This will automatically switch the printer mode. You may also select Switch To HPPCL Mode or Switch To Postscript Mode from the system menu, which you can display by clicking once on the icon.

CONFIGURATION

Print Switch includes default settings for Adobe and Pacific Page postscript cartridges. You may change the postscript cartridge by selecting Select postscript Cartridge from the system menu. If you have another postscript cartridge, you can select Other in the dialog box, and then type in the appropriate mode-switching command strings.

Shareware

This program is shareware. You may make copies of this program and give them to others as long as the documentation is included, both unaltered. If you like this program, a registration fee of \$15 would be appreciated. Add \$3.00 for a $5^{1}/_{4}$-inch diskette or add \$4.00 for a $3^{1}/_{2}$-inch diskette. Add \$1.50 for shipping outside of the United States. Please include your name, address, disk size, and current version number. Comments and suggestions (with or without the registration fee) would be greatly appreciated.

Please read the file PRODLIST.TXT for more information on other programs by the same author.

Disclaimer

Pswitch is supplied as is. The author disclaims all warranties expressed or implied, including, without limitation, the warranties of merchantability and of fitness for any purpose. The author assumes no liability for damages, direct or consequential, which may result from the use of Pswitch.

Regfind, Version 0.7

Copyright © Raju Varghese, Intellisoft, Inc., All Rights Reserved

Stoeckmattstr 3, CH-5316 Leuggern, Switzerland, Voice: +41 56 455149, Fax: +41 56 455140, CIS: 100116,1001, Internet: raju@inso.pr.net.ch

Type: Freeware
Crippled? No

Introduction

Regfind is a utility for searching through a Win32 registry. This is the first version of the program and is meant for use with Windows NT and Windows 95. It has been tested with NT 3.5. Regfind started off as a perl utility for Windows NT, but this version has been rewritten in C. It has not undergone exhaustive testing, and hence I would welcome any bug-reports you might have. This utility does not write to the registry and should, therefore, not cause any damage to it. Microsoft has stated over and over again that modifications to the registry can render the system unusable. Regfind does not modify the registry in any way. However, please read the disclaimer below.

Regfind is a console application: you can run it from a DOS box just like other command line programs. I intend to put a GUI front-end on it sometime, but I cannot promise when that will be. Regfind accepts various parameters and they are explained in the section below.

Thanks to this program I have been able to unearth vestiges of obsolete data. After I had changed network names on a few nodes, I noticed that my machine was extremely slow when certain programs were started. I searched for old machine names, deleted them from the registry, and speed was restored. Those applications were waiting for the old hosts to respond, and only after a timeout error was reported, did they continue. Thus removing those names from the registry caused the application to start faster.

The current version is 0.7, dated May 6, 1995.

Usage

The command line syntax for executing Regfind is:

```
regfind {<control argument>} [pattern]
```

Regfind may be followed by zero or more control arguments which, in turn, may be followed by a pattern for which to search. Omitting pattern and control arguments will result in all data in the registry being shown. This can be quite large; you can restrict it by turning on various filters by means of control arguments. Control arguments start with a - or a / character; in this document we will use -.

The generated output is displayed in the form:

```
Full\key\path\separated\by\slashes modification_time value1 = data1
value2 = data2
```

Modification_time is only displayed on Windows NT.

<control argument> may be one of the following:

-**key <key pattern>** The keyname specifies a pattern to search for in the registry keys. All subtrees which contain <key pattern> will be displayed.

-**value <value pattern>** The value pattern specifies a pattern to search for in values. All value names which contain <value pattern> will be displayed.

-**data <data pattern>** The data pattern specifies a pattern to search for in data. All string data which contain <data pattern> will be displayed.

-**any <pattern>** This is the same as typing <pattern> on its own; in other words, "Regfind -any xxx" is equivalent to "Regfind xxx". This will cause the program to display all value/data pairs and keys which contain <pattern>.

-hive <hive name> Hive name must be one of the four predefined hives:

HKEY_LOCAL_MACHINE

HKEY_CURRENT_USER

HKEY_USERS

HKEY_CLASSES_ROOT

-node \\nodename Nodename must be running a Win32 OS and must be accessible through a Microsoft supported network.

-before 19yy/mm/dd [hh:mm[:ss]] This will show all keys and their associated value/data pairs which were modified before the specified time. It is available only on NT. If you supply time as well, put the whole parameter in quotes (e.g., -before "1995/1/3 10:34"); the specified time is assumed to be the local time.

-after 19yy/mm/dd [hh:mm[:ss]] This will show all keys and their associated value/data pairs which were modified after the specified time. It is available only on NT. If you supply time as well, put the whole parameter in quotes (e.g. -after "1994/3/4 11:35"); the specified time is assumed to be the local time.

-hidevalues This does not show value/data pairs; useful if only keys are required

-depth <number> This does not go deeper than <number> levels deep when traversing the registry tree. <number> must be >= 1.

-case This makes searches case-sensitive; default is case-blind.

-showerror This shows errors which are returned from the API; these usually indicate security errors or that there is more data. The latter one is due to the fact that RegFind has a buffer of approximately 1 KB and there are large binary data in the registry (> 8 KB).

-help This shows a short help screen

`Pattern` is a text string which specifies the data to be searched for in the registry. For example, typing **regfind blue** will show you all keys and value/data pairs which have the string "blue" in the key, value, or data. This is the same as typing **regfind -any blue**. My favorite is **regfind raju** which shows me where the operating system has squirrelled away my name. Alternatively, **regfind -case raju** will perform a case-sensitive search. Try it out with your name.

To specify a parameter with embedded blanks, enclose it in double-quotes. For example **regfind -key "Control Panel"** will display the control panel subtree in all four hives.

The -key, -value, -data and -hive control arguments may be used to restrict the amount of information displayed. They are like filters; specifying more than one will cause the filters to restrict the displayed information even more. Thus, **regfind -key** *xxx* will show all keys, values, and data which are under a key which has xxx in it. **Regfind -key** *xxx* **-value** *yyy* will only show those keys values and data which have *xxx* in the keys and *yyy* in the value names. Similarly, **regfind -key** *xxx* **-value** *yyy* **-data** *zzz* will only show those which have *xxx* in the keys, *yyy* in the values, and *zzz* in the data. The search can be restricted even more by turning on the -hive control argument. Currently, there are only four hives predefined in the Win32 registry (refer to the win32 documentation for details). The -any control argument cannot be used with -key, -value, or -data.

Case-sensitivity can be turned on with the -case control argument. This affects the items specified by the -key, -value, -data, -any, and-hive. The value/data line is shortened, so that it fits into a normal window with 80 columns.

Examples

- Typing **regfind** on its own will display the whole registry: everything under all the four hives.

- Typing **regfind blue** (which is incidentally the same as typing **regfind -any blue**) will show you all subtrees where blue occurs in the full key name-, all value/data pairs where blue occurs in the value name-, all value/data pairs where blue occurs in the data field.

- If you are looking for a certain string in the key, value, or data, you could use the appropriate control argument. To see all subtrees of the control panel, type **regfind -key panel**. This will not show value/data pairs where the word *control* is in the data or value name.

- To turn on case-sensitivity, use -case. I prefer the default case-blind searches. To hide value-data pairs, use the -hidevalues control argument.

- To see everything under the HKEY_LOCAL_USER hive, type **regfind -hive local_user**. For just the keys under the same hive, type **regfind -hive local_us -hidevalues**.

- For remote registry access on node humbug, type **regfind -node \\humbug**. Note that only two of the four predefined hives (HKEY_LOCAL_MACHINE, HKEY_USERS) are accessible over a network. The command above will display everything in those two hives. Typing **regfind -node \\humbug humbug** will reveal where the machine stores the machine name.

Contacting Me

I would welcome any constructive criticism regarding the program, its usefulness to you, and any assorted ideas you have which might improve it. However, I cannot guarantee a response, and further, I cannot guarantee that I will fix bugs and/or incorporate your ideas into a future version. You may contact me at the address and e-mail numbers above.

Legalese

Regfind is supplied as is without warranty of any kind, either expressed or implied, including, but not limited to, the implied warranties of merchantability and fitness for a particular purpose. The entire risk as to the quality and performance of the program is with you. Should the program prove defective, you assume the cost of all necessary servicing, repair, or correction.

RipBAR, Version 6.2 for Windows 95

Copyright © 1993-95 by Jonathan Carroll, All Rights Reserved

SoftDesign, 28 Parkland, Point Claire, Quebec, Canada H9R 2E8, CIS: 74017,3242, Internet: 74017.3242@compuserve.com

Type: Shareware
Registration Cost: $34.95
Crippled? No

Introducing RipBAR

RipBAR is, in some ways, the Swiss Army knife of utilities. It combines an application toolbar, command line launching, drag and drop server, memory and system information display, Post-it–style notes, hot key support, and more, in a package that remains unobtrusive on your screen. What you have now is RipBAR for Windows 95—the most recent update to RipBAR. It is the culmination of many months worth of work and updates—I hope you enjoy it and find a permanent place for it on your system.

RipBAR is available in separate files for both Windows 3.1, Windows 95, and Windows NT. While the versions are similar in most respects, differences between them will be pointed out whenever necessary. In some cases, pictures in the help file may differ slightly from what you actually see on the screen.

RipBAR is an icon toolbar that you may set up with applications of your choice. Configuration options include the ability to set up startup directory and command line parameters. Additionally, files may be dropped onto the application icons sitting on the bar—causing the application to launch and open that file automatically.

The Windows 3.1 version displays the time, memory information, and the remaining resources available to the system. The Resource Tracker (Windows 3.1 only) is included to allow you to monitor an application's use of memory and resources.

The Windows NT and Windows 95 versions display the time, along with available physical and paged RAM.

In addition, RipBAR supports attaching sound to certain types of events, hot key activation, program groups, and much more. Be sure to take some time to review the entire Help file, so that you don't miss out on features!

Installation Guide and Release Notes

There are three specific editions of RipBAR, Version 6.2: a Windows 95 edition included in this book, and Windows 3.1 and NT editions. Each edition has slightly different installation steps.

INSTALLATION FOR WINDOWS 95

Installation in this release needs to be done manually, although there isn't really much to be done.

1. Create a new directory for RipBAR anywhere on your hard disk.
2. Copy RIPBAR95.EXE, MINIRIP.EXE, and RIP_BAR.HLP to the new directory. Copy RIPKH32.DLL to your \Windows\System directory.

You are now ready to run RipBAR. The first time it runs, it will let you know that it is setting things up with the default option settings and will offer to import Program Manager (or Windows 95 shell) items.

Please consult the help file for more information on how to work with RipBAR. Some of the very latest features are not documented there yet, but we'll leave them for you to discover!

INSTALLATION FOR WINDOWS 3.1

The following files should be installed in a separate directory, perhaps something called RipBAR or the like.

- RIPBAR16.EXE   The main application file
- RIP_BAR.HLP   The online help facility

The following file should reside in \WINDOWS\SYSTEM. It is essential to the proper running of RipBAR.

- RIPKHOOK.DLL   Hot key library

Finally, RipBAR creates and maintains the following files in your \WINDOWS directory.

- RIP_BAR.INI   RipBAR settings file
- RIP_BAR.NOT   RipBAR notes file

INSTALLATION FOR WINDOWS NT 3.5

The following files should be installed in a separate directory, perhaps something called RIPBAR or the like.

- RIPBARNT.EXE   The main application file
- RIP_BAR.HLP   The online help facility

The following file should reside in \WINNT\SYSTEM32. It is essential to the proper running of RipBAR.

- RIPKH32.DLL   Hot key library

The RipBAR settings are stored in the Windows NT Registry database under SOFTWARE\RIP APPLICATIONS\RIPBAR. Use REGEDIT to view or remove these settings. Finally, RipBAR creates and maintains a file called RIP_BAR.NOT in whatever directory you specified when you first installed

RipBAR. You can change the location where the Notes file is stored from Preferences in the Directories section.

New in Version 6.11

For those not using Windows NT, version 6.11 is the first version since version 6.02, so you can find out about more new features by looking at the Version 6.1 What's New list. This version includes the following enhancements:

- (Windows 3.1 only). When you run a DOS program from the bar, RipBAR will ensure that the icon you choose for the application will be the one you see when you minimize the console window, or use the Windows Alt-Tab feature to switch between applications. Additionally, the text you type for the title of the application will be set as the title of the window in which your console application runs.

- Clock text autosizing problems have been fixed.

- Double-Click Creates Group now works for those using RipBAR in horizontal mode.

- Problems with RipBAR staying tucked away (if Tuck-Away was enabled) are fixed.

- RipBAR's means of watching for application hot keys has changed. This means that things like Move on the system menu work properly and alternate. Task Managers (like Microsoft's Natural Keyboard task manager) should now work properly.

- RipBAR's method for becoming the system shell has changed somewhat. There is now a new utility (RipShell) that takes over launching RipBAR. See RipBAR As Windows Shell for more information.

- All menus in RipBAR now behave consistently, that is, menus appear as you click down on the mouse.

- A problem in Adobe Type Manager used to create problems for RipBAR when it was run as the Windows shell. RipBAR now contains a workaround that solves this problem.

- (Windows NT only). When an item is launched in Separate Memory Space, the Clock turns green instead of red.

- (Windows NT only). The Run Tool now contains an option to launch the requested item in Separate Memory Space.

Tips, Tricks and Things

Even if you never read manuals, read this! RipBAR offers a vast array of features and customization possibilities. You should really take the time to peruse the entire Help guide, but if nothing else, read this section to get an overview of things you should know about. Also, be sure to go through the many options in RipBAR's Preferences dialog. If you have trouble working with RipBAR, see the Troubleshooting section of the Help guide.

- RipBAR Hot Key

  One of the first things you might want to do is set up your preferred activation hot key for RipBAR—this let's you use a key sequence to bring RipBAR to the front of your screen. (This assumes RipBAR is actually running.) That way, you don't need to always have RipBAR on top of other windows—a plus for people with smaller screens. See HotKey in Preferences.

- Hiding Group Icons

  RipBAR supports Groups on the bar—icons that, when double-clicked, open up to display all the items in that group. Beginning with version 5.0, RipBAR has the ability to display Groups as tabs on the bar. You can turn the tabs off, but if you don't, it is probably redundant to also have the group icons on the bar as well. To save space, enable the Hide Group Icons option (see Customizing RipBAR (Preferences)).

- More about Group Tabs

  By default RipBAR displays tabs for Groups on the bar in a column down the left side of the bar. Should you want the bar to extend horizontally across the screen, you can reposition the Tabs to be horizontal also. See the Titles & Tabs section of Preferences.

- Drive Tools

  In addition to application and document icons, you can place Drive Tool icons on the bar—icons that display information about the free space on a particular disk on your system. Create Drive Tools from the Show Tools section of Preferences.

- Bringing Stuff over from Program Manager

  If your Program Manager is already set up with items or groups of items that you frequently use, use RipBAR's Import feature (see Importing Items From Program Manager) to quickly bring these items over to RipBAR.

- Autosizing

  When you first install RipBAR, the bar appears in a predefined size. You can resize the bar to whatever shape you want. If you find your groups are getting large, you might find that you can't see all the items in them because the bar isn't sized large enough. Also, in some groups there might be a lot of empty space on the bar. You can enable the autosizing option so that RipBAR automatically resizes the bar to fit all of the items—choose from one of two different autosizing modes in the Sizing section of Preferences (see Customizing RipBAR (Preferences)).

- Icon Sizing

  Depending on the size and resolution of your screen, you may want to take advantage of RipBAR's ability to display icons in one of three sizes on the bar. See the Sizing section of Customizing RipBAR (Preferences) for information on how to do this.

- Application Hot Keys

  As you add applications to the bar, remember that you can add an application hot key sequence for them too—this goes for any icon tool on the bar. You can get one-key access to things like the Run Tool for quick access to applications not installed on the bar. (The Notes Tool is the one exception—the hot key is Ctrl-N and can't be modified.) You can also assign hot keys to group icons. (See RipBAR Item Menu Popups.) You'll be pleased to note that the application key works whether the icon is visible or not, that is, you can be in any group and quickly access an application from another group.

- And Other Great Stuff

  Remember, there is a lot that may be configured—so go ahead and set your default Notes font, whether memory and resource tools display in numerical or graphical form, and the shape and size of RipBAR's bar. If you don't have a mouse, be sure to see Keyboard Usage.

Does RipBAR look a little boring when it's minimized? Turn on the Customized Minimize setting in Preferences, General tab. You can determine where RipBAR will minimize to and what gets displayed when it's minimized.

Old users should know that you can no longer add new applications to the bar by dragging files from the File Manager and dropping them on top of an existing application on the bar. You must now drag files to an empty space on the bar—this is so that users with applications that take .EXE files as parameters can launch them in this fashion.

Finally, you can choose between the half-height, customized title bar and System Menu, or the standard-height title bar and System Menu (the RipBAR Menu). So, go ahead and fool with RipBAR—but be sure to come back and read the rest of the documentation—there's a lot here in a small package!

Registration

I want to thank you for trying RipBAR. It is designed to provide the most convenient access possible to applications without having to remember hot keys and the like. Even for those who own Norton Desktop or some similar enhanced shell, the resource and memory displays, Post-it-style notes, and command-line utility are invaluable.

RipBAR is one of a number of applications written for the sheer pleasure of programming. It was originally designed on Windows NT, where I missed my Norton Desktop!

If you try RipBAR and like it, the registration cost is U.S. $34.95. In return for your registration, I'll provide you with support; I'll keep you notified of new releases; and best of all, I'll send you RipBAR Pro for free! RipBAR Pro is the completely loaded version of RipBAR—available exclusively for registered users and available for Windows, Windows 95, and Windows NT. For more information on the features and extra software included with RipBAR Pro, see About RipBAR Pro.

Registered users of RipBAR version 6.02 or earlier can upgrade to RipBAR Pro version 6.1 for U.S. $14.95.

We've made it easy to register. You can either use CompuServe's online registration service (see instructions below) or you can mail a check (in U.S. funds) to the postal address listed on page 537.

REGISTERING ONLINE

You may register your copy of RipBAR via CompuServe. Simply type **GO SWREG** at any CompuServe prompt, and follow instructions. You may search for RipBAR there by using the word **RIPBAR** as a keyword.

REGISTERING AND FEEDBACK VIA CONVENTIONAL MAIL

If you need a copy of RipBAR mailed to you because you don't have access to CompuServe, contact us about the possibility of having RipBAR sent to you via the Internet, or include U.S. $7 to have it mailed to you via conventional mail. Use the address shown on page 537.

RipSPACE Version 3.0 for Windows 95

Copyright © 1993-95 by Jonathan Carroll, All Rights Reserved

SoftDesign, 28 Parkland, Point Claire, Quebec, Canada H9R 2E8, CIS: 74777,2357, Internet: 74777.2357@compuserve.com

Type: Shareware
Registration Cost: $19.95
Crippled? Yes, printing is not available

Introducing RipSPACE

RipSPACE is an application written for Windows, Windows NT, and Windows 95 that analyzes a drive and the space that each subdirectory on it consumes. In other words, you'll now be able to find out how much space your Windows installation is taking up, or how much drive space you'll gain if you delete the WordPounder word processor you installed but never use.

RipSPACE also allows you to define file types that are to be included in a file report. You can then tell how much total space is being taken up by certain file types, for example, Bitmaps, Dynamic Link Libraries, and executable files.

Though RipSPACE is distributed as separate versions depending on whether you're running Windows, Windows NT, or Windows 95, the versions use the same interface and incorporate the same features. The help file is thus common among the versions.

Please see the section titled "Registration and Contacting the Author" for information on how to reach me should you like to provide some suggestions or feedback.

Registration

RipSPACE For Windows 95 is not free. If you like RipSPACE and continue to use it, I ask for a $19.95 registration. If this program could be more useful if something were changed or added, I'd like to hear from you (see above for ways that you can reach me). Either way, you have a complete and fully functional version of RipSPACE—there are no time limits, no annoying Register Me screens, and so I depend on your good will.

Installing RipSPACE for Windows 95

To install RipSPACE on your hard disk, use the following instructions:

1. Create a folder on your hard disk named RipSPACE or anything you want to name it.

2. Copy the files from the CD folder RipSPACE to your new folder.

3. Drag the RIPSPACE.EXE file to your \Windows\Start Menu\Programs\Accessories folder to create a shortcut there for RipSPACE.

4. Start RipSPACE by opening the Start Menu and choosing Programs, Accessories, and RipSPACE.

Analyzing a Drive or a Path

To get started, double-click on a drive letter in the Drive window. A new window will come up and RipSPACE will begin work. Depending on the size of your drive, this may take some time.

The last drive in the Drive window is marked Path. Double-clicking on this will prompt you to type a path; this generates a report for a path (including all subdirectories) instead of a physical drive.

DURING THE ANALYSIS

While RipSPACE is working, you can resume work elsewhere in Windows— RipSPACE can continue processing in the background even as you work elsewhere. Note however, that during an analysis, RipBAR's menus and toolbar are disabled. No further work in RipSPACE is possible during the analysis. You may, however, operate the scroll bars in the windows where the report is being generated, and you may switch to other report windows. In any case, you may switch to, or launch, other applications.

You may be able to speed up the analysis if you tell RipSPACE to minimize itself during the analysis process—this way, RipSPACE doesn't have to update and draw the contents of the report window. There is a Preferences option that automates the minimizing and restoring of RipSPACE's window; see Preferences for more information.

AFTER THE ANALYSIS AND INTERPRETATION

After the analysis is finished, you should see a display that shows the total contents of the drive and the total for each directory and subdirectory on the drive. There is one line for every directory on the drive. On the left is the space that a directory is using on the disk. Next are the number of files, followed by the path (name) of the directory.

RipSPACE distinguishes between two types of directories: those that contain only files (shown with a closed folder picture, and printed in black), and those that contain files and other subdirectories (shown with an open folder picture, and printed in red).

Directories that hold other subdirectories are listed twice. They get listed once to show you the number of files alone in the directory, and again to show all files in all subdirectories. Under Windows NT, or under Windows (when using a network), it is possible that you don't have access to certain directories. When RipSPACE encounters this situation, the directory name will be accompanied by an Access Denied message. The files in this directory will not be counted or added to the Disk Analysis Report.

Customizing, Saving, and Printing Reports

This is all you need to start generating analysis reports of your own, but if you want to customize your reports a little, see the Preferences section of online Help. Or if you'd like to print or save this report, see Printing A Report, or Saving A Report, again in the online Help.

Win, What, Where, Version 3.0

Copyright © 1993-95 by Basic Systems, Inc., All Rights Reserved

Basic Systems, Inc., 2103 West Canal Drive, Kennewick, WA 99336, Voice: 509-735-2386, Fax: 509-735-1730, CIS: 70034,1341, Internet: 70034.1341@compuserve.com

Type: Shareware
Registration Cost: $37.00
Crippled? No

Introduction

Win, What, Where™ (W³) tracks all applications you run in Windows. It logs when a program was launched and details how long that program ran. Multi-user capabilities let you gather usage information over the entire network. The new Project Tracking feature adds the ability to group your activities based on a project. Keyboard and Mouse Tracking give you a valuable insight into how your users are using the mouse and keyboard. This feature is invaluable for ergonomists.

Win, What, Where won't get in the way. Load it and forget it. Your time and activities are recorded automatically.

Registration:

Single-user License: $37; Network Starter Pak (three-user license) $99; Add-on user licenses (requires Net Starter Pak) $15 each user.

W³ Installation

1. From the Explorer, open the WinWhatWhere folder on the Windows 95 Power Tools CD, and double-click on Install.exe.

2. You will be asked a few simple questions, and then the installation will begin. You will always have the choice to proceed or cancel the installation. Install first asks for a destination directory (C:\WWW by default), displays the minimum amount of free space required, and advises if the selected drive doesn't have sufficient space. Throughout the installation, Install displays when a file is copied or a Program Manager group is created. The only intervention required is when a new disk needs to be inserted. You will be prompted for the disks and asked to continue the installation. You have the option of changing the source path each time Install prompts for a new disk. If the installation has been properly completed, you will be asked whether or not a Program Manager group should be created.

ABORTING THE INSTALLATION

The installation process can be aborted at any time by choosing Exit Install, Cancel, or Abort from any of the dialogs (varies depending on the situation). After confirming with the user, Install will report that the installation was not completed and that W³ should not be used in this condition. The files that have been created will need to be manually deleted. This is done as a precaution, since most users would not like the installer to delete files from their drive.

NETWORKS

On a network, W³ should be installed in one location accessible by all. Typically this is the server or a shared directory on a peer-to-peer network. Users will need to have read, write, and delete privileges to the W³ application directory.

Network Distribution   If your network has a MAPI-compliant mail, you may distribute W³ to the workstations by using MAILWWW.EXE. Mail WWW is placed in the W³ directory during installation. This program mails NETSETUP.EXE (also supplied during installation) to each defined recipient with a message explaining what it is and how to run it. When NETSETUP is executed from the workstation, it simply starts W³ and places a reference to it in the local workstation's RUN line of their WIN.INI file. If you do not have a MAPI system or MAILWWW fails, you can send NETSETUP.EXE as an attachment using any mail system capable of sending messages with attachments. If you decide to send NETSETUP using another facility, be sure to run MAILWWW.EXE once prior to sending. Starting MAILWWW causes NETSETUP to be modified for your particular installation of W³. This is very important!

Manual Network Distribution After Installation, starting W^3 from any workstation is sufficient to set up W^3 for that workstation. Doing this will cause W^3 to place a reference to itself in the local workstation's WIN.INI run= line.

How Win, What, Where Works

Win, What, Where tracks the start and elapsed times for each application when the application gains focus. W^3 captures the application's caption along with the program name (.EXE filename). The application that has the focus is the active window. The active window is generally the window in the foreground. The application's caption is the window title bar (the top line of a window).

WWW.EXE is the program that actually does the data gathering. It is normally run all the time by either selecting Load With Windows from Setup, or by selecting it from the Program Manager. All options, online help, registration, and history functions are available from here.

The Main Window displays

- Current Application and how long it's been active
- Listing of today's activities in either Summary or Detail format
- Summary information on today's times
- Summary information on Keyboard and Mouse usage
- Project Information

WinBatch 32, Version 5.1C

Copyright © 1990-95 by Morrie Wilson, Wilson WindowWare, Inc., All Rights Reserved

2701 California Ave. SW, #212, Seattle, WA 98116, Voice: 206-938-1740, Fax: 206-935-7129, CIS: 76702,1072, Internet: wwwtech@halcyon.com

Type: Shareware
Registration Cost: $69.95
Crippled? No

Introduction

WinBatch is the Windows Batch Language that you can use to write real, honest-to-goodness Windows batch files to control every aspect of your machine's operation. There are more than 350 different functions that allow you to do *anything* with WinBatch!

Overview

WinBatch can automate Windows and Windows NT. WinBatch manipulates the Windows interface, Windows applications, and network connections. So, any operations in or from Windows, or Windows NT, can be done at the click of a mouse button with WinBatch. WinBatch includes keystroke record and playback, and much more. WinBatch works from script files, so recorded events can be combined with advanced capabilities to automate operations impossible to record. Testing values, getting system information, working with directories, logging events, and manipulating files are just a few of these capabilities.

WinBatch is often used to assemble reports, install software, automate testing, control processes, acquire data, and add efficiency to the Windows workstation. WinBatch excels in tailoring the Windows interface to fit any user. Standard operations are easy to program in WinBatch. WinBatch utilities manipulate:

- The operating system
- The Windows interface
- Any and all Windows applications
- Most MS DOS applications
- Most networks.

WinBatch has two components:

- A system control language called WIL (Windows Interface Language)
- An interpreter that reads a text file written in the WIL language and performs the required manipulations

Separate versions of WinBatch are available for Microsoft Windows and for Windows NT or Windows 95. WinBatch is continually updated to function with future versions of Microsoft Windows.

It is easy to get started in Windows programming with WinBatch. Useful system utilities are produced quickly with WinBatch. All the things you couldn't do before in Windows are suddenly just a few minutes away.

When projects demand an advanced solution, the depth in WinBatch is ready to speed development. A visual dialog editor, a window information grabber, a debugger, and the power of structured programming are part of the WinBatch software.

WinBatch has these capabilities: engineering functions, text manipulation, binary file editing completely in memory, network connectivity, and Windows system manipulation.

Many WinBatch functions accomplish with one line operations what other programming languages take pages of forms design, property setting, and coding. WinBatch is optimized for making quick work of custom system management utilities.

What WinBatch Can Do

With 269 general functions and commands, 64 networking functions, 74 physical constants, 24 operators, and 397 exception handling routines, WinBatch can

- Solve numerous system management problems

- Run Windows and DOS programs
- Send keystrokes directly to applications
- Send menu items directly to Windows applications
- Rearrange, resize, hide, and close windows
- Run programs either concurrently or sequentially
- Display information to the user in various formats
- Prompt the user for any needed input
- Present scrollable file and directory lists
- Copy, move, delete, and rename files
- Read and write files directly
- Copy text to and from the Clipboard
- Perform string and arithmetic operations
- Make branching decisions based upon numerous factors
- Call Dynamic Link Libraries
- Act as an OLE 2.0 Automation client
- And much, much more

System Requirements

WinBatch requires an IBM PC or compatible with a minimum of 4 MB of RAM
(You really should have at least 8 MB), running Microsoft Windows, version 3.1
or higher.

Late-Breaking News

WinBatch 5.1 includes two new extenders:

- WILX.DLL

    Provides an assortment of general-purpose (non-network) functions.
    See WILX.HLP for details.
- WWENV16I.DLL

    Provides the ability to modify the PATH and other environment vari-
    ables from within Windows. See WWWENV.HLP for details.

FIXES FROM PREVIOUS 5.0 VERSIONS

The file FIXES.TXT details the many bug fixes and enhancements that have
been made to the program since the initial 5.0 release.

ANNOUNCING THE WINBATCH COMPILER

Also available is our WinBatch Compiler. With the WinBatch Compiler, you can
turn your .WBT files into stand-alone .EXE files that you can distribute on a
royalty-free basis.

Have a BIG network? Want all your users to run your .WBT files? Compile the .WBT files with the WinBatch Compiler and put the .EXEs up on the server.

Making specialized WinBatch files for clients? Don't want them modifying your files? Just compile the .WBT files, and give the .EXEs to your client.

Are you the corporate guru? Get a compiler. Compile those .WBT files, and hand them out like candy.

The WinBatch Compiler, a separate product from the WinBatch Interpreter contained in these files, is available for $395.00, plus shipping, if applicable. The WinBatch Compiler includes a copy of WinBatch. In addition, if you buy a copy of WinBatch, you have 90 days to upgrade to the Compiler and just pay the difference in price.

How to Install WinBatch

There are two ways to install WinBatch, one is automatic and very easy and the other is manual and very hard. Want to guess which we recommend?

AUTOMATIC INSTALL

The automatic install uses our WSETUP.EXE program, which will expand and copy the files for you and install a WinBatch group in the Program Manager (or Programs menu in Windows 95) with various sample files.

1. Shut down all extraneous Windows applications. (You do have to be in Windows to run WSETUP.EXE.)

2. Double-click on the WSETUP.EXE program in the WinBatch folder in the *Windows 95 Power Tools* CD or from Program Manager, use File/Run (or Start/Run in Windows 95), type the drive letter of your CD drive, the **winbatch** directory, and **wsetup** (e.g., **d:\winbatch\wsetup**, if *d:* is your CD).

3. The setup program asks for a directory. Specify a directory, or accept the given default.

4. The screen comes up that asks you what you want to install, do your selections, or just click on the Add All button. Click on the Install button to continue.

MANUAL INSTALL

If you cannot use the snazzy setup program and must do a manual install . . . good luck. Basically installing our products without going through the setup program is *unsupported*, as installation of Windows products does get tricky. However, as to not leave you completely in the lurch, try the following:

1. Most files to be installed by the installation program end in an underscore (_). The files *might* be compressed.

- If you received the files on a disk, the probability is HIGH that you must expand the files with our WEXPAND (see below) program before use.

- If you received the files packaged in a .ZIP file, the probability is LOW that the files need expansion and you may simply rename the files to the correct name.

- If you try to expand a file that was not compressed, the expand program will NOT give an error message, and it will NOT correctly process the file. In general, if the output from the expand program is smaller than the file that went in, the expand program should not be used.

- By examining the files with our Browser program (possibly included with the package), or basically any tool that allows you to look at the file in hex, you can quickly determine if the file is compressed or not. If you can read *any* text in the morass of funny-looking symbols, the file is probably not compressed. If the characters seem completely random, then it is probably compressed.

2. The files (generally) must either be expanded into files with the correct names or must be renamed prior to use.

3. In general, the .DLL files should go into your WINDOWS directory, or else some directory mentioned in your DOS path statement.

USING THE WEXPAND PROGRAM

1. Copy the files WEXPAND.EXX and WEXPAN1.EXX from the installation disk to a temporary directory on your computer.

2. Rename the files, so that they have a .EXE extension. The files were named with the .EXX extension to keep most people out of trouble.

3. Copy the files you wish to expand into the temporary directory. Let's say it's WINFO16I.EX_, in which case, type at the DOS Prompt

```
wexpand winfo16i.ex_ winfo16i.exe
```

4. Make sure the output file (WINFO16I.EXE in this case) is LARGER than the input file (WINFO16I.EX_); otherwise, the file was not compressed. In that case, delete the incorrectly expanded file. and rename the original file as follows:

```
erase winfo16i.exe
ren wininfo.ex_ wininfo.exe
```

5. Repeat for each of the six million files on the floppy.

UNINSTALL INFORMATION

The snazzy setup program will create a DOS batch file, UNINSTAL.BAT, in the target directory that will uninstall the product just installed.

You may either review the batch file and perform a manual uninstall, or, if you have not installed any products *after* installing this product, go ahead and run the batch file.

If you have installed several products before deciding to uninstall this one, the uninstall will *generally* work successfully. The only problem that occurs is when this product uninstalls a file that the other products use.

In general, this will only be a problem when you install several of our products, and it will be much less of a problem if you install products from other vendors. If problems occur, usually all that is required is to reinstall the product that is complaining about the lack of a file.

A quick review of the uninstall batch file, and deleting a line or two for files you know are used by other products may be all that is required to successfully run the uninstall.

How WinBatch Is Used

Activate one WinBatch icon or file and you can run from one to thousands of operations. One WinBatch script can squeeze any number of operations into a single batch file that runs just like a Windows program. It can run from a Windows shell or any application that can run another application.

WinBatch excels in controlling other software—both Windows and MS DOS. From getting system information, through controlling software, to accessing the network, WinBatch can do it all from Windows.

Special Example

A number of example programs are included with WinBatch. After installation, they can be found in the subdirectories under \WinBatch (if you use the default directory name). You can explore these programs using the Wilson WindowWare WinEdit program that is also included on the *Windows 95 Power Tools* CD.

As a special bonus to *Windows 95 Power Tools* readers, Wilson WindowWare has included an application scheduler program, APPSCHED, in both compiled .EXE form, and in interpreted .WBT form that you can edit. Try this program out and see the kinds of things that you can do with WinBatch. Also, you can compare the interrupted and complied versions.

Registration

Unlicensed copies of Wilson WindowWare products are 100 percent fully functional. We make them this way, so that you can have a real look at them, and then decide whether they fit your needs or not. Our entire business depends on your honesty. If you use a product, we expect you to pay for it. We feel that if we treat you well, you will treat us well. Unlicensed copies of our products do have a registration reminder screen that appears whenever you start the program. This shouldn't really affect your evaluation of our software.

We're sure that once you see the incredible quality of our software, you will dig out your credit card, pick up the phone, call the nice people at our 800 number, and register the software.

If you work for a large corporation, you can purchase most of our products the same way you buy your retail software. Just send the purchase request up the line. Most all the corporate software suppliers (Egghead Corporate, Software Spectrum, Corporate Software, Programmers Shop, and many others) purchase considerable volume from us on a regular basis.

When you pay for the software you like, you are voting with your pocketbook, and you will encourage us to bring you more of the same kinds of products. Pay for what you like, and then, more of what you like will almost magically become available.

Legal Matters

Of course the usual disclaimers still apply. We are not responsible for anything at all. Nothing. Even if we are held responsible, the limit of our liability is the licensing fees you paid. The full text of our license agreement is at the end of the README2.TXT file that you will see after installing WinBatch.

Update Policy

Wilson WindowWare frequently updates its products. There are various kinds of updates, including major updates, minor updates, and bug-fix updates.

Minor and bug-fix updates for our shareware products are free—subject only to our reasonable shipping and handling charges for disks. As we are not in the disk-selling business, you may find that shareware vendors specializing in disk sales can easily sell disks cheaper than we can. On the other hand, we *always* have the most recent versions of our software. Our shipping and handling charges for update disks are as follows:

$10.00 U.S. and Canada for the first product

$5.00 U.S. and Canada for each additional product

$9.50 Surcharge for shipping outside of U.S. and Canada

If you obtain a minor or bug-fix update from CompuServe or other online service, a BBS, a shareware disk vendor or from another source, there is no charge from us (of course you will have to pay the online service fees, disk vendors fees, or at least pay your phone bill for downloading from a BBS). In addition, you may use a single disk to update any number of copies of a product.

The policy and pricing for major shareware updates vary. Depending on the nature of the upgrade, length of time since the previous major upgrade, desirability of new features added, the extent of revisions to the printed manuals (if any), work involved, and possible price changes for new users, we may or may not charge fees.

Online Support

Wilson WindowWare has online support! The home of all Wilson WindowWare is on CompuServe, in the WINAPA forum, in the Wilson WindowWare section (#15 currently). Also, the latest and greatest downloads are available from DL15 of the WINAPA forum. The Wilson WindowWare section of the WINAPA forum is checked on a daily basis, and we will respond to all questions.

Wilson WindowWare also lives on the Internet. We maintain a World Wide Web Server and an anonymous FTP site:

WWW URL http://oneworld.wa.com/wilson/pages/

FTP Site oneworld.wa.com /wwwftp/wilson/

Registered users may also call our BBS for the latest versions of our products: (206) 935-5198 USR HST/V.32bis V.42bis 14,400+ 8N1. Although we still allow 2400-baud connects as of September 1994, we are considering requiring at least a 9600-baud modem in the very near future—probably when we install our new 28,800 modems. Connects at 1200 baud and below are not currently permitted to log on.

ASSOCIATION OF SHAREWARE PROFESSIONALS OMBUDSMAN STATEMENT

Wilson WindowWare, the producer of Wilson WindowWare software, is a member of the Association of Shareware Professionals (ASP). ASP wants to make sure that the shareware principle works for you. If you are unable to resolve a shareware-related problem with an ASP member by contacting the member directly, ASP may be able to help. The ASP Ombudsman can help you resolve a dispute or problem with an ASP member but does not provide technical support for members' products. Please write to the ASP Ombudsman at 545 Grover Road, Muskegon, MI 49442, or send a CompuServe message via easy-plex to ASP Ombudsman 70007,3536.

Ordering Information

Licensing our products brings you wonderful benefits. Some of these are

- Gets rid of that pesky reminder window that comes up when you start up the software
- Entitles you to one-hour free phone support for 90 days (your dime)
- Ensures that you have the latest version of the product
- Encourages the authors of these programs to continue bringing you updated/better versions and new products
- Gets you on our mailing list so you are occasionally notified of spectacular updates and our other Windows products
- And, of course, our 90-day money back guarantee

INTERNATIONAL ORDERING INFORMATION

Our international customers may wish to order our products from their favorite dealers. The following shareware vendors will be happy to provide you with registered copies of any of our products. If your favorite vendor is not listed, ask them anyway. If you wish to order direct from Wilson WindowWare, please see the note on the order form for international customers.

AUSTRALIA and NEW ZEALAND: Budgetware (George Margelis), 9 Albermarle St., Newtown NSW 2042, Australia, Phone: 61 2 519 4233, Fax: 61 2 516 4236

DENMARK: Pro—Soft (Jens Rex), Benloese Skel 4 G, 4100 Ringsted, Denmark, Phone: 45 53 61 90 42, Fax: 45 53 61 93 91

FRANCE, SWITZERLAND, BELGIUM: WinShare (Jean Guy Ducreux), 32 rue des Frières, BP 2078, 57051 METZ Cedex 2, France, Phone: 33 87 30 85 57, Fax: 33 87 32 37 75

NETHERLANDS: BroCo Software (Eric van den Broek), Ereprisstraat 26, P.O. Box 446, 3760 AK SOEST, Netherlands, Phone: 31 0 2155 26650, Fax: 31 0 2155 14012

England, UK: Omicron (Mick Ekers), Omicron Systems Ltd., 45 Blenheim Crescent, Leigh-On-Sea, Essex SS9 3DT, England, Phone: 44 70271 0391, Fax: 44 702471113

An order form may be found in the application help file. Once you are viewing the order form, you can then select the File. Print Topic menu item to obtain a hard copy.

WinClock, Version 4.03

Copyright © 1990-95 by David Feinleib, All Rights Reserved

30 Hamilton Rd., #401, Arlington, MA 02174, Voice: 617-648-1457, Fax: 617-648-1561, CIS: 76516,20, Internet: 76516.20@compuserve.com

Type: Shareware
Registration Cost: $16.00
Crippled? No

Introduction

WinClock is a digital clock for Microsoft Windows that has the following features:

- Display of time and date in many different formats
- 25 alarms (which can be set for daily or only a specified date)
- Date display in any of six languages
- Run Program Timer (ability to run programs at specified times)
- Optional hourly beep
- Allows user to set date and time easily
- Optionally stays in front of other applications
- Remembers its position on the screen
- Two stopwatches and two countdown timers
- Colon separating hours and minutes may be set to blink
- Context sensitive help

- Direct screen saver compatibility (autodetects the active screen saver)
- Cascade and Tile compatibility
- Alarms can use the speaker or wave files

Running/Installing/Upgrading WinClock

Please note that the following directions assume you are using a mouse. If you are not using a mouse, please refer to your Windows documentation for equivalent keystrokes.

UPGRADING WINCLOCK

If you are upgrading from a previous version of WinClock, you should copy this version of WinClock to the same directory in which the old version is. Since configuration files of previous versions of WinClock are not compatible with this version, the first time you run WinClock you will see a message which tells you that your configuration file was created by a different version of WinClock and that your preference settings have been reset to the default. You may want to change the settings back to your preferred settings.

1. Copy WINCLOCK.EXE, WCHOOK.DLL, WINCLOCK.HLP, WSAVER.DLL, DATEFUNC.DLL, DAFLIB.DLL, and DAFLIB.HLP (all but the .TXT or .DOC files on the CD) to your Windows directory or another directory of your choice. Note that all of the files must be copied to the same directory.

2. Do one of the following (Note: Option D is highly recommended over A, B, and C.):

    A. Open the Run dialog box from the Start menu and type winclock (including the path if it's not in your \Windows directory) in the Open text box, and click on OK. If you use this option, you will have to do this every time you want to run WinClock.

    B. Using the Explorer, drag the WINCLOCK.EXE file to your \Windows\Start Menu\Programs\Accessories directory to create a shortcut there. This allows you to start WinClock by opening your Start menu and choosing Programs, Accessories, WinClock.

    C. Using the Explorer, drag the WINCLOCK.EXE file to your \Windows\Start Menu\Programs\Startup directory to create a shortcut there. This will automatically start WinClock each time you start Windows.

    D. Do both B and C, which will automatically run WinClock and allow you to run WinClock easily if you close it.

WinClock Options

To bring up a list of options, click once on the WinClock system box or right-click on the clock itself.

HELP...

This will bring up help about WinClock and explain how to use context sensitive help. It will also display an index of all help available for WinClock.

SET TIME/DATE...

This allows you to easily enter the time and date. When the window pops up, enter the correct time and date as follows:

- Click on AM or PM to set the time in 12-hour format, or click on 24-hr and enter the time in 24-hour format. WinClock will automatically convert 24-hour format to 12-hour format if you click PM after 24-hr was selected. WinClock will also convert from PM to 24-hour format.

- The current time and date will be shown in the edit boxes when the window originally appears. To update the time and date displayed in the edit boxes to the current time and date, click on the Time or Date button depending on which you want to update.

- When you have made all your choices, click on OK (or press Enter). If you want to leave the old time and date, click on Cancel.

- You should select Auto Advance Date only if you are using a version of DOS that does not advance the date correctly at midnight.

ALARM...

This allows you to configure one of WinClock's 25 alarms. To set an alarm, click on the spinner arrows, or type a number in the box. When you have made your choices, click on OK. If you want to leave the alarms the way they were, click on Cancel. You can set the following options:

- **Enabled** If you want the alarm to be on, select Enabled (so that there is a check mark in the box). If you do not want the alarm to be on, but only want to set it for use at a later time, click on Enabled until there is no check mark in the box.

- **Time** Enter the time for the alarm to go off in the edit box. If you select AM or PM, enter the time in 12-hour format. If you select 24-hr, enter the time in 24-hour format.

- **Date** Select One Date to have the alarm go off on a single date, and then type the date in the edit box. Select Enhanced Alarms, and enter the start date in the edit box, and select the Day and the Week Interval. The start date is the date from which the alarms start.

  - **Week Interval:** Periodic causes alarms to go off on dates such as every Thursday, every other Wednesday, and so on. Select the periods that you want, and choose the dates with which they should be combined. Of Every Month causes alarms to go off on dates such as the first Thursday of every month, the second Wednesday of every month, and so on.

  - **Day** is combined with options you select in the Periodic and Of Every Month sections.

- **Alarm Sound** To have the alarm beep when it goes off, select Beep. Select high or low pitch. Select the duration of the beep. Short is about eight seconds; Long is about 30 seconds. Both beeps may be stopped by clicking on OK when the box alerting you to the alarm appears.

Examples

- **Periodic** To have an alarm go off every other Tuesday, you would select Every Other in the Periodic section and Tuesday in the Day section.

  If you entered 5-15-90 in the Start Date edit box and selected Every and Tuesday, since 5-15-90 is a Tuesday, the alarm would go off on 5-15-90, 5-22-90, 5-29-90, 6-04-90, and so on.

- **Of Every Month** To have an alarm go off on the second Wednesday of every month, you would select Second in the Of Every Month section and Wednesday in the Day section.

  If you entered 5-15-90 in the Start Date edit box and selected Third in the Of Every Month Section and Monday in the Day section, the alarm would go off on 6-17-90, since that is the third Monday of the month.

- **Note/Run Program** If you want to, enter a note to display when the alarm goes off. Select Run Program to run a program at the time for which you have set the alarm. Type the full pathname of the program you want to run. Select Max if you want the program to be maximized when it is run, Min to have it minimized, or Normal to have it shown in its normal size.

  If you type the name of a program that does not exist on your hard disk, a warning message will appear when you click on OK. You may then choose to edit the name of the program to run or to leave it unedited.

TIMERS . . .

WinClock has two stopwatches and two countdown timers. By selecting different options you can have WinClock display some or all of the timers as well as the time and date. In order to use a countdown timer, you must type a number from which to countdown in the Countdown from edit box. This number must be in the HH:MM (hours:minutes) form. If it is not in this form, any number found (that is before non-numeric numbers, excluding the colon) will be used as the minutes.

- Select Display Timer individually for each timer if you want to display it (or to not display it). Select Display Date and/or Display Time if you want to display the date and/or time while one or more of the timers are running. The display of the date and time are not dependent on the timer that is currently selected.

- Display seconds is selected by default. If you do not want to display the seconds, click on it so that there is no check mark in the box. You can choose to display the seconds individually for each timer. The seconds will only be displayed if Display Timer has been selected.

- The settings that you make in the Timer dialog box only affect the WinClock display while one or more timers are running. The settings will be saved while WinClock is running but will be reset to the default when WinClock is restarted.

- When you have selected to display a timer, the first stopwatch appears as S1 00:00:00 and the second as S2 00:00:00. The first countdown timer appears as C1 00:00:00 and the second as C2 00:00:00.

- The current count (time elapsed) of the selected timer will appear in the Current Count box while the Timers dialog box is displayed.

- When a timer is stopped, its current count will be displayed in the Current Count box until you switch to another timer. The stopped timer will then reset itself to zero.

- The Start/Stop button will reflect whether the currently selected timer is running. If the current timer is running, the button will display Stop so that you may stop the timer. If the current timer is not running, the button will display Start so that you may start it.

- Each countdown timer may be set to beep or not to beep. Select beep so that there is a check mark in the box if you want the countdown timer to beep, when it finishes. Select the pitch and the duration of the beep. The short beep lasts about eight seconds; the long beep lasts about thirty seconds. Both beeps may be stopped by clicking on OK when the window alerting you that the timer has finished appears.

HOURLY ALERT

Select this option if you want WinClock to sound a short beep and flash on the hour. A check mark will appear next to Hourly beep if it is selected. To turn off the hourly beep, click on Hourly beep. The check mark will disappear.

- Special note for 386 Enhanced mode:

  If a DOS box is active and hourly beep is enabled, WinClock will, by default, return you to Windows and beep. You must then return to the DOS box. If you do not want to be returned to Windows when an hourly beep occurs, deselect the For Hourly Beep check box in the Preferences dialog box.

- New! WinClock now includes support for wave files when sounding the hourly alert.

PREFERENCES . . .

Preferences allows you to change how the date and time are displayed. Select the options you want and click on OK.

Time Format

- **Separator** You may change the character that separates the parts of the time by typing a different character in the Separator edit box. Although it is possible to type more than one character, only the first character you type will be used.

- **Blinking Colon** If you would like the colon that separates the hours and minutes of the time to blink on the second when the seconds are not displayed, select Blink Colon so that there is a check mark in the box.

Screen Saver Compatibility WinClock is compatible with most available screen savers. (Note that WinClock itself is not a screen saver.)

- **Auto** Setting this option will cause WinClock to be hidden when a screen saver saves the screen. This option is compatible with most screen savers; it is recommended that you try this option first if you would like screen saver compatibility.

- **Delay** Setting this option will cause WinClock to be hidden (not displayed on the screen) after the amount of time that you specify in the edit box, when the mouse and keyboard have not been activated. You must set the delay in the form MM:SS (minutes:seconds). If it is not in this form, any number found (that is before non-numeric numbers, excluding the colon) will be used as the seconds.

  It is recommended that you use this option if the Auto option (see above) does not work correctly with your screen saver.

- **None** This turns off screen saver compatibility, which means that WinClock will not be hidden if you have a screen saver.

Display

- **System Box** If you want WinClock to display a system box, select System Box. Hiding the system box reduces the area that WinClock takes up on the screen. See "Displaying/ Hiding the System Box" for more information.

- **Anti-Cascade** You should select Anti-Cascade if you do not want WinClock to be cascaded when you cascade the open windows.

- **Stay In Front** If you want WinClock to appear over other applications, select Bring To Front.

Remember Screen Location

- **One Location** WinClock remembers one screen location by default. This means that when you move WinClock it remembers its position on the screen so that the next time you run WinClock, it will go to the position where it was when it was closed.

- **Return To Lower Right Corner On Startup** If you want to move WinClock to a certain location for only the current time that WinClock is running but then revert to the default screen position, select this option. The next time you run WinClock, it will revert to its default location.

- **Lock Location** This will lock WinClock's location on the screen, so that you do not move it accidentally.

DOS boxes, Alarms, and Hourly Beep The following information only applies when Windows is running in 386 Enhanced mode (or when running Windows 95).

- If a DOS box is active and an alarm is enabled and set to go off, WinClock will, by default, return you to Windows and display the message, beep, and/or run a specified program. You must then return to the DOS box. If you do not want to be returned to Windows when an alarm occurs, deselect the For Alarms check box in the Preferences dialog box.

■ If a DOS box is active and Hourly Beep is enabled, WinClock will, by default, return you to Windows and beep. You must then return to the DOS box. If you do not want to be returned to Windows when an hourly beep occurs, deselect the For Hourly Beep check box in the Preferences dialog box.

ABOUT . . .

Select About... to display information about WinClock.

GETTING HELP

WinClock help may be accessed in three ways:

1. Select Help from the WinClock system menu. This will display an index of all help available for WinClock. It will also explain how to use WinClock's context sensitive help.

2. You may access context sensitive help by clicking on one of the WinClock system menu items, holding down the mouse button, and pressing F1.

3. You may access context sensitive help from most of WinClock's dialog boxes by clicking on the Help button if one is displayed.

DISPLAYING/HIDING THE SYSTEM BOX

You may display/hide the system box in the following ways:

1. Open the Preferences dialog box and select System Box, so that there is a check mark in the box. This will display the system box. To hide the system box from the Preferences dialog box, select System Box so that there is no check mark in the box.

2. Double-click on the WinClock caption (the caption is the area in which the time and date are displayed). If the system box is hidden, it will appear; if it is displayed, it will be hidden.

Avoiding Cascading or Tiling WinClock

CASCADING

If you want to cascade the open windows, it is useful to have the Anti-Cascade option selected (in the Preferences dialog box), so that WinClock does not get cascaded. To select Anti-Cascade, select Preferences... from WinClock's system menu. In the Preferences dialog box, select Anti-Cascade so that there is a check mark in the box.

TILING

If you want to tile the open windows, you should click once with the right mouse button on the WinClock client area (the area where the time and date are displayed). This will cause WinClock to be hidden for about seven seconds, during which time you may tile the open windows.

Moving WinClock

To move WinClock, click on WinClock and, while holding the mouse button down, drag WinClock.

Closing WinClock

To close WinClock, do one of the following:

1. Click on the Close button.
2. Double-click on the WinClock system box.
3. Click once on the WinClock system box, and then click on Close.

How to Contact Me

Comments and suggestions (and reports of problems) would be greatly appreciated. You can contact me at the address and numbers listed above.

How to Pay for and Register WinClock

WinClock is shareware. You may make copies of this program and give them to others as long as the documentation is provided with the program, both unaltered.

Please refer to the About Box for information on registering the program. From the About Box you can print out a registration form. Alternatively, you can print out the file REGISTER.DOC.

Please include your name, address, and current version number, as well as the name of the program that you are registering. (The version number may be found in the About Box.) See above for the address.

Thanks!

My thanks to those BIX users who, by downloading WinClock, inspired me to write this version. Credit is due to John Ogren for suggesting the addition of international date formats. Thanks to Guy J. Gallo for his suggestions (most of which were implemented) on the alarms. Thanks to Steve Garcia, Ernest Karhu, Mark Lutton, and William Saito for their suggestions, which greatly influenced this version of WinClock, and especially to Peter Kaminski for help with the icons and for his numerous comments, suggestions, and support from the beginning and all through the testing stages, which resulted in many of the changes in this version. My thanks to Peter W. Meek for his encouragement, sense of humor, testing, and suggestions for the new alarm options. Thanks to Steve Moshier for help with the algorithms used in the new alarm options. Thanks to

Bruce Wheelock for his extensive testing. Thanks to Arlan Fuller for his sense of humor and help with various parts of WinClock.

Error Messages and Solutions

Following are the error messages that you may encounter and their solutions:

W1000   No system timers available

WinClock must use one of the Windows Timers to update the time. You should try closing another application, closing WinClock, and running WinClock again.

W1010   Unable to save WinClock configuration file

WinClock was unable to save the information you entered in the Preferences box.

W1020   Invalid time entered

You entered an invalid time. Enter a valid time.

W1021   Invalid date entered

You entered an invalid date. Enter a valid date.

Disclaimer

WinClock is supplied as is. The author disclaims all warranties expressed or implied, including, without limitation, the warranties of merchantability and of fitness for any purpose. The author assumes no liability for damages, direct or consequential, which may result from the use of WinClock.

WinEdit 32, Version 3.1a

Copyright © 1990-95 by Steve Schauer, Wilson WindowWare, Inc., All Rights Reserved

2701 California Ave. SW, #212, Seattle, WA 98116, Voice: 206-938-1740, Fax: 206-935-7129, CIS: 76702,1072, Internet: wwwtech@halcyon.com

Type: Shareware
Registration Cost: $99.95
Crippled? No

Welcome to WinEdit!

WinEdit is a fast and powerful ASCII/ANSI text editor. It is available in three different levels of functionality for Windows 3.1 and at the Professional level for Windows NT and Windows 95:

- **WinEdit Lite** provides super fast editing of any size text file. It has a handy button bar for common operations. $29.95

- **WinEdit Standard** adds the ability to compile programs directly from WinEdit and view the output to fix errors. $59.95

- **WinEdit Pro** adds a complete macro scripting language to allow professional users to write their own WinEdit menus. $89.95

- **WinEdit 32 Pro**, a native 32-bit application for Windows 95 on Intel and Windows NT on Intel, DEC Alpha, and MIPS platforms, includes a FREE copy of WinEdit Pro for Windows 3.1. $129.95 ($99.95 special for *Windows 95 Power Tools* readers)

All three levels are contained within the same executable program, in both the evaluation and registered versions. By selecting Lite, Standard, or Professional from the File ... Settings menu, you enable all features at that level. When you register WinEdit, you will receive a registration number which will allow you to use WinEdit at the registration level you have selected, although you will still be able to use features belonging to a higher level on an evaluation basis. For example, if you register WinEdit at the Standard level, you would select Standard from the Settings menu, so that only Standard-level functions will appear on the WinEdit menus, and everything would operate normally. If you decided to select Professional from the Settings menu, additional functions would become available, but if you used one of those Pro-level functions, you would first receive a message informing you that the feature you had selected is not included in the Standard level, and that you should upgrade to the higher level if you plan to continue using that function. You can upgrade to a higher level at any time; the cost is the difference in registration price between the level for which you are currently registered and the level to which you are upgrading, plus $5.00.

New Features

The following summarizes the new features in version 3.1. The online help has not yet been updated.

- New command line options:

/M:\<text\>	Run the named macro before doing anything else
/P:\<text\>	Print the named file, then quit
/W:\<text\>	Set the project to the named file
/L:\<0|1|2\>	Set the feature level to LITE, STANDARD, or PRO
/#:\<number\>	Go to line number
filename(s):	Load the named file(s); can include wildcards

- Print a selection
- File difference utility
- Read and write Unix and Macintosh text files
- Turn status bar and horizontal scroll bar on/off
- Improved memory management for large files
- Shift + click to extend selection
- Brace matching

- Multiple views of same file
- Accessed via the Window, New menu item
- Toggle case of selection (this is on the Utility menu)
- Save all files option
- Syntax coloring of source code files

  Fully configurable syntax coloring highlights keywords, quotes, and comments in C, C++, WIL, Basic, dBase, and DOS and NT batch files. Most any language can easily be added.

- Easy to use key reassignments

  You can now reassign command hot keys from an interactive dialog in WinEdit. Menus are automatically updated to reflect the new hot keys. You can also define more than one hot key for a command, such as Ctrl + y and keypad - to delete a line.

- Improved compiler support

  Choosing a compiler from the Project dialog's drop-down combo box automatically configures WinEdit's error parsing logic for that compiler. WinEdit supports Microsoft, Zortech, Watcom, Borland C++, Turbo Pascal, Borland TASM, and Clipper and is user-configurable for any other compiler.

- Improved macro recording

  In the Pro version, the Macro Recorder now records all commands as WIL scripts. When recording is concluded, the recorded script is loaded into a document window for easy editing. WinEdit is preconfigured to automatically add the newly recorded script to the Macro Menu, or you can fine tune your macro with any of over 400 WIL and WinEdit macro functions.

- Other new features:

  Backup file creation, location, and name are configurable

  Changed (unsaved) files indicated on screen

  Improved support for read-only files

  Improved network support

  Captured compiler output file location configurable

  Regular expressions in search can be disabled

We have also corrected dozens of minor bugs that have been reported in earlier versions of WinEdit.

System Requirements

WinEdit requires an IBM PC or compatible with a minimum of 4 megabytes of RAM, a rodent, 1.5 MB of hard drive space and Microsoft Windows, version 3.1 or higher.

How to Install WinEdit

Use our WSETUP.EXE program, which will copy the files for you and install a WinEdit group in the Program Manager.

The following steps use our WSETUP.EXE program (manual install instructions below):

1. Close down all extraneous Windows applications.

2. From the Explorer, open your CD-ROM drive and the WinEdit directory, and then double-click on the WSETUP.EXE program

3. When the setup program asks for a directory, specify a directory, or accept the given default (C:\WINEDIT).

The setup procedure creates a WinEdit group in the Program Manager of Windows 3.1 or WinEdit 32 entry in the Programs menu of Windows 95.

Using WinEdit

As an ASCII text editor, WinEdit allows you to open numerous text files at once, print half-sized two-up pages side by side in landscape orientation, print headers and footer text (see document name, date and time, page number in README2.TXT), merge files together, and word wrap your text to the size of the window (see word wrap in README2.TXT). In particular, WinEdit lets you edit Wilson WindowWare's WinBatch .WBT files.

STARTING WINEDIT

You can start WinEdit from either the Programs menu (Program Manager group if you are using Windows 3.1) or the Run command line. You can use one or more of the following switches if you start WinEdit from the Run command line:

/M:<text>	Run the named macro before doing anything else
/P: <text>	Print the named file, then quit
/W: <text>	Set the project to the named file
/L:<0|1|2>	Set the feature level to LITE,STANDARD, or PRO
/#:<number>	Go to line number
filename(s)	Load the named file(s); can include wildcards

Technical Support

Wilson WindowWare has online support for WinEdit! The home of all Wilson WindowWare is on CompuServe, in the WINAPA forum, in the Wilson WindowWare section (#15 currently). Also the latest and greatest downloads are available from DL15 of the WINAPA forum. The Wilson WindowWare section of the WINAPA forum is checked on a daily basis, and we will respond to all questions.

Wilson WindowWare also lives on the Internet. We maintain a World Wide Web Server and an anonymous FTP site.

- WWW URL http://oneworld.wa.com/wilson/pages/
- FTP Site oneworld.wa.com /wwwftp/wilson/

Registered users may also call our BBS for the latest versions of our products: (206) 935-5198 USR HST/V.32bis V.42bis 14,400+ 8N1. Although we still allow 2400-baud connects as of September 1994, we are considering requiring at least a 9600-baud modem in the very near future—probably when we install our new 28,800 modems.

Connects at 1200 baud and below are not currently permitted to log on.

ASSOCIATION OF SHAREWARE PROFESSIONALS OMBUDSMAN STATEMENT

Wilson WindowWare, the producer of Wilson WindowWare software, is a member of the Association of Shareware Professionals (ASP). ASP wants to make sure that the shareware principle works for you. If you are unable to resolve a shareware-related problem with an ASP member by contacting the member directly, ASP may be able to help. The ASP Ombudsman can help you resolve a dispute or problem with an ASP member but does not provide technical support for members' products. Please write to the ASP Ombudsman at 545 Grover Road, Muskegon, MI 49442, or send a CompuServe message via easyplex to ASP Ombudsman 70007,3536.

REGISTRATION REMINDERS

Unlicensed copies of Wilson WindowWare products are 100 percent fully functional. We make them this way so that you can have a real look at them, and then decide whether they fit your needs or not. Our entire business depends on your honesty. If you use a product, we expect you to pay for it. We feel that if we treat you well, you will treat us well. Unlicensed copies of our products do have a registration reminder screen that appears whenever you start the program. This shouldn't really affect your evaluation of our software.

We're sure that once you see the incredible quality of our software, you will dig out your credit card, pick up the phone, call the nice people at our 800 number, and register the software.

If you work for a large corporation, you can purchase most of our products the same way you buy your retail software. Just send the purchase request up the line. Most all the corporate software suppliers (Egghead Corporate, Software Spectrum, Corporate Software, Programmers Shop, and many others) purchase considerable volume from us on a regular basis.

When you pay for the software you like, you are voting with your pocketbook, and you will encourage us to bring you more of the same kinds of products. Pay for what you like, and then, more of what you like will almost magically become available.

LEGAL MATTERS

Of course the usual disclaimers still apply. We are not responsible for anything at all. Nothing. Even if we are held responsible, the limit of our liability is the licensing fees you paid. The full text of our license agreement is at the end of the README2.TXT file that you will see after installing WinEdit.

INTERNATIONAL ORDERING INFORMATION

Our international customers may wish to order our products from their favorite dealers. The shareware vendors shown above, under WinBatch, will be happy to provide you with registered copies of any of our products. If your favorite vendor is not listed, ask them anyway. If you wish to order direct from Wilson WindowWare, please see the note on the order form for international customers.

An order form may be found in the application help file. Once you are viewing the order form, you can then select the File, Print Topic menu item to obtain a hard copy.

WinImage, Version 2.0a

Copyright © 1993-95 by Gilles Vollant, All Rights Reserved

13, rue François Mansart, 91540 Mennecy, France, Voice: 33-1-6499-7523, CIS: 100144,2636, Internet: 100144.2636@compuserve.com

Type: Shareware
Registration Cost: $20.00
Crippled? No

Introduction

WinImage is a disk image management utility. A disk image is a file which contains all the floppy data (files, FATs, boot sectors, directory, and so on). By making an image of a floppy disk and writing it on another, you get an exact copy (as with the DOS DiskCopy command). You can also read a floppy and write the image on the hard disk. The day after, without using a floppy, you can extract a file from the image. The week after, you can write the image on two new floppies, for instance, without needing the original, and create two exact copies of it.

You can also create disk images with WinImage. If you want to put five files (taking 1.3 Mb) on a $3^1/2$-inch HD unformatted floppy, you create an empty 1.44-Mb image, inject the five files into it from the hard disk (this is very fast), and in one operation, you format the floppy and write the image on it.

WinImage can format and use very large-capacity nonstandard disks ($3^1/2$-inch HD 1.72 Mb and $5^1/4$-inch HD 1.44 Mb). To use them, you must load, before Windows, the TSR FdRead, a shareware from Christoph H. Hochstätter, which you can get with the FdFormat utility. I think that having a look at it is a must. You don't need this TSR if you use only standard formats with WinImage.

You can load an image by reading a floppy, or reading an image file, or creating an empty image. You can extract the files of an image onto any device (hard disk, network unit or a floppy). You can also add files to the image. The image can be copied onto a floppy (which must have the same format) or saved in a file. An image file contains all the floppy sectors. If it's not full, you can truncate it.

WinImage can read the images of a lot of disk copy utilities: Wimage (in FdFormat utility) from C.H. Hochstätter, CopyVit from Sébastien Chatard, DrDos 6 and OS/2 2.x disk image utilities, DCF (Disk Copy Fast) from Chang Ping Lee, DF (Disk Image File Utility) from Mark Vitt, Super-DiskCopy from Super Software, SabDu from S.A. Berman, Disk-RW from K. Hartnegg, DiskDupe from Micro System Design, internal disk Microsoft and Lotus image utilities and the MFMT sample Windows NT application that comes with Windows NT SDK.

Installing and Running WinImage

Use the following instructions to install and start WinImage:

1. Create a directory on your hard disk where you want to store the WinImage files.

2. Insert the *Windows Power Tools CD* in your CD-ROM drive.

3. Open the Explorer, open the CD-ROM and the WinImage directory, and copy all the WinImage files to the new directory you just created.

4. Again from the Explorer, open the directory that contains the WinImage files.

5. Double-click on the WINIMANT.EXE (for Windows 95 and Windows NT) or WINIMAGE.EXE (for Windows 3.x) file. The WinImage window will be opened.

Using WinImage

WinImage shows in its main window the files and directories present in the image. You can go into a directory by double-clicking on it. To return to the parent directory, double-click on the first entry (..).

WinImage runs with the image in memory. When there is no image, some icons and menu entries are grayed.

You can create a directory, and delete or add files in the image with the icons or the Image menu. You can use drag and drop from the Windows File manager to WinImage to inject data into an image, or from WinImage to another application to extract from it.

You can extract files in three ways: by extracting in the Image menu (or its icon), by launching a file by double-clicking on it, and by dragging it to another application.

WinImage allows you to drag the image file from WinImage to another application: You put the mouse pointer in the status bar or in the toolbar background.

You press the left mouse button and keep it pressed, put the mouse pointer onto another application (drag-and-drop client), and release the mouse button. This original function allows you to add the image in a .ZIP or .ARJ file with Nico Mak's WinZip utility, or attach the image to an e-mail created with Microsoft™ MS-Mail, or Lotus™ Notes or ccMail.

MULTILINGUAL

WinImage is completely multilingual. All of its titles, menus, and dialog boxes can display one of four languages: English, French, German, or Spanish. To change to a different language, open the Option menu and choose Preference. At the bottom of the dialog box you will see the Language drop-down list box.

Registration

WinImage is shareware. You can copy, distribute, and try it, and it is available on BBSs and CD-ROMs. If you use it, you must register it. You will receive a license, the latest release, and the next two releases, DOS Extract and Inject tools.

If you register WinImage, I will send you a registering number. You can choose Registering in the Option menu, and enter this code. After, you can, in the Preference (Option menu), ask to hide the first screen.

The licence price is still 100 French francs or U.S. $20.00.

Site Licence : You can contact WindowShare B.P. 2075 / 57051 Metz cedex 2 France, Fax : (33) 87 32 37 75.

You can also use the CompuServe shareware registration service (GO SWREG). The WinImage registration number is 1233.

CREDIT CARD ORDERING:

To order by MasterCard, Visa, American Express, or Discover, call the Public (software) Library at 1-800-2424-PsL or 1-713-524-6394 or send your order by Fax to 1-713-524-6398 (USA phone number) or by CompuServe e-mail to 71355,470. You can also mail credit card orders to PsL at P.O. Box 35705, Houston, TX 77235-5705. The WinImage number on the PsL registration service is 10976.

Use these numbers only for credit card orders. For site licenses or WinImage information, contact me at CompuServe 100144,2636.

This software is produced by a member of the Association of Shareware Professionals (ASP). ASP wants to make sure that the shareware principle works for you. If you are unable to resolve a shareware-related problem with an ASP member by contacting the member directly, ASP may be able to help. The ASP Ombudsman can help you resolve a dispute or problem with an ASP member but does not provide technical support for members' products. Please write to the ASP Ombudsman at 545 Grover Road, Muskegon, MI 49442-9427 USA, Fax 616-788-2765 or send a CompuServe message via CompuServe Mail to ASP Ombudsman 70007,3536.

WinPrint, Version 1.53

Kindel Systems, 4522 194th Way NE, Redmond, WA 98053, Voice: 206-868-9591, Fax: 206-868-9591, CIS: 71551,1455

Type: Shareware
Registration Cost: $25.00
Crippled? No

What is WinPrint?

WinPrint is a Windows shareware application that allows you to easily print ASCII text files from within Windows. It allows you to specify headers and footers with page numbers, fonts, margins, landscape versus portrait mode, and multiple pages up printing. See the WINPRINT.HLP file for a more complete description. WinPrint was designed from the very beginning to be a tool for printing plain text files. Version 1.3 and Version 1.4 do not support the printing of graphics, word processing documents, or spreadsheets. The goal from has been to keep WinPrint as small, efficient, and simple as possible.

If you want to print graphics, use PaintBrush. It works just fine. If you want to print your word processing documents, use your word processor; and if you want to print spreadsheets, use your spreadsheet package. They both print nicely. But, if you want to print plain ASCII text files, use WinPrint!

The WINPRINT.HLP file contains all the documentation you will need. It also contains information on how to register WinPrint.

Overview

WinPrint is a Windows 3.1 utility for printing ASCII text files easily and efficiently in Windows. It allows you to easily select the files to print, choose formatting options, and print to any printer supported by the Windows environment. WinPrint provides the following major features:

- Spooling
- Multiple Columns (or *n* pages up)
- Headers and Footers
- Margin Control
- Font Control
- Tab and Form-Feed Support
- Multiple Saved Configuration
- Command-Line Invocation
- Online Help
- Overview of Fonts
- Overview of Printer Drive

Getting Started

A few quick notes on what is needed to run WinPrint:

- Under Windows 3.0 and 3.0a you need the following Dynamic Link Libraries (DLLs) in your path:

  TDUTIL.DLL - WinPrint Support DLL

  COMMDLG.DLL - Microsoft Common Dialogs DLL (you only need this file if you are running on Windows 3.0)
- You will also need the main WINPRINT.EXE executable file and the help file (WINPRINT.HLP).

I recommend that you create a WINAPPS directory off of your root directory in which you place all of your small Windows applications such as WinPrint. Copy the above files into this directory and make sure that the directory is in your path statement. You can now run WinPrint just as you would any Windows application.

STARTING WINPRINT

WinPrint can be started in any of several ways: from the Programs menu or a Program Manager icon, from the Explorer or the File Manager, from the Run command line, or by another application.

Once WinPrint begins executing, several things happen. First, WinPrint checks to see if you are a registered user or not. If you are not, two windows will appear, one after the other. The first window gives you information regarding WinPrint, such as the version number and registration instructions. Click on the OK button to continue.

The second window is the Registration window. This window is provided to give you an opportunity to enter your registration number if you are registered user. It also provides a button that will allow you to print a registration form that you can send in along with your registration payment. See "Registering Information" for more information on registering WinPrint.

After WinPrint checks the registration information, it checks to see if you have used WinPrint before. If you have, the configuration WinPrint used the last time it was run is loaded. Otherwise, WinPrint sets all options to their Factory Defaults.

WinPrint can also be started with command-line options. See "Command Line Options" in the online Help for more information.

Drag and Drop

WinPrint fully supports the Windows drag and drop interface from the Explorer or File Manager. This means that you can select files in the Explorer or File Manager, drag them to the WinPrint window (or icon), and drop them by releasing the mouse button. If WinPrint is minimized when you drop files on it, WinPrint will begin printing those files immediately. If WinPrint is not minimized, the files will be added to the Selected Files list-box.

WinPrint has been optimized to work closely with the Windows 95 Explorer or the Windows 3.1 File Manager. It fully supports drag and drop operations. In fact, the recommended way for using WinPrint is to set it up with your favorite options, minimize it, and drop files on it at will! You can even have several copies of WinPrint minimized, each with a separate configuration loaded (see "WinPrint Command Line Interface" in online Help for information on how to start WinPrint with a specific configuration).

Notes to Users of Previous Versions of WinPrint 1.x

WinPrint 1.32 was designed as a Windows 2.x application. It worked correctly under Windows 3.0 because it adhered to Microsoft's programming guidelines for Windows.

WinPrint 1.4 has been designed as a Windows 3.x application. It takes advantage of features found only in Windows 3.0 and above. As such, it will not run on Windows 2.x, and will not operate correctly with printer drivers that have not been updated to the Windows 3.0 specification.

Versions of Windows previous to Windows 3.0 provided no way for applications to store printer settings locally. For example, any change made to printer settings from within an application (such as landscape mode) were made systemwide. The Windows 3.0 printer driver specification allows for applications to change printer settings locally. WinPrint 1.4 takes advantage of this and adheres to the policy that no application, except Control Panel, can make systemwide printer-setting changes.

Technical Support

Technical support for WinPrint is provided to registered users only via electronic mail.

If you are a registered user, you can contact the author for support on CompuServe. Send CompuServe mail to 71551,1455.

Registration Information

WinPrint is not and has never been public domain software, nor is it free software. WinPrint is a commercial application distributed as shareware.

Nonlicensed users are granted a limited license (registration) to use WinPrint on a 21-day trial basis for the purpose of determining whether WinPrint is suitable for their needs. The use of WinPrint, except for the initial 21-day trial, requires registration. The use of unlicensed (unregistered) copies of WinPrint by any person, business, corporation, government agency, or any other entity is strictly prohibited.

A single-user license permits a user to use WinPrint only on a single computer. Licensed users may use the program on different computers, but they may not use the program on more than one computer at the same time.

There are two methods for registering WinPrint. Method one involves using the Shareware Registration System on CompuServe, and method two is by mail.

METHOD ONE: ONLINE VIA COMPUSERVE'S SHAREWARE REGISTRATION FORUM

Method one is by far the easiest and fastest way to register shareware. The process is as follows:

1. Connect to CompuServe and go to the SWREG forum (type **go swreg** at any ! prompt).

2. Once you have entered the SWREG forum, choose menu item 2 Register Shareware.

3. Choose 1 Registration ID, and enter **546** (which is WinPrint's registration ID).

4. The system will ask you to confirm.

5. If you confirm, a CompuServe mail message will be sent to me (Charles E. Kindel, Jr. at 71551,1455) indicating that you have registered. At the same time, your CompuServe account will be charged the $25.00 registration fee.

6. I will respond to the mail that CompuServe sends with your registration number. Note that this will be the only notification you will receive with your registration number. You will not receive one by mail.

METHOD TWO: BY MAIL

To register send a check for $25.00 (U.S. Dollars) drawn on a U.S. bank made out to Charles E. Kindel, Jr. at the address above.

Important points to remember when registering:

■   The only forms of payment currently accepted are by check for United States dollars drawn on a United States bank (the cost of cashing a check drawn on an international bank is typically $25-$30, which is prohibitively expensive) or cash. If you do send a check drawn on a U.S. bank, but from an international branch, make sure the check clearly states where a U.S. branch of that bank is located.

■   You can print a registration form from the Registration dialog box or by selecting the registration form topic in WinHelp and using the File, Print... menu item. Using these forms makes processing orders much easier.

■   Make sure your name and address are clearly legible on the registration form and that you include a first and last name.

The single-user registration fee for WinPrint 1.5 is $25 (U.S. dollars). Payment of this fee entitles you to the following:

■   Registration number that will disable the startup shareware reminder windows contained within the program

■   Technical support via electronic mail

Diskettes containing the latest version of WinPrint are available for $15. The most recent version of WinPrint can always be found in the WinShare forum on CompuServe.

Site licenses for WinPrint are available. Contact the author for more information.

No one may modify or patch the WinPrint executable and documentation files in any way, including but not limited to decompiling, disassembling, or otherwise reverse engineering the program.

A limited license is granted to copy and distribute WinPrint only for the trial use of others, subject to the above limitations, and also to the following:

1. WinPrint must be copied in unmodified form, complete with the file containing this license information.

2. The WinPrint product consists of the following files:
    WINPRINT.EXE, TDUTIL.DLL, README.TXT, and WINPRINT.HLP. All of these files must be copied in unmodified form.

3. WinPrint may not be distributed in conjunction with any other product without a specific license to do so from Charles E. Kindel, Jr.

4. No fee, charge, or other compensation may be requested or accepted, except as authorized below:
    a. Operators of electronic bulletin board systems (sysops) may make WinPrint available for downloading only as long as the above conditions are met. An overall or time-dependent charge for the use of the bulletin board system is permitted as long as there is not a specific charge for the download of WinPrint.
    b. Vendors may charge a disk duplication and handling fee, which may not exceed eight dollars.

Zip Manager, Version 5.2

Copyright © 1990-1995 by Software Excellence By Design Inc., All Rights Reserved

14801 North 12th Street, Phoenix, AZ 85022, Voice: 602-375-9928, Fax: 602-375-9928, BBS: 602-375-9945, CIS: 72200,2276

Type: Shareware
Registration Cost: $49.95
Crippled? Yes, won't capture directly to printer without registration

Welcome to Zip Manager

This version represents a whole new class of applications for Microsoft Windows NT 3.5 or higher and Windows 95—file compression without the dependence on any DOS third-party applications for ZIP and UNZIP operations!

New Features in Version 5.2

- **ZMZIP and ZMUNZIP**—Our Native Windows File Compression Utilities, ZMZIP and ZMUNZIP are the first 100 percent PKZIP 2.04-compatible compression utilities designed especially for Windows from the ground up! ZMZIP and ZMUNZIP are built-in to Zip Manager, which means you have two less files to worry about and more free disk space. These utilities take full advantage of the Windows operating system to give you the best performance in speed and compression.

- **Right Mouse Button Popup Menus**—Now you can press the right mouse button to activate a popup menu for the directory and archive windows.

- **Window and Archive Memory on Shutdown**—When you close Zip Manager, it will remember all of the child windows that were open and their positions. It even remembers the .ZIP or .ARJ file that was in each window! So the next time you start the program, it will reopen the windows and the .ZIP or .ARJ files with which you were last working. You can specify in the Setup dialog box whether you want to use the Window Memory feature or not. As with the rest of Zip Manager, we have designed it to give you the utmost in flexibility and options.

- **Drag and Drop Server Capability**—Zip Manager is now a drag-and-drop server. What this means is that you can drag files FROM Zip Manager and drop them ON any application that will accept a file drop. One of the best ways to use this ability is to drag a file from a .ZIP and drop it on a Program Manager group window. Zip Manager will ask you which directory should receive the file and then extract it and add it to the group window! Note, the Windows File Manager is NOT a drag-and-drop client. Any attempt to drag files from Zip Manager to the Windows File Manager will display the No Drop cursor. Most other file manager replacements are, however, drag-and-drop clients.

- **Open and Work with Self-Extracting .EXE Archives**—Zip Manager now recognizes self-extracting .EXE files as if they were normal archive files. You can add, move, and delete files in them just as you can with other archive files.

- **Directory Creation on Extraction**—Zip Manager will create a new directory on Zip Extraction. All you have to do is enter the new directory name as the target directory.

- **User-Selectable Compression Program Option**—Zip Manager will allow you to specify whether you want to use our ZMZIP and ZMUN-ZIP, or to use PKZIP and PKUNZIP. We realize that there may be times when you might have to use PKZIP, and we wanted to make sure that you could easily do so.

- **True Multitasking with ZMZIP and ZMUNZIP**—Now you can finally take advantage of multitasking with our ZMZIP and ZMUN-ZIP. Zip Manager loads a *unique Arrow and Hourglass cursor* to let you know that it is processing files in the background, while you continue to work with another program. When it is finished, you will see your cursor change back to the normal Windows arrow cursor, letting you know that your file compression or extraction is complete.

- **Other Enhancements**—Users of version 5.2 will notice some subtle performance and cosmetic enhancements over version 4.0. We have reduced overall program size requirements by more than 117 KB.

General Features and Information

Zip Manager is a Microsoft Windows-based utility that allows you to create, extract, and manage compressed files. Zip Manager uses the popular .ZIP and .ARJ file compression formats, and supports .ARC, .LZH and .LHA file formats for conversion to .ZIP or .ARJ format.

Zip Manager allows the Windows File Manager to directly open .ZIP and .ARJ files by just double-clicking on them! This functionality is available to any Windows program that uses the file associations in the [extensions] section of WIN.INI.

Zip Manager still allows you to use the DOS-based PKZIP 1.10 or 2.04G versions of ZIP.

Zip Manager takes full advantage of the Windows multitasking environment with its ZMZIP and ZMUNZIP file compression utilities. You will be able to compress files in the background while continuing to work with your graphics, spreadsheet, word processing, or communications program in the foreground.

FEATURES OVERVIEW

- ZMZIP and ZMUNZIP are built into Zip Manager.
- Right Mouse Button Menus are available for the directory and archive windows.
- Zip Manager allows the File Manager to directly open .ZIP and .ARJ files.
- Manager Mode works and functions almost exactly like the Windows File Manager.
- Express Mode retains the simplicity of version 3.01 but drastically improves the ease of use.
- A File Manager Extension allows placement of Zip Manager on the File Manager Menu.
- User can create New Groups and Add items to any existing group.
- Full drag-and-drop server and client capability is available between most Windows-based file managers and Zip Manager.
- Most virus scanning programs, both DOS- and Windows-based, are supported.
- A macro feature allows you to save and run special command-line switch options from the Menu.
- An application launch feature allows you to set up and run other programs from the menu.

- Complete e-mail capability is available in the network and Windows NT 3.5 or higher versions.
- Zip Manager is fully compatible with MS DOS Version 6.0, Stacker, DoubleSpace, and similar programs.

Express and Manager Modes Zip Manager allows you to choose between the power of drag-and-drop file management and the quick and easy interface of the dialog-driven Express Mode. If you need to quickly extract all of the files in an archive, or compress all of the files in a directory, Express Mode lets you do this with a minimum of effort, while Manager Mode gives you complete control of every file on your hard disk or floppy disk.

Smart Switches Zip Manager knows by looking at the current switch settings whether you want to extract files as a background task. If you have the Overwrite All switch checked, then Zip Manager knows that you won't need to interact with the archive program and will run it in the background. On the other hand, if the Don't Overwrite Existing Files switch is checked, then it will run the task in a window so you can respond to file overwrite warnings. The same is true for the multiple volume switches; if one is checked, then Zip Manager knows that you will need to respond to the prompt for the next diskette.

The Last Mode Used Zip Manager remembers the last mode you were in when the program was closed. When you restart, it will come up in either Manager Mode or Express Mode.

Automatic Directory Creation When you are creating a new archive, or extracting an existing archive, you can specify a target directory that doesn't exist. When Zip Manager runs the archive command, it will create the new directory for you. When copying or moving files, if you specify a new directory, Zip Manager will create it for you and copy or move the files into it. Zip Manager will create a new directory on Zip Extraction. All you have to do is enter the new directory name as the target directory.

Viewing Archive File Contents To view the contents of any .ARJ or .ZIP file, double-click on the *A* or *Z* red bitmap in the directory window. Zip Manager will then open the archive into the archive window. You can then view any file in the archive as long as it has a corresponding association. You can associate a new file at any time right from the File Menu.

Full Use of File Associations Zip Manager uses file extension associations exactly like the Windows File Manager, in both the directory window and the archive window. This enables you to double-click on any file in an archive or directory and launch it with the associated application. You can run and view files in an archive without having to extract them first. Zip Manager will extract all the files needed to run any executable file in an archive.

Norton Desktop for Windows and PC Tools for Windows If you plan to use Norton Desktop for Windows, you must have version 2.2 or later. Previous versions have a bug which prevents them from sending a correct Drop Files Message. Version 1.0 or greater of PC Tools is fully compatible.

Installation and Setup

Zip Manager, Version 5.2 requires no special setup since it is a stand-alone file compression program. Use the following steps to install Zip Manager:

1. Place the *Windows 95 Power Tools* CD-ROM in your drive, and with the Explorer, open the ZipManager directory.
2. Double-click on the ZMSETUP.EXE file, and follow the instructions on the screen.

There are a few features that either were impractical to implement in a Windows environment (self-extracting .EXE files), were proprietary (password encryption), or were of marginal benefit (multiple volumes). It was important for Zip Manager to support these features as it always has. If you need to use any of the features listed below, please refer to Appendix G in the MANUAL.WRI file before proceeding.

Feature	Support Program Needed
Creating Self-Extracting Archives	ARJ or ZIP2EXE
Extracting Password-Protected Zip Files	ARJ or PKUNZIP
Multiple Floppy Disk Volumes	ARJ or PKZIP or PKUNZIP

If you don't plan on using any of these features, then continue with the rest of this section now.

SETTING UP THE ZIP MANAGER PROGRAM DEFAULTS

It's time to configure Zip Manager. Start the program by double-clicking on the program icon in its Program Manager group window.

1. After starting Zip Manager, open the Options menu.
2. Select Setup.

Defining the Default Directories   Zip Manager allows you to define the following:

- **The Default Extraction Directory**   Enter the drive and directory where you want Zip Manager to extract the files stored in the archive(s)with which you are working. You may want to set this to a RAM drive to speed up the extraction process.

- **Default Archive Directory**   Enter the drive and directory where you want Zip Manager to create new archives. You may want to create a directory dedicated to archive storage. This option will allow Zip Manager to create all of its new archives in this directory, saving you the time and trouble of copying them to this directory later.

- **Default Work Directory**   Enter the drive and directory where you want Zip Manager to start. You may want to set this to your default archive directory, so that all of your archives will be readily available in the directory list box when the program starts. The program will start in this directory each time it is run.

VERY IMPORTANT! Make sure that you do NOT set conflicting work directories! To check this, highlight the Zip Manager icon, and press ALT + ENTER. Look at the Work Directory edit field; MAKE SURE that this field is EMPTY. Failure to do so may cause Zip Manager to start in the wrong directory.

- **ARC Archive Extraction Program** If you want to convert files from ARC format to ZIP format, enter the program name to use for ARC extraction: C:\ZIPMGR5\ARC-E.COM for example. You can leave this set to NONE if you don't need this option.

- **LZH Archive Extraction Program** If you want to convert files from LZH format to ZIP format, enter the program name to use for LZH extraction: C:\ZIPMGR5\LHARC.EXE for example. You can leave this set to NONE if you don't need this option.

- **Save Open Archive Windows at Program Shutdown** You can specify in the Setup dialog box whether you want to use the Window Memory feature or not. As with the rest of Zip Manager, we have designed it to give you the utmost in flexibility and options. When you close Zip Manager, it will remember all of the child windows that were open and their position. It even remembers the .ZIP or ARJ files that were in each window! The next time you start the program, it will re-open the windows and the .ZIP or .ARJ files you were last working with if this option is checked.

If you enable this option, it will take Zip Manager longer to start, since it must open the child windows and check for the existence of the archive file you had open last.

- **Virus Detection Programs** This is an optional program and is not required. Enter the name of the program executable: for example, SCAN.EXE. Also check the appropriate radio button to tell the program if your virus detection program is Windows or DOS Based.

In order for your virus detection program to work with Zip Manager, it MUST be able to accept command-line arguments. The tests outlined below will help you to determine if your virus detection program does accept command-line arguments. You MUST enter the full path and drive in addition to the filename. For example, if you use SCAN, you would enter C:\ZIPMGR5\SCAN.EXE. Now check the appropriate radio button for DOS- or Windows-based virus detection program.

See the instructions in MANUAL.WRI for testing DOS and Windows virus programs for compatibility.

Using Zip Manager's Drag and Drop Effectively

With Zip Manager you can drag .ZIP files, .ARJ files, and normal files from the Windows File Manager, or any replacement file manager, and drop them on the Zip Manager window *all at the same time!!* Zip Manager will open a new archive window for each .ZIP or .ARJ file that was dropped. Zip Manager will then prompt you for a new filename for the compressed file that will contain the remaining files and then compress them. This feature gives you unparalleled power to work with compressed and normal files at the same time. You are able to view existing archives and create new archives with just ONE drag-and-drop operation.

It makes no difference if Zip Manager is running as a visible window or is minimized. You can still drag files and drop them on the Zip Manager icon. If Zip Manager is minimized, you can't, however, drop files from the file manager into a specific archive. To do this, Zip Manager must be running in a visible window, so you can drop the files on the exact target archive.

By *default* Zip Manager will *copy* files, instead of moving them like the Windows File Manager. This affords you added protection from accidentally moving files you intended to copy. The drag-and-drop options listed in this section apply to Manager Mode Only. Express mode does NOT accept drag-and-drop commands.

The MANUAL.WRI file lists many different ways you can manipulate files and archives using Zip Manager's built in drag-and-drop support. In addition you can drag files from any Windows-based file manager and drop them on the Zip Manager window or icon.

DRAG-AND-DROP SERVER CAPABILITY

Zip Manager is a drag-and-drop server (sender) as well as a client (recipient). You can drag files to any application that is programmed to accept them.

You can easily add a program contained in a .ZIP or .ARJ file to a program manager group by simply dragging it from the .ZIP file and dropping it on the correct group window. Zip Manager will ask you where you would like to store the program file. It will then extract the file to that directory and add the icon to the group window! You can do the same thing with any file or program that is visible in the Zip Manager directory window also. *Remember* that you can always have Zip Manager create a new directory for you by entering its name as the target directory.

Express and Manager Mode Reference

Express Mode is an improved and more flexible version of the dialog box interface that was so popular with users of Zip Manager, version 3.01. The MANUAL.WRI file covers each operation available from the Express and Manager Mode menus.

Important Tips and Tricks

Listed below are some of the really slick features of Zip Manager you can use to get the most out of your program.

- **Right Mouse Button Popup Menus** Now you can press the right mouse to button activate a popup menu for the directory and archive windows.

- **Open and Work with Self-Extracting .EXE Archives** Zip Manager recognizes self-extracting .EXE files as if they were a normal archive file. You can add, move, and delete files in them just as you would with any other archive file.

- **Drag a Directory or Directories to Compress Their Contents.** When you want to compress the contents of an entire directory, don't go into the directory itself. Instead move up one level, so the directory you want to compress is displayed as a yellow folder. Then follow the steps outlined below:

  1. Highlight the subdirectory folder in the directory window, and drag it over the archive window. When the left mouse button is released, the New Archive dialog box will be displayed.
  2. Enter the name of the new archive to create; you don't need to enter the extension (i.e.. .ZIP or .ARJ).
  3. Click on the ZIP or ARJ radio button.
  4. Enter the directory where you want the archive to be created. If you want to leave it in the same directory, just enter that directory as the target.
  5. Select the OK button.

The example above works equally well when you need to compress several directories that are beneath each other. In this case, select the Recurse Directories button in the Switches dialog, which is directly accessible from the New Archive dialog box.

- **Drag-and-Drop Server.** If you are using a file manager that is a drag-and-drop client (NOTE: the Windows File Manager is NOT a client), you can drag files from Zip Manager and drop them directly on your file manager directory window, or any subdirectory displayed in its directory tree window. This drag-and-drop power includes dragging files directly from .ZIP and .ARJ files.

Trouble Shooting Help

Appendix A in the MANUAL.WRI file lists the most common problems and questions you are likely to have.

Registration Information

Thank you for taking the time to find out how to register your copy of Zip Manager. To do so, please use the file called REGISTER.FRM that is supplied with the program, or you can print a registration from the Zip Manager help file. When you register you will receive the following:

- The most current version of the program
- Free telephone support

- You will be notified of any future upgrades by mail, and will be eligible for discounts on our other programs
- No more of those pesky nagware screens
- You will be able to tell your computing associates that you like the program and that you registered it. In order for new and higher quality shareware to become available, end-user support is vital!

The registration fee for the Single-User Version of Zip Manager is $49.95 + $3.00 shipping in U.S. Funds. We welcome Visa, Master Card, American Express, checks, money orders, and foreign checks drawn on a U.S. BANK. You can phone in your order using your Visa or Master Card Monday–Friday, 8:00 AM–4:00 PM MST. The TOLL FREE order phone number is 1-800-468-1438.

Questions, correspondence, bug reports, and suggestions should be directed to the address and number shown above.

Obtaining Technical Support

Please read the MANUAL.WRI document and check Appendix A FIRST. We are a small company and don't have the manpower to handle a large volume of support calls. Telephone support is available to registered users ONLY.

Shareware Evaluation Users can get help by calling our BBS at 602-375-0531 (9600 baud) or 602-375-9945 (14,400 baud). Leave a message to the sysop regarding your problem. You will have an answer in a few days. You can fax us with your problem at 602-375-9928. We will return your answer by fax only, so be sure to include your fax number with your question. You can leave a message in our CompuServe mailbox. Our CIS ID number is 72200,576.

Registered Users can use the options outlined above, and they can also get direct phone help. Before you call for help YOU MUST HAVE YOUR REGISTRATION NUMBER READY. It will be the first thing we will ask you for when you call. The technical support phone number is 602-375-9928 and is available from 9:00 AM until 3:00 PM, Monday–Friday.

Arizona is on Mountain Standard Time *all year long.* **When daylight savings is in effect, we are the same time as the West Coast. The rest of the year we are on the same time as Denver, one hour later.**

RRKeyFonts/PC

Copyright © 1993-95 by Elizabeth A. Swoope, All Rights Reserved

RoadRunner Computing, P.O. Box 21635, Baton Rouge, LA 70894, Voice: 504-928-0780, Fax: 504-928-0802, CIS: 76436,2426, Internet: 76436.2426@compuserve.com

Type: Shareware
Registration Cost: $49.00
Crippled? No

Introduction

The shareware version of RRKeyFonts/PC includes a complete set of RRKeyCaps plus a sampler font (RRKeySampler) containing characters from additional fonts that you receive when you register your copy of RRKeyFonts.

RRKeyCaps and the companion typefaces are designed specifically for use in computer documentation and tutorial material. I have written hundreds of pages of those materials, and I created the keycap fonts and the companion fonts after being frustrated with the keycap fonts that currently are available to Windows users.

My typefaces are plain 2-D characters that print well and are readable at standard body text sizes (10–12 points). They are readable at smaller sizes. Because they lack embellishments like 3-D or drop shadows or reverse, they are not as attractive at larger (display) sizes as typefaces from other vendors, and I don't recommend that you use them as display faces.

While the current crop of 3-D, drop shadow, and reverse keycap typefaces are quite attractive and interesting, they don't work well at standard text sizes. The reverse keycaps may not reproduce well when copied, and the lettering in the 3-D and shadow typefaces is hard to read at body text sizes because some of the character height is occupied by the 3-D or drop shadow effect.

Many of the typefaces are cumbersome to use, too. Either you have to compose each key by typing each character (as well as opening and closing characters) and accessing graphics elements using the numeric keypad; or many keys are mapped to characters above 127, which forces you to use the numeric keypad; or the keys aren't mapped logically; or some of the keys are missing.

All characters in all the keycap and winsym typefaces can be accessed in one or two keystrokes (one of which is [Shift]). Most of the keys are mapped mnemonically, so you probably won't need a character map to remember which keycap is mapped to which key or what [Alt]-number pad combination to use.

There are alternate versions of some keys, so you can use the version that you prefer.

These typefaces have been designed so that you can access them efficiently while developing documentation without wasted keystrokes or mouse use. With a simple macro or two, you can use these typefaces with minimal effect on your typing speed. The documentation you will receive when you register the fonts includes many hints, tips, and instructions on using the fonts.

All keycap sets are available in both PC and Mac format, and you will get both TrueType and PostScript Type 1 versions of all the fonts in the set.

There is a section of comments at the end of this file. If you have an HP LaserJet 4 printer and your printouts show the missing-character box instead of the actual keycap character, or if you are a Word for Windows 6 user and you like to use Insert Symbol, important information for you is included in that section.

Explanations of which characters are mapped to which keys on the keyboard follow.

RRKEYCAPS MAP:

A	Alt
B	Backspace
C	Ctrl
D	Delete
E	Esc
F	text-only Tab
I	Insert
J	text-only Enter
M	Space
N	Fn (notebook users)
O	OMNI (Northgate keyboard users)
P	Pause
R	Enter (Return)
S	Shift
T	Tab
V	text-only Shift
X	Del
Y	text-only Bksp
Z	Ins
b	down arrow (*b* for bottom)
t	up arrow (*t* for top)
l	left arrow
r	right arrow
h	home
e	end
d	PageDown
u	PageUp
c	CapsLock
n	NumLock
o	ScrollLock (this is the only one that's *really* weird)
p	PrtScr
k	Break
s	Spacebar
q	SysRq
f	graphics-only Tab
j	graphics-only Enter
v	graphics-only Shift
x	PgDn
z	PgUp
1	F1

2	F2
3	F3
4	F4
5	F5
6	F6
7	F7
8	F8
9	F9
0	F10
!	F11 (shift of 1, or shift of F1)
@	F12
#	F13 (Northgate keyboard users)
$	F14 "
%	F15 "
&	blank single-width key frame (like arrow keys)
*	blank one-and-a-half-width key frame (like F keys)
(	blank double-width key frame (like Tab)
)	blank triple-width key frame (like Enter, Shift)
=	two-button mouse w/no buttons pressed
[	two-button mouse w/left button pressed
]	two-button mouse w/right button pressed
;	two-button drag mouse
.	two-button mouse double-click
/	two-button mouse, different version of double-click
\	two-button mouse w/no buttons pressed
`	two-button mouse w/both buttons pressed
{	three-button mouse w/left button pressed
}	three-button mouse w/right button pressed
:	three-button drag mouse
<	three-button mouse w/ middle button pressed
>	three-button mouse double-click
?	three-button mouse, different version of double-click
|	three-button mouse w/no buttons pressed
~	three-button mouse w/all buttons pressed
- -	(this is not a keycap hyphen, but a regular hyphen for use between keycaps, as in [Ctrl]-[Alt]-[Del], so that you don't have to switch out of the keycap font just to get a hyphen, then switch back in)
+ +	(regular plus for those who prefer to use a plus, rather than a hyphen, between keys)
,	regular comma for use between keys in a sequence

RRKEYSAMPLER MAP:

The RRKeySampler typeface is a mixture of RRKeyLetters and RRWinSymbols designed to be used with this typeface for combinations like [Ctrl]-[Y]. You get a complete set of RRKeyLetters and RRWinSymbols when you register.

From RRWinSymbols:

N	No button
O	side-by-side unshaded spin button
R	right scroll bar arrow (unshaded)
S	slider (unshaded)
T	up scroll bar arrow (unshaded, *t* for top)
V	pull-down list (unshaded)
X	un-*x*-ed X box
Y	Yes button
Z	maximize (unshaded)
a	radio button on
b	down scroll bar arrow (shaded, *b* for bottom)
c	system menu control box
d	document menu control box
e	restore (shaded)
f	frame (clear selected object with handles)
g	magnifying glass, plain
h	hourglass
i	I-beam cursor
j	magnifying glass w/+
l	left scroll bar arrow (shaded)
m	minimize (shaded)
n	magnifying glass w/-
p	hand "pause" cursor
r	right scroll bar arrow (shaded)
s	slider (shaded)
t	up scroll bar arrow (shaded, *t* for top)
v	pull-down list (shaded)
x	X-box *x*-ed
z	maximize (shaded)
1	open arrowhead
2	solid arrowhead
3	another solid arrowhead
4	horizontal two-headed arrow
5	four-headed arrow
0	side-by-side spin button, shaded
-	spin button

    =   another spin button

    +   crosshair cursor

All other characters are a key outline with that character in the middle (keyletters).

Association of Shareware Professionals Ombudsman Statement

This program is produced by a member of the Association of Shareware Professionals (ASP). ASP wants to make sure that the shareware principle works for you. If you are unable to resolve a shareware-related problem with an ASP member by contacting the member directly, ASP may be able to help. The ASP Ombudsman can help you resolve a dispute or problem with an ASP member but does not provide technical support for members' products. Please write to the ASP Ombudsman at 545 Grover Road, Muskegon, MI USA 49442-9427, Fax 616-788-2765, or send a CompuServe message via CompuServe Mail to ASP Ombudsman 70007,3536.

Registration:

When you register, you'll receive:

- A diskette containing:

    a. the keycap font RRKeyCaps
    b. the complete matching RRKeyLetters font
    c. the complete RRWinSymbols font

- Extensive documentation (Hey, these keycaps are for documentation writers, so I'd be remiss if I didn't provide GREAT documentation! I've had more than one person say that the docs alone were worth the registration fee. The PC documentation is approximately 60 pages, and it includes installation instructions; guidelines and tips for using the typefaces; detailed instructions and tutorials for using the fonts in Ami Pro 2 and 3, WinWord 6 and 2, WPWin 6 and 5.*x*, and WPDOS 6 and 5.1; extensive reference pages that show characters in each font, keyboard layouts, etc.

Registration is $49 per font set, with quantity discounts available for two or more copies (mix and match okay). Shipping is $5 per order.

To register, print the RRKEYORD.FRM form, complete it, and mail the form and payment to the address on page 582.

Note

The shading on the shaded windows symbol characters in RRKeySampler is much less robust than on the same characters in RRWinSymbols that ships with the registered version of the keycaps. This has to do with the light strokes in the keyletters that are in the sampler. The characters in RRKeySampler were copied directly from the shipping version of RRWinSymbols, but the font generation program renders them differently in the two fonts.

Important Information for Word for Windows 6.0 Users!

Many of you like to use Insert Symbol to choose characters to insert into your documents. Although RRKeyFonts can be used this way, there are two reasons why it is not recommended.

First, the TrueType version of the keycap fonts does not show in the character map windows. Instead, you simply see the regular letters, digits, etc. On some computers, when you click on a character in the character map, you do see the actual character that will be inserted, but on others, you still see just the character that you type rather than the character that will be inserted.

If you use the PostScript Type 1 version of the fonts, you can see the characters in the character map windows. Unfortunately, the characters are so small that they are unidentifiable in most cases. This has been tested at both 640×480 and 1024×768 resolutions.

The documentation that you receive when you register the fonts gives complete step-by-step instructions for setting up styles and assigning shortcut keys to those styles. Because most of the characters are mapped mnemonically, most people become comfortable in no time with using the fonts (even without the Insert Symbol).

Hop, Version 1.02

Copyright © 1990-95 by David Feinleib, All Rights Reserved

30 Hamilton Rd., #401, Arlington, MA 02174, Voice: 617-648-1457, Fax: 617-648-1561, CIS: 76516,20, Internet: 76516.20@compuserve.com

Type: Shareware
Registration Cost: $7.50
Crippled? No

Installing and Running Hop

To install Hop, copy its files from the *Windows 95 Power Tools* CD to a directory on your hard disk. (You can also run Hop directly from the CD.) To run Hop, use the Explorer and double-click on HOP.EXE, and follow the directions. If you wish, you can drag the HOP.EXE program to the \Windows\Start Menu\Programs\Accessories\ Games directory to place a shortcut there. You will then be able to start Hop from the Programs menu.

Registration

If you like Hop, please register to receive information to disable the shareware reminder message by sending $7.50 to the address above.

Appendix A

Preparing for and Installing Windows 95

The actual installation of Windows 95 is very easy. What you need to do to prepare for the installation and what decisions you need to make as you progress through it make the installation process a little more difficult. This appendix, though, will quickly guide you through that process. First, however, look at the requirements for Windows 95.

Requirements for Windows 95

Windows 95 will run on a large number of the computers in use today, although it runs better on some systems than it does others. Table A–1 shows the minimum and recommended system requirements.

Although Table A–1 recommends a 486-66 processor, any 486 processor is better than a 386; you don't have to have a 486-66. After the processor, the next most important component of your system is memory; the more you have the better Windows 95 will operate. With a 386 processor and 4 MB of memory, you will see about the same performance between Windows 3.1 and Windows 95. With a 486 and 8 MB, Windows 95 will perform better than Windows 3.1, and as you add memory, Windows 95 will widen its distance from Windows 3.1.

Certain components of Windows 95, such as the Microsoft Network and the Microsoft Exchange, require 8 MB. If you get Microsoft Plus! for Windows 95, you will need a 486, 8 MB, and a 256-color display.

589

Table A–1.

Requirements for Windows 95

Component	Minimum	Recommended
Operating system	MS- or PC-DOS 3.2 (partitions over 32 MB)	MS- or PC-DOS 5.0 and Windows 3.1 or above
Processor	Intel 386DX, 20 MHz or higher	Intel 486DX, 66 MHz or higher
Memory	4 MB	8 MB or more
Free conventional memory	417 KB	500 KB
Disk space (Win 95)	40 MB	80 MB or more
Video display and adapter	VGA (640 × 480, 16 colors)	SVGA (800 × 600, 256 colors) or higher
CD-ROM	None	Double speed (2x) or above
Audio board	None	16-bit
Modem	None	14.4 Kbps fax/modem
Mouse	None	Any pointing device

When you are figuring disk space, remember that most of the space used by your current version of Windows will be replaced by Windows 95, so you can subtract that from the disk space needed. (You can use RipSPACE on the *Windows 95 Power Tools* CD to determine how much space is taken up by your current Windows files.)

If you use the Windows upgrade version of Windows 95, you must have Windows 3.1 or above, any version of Windows for Workgroups, or OS/2 version 2 and above installed, or have a distribution disk from one of those products.

You can also get a DOS upgrade version of Windows 95 and install it over any version of Windows, over any version of DOS, 3.2 and above, or Novell DR DOS, over any version of OS/2, or in a dual boot configuration with Windows NT. If you install over OS/2, the system must have MS- or PC-DOS also installed, and you must run the installation from DOS.

What Do You Currently Have?

Your first step in the installation of Windows 95 is to find out what are the hardware and software components of your current system. You may already know all this, so it isn't a problem. If you don't know, and you have DOS 5.0 or above, there is a DOS program called Msd.exe that you can run at any DOS prompt (just type msd) or from the Windows Program Manager's Run command line. If you don't have Msd.exe, you will have to dig to find the answers. The first place to start is with the dealer that sold you the system.

Preparing for Installation

The installation of a new operating system is a milestone that you can use to do some major housecleaning or that you can simply ignore. At the very least you should back up your data files and some Windows settings files. Since you will be needing a lot of disk space, it would also be a good time to clean off files and older programs you are no longer using.

If you have been using Windows for some time and have been adding and removing a lot of programs, you probably have a number of files in your Windows directories that are not being used. Since these files do not belong to Windows, Windows 95 will not replace them when it is installed. To recover this space, you can do one of two things: you can buy an uninstall program that looks for stray files that are no longer in use, or you can wipe out all of your Windows directories and install Windows 95 from DOS. The latter is a very drastic step because it requires that you *reinstall* all of your Windows applications, and you will lose your program groups and other settings that you have made in Windows. While this is a drastic step and should not be underestimated, it is the best way to really clean up your hard disk. You basically erase Windows and all your Windows applications and reinstall them. You'll be amazed at how much disk space you'll recover.

If you delete your Windows directories, you'll have to reinstall your Windows applications, and you'll lose you Windows settings.

Backing Up Files

No matter what else you do, use the excuse of installing Windows 95 to back up all of your data files (such as the files *created by* your word processor, spreadsheet, database, and other programs). Since you supposedly have all of your program files on the floppy disks or CDs from which you loaded them, you do not have to back up these files, but you do need to back up the product of these programs.

In addition to your data files, if you don't choose to wipe out your Windows directories, you should back up your Windows settings files. These include the following, which are all in your Windows directory:

.INI initialization files

.DAT Registry data files

.PWL password files

In any case you should back up your Config.sys and Autoexec.bat files in your root (\) directory as well as all the files they reference. To see the files in Config.sys and Autoexec.bat, use NotePad in Windows, or Edit in DOS, to view the files. If you are connected to a network, you need to back up your network configuration files and any logon scripts that you use.

Creating a Bootable Floppy

Another precaution prior to installation is to create a bootable floppy, if you don't already have one. If something prevents you from booting off of your hard disk, you can still boot your computer from a floppy and see what is going on on your hard drive. To make a bootable floppy, use the following instructions:

1. Put either a new floppy disk or one that can be erased in your A drive.

2. At a DOS prompt or at the Windows Program Manager's Run command line, type **format a:/s**. This will format the disk and place on it the files necessary to boot your computer.

3. Either from the DOS prompt using **copy** *filename* **a:** or from the Windows File Manger, copy some of your more important DOS files to this disk, so they are also available to you. Such files in DOS 6.2 include the following:

Ansi.sys, Chkdsk.exe, Defrag.exe, Deltree.exe, Diskcomp.com, Diskcopy.com, Doskey.com, Edit.com, Emm386.exe, Expand.exe, Fdisk.exe, Format.com, Himem.sys, Memmaker.exe, Mode.com, Mscdex.exe (if you have a CD-ROM), Msd.exe, Qbasic.exe (so you can use Edit), Scandisk.exe, Share.exe, Smartdrv.exe, Sys.com, and Xcopy.exe.

You may have your own set of files. If you are using disk compression, like Stacker, DoubleSpace, or DriveSpace, be sure to include those files. Also, you may want to include your favorite utility programs. In any case, create a bootable floppy disk with the DOS and/or utility files that you use most often.

Optimizing Your Hard Disk

After you have removed all of the files that you want to remove from your hard disk, it is worthwhile to defragment or optimize the disk. To do this, you need to first run ScanDisk and then run Defrag. ScanDisk looks both for problems with your current files and for problems with your hard drive itself. It fixes many of the problems and alerts you to the remaining situation. Defrag defragments the files on your hard disk. As you store files on the disk, they are broken into segments, and the segments may be scattered around the drive. Defrag gathers all of those segments into one contiguous area of the disk, which greatly speeds up disk reading.

ScanDisk is available on your Windows 95 CD or the first floppy disk without having to install Windows 95. It is strongly recommended that you use this version, as it is considerably superior to the DOS 6.2 version. You will have to use the DOS 6.2 version of Defrag until Windows 95 is installed. If you have DOS 6.2 or later, you can use the Defrag file found there. If you have a recent version of Norton Utilities, you can use Norton Speed Disk to defragment your hard drive.

It is strongly recommended that you run the Windows 95 ScanDisk Thorough option and a recent version of Defrag or its equivalent, BEFORE running Windows 95 Setup.

Making Installation Decisions

When you install Windows 95, you have several major decisions to make. Among these are whether to

- Run the installation from Windows 3.*x* or from DOS
- Install to the same Windows directory or to a new directory
- Use the Typical, Portable, Compact, or Custom installation

Run Setup from Windows or DOS?

If you have Windows 3.1 or above, or any version of Windows for Workgroups, then the recommended approach is that you start the Windows 95 Setup program from Windows. This allows you to preserve the current settings in your Win.ini, System.ini, and Protocol.ini files, which are copied to the Windows 95 Registry along with your Windows 3.*x* Registry information. Also, your Windows 3.*x* Program Manager groups and their contents are converted to folders and files in the Windows 95 Programs menu, and the application files in your Windows directories are preserved, so your applications do not have to be reinstalled.

If you are running Windows 3.0 or below, any version of DOS 3.2 and above without Windows, any version of O/S 2, or Windows NT, then you must install Windows 95 from DOS. Your Windows settings and Program Manager groups, if any, will be lost, and you must reinstall any Windows applications you want to run under Windows 95.

As was mentioned earlier in this Appendix, installing from DOS has the added benefit of allowing you to erase all of your old Windows files and do a major housecleaning on your hard disk. While it sounds scary to erase your settings and Program Manager groups, these have only marginal value in Windows 95, and their functions are quickly and easily restored. It is admittedly a pain to flip all the floppies necessary to reinstall your Windows applications, but the gain in hard-disk space is generally worth it.

There is another reason for installing from DOS—a new hard disk. With the demands for huge amounts of disk space (Microsoft Office 95 can easily use well over a 100 MB) and the great disk prices that are available, you may well decide to get a new, large hard disk. In that case, *after* making the bootable floppy described above, and *then* installing the new drive, use the following instructions to format and put DOS on it prior to installing Windows 95:

1. Put your bootable floppy in drive A and turn on your computer. DOS will boot.

2. At the DOS prompt, type **format c:/s**. This will format the drive and place the DOS system files on it.

3. When formatting is complete, remove the bootable floppy and reboot from the hard disk.

4. Again at the DOS prompt, type **md \DOS** to make a directory named DOS.

5. Finally, type **copy a:*.*** \dos to copy the files you put on the bootable floppy to your new hard disk.

Use the Same Windows Directory?

One of your first questions in Windows 95 Setup is to select the directory into which you want to install Windows 95. The default and recommended choice is the current directory in which Windows 3.*x* is installed (usually C:\Windows). If you do that, Windows 95 will replace Windows 3.*x*, and all your settings, Program Manager groups, and Windows applications are preserved under Windows 95 as they existed under Windows 3.*x*.

If you want to preserve and be able to run Windows 3.*x*, then you will need to install Windows 95 into a new directory. If you do this, your Windows 3.*x* settings will not be transferred, and any applications that you want to use under Windows 95 will have to be reinstalled. (Most probably, the applications you reinstall will *not* be usable under Windows 3.1.)

Unless you have a very special application that absolutely requires Windows 3.*x* (and I have never heard of such an application), then the only reason not to install to the same directory is a fear of the unknown—a fear of Windows 95. While this is most understandable, it is unwarranted. Windows 95 has been tested far more than any other piece of software, more than 75 million hours of testing. I personally have used Windows 95 for over 18 months. I am very comfortable with it and cannot conceive of going back to Windows 3.1. Windows 95 is a mature product that is ready for general use.

Type of Setup	Description
Typical	Installs what Microsoft believes are the most commonly selected options in a manner that requires the least amount of interaction with you. It is the default.
Portable	Installs the options typically selected by portable, or mobile, computer users. It combines lower disk usage with features needed in a mobile environment.
Compact	Installs the minimum files needed to run Windows 95.
Custom	Allows you to choose the options you want to install and to confirm the configuration settings as they are made. This gives you the most flexibility, but it also requires the most knowledge about your system.

Use Typical, Portable, Compact, or Custom Setup

The second major question in Windows 95 Setup is the type of setup that you want to perform. You have four choices, which will determine the Windows 95 features and options that are installed and the amount of disk space that is used by them. Table A–2 describes these choices, and Table A–3 shows the Windows 95 options that are available in each.

Most of the options can be installed after you have Windows 95 installed and you have had a chance to read the rest of this book and learn what the options do. The Windows 95 Control Panel has an Add/Remove Programs capability that allows you to do that (and one option, Clipboard Viewer, is only available there). Therefore, the decision on which options to install during the initial setup is not critical.

Since you can add any options you may want after the installation, and the Typical installation is so much easier, that is the recommended choice. Study Table A–3 to see what is not included in the Typical installation and then use the Add/Remove Programs control panel to add the missing programs after you have completed the installation of Windows 95.

Notes on Table A–3   All of the options in Table A–3 are included on the Windows 95 Upgrade CD. The options down through Multimedia can be selected for installation in a Custom install. The only exceptions to that are the Clipboard Viewer, which can only be installed through the Add/Remove Programs control

Table A–3. *Options Available in Different Types of Setup*

Setup Option	Typical	Portable	Compact	Floppy	Online
Accessibility Options	Yes	Yes		Yes	
Accessories					
Briefcase		Yes		Yes	
Calculator	Yes			Yes	
Character Map					Yes
Clipboard Viewer				Yes	
Desktop Wallpaper				Yes	
Document Templates	Yes			Yes	
Games				Yes	
Mouse Pointers					Yes
Net Watcher					Yes
Online Guide					Yes
Paint	Yes			Yes	
Quick View					Yes
Screen Saver	Yes (1)			Yes	
System Monitor					Yes
Resource Meter				Yes	
Windows 95 Tour					

Table A–3. *Options Available in Different Types of Setup*

Setup Option	Typical	Portable	Compact	Floppy	Online
WinPopup	(2)	(2)	(2)	Yes	
WordPad	Yes	Yes		Yes	
Communications					
Dial-Up Networking		Yes		Yes	
Direct Cable Connection		Yes		Yes	
Hyper-Terminal	Yes	Yes		Yes	
Phone Dialer	Yes	Yes		Yes	
Disk Tools					
Backup				Yes	
Disk Compression	(3)	(3)	(3)	Yes	
Scan Disk (4)	Yes	Yes	Yes	Yes	
Defrag (4)	Yes	Yes	Yes	Yes	
Microsoft Exchange					
Microsoft Exchange				Yes	
Microsoft Mail				Yes	
Microsoft Fax				Yes	
Fax Viewer				Yes	

Table A–3. *Options Available in Different Types of Setup*					
Setup Option	**Typical**	**Portable**	**Compact**	**Floppy**	**Online**
Microsoft Network				Yes	
Multilingual Support					
Multimedia					
Audio Compression	(5)	(5)		Yes	
CD Player	(6)	(6)		Yes	
Media Player	Yes	Yes		Yes	
Sample Sounds					
Sound Recorder	(5)	(5)		Yes	
Sound Schemes	Yes	Yes		Yes	
Video Compression	Yes	Yes		Yes	
Volume Control	(5)	(5)		Yes	
CD-Admin Directory					
AppTools					Yes
NetTools					Yes
Resource Kit					Yes(7)
CD-Microsoft Exposition					

Setup Option	Typical	Portable	Compact	Floppy	Online
Table A–3. *Options Available in Different Types of Setup*					
CD-Funstuff Directory					
Hover!					
Pictures					
Videos					
CD-Datalink Directory					
Datalink					
CD-Other Directory					
Chat					Yes
ClipBook Viewer					Yes
Microsoft Diagnostics					Yes
Old MS-DOS Utilities					Yes
Wordview					Yes

panel, and ScanDisk and Defrag, which are automatically installed in all cases. The options beginning with CD-Admin Directory must be copied off of the CD. A Yes under Typical, Portable, or Compact means that the option is automatically installed in that type of installation. A Yes under Floppy means that option is available on the floppy upgrade package. A Yes under Online means you can get the option off of the Microsoft Network, CompuServe, and Genie online services as well as off the Internet at Microsoft.com.

A blank space in a column is the same as a No. Other notes on Table A–3 are as follows:

(1) Only the Flying Windows screen saver is installed in a Typical install. Other screen savers are available in both the CD and floppy packages.

(2) Only installed if networking capability is detected and other networking software is installed.

(3) Only installed if DoubleSpace or DriveSpace is detected.

(4) Automatically installed in all situations.

(5) Only installed if a sound card is detected.

(6) Only installed if a CD-ROM drive is detected.

(7) Available by purchasing the *Windows 95 Resource Kit* book from Microsoft Press.

Checking Your Current System

Windows 95 Setup looks at your current system and gets a lot of information based on what it finds. This is especially true with networking. It is therefore important that your system and networking configuration and related software are the way you want them prior to running Windows 95 Setup. One part of this is to read the Windows 95 Readme.txt and Setup.txt files on the installation disk (CD or first floppy) and see if any notes apply to your hardware or software, especially those that are networking related.

A second aspect of checking your current system is to look at your Config.sys and Autoexec.bat files and remove any programs other than those that are necessary for hard disk control or partitioning, networking, and device drivers for your CD-ROM, sound card, or other devices. No other programs or utilities should be started by Config.sys, Autoexec.bat, or your Windows initialization files, or somehow otherwise be running when you start Windows 95 Setup.

Running Windows 95 Setup

After all the preparatory work to get ready for installing Windows 95, running Windows 95 Setup is definitely anticlimactic! There are only slight differences between the Windows and DOS starting locations.

Running Windows 95 Setup from Windows 3.x

If you have Windows 3.1 or above or any version of Windows for Workgroups, use the following instructions to install Windows 95:

Make sure no other programs or utilities are running.

1. Start your computer and Windows in your normal way.
2. Put the Windows 95 Setup CD or first floppy disk in the appropriate drive.
3. Using the Windows File Manager, select the drive and double-click on Setup.exe. Alternatively, from either the Program Manager or File manager, open the File menu, choose Run, type **d:\setup** (where d:\ is the drive you are using), and click on OK.
4. Follow the directions as they appear on the screen. If you use a Typical installation, the only questions you'll be asked are the installation directory, the type of installation, the user and computer identification, and whether to create a startup disk (recommended).

Running Windows 95 Setup from DOS

If you want or need to run Setup from DOS, use the following instructions to install Windows 95:

Make sure no other programs or utilities are running.

1. Start your computer in your normal way.
2. Put the Windows 95 Setup CD or first floppy disk in the appropriate drive.
3. At the DOS prompt, type **d:\setup** (where d:\ is the drive you are using), and press (Enter).
4. Follow the directions as they appear on the screen. If you use a Typical installation, the only questions you'll be asked are the installation directory, the type of installation, the user

and computer identification, and whether to create a startup disk (recommended).

Running Windows 95 Setup across a Network

If you are connected to a network, the Windows 95 Setup programs may reside on a hard disk or a compact disk on a network server. In that case, you can still install Windows 95 from either Windows or DOS and replace Step 2 above with the following steps:

1. Start your networking software if it isn't already running, and connect to the server.

2. Make the drive and directory that contains Windows 95 Setup the active drive.

3. Follow the remaining instructions for either Windows or DOS installation.

 If you install from a network server, Windows 95 will automatically go there for any optional files or device drivers that you need in the future. This can be very handy and can save having to keep track of many sets of disks in even a modest size organization.

Index

A

About Information Service dialog box, 268
About Windows, system optimization and, 436
Accelerating graphics, 440
Acceleration, of mouse, 109
Access, to disks and folders, 193
Access data source, 122
Accessibilities Properties dialog box, 103–104
Accessibilities Sound tab, 107
Accessibility options, 103–111
Accessories, 373–406. *See also* CD-ROM
    companion disk; HyperTerminal
    telecommunications package
  for multimedia, 357–365
  for networking, 210–217
Add a Fax Modem dialog box, 304
Add Fonts dialog box, 151–152
Adding fonts, 150–152
Adding icons to desktop, 88
Adding programs, 113–115
Add New File Type dialog box, 61
Add New Hardware control panel, 111–112
  adding network adapters with, 182–183
  installing multimedia cards and, 355–356
  setting up networks and, 177–178
Add New Hardware Wizard, 177–178
Add Port button, 134
Add Printer Wizard, 126–127
  capturing network printer ports with,
    202–203
  installing local printers with, 128–130
  installing network printers with, 130–131
Add/Remove Programs control panel, 113–115
Add/Remove Programs dialog box, 114
Add/Remove Programs Properties dialog box,
  installing Microsoft Network and, 310

Add/Remove Programs Properties window,
  installing Microsoft Exchange with, 262–263
Add/Remove Properties dialog box, 113
Address Book dialog box, 288–290
Address Book Properties dialog box, 283
Address Book tab (Microsoft Network), 281–282
Addressing tab, 282–283
Add Scheduled Session dialog box, 274
Adjust Free Space dialog box, 78–79
Administration
  of postoffices, 258–262
  of systems, 409–433
Adobe Type 1 font technology, 154
Adobe Type Manager (ATM), 154
Advanced button (ScanDisk), 69–71
Advanced Connection Settings dialog box, 232
Advanced Fax Security dialog box, 305
Advanced Graphics Settings dialog box, 440
Advanced Options dialog box, 69–71, 73–74
Advanced Program Settings dialog box, 448–450
Advanced tab (Multimedia), 365, 366–367
Airbrush tool (Paint), 397
Alarm, setting with WinClock, 556–557
Aliases for filenames, 52–53
Allow screen saver check box, 453
Alt key, 14–16
Always on top option, 89–90
America Online (AOL), 308
  HyperTerminal and, 243
Analyzing disks with ScanDisk, 67–72
ANSI text, 487
Answer mode section (Fax Modem Properties),
  278–279
Appearance tab, 118
Applets, 35–39
Applications. *See also* Accessories; Programs
  capturing, 496

605

T

Project Tracking

Ergonomics   Activity Log

Computer Usage

Productivity

Networks

Time

Billing

Security

* Just a few uses for

Win, What, Where quietly monitors every activity on your computer. The sophisticated Project Tracking feature allows you to group activities and easily generate billing information. Extensive configuration options let you track what you want and how you want it. The History module creates custom summary and detail reports from every workstation on your network. Win, What, Where also logs keyboard and mouse activity giving you invaluable ergonomic information.

Try the fully functional 30-day evaluation copy on the enclosed CD and experience for yourself the power of Win, What, Where.

basic
systems, inc.

Single User	37.00
Network Starter Pak (3 User License)	99.00
Additional Users (requires Network Starter Pak)	15.00 each

1.800.242.4775 (orders only, please)
509.735.2386 fax 509.735.1730
70034.1341@compuserve.com

2103 West Canal Drive
Kennewick, WA 99336

GREAT UTILITIES, GAMES, AND SCREEN SAVERS
FOR WINDOWS 95

WINCLOCK - Digital alarm clock

> ▬ **9 51 pm Tue 6.13.95**

- Display date and time in many different formats
- Date display in any of six languages, 25 alarms
- Ability to run programs at specified times (backup programs, etc.)
- Optional hourly beep, stopwatches and countdown timers

MEM - Memory and Disk Space Display

> ▬ **28,615; C: 25,600; 67%**

- Amount of free memory, percent of free system resources, free disk space
- Alarms in case free disk space or memory go below a specified amount

HOP - A cool Chinese checkers like game

RANDSCRN - Randomize Windows 95 and Windows 3.1 screen savers
- Comes with several new savers, including Random Pixels, Bouncing Lines, Balloons, Raindrops, and Laser Show

---

Please make check or money order payable to:
Tel: (617) 648-1457
Fax: (617) 648-1561

David A. Feinleib
30 Hamilton Road #401
Arlington, MA 02174-8271

PROGRAM	QUANTITY	AMOUNT
WinClock	_____ @$16.00 each	$_____
RunProg	_____ @$12.00 each	$_____
PrintSwitch	_____ @$16.00 each	$_____
EndPrint	_____ @$16.00 each	$_____
Mem	_____ @$12.00 each	$_____
IconCalc	_____ @$12.00 each	$_____

Add $4.00 for shipping inside U.S. or $6.00 outside U.S.

TOTAL: $_____

Register WinImage 2.10 Now !

WinImage - The Windows disk imager for Windows 95 and Windows NT!

The registration of WinImage 2.10 is $20 until the end of 1995!

You can register by:

- Sending $US 20 to Gilles Vollant, 13 rue Mansart, 91540 Mennecy - France
- By credit card to PsL at 1-800-242-4PSL, Fax to 1-713-524-6398, mail to P.O. Box 35705, Houston, TX 77235-5705; registration number is 10976
- By Compuserve shareware registration service (GO SWREG). The WinImage registration number is 1233.

Name: _____

Company: _____

Adress: _____

City, State ZIP: _____

Country: _____

Version(s) used : ☐ Windows 3.1 ☐ Windows NT ☐ Windows 95

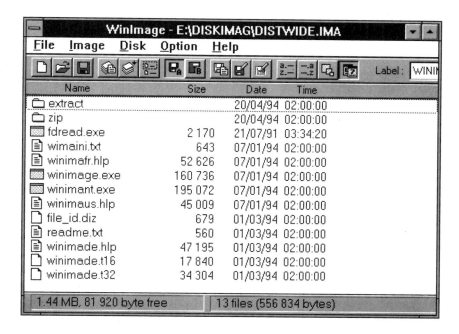

Have You Gotten All The Power Out of Windows 95 PowerTools?

Not until you take a look at **PAINT SHOP PRO v3.0!**

Paint Shop Pro version 3 (evaluation version included with this book) is designed to be the only Photo Retouching, Painting, Image Format Conversion and Screen Capturing program you will need. *Now that sounds like a PowerTool!*
Features include: Painting with 8 brushes, photo retouching, image enhancement and editing, color enhancement, image browser, batch conversion, and scanner support. Included are 20 standard filters and 12 deformations. Supports plug-in filters. Over 30 file formats supported.

Other programs from JASC included with this book:

Jasc Media Center - The Easiest Way to Catalog Your Multimedia Files
Features include: Organize your multimedia files into albums of thumbnails. Catalog, search, sort by keyword, comment, or file properties. View files using the powerful slide show feature. Full file manipulation capabilities from within the program. Print high quality contact sheets. Support for over 35 file formats, removable disks, and CD ROMs.
Professional Capture Systems - Complete Screen Capturing for Windows and DOS.
Features include: PCS is 2 programs: JasCapture and DosCapture.
JasCapture for Windows allows for the capturing of a defined area, full screen, window, client area, and objects. Captures can be sent to disk, printer or clipboard. DosCapture will allow you to capture standard and extended VGA text modes and standard VGA graphics modes. Captures are saved as PCX files. Req. 286 & VGA.

For Additional Information or a Catalog...

JASC, Inc.
10901 Red Circle Drive, Suite 340
Minnetonka, MN 55343
Phone: 612-930-9171 Fax: 612-930-9172
WEB Page http://www.winternet.com/~jasc
CIS: GO JASC

KINDEL SYSTEMS

WinPrint 1.53 is a text file printing utility which makes printing ASCII or ANSI text files in Windows™ incredibly simple. Without changing a single option text files can be dropped on *WinPrint's* minimized icon from File Manager and those files will print, formatted with headers and footers including the filename, date printed, date revised, and page numbers. Of course WinPrint also allows the user to change all imaginable options via an elegantly designed user interface.

WinPrint is the perfect tool for printing reports generated by legacy systems, source code, shareware documentation, or any standard text file. It was designed to be operated either interactively or in "batch mode" making it perfect for single users or complete enterprises.

INIedit 1.31 is the quickest, most efficient way to modify Windows™ "INI" files. Most Windows™ programs save configuration information in INI files and, unfortunately, users are often required to edit them manually. The simple and elegant user interface makes a sometimes scary task easy.

INIedit follows the "Keep it simple stupid (KISS)" principle by not trying to solve all the problems of Windows™ configuration. It won't un-install software. It won't detect interrupt conflicts. But it does make it easy to change INI file settings.

WinPrint Single User License	$25.00
INIedit Single User License	$25.00

Special Offer: Buy Both *WinPrint* and *INIedit* using the coupon below and save $10.00!

To Order: Mail the coupon below, along with your check made out to "Charles Kindel" (Payable in U.S. funds drawn from a U.S. bank) to (sorry, credit cards not accepted):

Charles E. Kindel, Jr., 4522 194th Way, N.E., Redmond, WA 98053-4648

Windows 95 Power Tools Special Offer

$10 OFF

WinPrint & INIedit Purchased Together

Send this coupon along with your order.

Volume discounts are available. Call or fax for more information.
4522 194th Way, N.E., Redmond, WA 98053-4648. (206)868-9591 (voice/fax). CIS: 71551,1445

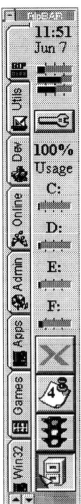

There are a couple of things that Microsoft forgot to include in Windows 95...

Presenting

RipBAR Pro & RipSPACE for Windows 95.

RipBAR Pro for Windows 95 $34.95

RipBAR is an application toolbar where you can store applications and documents. Launching your favorite utility is but a mouse click away. It also sports features like memory gauges, resource gauges, disk space gauges, time & date display, program groups with a unique tab dialog interface, Post-It style Notes, and much more. RipBAR is the perfect addition to your Windows 95 desktop!

RipSPACE for Windows 95 $19.95

Ever wonder what happened to all the free space on your hard disk? RipSPACE will tell you-- RipSPACE can scan your disks and report on the space used by directory. Many options are available for customizing the reports.

And More!

We sell a number of other utilities as well :

RipSwitch: The Windows 95 style task bar for people with Windows 3.1 and Windows NT.
RipTABS: The tab dialog library for programmers who would like to implement tab-style dialogs on Windows 3.1 and Windows NT.

Software By Design

1.45"

SoftDesign can be reached at:
Fax: (514) 630-6395
Internet: 74777.2357@compuserve.com
CompuServe: 74777,2357
Visit our CompuServe forum: GO SOFTDESIGN

Buy any of our Windows 95 programs
and get a second one _FREE_!

When you buy any of our Windows 95tm programs at the regular price you get a second program of your choice _free_! This applies to all of the programs we sell so don't wait, mail this coupon with your order today.

Notes

Notes

Notes

Notes

Notes

Notes